In the Beauty of the Lilies

The Wartime Journals
of Confederate Correspondent
Royal K. Chapman
1862-1864

By

R.A. Busse

Order this book online at www.trafford.com
or email orders@trafford.com

Most Trafford titles are also available at major online book retailers.

Printed in the United States of America.

ISBN: 978-1-4269-2555-9 (sc)

Library of Congress Control Number: 2010902920

Trafford rev. 04/14/2011

 www.trafford.com

North America & International
toll-free: 1 888 232 4444 (USA & Canada)
phone: 250 383 6864 ♦ fax: 812 355 4082

CONTENTS

The Premise

Save for weaponry, nothing about
war changes, nor does its predations
of the human soul.

* * *

Dedication

To my parents

Arthur & Mary Busse
for their inspiration,
who did not live to see
In the Beauty of the Lilies,
and to Royal K. Chapman,
late teacher and family friend,
who took me to Gettysburg
where I discovered
Seminary Ridge
and who, if he had lived
between 1860 and 1865,
would have worn Gray
and undoubtedly have followed
the armies of the South
with pen and journals.

*   *   *

Acknowledgements & Thanks

For their assistance in the completion
of this work

Mary K.Emmrich
Director
Newton County, IN Public Libraries
Advisor, editing & formatting

David Spencer
Indianapolis, IN
Ball State University
Typing & collating

Bill Herbert
Artist
Remington, IN
Cover design

Dave Alm & Associates
Dave's Computer World
Brookston, IN
Equipment usage & direction

Prof. Don Kreilkamp
St. Joseph's College
Retired
Rensselaer, IN
Concept & criticism

Connie Kingman
Director
Prairie Writers Guild
Rensselaer, IN
Technical assistance

Prairie Writers Guild
Support & encouragement

*   *   *

Of Interest

Long before beginning this work in earnest, I sent numerous entries entitled, "Blue Shadows, Gray Ghosts," to noted Civil War historian, Shelby Foote, hoping he might comment on them. He admitted to me via a phone call later that although he "never reads manuscripts sent to him in the mail," he read mine and found them "powerful." When he returned the manuscript to me, he included the following note:

> "Dear Mr. Busse: All I can do is wish you well and advise you to pay not attention whatsoever to what anyone else will say or think; it's altogether your own private war & you must fight (or write) it in your own way. So far as I can see, so far you've done just that & I hope you will continue with that in mind.

> Regards & Best Wishes,

> Shelby Foote

Taking his advice, I continued with that in mind, the work eventually becoming <u>In the Beauty of the Lilies</u>.

R. A. Busse

A Thought

Found at Franklin, Tennessee,
Amongst Chapman's Journals In
November 1864

*   *   *

Perhaps, it is because
within us all
an ember glows,
that ever-compelling,
warming urge to,
with our hands and good will,
create that which
will contribute most
to the peace the Almighty
wishes us to establish
on this tortured Earth;
that we, with conviction,
ever-bridle our
contradictory natures
that deny free will
for good, but yield to such
crimson failures as war.
Yet, as long as the strong
victimize the weak
shall the weak find no recourse
but to seek allies in God by
whatever means.
Perhaps, before we strive
for universal passivity,
we must search for those seeds
within our negative nature
that poison the most noble
of our enterprises,
and, at last,
excise them forever
from our mortal souls.
And thus might we achieve,
under His gracious auspices
the grace and immortality
He intends for us.

A Time of Leaves

It was their four-year autumn, when the leaves fell from the boughs of an entire generation. Theirs was a soldiering world. Their closest enemies of that season were constant...sun, snow, wind and rain...heat, dampness, cold and misery, and, always lurking in time - iron, lead and bayonets. Their worries and fears for themselves were compounded by those for their families, victimized at home by marauding hordes in blue. Hunger and privation served at their sides.

Neither rifles nor cannon killed as many as the microscopic things we are only now coming to know. They wept for and yearned to know again the love of those families we so dearly missed, yet they were not strangers to distracting songs and laughter.

Sleep, ever a luxury for some, became for others a dreaded reply of war's indelible horrors. Many escaped to pen and paper, books and writing. Some endured loneliness and moral confusion. Tomorrows were beasts in the unknown's mists. Some possessed great conviction, others not. Of the war, many asked why? Battle humbled even their strongest. All struggled with personal demons and survival's imperatives, some never able to reconcile war's indifference to goodness and faith. Many times, their consciences bled. Horror killed faith and tormented souls even as adversity made others stronger.

They learned to live for the hour only. To do more was dangerous. Some gave up hope that the war would ever end. As moths to light, they searched for redemption while longing for salvation. Through it all, many ironically found abiding courage and some were touched by Providence.

For the most part, they stayed and fought because those around them stayed and fought. And they survived or died surrendering themselves to that most imponderable of all constants — the Lord's promise of a merciful Eternity.

In all of the above regard, we and our enemies shared the war in common.

Former Private Will Hoskins
Infantry--CSA
1885

Their Battle Hymn

In their Battle Hymn of the Republic, they have made the quality of war reverential, ascribing the principle of Christ's ultimate sacrifice to their cause - even ensconcing it with the beauty of lilies. I have wondered since why men apply such religious attributes to war. Never during my service in the war with Mexico did I see or find beauty, neither on its battlefields nor in its hospitals afterward. The only holy enlightenment I discovered emanated from the souls of dying men or those about to die, victims of circumstance that denied them their humanity until, in the end, it tearfully sprung from their physical and spiritual pain with a childlike innocence that left me humbled and spiritually spent. And so it is again in this ever more savage contest of blood against blood. In the "Beauty of the Lilies?" If beauty exists, I must search for it not without but within men's souls.

RKC

A Reflection

"Some of us, even some of our religious boys, eventually felt that Christ, for the whole war, remained where he was born - somewhere across the sea or jest so distant we nary could reach Him, like He was so put off by the noise 'er horrified by the slaughter that He only sometimes made himself apparent - that mostly, He were hidden in 'er behind what the Yankees sung about but there never much was - the beauty of lilies."

Private Homer Payne
Infantry
CSA

They Adore Him

"My husband, Will, went for soldier today. I saw him off. He appeared so confident and brave. But it was all a sham. He did not want to go — I know he did not. But the certainty of losing face or otherwise being thought a coward by our community if he did not forced his hand. He is not a soldier, not hardly. He could never kill anything, let alone another human being. He is a cabinet-maker and wood carver. Creating works of beauty is all he knows to do. How can they ever make made him a soldier? He thinks the war is a tragedy, yet it shamed him into violating his very nature and truest conviction against war-making. How many must there be just like him going to war at this very hour, who are artisans of peace, instead? We are going to lose too many who have great talent to give to the world. And I fear we will lose my husband. What to do then, except die inside at that moment for the rest of my life? What will Johnathan, 6, and Maybelle, 4, do without him? They adore him so.

Mrs. Bethune Powers
Homekeeper

Author's Comment

People ask me, "Why did you write this work?" I answer simply, "To commemorate the Confederate soldier." For too long, owing to the many misleading myths propagated in the North about the Southern "Cause" and afterwords promoted by the general culture (via entertainment and formal education), he's been made the war's villain. Yet, he lost everything in *defense* of his home and hearth against *invading* federal armies, besides suffering a grim social and economic aftermath.

"Johnny Reb" was as genuinely American as any soldier in blue. He fought doggedly and ultimately against overwhelming odds for the Southern states in what he perceived and believed was the defense of the Constitution as he and learned men then interpreted it. The war never truly resolved the Constitutional issue of states' rights versus federal authority, having merely stifled the debate via force of arms.

The words in these seemingly apocryphal journals came to me as if those forgotten Southern veterans stood at my side whispering their lingering recollections to me, each contributor thereby diminishing his haunting anonymity - having died either unknown or buried in places obscured by time or otherwise unrecorded. And having found a living communicator, who's to say their actual spirits did not. I chose the fictional Chapman to be their eyes, their consciences and their spokesman.

As I wrote, sometimes moved and chilled by the descriptions pouring forth, I wondered if what I was recording might ironically have been factual after all. I'm satisfied that the words herein are theirs and that I served only as their obedient transcriber.

In 1958, the real Roy K. Chapman, teacher and close family friend, who inspired me to someday write this work, took me and high school classmate James North to Gettysburg. Jim gravitated to Cemetery Ridge, I to Seminary. Later, we trudged solemnly from Seminary to and across the Emmitsburg Road and on to the stone wall before Cemetery's fabled clump of trees. But my heart remained on Seminary. In 1969, "Chappy" left for soldier, to bivouac with those tale-telling souls in butternut and gray he so admired and whose sacrifices he moved me to honor as well. May he be pleased.

R.A. Busse
July 2007

In the Beauty of the Lilies

This work is intended to be a "browsing" adventure.

Unless the reader chooses otherwise, it is not intended that he or she read from the beginning to the end. Royal Chapman's entries are voluminous, but each is its own story. Browsing will not compromise the impressions he attempted to convey concerning war's effects upon the soldiers and civilians he wrote about. Had he survived the war (it is generally assumed but not proven that he did not), his intent might well have been to interest readers, South and North, in viewing his works as an insightful testament to both war's waste and its predations upon the human soul. At the same time, they are a window into the common man's search for himself amidst the worst instrument of adversity man forces upon his kind.

*   *   *

The War Between the States

1861-1865

We were not there...we did not see...
we could not feel it nor know it...
and yet, it haunts us still
and we are prisoners of its times.

*   *   *

Insight

Royal Chapman believed it was his mission to record the trials and sacrifices of his people at war that their posterity might understand. It was his aim not to write of great battles nor of generals' fateful decisions, but to peer into the souls of the common soldiers bearing the poor man's fight. And thus he marched with the armies, going into combat with them armed only with pen, paper and sketch pad that he might write and illustrate with authority, braving all they braved, even if it meant suffering the worst with them. He was an unusually dedicated yet conflicted man in search of those redemptive qualities that raised morally beleaguered soldiers above their conditions even amidst the predations of war upon their humanity. And he searched no less for his soul's identity...
In the Beauty of the Lilies.

* * *

Commentary by a Veteran

Pvt. Ezra Cooley

Infantry

"Best to rememba the war nobly if'n ya ken, and what cha done in it and had t'do fer yer country, and then move on, cause tryin' t'fergit all the many horrors ya seen and the killin' ya done'll turn yer insides sour and yer heart cold and yer soul as rancid as spoilt butter. Lotsa men cain't fergit them details and they jest dry up and die t'life and t'God and wander like they be in a trance, takin' t'bad drink and worst, like haunted beggars tryin' t'hide from their own shadows in the light of an accusin' sun."

Something to Consider

Before the War Between the States, Americans generally referred to the nation in the following manner, the United States "are." Only after the war did it become the norm to say of the nation the United States "is." Especially in the prewar South, this implied that the term "United" did not necessarily convey agreement that the Constitution mandated that the states be wholly subordinate to a central federal authority, the states, instead, being free to remain loyal first to themselves, their association to a central federal government being voluntary.

The South remained suspect of absolute federal authority, considering that it smacked too closely of monarchical-like dominance, a holdover attitude dating to our Revolution and our colonial struggle against the supreme power of the English Throne. Understanding this prewar mindset is crucial to appreciating how the South viewed and interpreted the Constitution's word and spirit — and consequently to why it stood by its rationale for, and the righteousness of, secession.

In other words, it believed the federal government was not empowered to force states into compliance with every federal policy, the states instead possessing the right to reject federal measures they considered detrimental not only to their citizens' welfare but a usurpation of their decision-making liberties.

Even today across the nation, many worry that the federal government has assumed and continues to assume powers exceeding the Constitution's word and violate its spirit. Just as in 1860, the question of absolute subordination of the states and their self-determination to federal authority simmers beneath the surface of growing disillusionment with all-powerful federal regulation. Southern states maintained their "right" to deal with and rid themselves of their "peculiar institution" in their own time, in accordance with changing economic times and necessities. They also concurred that they were free to trade with European nations under conditions advantageous to the South and free of manipulation by the Northern business community and its controlling influence on the federal government.

*　*　*

In Retrospect

"If'n ya ask me, when a man crosses another's fences with a gun in his hand and fire in his eyes and intent to do his neighbor damnable harm, he spits in God's eye."

A Veteran

In the Beauty of the Lilies

-Sentiments in Passing—

Commentaries & Perspectives

A Conviction

It is said the past is prelude.

"I for one say this of war: We all are pawns in the chess game of mad gods."

Major Tory Smith
Infantry
CSA

Through One Man's Eyes

"No matta how this here war comes out, one thing's the truth: them Yankees invaded us. We din't invade them. Sumpta was Southun' territory and it were jest a pile a bricks. Any goose with a grain a'sense'd know that wars don't b'gin lessen somebody sends armies, not cannon balls, somewheres. Their armies was sent south and that was worse than Sumpta eva was and that's what trula begun it all. And the big brave gin'rl who sent it weren't 'old Jeff Davis. That were akin to havin' an uninvited stranga bustin' through yer door one mornin' with a gun-totin' mob behind him. The crim'nals up North who been achin' to put the South down fer a hundred year talked 'ole Abe inta it and gived him the excuse - and now he's in it up to his britch's shiny bottom."

Sergeant Rubin Teague
Infantry
CSA

The Inner Chapman

Royal Chapman, whom I knew, was a conflicted man. He did not approve of the war, yet, when the North invaded us, he understood that a knife had been put to his peoples' throat. And, dutifully, after Sumter, and still with grave misgivings about our infant government's ability to properly conduct a war of the scope he envisioned, let alone comprehend its titanic necessities, he threw himself into his self-appointed task with incredible dedication, viewing it as a tribute to those who, for the South, would sacrifice everything. I was associated with him for only a short while, as we met when he joined-up with our regiment before Second Manassas. Still, we struck a symbiotic relationship and much discussed the war and its prospects. Yet, while with us, he earned our troops' eternal respect by going with them into the fighting, armed with his journals and pencils, tending to our wounded for hours afterwards. For the remainder of the war, no other civilian, to my knowledge or memory, attempted anything similar with our brigade. If he actually perished in the Battle of Franklin in November, 1864, as many believe he did, he did so staying true to that to which he had pledged himself - chronicling the common soldiers' war. If, on the other hand, he has survived to this day, even if broken by his wartime experience, I salute him sympathetically and with respect.

Augustus James
Former Quartermaster
Confederate States Army

A Different Soldier

Royal Chapman became a soldier who armed himself with pen and paper. Like all soldiers, he struggled with mixed emotions to understand the war. Cursing it while at the same time dedicated to seeing the south delivered from its powerful enemy's depredations, he chose to fight by chronicling his countrymens' story for whoever might eventually read his journals. Never mentioning that he suffered intensely with the after effects of serious leg wounds received many years earlier in the war with Mexico, he followed the South's armies for three years with unwavering faithfulness, sharing its soldiers' hunger, dangers and tribulations. And yet, he has remained virtually unknown until now, twenty years after the guns have fallen silent. He toiled with my regiment for two months in 1863 and went with Trimble's men into the cauldron the third day at Gettysburg. I think Chapman survived that slaughter only because the Lord granted him more time to poignantly describe and record for posterity the human costs of that war and of war itself.

Former Major Everett Souleen
Confederate States Army

Secession & Worst Apprehensions

Not all of us were for it, its perils being too great to contemplate should our independence not be quickly secured and our lands and people be subjected to Federal retribution.

I quaked at the zealous, pro-secession sentiment expressed by so many of our young men who had never seen war nor, with bodies savaged by hot iron and lead, survived a war.

The fictions they entertained astounded me; that the Americans who would become our enemies were of a lesser moral and spiritual quality, and, should they invade us, could be rapidly subdued because of their inferior military talents. In fact, our enemies possessed not only overwhelming material and financial resources but a far greater population, ergo much more abundant manpower. These firebrands could not see that the longer a war might last, the stronger the North would grow until it fielded a monstrous military machine single-mindedly dedicated to our suppression.

I could not persuade them that while the North could overcome its manpower losses, we could not, nor could we indefinitely sustain and replace ours. A prolonged conflict would drain our war potential, forcing us onto the constant defensive, while eventually bankrupting us and collapsing our society.

These arguments persuaded few who refused to see beyond their fiery enthusiasm for confrontation with Washington. Many of us believed that if we seceded, we should eventually have abandoned secession under certain conditions in exchange for amendments to the Federal Constitution guaranteeing the South economic safeguards, with the South committing itself to the abandonment of slavery within a specific time period - but without Federal coercion--as our economy and society readjusted and mechanized.

Our citizens had long suspected that the North's industrialists so feared competition from the expansion of our small industrial base - and our liberal trade policies with Europe - that they would use war as an excuse to take us low and impotent for a century. As it was, by revolutionizing our cotton production and harvesting methods, machinery promised to lift us from our agrarian status, eventually rendering our "peculiar institution" obsolete.

We had long been assailed for perpetuating and profiting from slavery. Yet, our countless thousands of scratch farmers and share-croppers now in ranks would argue that they subsisted by their own hands and slave-like labor, not by any Black man's. That our enemies now exploit the issue to gild the purity of their moral lilies is a tarnishing hypocrisy that must embarrass even our Lord, for the North cannot conscientiously assert that it did not immensely profit from the institution as well.

The tragedy of this war is not only that it should never have been pursued by either side, but that both sides' leaderships turned for their own justification to human counsel. Had they respected the Lord's Word, both sides would have been spiritually compelled to quell their passions even after the first shots were fired.

Now, the South has realized its worst apprehensions.

The war brings destruction and destitution even to our humblest people, even to freed black men whose farms and holdings the enemy either burns, confiscates or both in common with all others. "Total War," as he calls it, has been instituted to compensate for his battlefield failures and, unto Grant's prominence at a time of our debilitation, the ineptitude of Lincoln's generals. But, to our people and our innocent, it constitutes unnecessary brutality. More than any other factor, their Total War is why we fight and *have* fought with such dedication for so long and *will* fight until Lee or Davis says, "Enough."

Although our boys have long since despaired of achieving Southern independence, and despite their physical and spiritual dissipation, they have determined to indefinitely resist Total War and the North's violation of Southern soil.

Daily, they subsist on two sustaining rations - sacrifice and honor.

RKC

In the Beauty of the Lilies

A Pertinent Reflection

Thomas Carlisle

Former Colonel
Confederate States Army
Army of Northern Virginia

Twenty years have passed since the war's end. Yet, I find it painful to attempt to reconcile time's passage. The war's impressions haunt me still with a brilliant clarity that will remain so for the rest of my dwindling days. Age has not only mellowed me but helped me view the past more perceptively.

In past years, I tried to put pen to paper, lest I sacrificed to oblivion impressions garnered between 1861 and 1865 that I believed were important to posterity. I would have sought neither recognition nor fame. Yet, I bore a responsibility to the men with whom I served and who had so loyally served me, whose deeds might otherwise have been lost to time and the pain-calloused conscience of a reconstituted nation. But my attempt was only that. I discovered I was not yet far enough beyond those matters to avoid the tears that blinded me to my task.

The memoirs of so many veterans since have spoken to everything I might have written. Ironically, though enough time now has passed that I have checked my emotions and should have been able to write, my health abandons and weakens me and I haven't the endurance for it. Yes, I still hear battle noises - artillery's thunder, the desperate musketry - and reluctantly recall the carnage, the soul-rendering cries of the mutilated and all those numberless faces that conveyed every possible fear and emotion or resided in death's contorted oblivion. And, yes, I will never be able to rid my nostrils of putrefaction's and gangrene's stench. But, I also remember the comradeship and devotion I witnessed on both sides of that invisible line separating countrymen. Despite their contesting flags, their experiences were universal and commonly poignant.

So many lives lost...

Colonel Carlisle's Thoughts, Concluded by His Wife

Amanda Carlisle

What was done in those war years is done. Scars still remind us. Emotions have not truly quieted. And the roaring issue of that tribulation - states' rights versus federal authority, stilled only by force of arms - remains to future generations to Constitutionally resolve. The present quiet is a contemplative period born of exhaustion. Reasonable men now realize they should have thought more intensely and consulted each other more before taking up arms. But, what "should have been" hardly persuades a universe indifferent to men's mortal follies.

Thankfully, in Royal Chapman's writings, my husband found a voice that could have been his own. But, owing to his rank, he was never able to be as in touch with the war's grit and poignancy, and he regrets that he never knew him. Chapman's words bring Thomas together with the common soldiers he commanded as he could not have been then but still thirsts to be.

We understand that Chapman dedicated his journals not only to our Southern soldiers, their progeny and our people, as symbols of his devotion to all, but also to those of the North--and to the combined hundreds of thousands of both sides who might have challenged destruction's trumpet had they understood beforehand the cataclysm breaking upon them. But, owing to stubbornness or ignorance, much of it forgivable in retrospect, they perished instead. And what of the star-crossed innocents of both sides caught-up in that whirlwind.

One final reflection: As my husband penned his comments, which could well have been his last, a bird sang beyond his window. He paused to listen. If only both sides then had listened to such harmonies and had interpreted them to mean that God was appealing to both to pause - to have remembered the Sermon on the Mount and all that its haunting message of peace promised our generation's then untarnished soul. Had we, the war might never have come and we might have found an equitable path around those mountains of hubris that cost so many so much. Thomas deeply regrets that they did not. He wonders what, if anything, they have learned in these decades since, and from those awful years - or what future generations will have learned from what should never have been our tragic American impasse.

May our Master grant both sides forgiveness, for, even now, after all their sufferings, both remain too proud to pray for it.

I am honored, in lieu of my husband's exhaustion, to have concluded his poignant thoughts, which I know so well.

Amanda Carlisle

In the Beauty of the Lilies

How the Book Originated
Explanation and Commentary

By

<u>The Editorial Staff</u>

Jay Albright Fuller
Publisher
Former Colonel of Infantry
Confederate States Army
Army of Northern Virginia
1862-1865

Simon Stockman
Assistant Editor
Former Cavalry Lieutenant
Confederate States Army
Army of Northern Virginia

Jerimiah Connerly
Researcher
Former Captain of Artillery
Confederate States Army
Polk's Corps
Army of the West
1863-1865

*   *   *

Insight

Other than what his journals have revealed about him, Royal Chapman remains an enigma.

Apparently, he was a private citizen and veteran of the war with Mexico, who took it upon himself to travel with myriad Confederate units during the war, chronicling the war from the soldier's viewpoint. It is believed he hailed from Georgia, but this, his age and family relationships have never been confirmed. Occasionally, he hints that he was married but never mentions offspring.

It is fact that during the War Between the States, he traveled with the Army of Northern Virginia and later with its Army of the Tennessee, where he ultimately met a puzzling fate at the Battle of Franklin, Tennessee in November, 1864. Armed with pen and ink, he spent at least three years living and going into battle with common soldiers to lend what he termed "credibility" to his observations. What credentials he used to establish himself with those commands is unknown.

Before his disappearance during the Franklin battle, Chapman entrusted the bulk of his writings to Regimental Chaplain James McKenzie. Ironically, while ministering to wounded troops during the fighting, Chaplain McKenzie was mortally wounded but survived long enough to inform fellow officers of the journals' whereabouts and to ask that they be submitted to the Brigade's commanding officer, Colonel Ezra Hayes. After the battle, Hayes hurriedly packed them in a trunk with other personal effects. However, Chapman habitually carried additional journals with him into every fight, and these (in whole or in part) were discovered on the battlefield by enlisted survivors. In the meantime, thinking the documents to be of military value, they sped them by coincidence to Hayes who hurriedly added them to his collection. Having no time to study them, Hayes sent the trunk home where, because of ill-health for years after the war, they remained unread and forgotten for nearly two decades.

Then, one inclement day while rummaging through those effects and war memorabilia near the end of his life, Hayes rediscovered them. Impressed with their significance, he had them delivered to me, a close personal friend, another irony. Their content greatly moved me and I immediately arranged for their publication.

The sketch-work Chapman often refers to was never located. Neither was an apparent index of units he marched with that probably contained the names of the numberless veterans he interviewed or whose conditions he described. We believe he intended to insert sketches, units and names into the appropriate journal entries at a later date, perhaps after the war. In the meantime, he left all journal entries, including those given to Chaplain McKenzie, haphazardly arranged.

Given the circumstances surrounding their recovery, it was neither possible to divine his work's original or intended chronology nor to determine whether it represented his entire effort. Some entries, including sketches and indexes, might well have been lost on the Franklin battlefield. Witnesses to the fighting theorize that artillery fire may have rendered Chapman's body unrecognizable, resulting in his mass grave internment with hundreds of other victims. In the case of the journals' formatting, traditional literary structure and continuity, his entries speak for themselves. It also is noteworthy that his journals give little insight into his private life.

Former Infantry Major Herbert Strong, of Richmond, who associated with Chapman for many weeks during the war, told us that, for the sake of the laymen he hoped his stories might benefit, Chapman avoided burdening his journal entries with confusing military minutiae and terminology, having intended to produce an ongoing chronicle of human endurance, not a military history. Nonetheless, his devotion to his self-ordained mission has become our unique inheritance.

J. Albright Fuller
Publisher
Richmond, Virginia
1885

Addendum

Why Chapman carried his voluminous journals into battle remains baffling, but Strong recounts that Chapman did so regularly. We can only speculate that after years of conscientious and laborious journaling, Chapman trusted his works only to his own safekeeping. At Franklin, however, he apparently sensed his fate and entrusted them to Reverend McKenzie's care, confident of the Godly man's fidelity.

The journals' bulk and weight should have been an excruciating burden, not to mention that toting them everywhere, as he must have, was a feat of extraordinary stamina and willpower.

It is intriguing that Chapman's fate at Franklin cannot be confirmed. Some believe the strain of his endeavors, or, perhaps, severe wounds may have left him wandering in shock and exhaustion somewhere in the war's backwaters, his mind displaced. All we have left of him are his works. We have effected all deciphered and legible notations, corrections, additions and deletions. In all else, we have left his copy intact.

Finally, throughout his writing, Chapman honestly discloses his ongoing dilemma - his struggles with conflicting and sometimes contradictory emotions concerning the war's necessity and conduct, even as he sympathizes with the South's need to defend itself. And though some reviewers have criticized the work's paucity of names, dates, and locations, it could be said, concerning names, that rather than risking inadvertent omissions and slighting anyone, he has treated all collectively, thereby anointing each with transcending immortality.

In his honor, we have featured his recovered labors in their entirety, having preserved all entries in the order of their recovery.

Fuller

Stockman's Note

1885

Those with whom Royal Chapman associated during the War Between the States speculate that he trekked with the Army of Northern Virginia and later with Army of the Tennessee to escape the pain of having lost his wife to a cancer shortly before the contest began, an ordeal for him which they termed emotionally excruciating. His wife's identity and lineage remains unknown, though it is believed she may have taught school in Georgia. But, in a personal sense, he remains an enigma.

Whatever his motivations for persevering in his passionate quest to illuminate the common soldier's ordeals, he sought no personal acclaim for it and apparently felt intensely about maintaining his private life's confidentiality. As a former army chaplain put it; "He came to us and other commands from nowhere and vanished just as mysteriously, as a phantom on the wind." Even so, his willingness to share enemy fire with those he wrote about endeared him even to soldiers who remembered him in passing.

It has also been noted that his journals contain a paucity of names, units, etc. The Reverend William Hirsch, of Atlanta, who served as a chaplain in the Army of Northern Virginia, knew Chapman, and confirms that Chapman kept a separate journal of names, places, dates, and units that he intended, at a later date, to insert in the appropriate journal entries. Reverend Hirsch believes that Chapman lacked a good memory for such details, thus his proclivity for avoiding them as he hurriedly made his initial daily entries. That detailed record has never been found.

Though haphazardly arranged, making their proper chronology difficult to divine, the disorganization of Chapman's journal entries speaks not only to the urgency of his efforts, but also to his prolific pace. Then, too, perhaps, such details prove essentially irrelevant when measured against the collective grist of men's wartime lives, as Chapman apparently believed, by virtue of the tone of his entries and their contents.

As previously mentioned herein, after the Battle of Franklin, Tennessee, in November of 1864, Chapman was never heard from again. It cannot be confirmed that he died in the battle, but it is likely. Either that or he finally cracked, as he feared he might, and to this day is lost in anonymity. The journals themselves were heavily stained, written in pencil and ink, and extensively annotated. The nature of those annotations amply indicates that, before fate intervened, he had planned to do considerable editing.

Finally, it may be considered, that the journals' scarcity of names, dates, and locations, rather than slighting the men he wrote about, has poignantly gilded all he observed with immortality in common.

Simon Stockman
Assistant Editor
Former Cavalry Lieutenant
Confederate States Army
Army of Northern Virginia

A Retrospective

By

Wilfred Gaines

Atlanta Constitution

<u>Remembering Chapman</u>

I was honored to have been asked by the publisher of *In the Beauty of the Lilies* to preview Royal Chapman's journals. Though Chapman wrote neither for newspapers or magazines, he has written something extremely important to all of us, and thus he is entitled by every measure to the honor of being called "correspondent." His impressions are indelibly singed into our memories as profoundly as the war he wrote about. Though humbled in defeat, we are inspired anew by his humanity and left uplifted by his record of our veterans' valor and our fallen's sacrifice. What a sad irony that after all of his dedication and travail he is lost to history, save for his works, and otherwise veiled in anonymity. I assume he would not have been disappointed if the war had eventually claimed him, his quest having been nobly accomplished. Yet, we shall always wonder what, indeed, was Chapman's fate that day at Franklin? Perhaps, as I suspect, our quandary was predestined and intended for the perverse amusement of those who conjured the tragedy of it all - those jackal-gods of war.

*   *   *

Connerly's Note

The Battle of Franklin haunts me still, as I lost a leg there commanding an artillery battery of four guns. For that reason and others, I feel a sympathetic attachment to Royal Chapman, who was reported to have perished there or, at the very least, to have gone missing. In fact, I vaguely remember noticing a civilian wearing a long white dust coat far down the line from our artillery battery's position, my vision being quickly obscured by smoke. It was only minutes thereafter that solid enemy shot took off my leg as I directed battery fire. But I remember thinking it odd, even as bullets snapped around us and shots and shells whirred past, that anyone should make such an inviting target of himself wearing white.

Those acquainted with Chapman said he never carried a weapon, it being remarkable that he continually exposed himself to maiming and destruction by faithfully following the men and boys he wrote about into hails of lead and iron--that his journal entries, as he preferred, might "ring" with authenticity. I cannot remember any other correspondent (and there were many) during the war who so heroically braved such fire or made such a memorable commitment.

Like countless soldiers who perished in battle, he apparently experienced a powerful intuition that told him he would not survive the day, and thus he gave the bulk of his works to Reverend McKenzie. I also think it exemplary of courage that the Reverend, as so many of his calling and devotion, regularly went into the cauldron to minister to the wounded and dying, chancing his life there and dying faithful to his mission. These servants of God received little if any praise for their efforts during the war, much to my discouragement and continuing embarrassment.

It amazes me that Chapman's works went unexamined and virtually unknown for twenty years. By another coincidence, and because I had written two wartime histories published by Mr. Fuller, he asked me to read Chapman's journals before he took them to press. I was one of several who read them and whose opinions he considered. Pouring through them, I was stunned to discover one entry in which he described himself as wearing a white coat. I gave the work my profound endorsement. It might not have comprised classic literature, but I immediately realized it was nonetheless a treasure, a poignantly human and stirring chronicle of the unforgettable dedication and bravery of our soldiers' and of Chapman's.

John Connerly
Army of Northern Virginia
CSA

Faces Of War

Comment by Ephram Walsh, Who Lost a Leg
Fifteen Years Earlier at Vera Cruz
in the War with Mexico

"Took our son to Atlanta's train depot to watch the coffins being unloaded for relatives to collect. I wanted him to see and remember it, as part of his education, for boys barely older were fighting across our land, and some may have been in those boxes. He understood that I did not wish to shame him for not being old enough to fight, but that I wanted him to remember the war's costs - to see the grief and hear the wailing of mothers and widows that day and to remember it on future solemn and patriotic occasions, when the fallen would be honored for their sacrifices. He returned home older and sobered that day, and I am satisfied that he thought deeply about his experiences. A year later, at sixteen, he joined-up, unbeknownst to us, but never came home."

Former Captain Daniel Boden
Cavalry-CSA

"I watched the partially yellow moon that memorable night, that peeked through rain clouds silhouetted against it - an ominous orb for us and omen-filled. Even our horses had grown skittish on their tether lines. In the morning we would fight, yet I doubted myself. I knew not whether I would lead my troop as I always had or whether, this time, my blood would freeze and I would falter, dishonoring myself before my men and the enemy. Pistols and sabers do terrible things to muscle, tissue and bone - shotguns worse. And a fallen body deflates terribly under the pounding of panicked hooves that turn it to pulp. I saw a thousand horrible images of myself beneath them, as I had witnessed that indelible metamorphosis occur a hundred times to unfortunates in our command and to the enemy's. No, nothing comforted me, no thought of home nor my sweetheart nor of pleasant times before the war. The air that night felt ominously cold and damp, unnerving me, as if the clammy hand of death were upon us. A chilling wind blew from the north. My body shook, but not from the chill. Rank aside, I felt too nakedly human, but I knew that in the morning I must be more - superhuman to do what my men, who depended upon me, expected of me - to lead them fearlessly even, if tactically necessary, in doomed or hopeless charges, as if I were made of iron. But, oh lord, was I terrified. Why did not my men appreciate that I was only made of flesh?"

**An Excerpt from a Memoir by
Mrs. Betsy Alberts, Concerning
a Sentiment Related to Her by
Her Sister Whose Husband, a
Scratch Farmer, was Away at War**

"I fret my Owen won't know me n'more - that we been apart too long t'rememba who we used t'be together b'fore he went for soldier - that he won't be a'knowin' his own youngins' and'll have t'learn togetherin' all ova agin. I ain't perdy n'more. Takin' care of'n 'ar farm fer three year near ruin't me. Ain't no woman n'more. Been too long a horse and pack mule. Frets me, it does.

If'n he come a'tall, he'll be a'catchin' me at m'worst fer sure - I knows it. Won't be a'wanting' me n'more and be shed a'me. Lord, this war be cruel."

**A Poem
Written by Private Tucker Smith
Infantry-CSA
1864**

And now, as soft rains fall
from a new spring's embrace
and memories tap upon my rifle,
I cherish in sweet-bitter reveries
joys and loves long gone
yet diminished not within me
that I wish to reclaim and relive
that, by God's grace,
the better I might do by them
and be forgiven for all my lapses then,
as I, at last,
have forgiven others theirs,
and that one compassionate night
while mercifully asleep
upon this Earth, my pillow,
I awaken humbled
and with charity for my enemies
and with, for myself,
abundant wisdom.

Comment by
Chester Putnam

Virginia Veteran

Confederate States Army

1861-1865

"I rememba' Chapman. He was at m'side at that slaughta pen, Malvern Hill. I was a Private then. He stayed with our compana' and endured. We lost thirty of our compana's' sixty that day. B'fore and afta' the battle, he and I talked at length about mana' things. He confided things to me. Why me? Neva knew - the stress of the moment, I suppose. He became a soldja armed with pen and paper and, like all soldjas, struggled to unda'stand the war, often with mixed emotions, like the rest of us. He cursed it while dedicated to seein' his nation delivad' from its powerful enemy's depredations. He chose to write that story for whoever might eventuala' read his journals. Did he eva' mention that he suffad' intensely from the afta' effects of a serious leg wound he received durin' the Mexican War? No, I spose not. At times, his painful leg swelled so badla', he was forced to split his trousa' seam. He followed our armies with incredible dedication. I could neva' have done as he did. It was bad enough bein' an armed soldja. He shared our soldjas' hunga, tribulations and sufferins'. And yet, he has remained unknown to posterity until now, two decades hence. Like the Lord, Fate, too, works in m'sterious ways, but unlike the Lord, not always justly."

Note By

The Reverend William Hirsch

Former Chaplain

Army of Northern Virginia

1861-1865

"I knew Royal Chapman. Met him during our Pennsylvania campaign. I can confirm that he kept a separate journal of names, places, dates, and units. I believe Chapman always felt rushed, thus his proclivity for trusting them to another venue as he hurriedly made his daily entries. Curiously, he came to our regiment and other commands seemingly from nowhere, stayed with us for a time, then vanished. Even so, his willingness to share enemy fire with us endeared him, even to soldiers who remembered him only in passing. I think he was supernaturally courageous patriot and the most unique human being I ever met. His spirituality left me feeling painfully inadequate and deeply introspective. Ironically, he was, in a unique sense, a greater spiritual inspiration to me than many men of deep conviction who were also servants of God's white collar.

* * *

A Legend Remembers

Gettysburg - Dusk - Day Three

July 3, 1863

We were gazing upon the wreckage of our once splendid divisions. No one could speak, for nothing was left to say. Acrid powder smoke hung everywhere. Even where our assault had been aimed - the cluster of trees along the opposing ridge - the air remained blurred beneath a grim, misty pall, as if we were staring into doom's lifeless realms, our massive assault having been turned back. The metallic scent of death crept everywhere. Standing alongside me, an ordinary citizen, who had gone with our troops into maelstrom but miraculously returned, jotted the following, tears streaming down his dirt and powder-blackened face. I believe his name was Chapman:

"Before this event, both armies prayed to the same God that He might side with them against the other. Did He answer only one or did He allow fate to have its way? We shall never know which, if either, He favored. Widows now on both sides will perish with grief, too overcome by the madness of it all to live forever alone and desolate. We, on our side, now see our fortunes imperiled as never before, our farms and mills threatened with fire and utter destruction by an enemy run rampant, our homes and cities burned or turned to rubble and our kin and livelihoods ruined, while our enemies have but to return to all they have safely left behind. On these fields for the past three days, we have both fought for liberties by different definitions, having condemned each other's motivations for three years. They decry slavery, for which the bulk of our men at arms do not lay down their lives, yet, they would admit to a perfect society while subjugating us and our land as if we, not they, were the perennial invader to be smashed--and they will now call foul our failed attempt to stave off their predations by bringing war to their soil as parity, as they have so egregiously brought it to ours. And yet, despite all, on this and other battlefields, in intervals of quiet and escape from the mutual slaughtering, we and they have individually met on neutral ground to greet each other and speak as old friends and about old friends and to engage in friendly discussion and trade tobacco for coffee, looking upon each other not as enemies but as countrymen in common. There and then, in the eyes of our Maker, both sides have stood exposed, naked and embarrassed, their consciences aflame with the knowledge that they have shamefully tread upon His Word and exceeded all moral authority. If the issues of this war had been left in the beginning to the privates of both sides to settle, with reasonable concords thereafter to celebrate with song and drink, this carnage today would never have transpired. Too carelessly does

the common man surrender his fealty to mortal powers above him and, as this war demonstrates, to hidden purposes and lofty egos that chant the septic spells loosing the mocking Devil's brutal scythe."

A weeping Chapman gave me that writing. I have done much meditation about that day and his words and will, until, for me, the Lord calls retreat.

J. Longstreet
General
CSA

Written by Royal Chapman
to fellow journalist
William Edgerton in May 1864

The Wilderness - Virginia

Dear William,

I have campaigned with a single regiment for two months and can testify that it is bone-weary and nearly fought-out. It has participated in some of the hardest fighting of the war and its losses over time have been severe.

Having originally enlisted 846 men in late '61, its numbers are down to 222. Note that this figure includes recent replacements, whose exact numbers are unknown to me.

The proof of the regiment's exhaustion lies not so much in its numbers of dead and wounded as much as in the eyes and faces of its veteran survivors. Even then, considering how much action they have seen its desertion rates have been mercifully miniscule.

Once again engaged with the enemy - this time for days in deviously treacherous terrain hidden within miles of burning wooded wilderness - these veterans have become ever more grim and sullen. They were a dispirited lot when I linked up with them, but the last two months of campaigning have drained them almost completely. They fight without the dash and spirit that once marked our Army's character. Even the least experienced among the newcomers proceeds slowly and cautiously, reluctant to blindly stride into this tangled Hell. There was a time when these proud fighters would have done so. No more.

Everywhere, fires, ignited by combat, burn out of control, consuming the trapped able-bodied and wounded with equal frenzy. The screaming agonies of those burning to death panic even our most steadfast. Our troops and the enemy's collide by accident in the underbrush and smoke, each side's lines being entwined and out of sight of their own. Companies become detached from regiments, lost and blinded in the smokey confusion and unable to communicate.

This battle is very much a struggle between individuals and individual effort. Never have I witnessed such attrition. I'm told it contravenes the most fundamental rules of tactics and organization, but convention hardly applies here. And we are suffering greatly for it. Officers have lost control. I regularly see men break down and weep with frustration and fear. Many refuse to move. Some menace their officers when ordered to do so - "To where?" they ask; "to what?" ...to inevitable death or capture? Some have gone mad.

Officers, commissioned and non-commissioned, are no less affected. It is impossible for some to deliver cogent orders, let alone know the tactical situation, that they might properly direct their men - and many are gripped by an infectious mental paralysis that defies them to act.

But I fear something more debilitating is abroad in the ranks - a fatalism seen in all eyes and faces - an acceptance of inevitable destruction stemming from a nearly tangible belief that it will forevermore liberate them from their constant terrors. Captured enemy troops suffer no less from it. Some become catatonic.

Many of our boys appear to wait for death and even to desire it. The waiting simmers quietly in their blank expressions. They stare soullessly into infinity and, like lumps of stone, passively resist orders - dumb and deaf. Many must be manhandled and carried by their comrades or shaken until their stupors are broken. Either that, or be consumed by the creeping flames.

Men become separated into groups of twos and threes that must constantly maneuver to flee the fires, with only a passing thought of the enemy, who is doing the same. Those who lose their bearings to hopelessness huddle in gaggles to await destruction - or surrender to death by their own hands. But the fighting's most contradictory nature comes when enemies, fleeing the fires, come face to face. At that moment, they either succumb to instinct and reflexively kill each other point-blank or, after a moment's hesitation, assert their common humanity by pulling together or carrying each other's wounded to safety - instantly reducing the war to absurdity - and just as instantly discovering the unity their politicians rejected before the first wartime shots were fired - or because pride and obstinacy pledged them to betray it. Those self-serving felons should be dragged here - today!

The fires burn day and night. No one sleeps. To sleep is to burn. Our boys pray for rain. Our generals and theirs are on their knees for it, asking that the flames might be quenched and their respective armies be delivered from this nightmare - so that they might organize the killing again!

How all their wounded and ours will be recovered without hundreds being consumed first, I cannot guess. These wooded tangles are impossible and the smoke is self-defeating. I fear that most who die in the flames will perish undetected.

Though not a combatant and worth nothing to the Army, I, too, am exhausted and as fearful as those about whom I write. I've composed this letter over a three-day period in brief moments of respite and in my head while on the move. Not to mention the fire's dangers, the enemy will spare no minié-ball on me because I carry only pencils and notebooks. After a time in conditions like these, killing becomes a thing of spiritual blindness. Stupefied soldiers do it by rote without conscience, never mind discretion. So-called "civilized" and "humane" rules of warfare blur and are lost to animal reactions. Killing becomes a reflexive exercise, as terror overcomes even the most reticent and turns them into near-mindless machines. A "no prisoners" mentality spawns an insidious blood lust that turns men's souls into rusted, disintegrating metal. The wounded are sometimes shot down or shot dead where they lay.

This war will claim thousands, William, long after the guns are stilled and the drums and banners put away. Even now, the seeds for that calamity are being sowed. Posterity will reap the after-winds of these times in lost and mutilated hearts that will not soon heal. We cannot know what the inevitable or final costs will be, except to surmise that all will be great. And I fear that my chronicling of these times, if I survive them, will continue as their ripples fan into the distant future.

Let us hope, that when it all ends, the decency and humanity, robbed from our people by these events, will Providentially reassert themselves, and that passions will cool in time - so that good men on both sides might at last look to Higher Authority for guidance, as both should have done initially - and as the killing has so poignantly proved - before taking up their soulless swords so long, long ago.

Your obedient servant,

Royal K.

* * *

In Chapman's Defense

Preachers who have read portions of his works suggest that he concentrates too repetitiously on mentioning gore and carnage, and that by repeating himself he risks putting off his more sensitive readership. Somewhere in that criticism hides the implication that he offends the clergy's sensibilities. Let me say that although I appreciate the moral broodings usually associated with preachers, war is not an incense-graced tabernacle - and Chapman's descriptions are far less repetitious and far more insightful than threadbare rituals commonly and patiently endured by parishioners for lifetimes of Sundays. I ask readers to attempt to place themselves in the fighting man's position because a soldier at war repeatedly experiences and endures what Chapman describes. Campaigning troops must so commonly associate with such horrors that each becomes part of his waking existence. He absorbs them into his psyche until he grows calloused and inured to them as he graduates from civilian virgin to blooded veteran. He lives around them - to the extent that treating with fellow soldiers in such an atmosphere can be called "socializing" in a civilian sense. And just as the uninitiated might be initially repulsed by them, the reader might more quickly begin to appreciate not only the veteran combat soldier's world view but how and why such matters become mundane to him and why he grows fatalistic about them and his chances for survival. At that moment, the reader will have vicariously entered upon that soldier's fractured existence, while, by far, having the better of things. As Chapman's works make obvious, while maintaining a chaplains' heart, he became that soldier.

Clifford Yancy
Captain of Artillery
Confederate States Army

From the Diary of Lieutenant Avery Gardner

CSA

Killed at the Battle of Murfreesboro, Tenn.
7 December 1864

Diary Entry:
Franklin, Tennessee - the evening of November 30, 1864

The fighting today was horrific, some of the worst this veteran has seen. We prevailed, but barely. The cost has been intolerable. Among those missing is Royal Chapman. Though we know not where he is, and fear the battle has claimed him, he remains with us in spirit. Though he was with us only briefly, two days, perhaps, his effect on us has been memorable. He was with us in the line and everywhere at Spring Hill before today, and after that fighting - in the glow of evening campfires - brought our hearts to pen. In that compacted time span, and with touching humility, he saw into our exhausted souls and those of our people.

He wrote as we might have written had we the ability, and read his writing to us, even as many of our boys tended to wounds. At our request, he read other pieces from his journals that he had written elsewhere, and we realized that he spoke with the voices of the living AND the sacrificed. Yes, he saw into our souls and those of our people. As he read, I pictured him filling his journal entries in summer heat and winter cold, in rain and wind, and was convinced that angels must have sat upon his shoulders dictating every word. His words gave comfort to our company's wounded, solace to the grieving who suffered the loss of long-time friends and encouragement to our war-weary.

He wrote not of great battles, nor of self-seeking generals, as have so many, but of haggard privates and equally set upon officers, illuminating their inherent humanness.

We miss his writings tonight, for we would once again have relished his poignant observations. Some say he is anonymously with our fallen now being buried. Others conjecture that he might have been taken prisoner or that he is wounded and under the care of enemy surgeons. If he IS hurt but alive, I wish him swift healing and much tranquility. And yet, my gut tells me that he is gone. At least, his words remain with us.

The end looms for us every day this war continues. Come morning or the next day or the day after that, we will meet our enemies again somewhere, for they are locust upon our lands - perhaps at a small settlement, near a town or at a wilderness road junction - or perhaps in a now pristine meadow or upon a panoramic vista. We fight on because we must, even though in their heart of hearts our soldiers know our cause is greatly imperiled. We struggle not fanatically but to make our point. Honor demands it and our enemies know it. We fight for the South's honor. If the victors ultimately be the Federals, history, being truth's concubine, will praise and honor them for their effort and call it righteous - while Northern posterity, if we are defeated, will cast us down and trample ours forever. But, we will always know differently and remain devoted to our disparaged dead and their days of glory. May the future be reminded that we are Americans, too.

In that regard, Chapman will have made us noble and honored us with immortality.

Excerpts From
In the Beauty of the Lilies

From the Recovered Journals of

Royal K. Chapman

Army of Northern Virginia

1862-1864

In The Beauty Of The Lilies

Said a young soldier to me today: "I love the land. It soothes me. It comforts m'spirit. I look on it as I look on all things a'beauty. I don't have none but someday I'm gonna git me some with woods on it and meadows a'long grasses and fields and hills. A man's gotta have land. It's the onla thing that mattas. He can have a wife and youngins and even his health, but land lives afta him foreva. It's something he ken leave to his kin that's a part a'him. And as long as he's alive, he ken walk it and know it's his and a part a'him as much his very own soul. Guess I'm dreamin' some, but'cha gotta dream a little jest t'git by day t'day in war, don'tcha? Leastwise, I do. My pa was onla a scratch farma and he din't have much save for five acre of no good bottom land, but he lost it fer debt and then he died. Ma died b'fore him three year. I buried both there 'cause the new owner let 'em be. But when I git MY land, I'm gonna move 'em to it even if they be onla bones. And there they're gonna stay for as long as there's an Earth. And when my time comes, I'll be there next to 'em."

But he would not be. Two days later, he perished with much of his company at Malvern Hill and now lies in the only land destiny would ever allow him and scores piled in with him.

*   *   *

How it is to Sacrifice

That you might understand the costs of this war in human terms, I am going to describe that which will offend and repulse many who read on. Yet, your cushion of safe distance from our battlefields should not protect you even from secondhand knowledge of the fighting's realities. You must know what your loved ones know who faced the "elephant" (a soldier's term for battle) in all its horrors. Thusly, will you be enabled to explain it to your progeny. In a spiritual sense, you, too, will have served.

Have you, who have never seen war, considered what it must be to be struck by a minié-ball, solid shot, canister balls or shards from exploding shells or pierced by bayonets? I will describe these conditions for you, not from personal experience, but from long observation.

Standard issue minié-balls, used by both sides, are conically-shaped bullets made of soft lead that mushroom around themselves when boring into tissue and bone. They devastate flesh and muscle and smash or splinter bones and joints, generally necessitating the amputation of limbs. They hit men like the hooves of bucking horses. I have seen struck soldiers lifted off their feet, spun 'round, bludgeoned to the ground, or heads exploded like watermelons. I have witnessed men, wounded by them, writhe on the ground like snakes run over by wagon wheels. And I have listened to men, whose innards they have torn away, swear in frustration, knowing they are as good as dead. I have observed others whose muscles have been gouged from their limbs by minié-balls, and left exit wounds that literally are crimson craters devoid of all living matter. And I have watched others, suffering chest wounds, turn deep blue in agony while suffocating because a ball's impact has collapsed their diaphragms and lungs. And I have seen others men with shattered spines poking from their backs after minié-balls have passed through their chests or jagged, broken ribs pointing through their torsos because minié-balls have passed through them from behind.

I have witnessed the effects of solid shot, fired from artillery, ripping obliquely through ranks, shearing away limbs or tearing a dozen bodies to pieces in misty clouds of blood, bone, tissue, and uniform parts. I have seen canister (iron balls of varying diameters packed together in compressed stacks and fired from cannon) mow shotgun-like through ranks, taking down hapless troops in mutilated heaps, arms, legs, heads and entrails flying. And I have observed jagged, razor-sharp iron chunks from exploding shells slice heads apart, sever limbs and, like whirling scythes, slash into and eviscerate bodies. And I have watched and heard men's supernatural agonies as bayonets plunge through their guts, rib cages, throats, sides and even eyes. Hauntingly, the dull, thudding impacts of rifle butts crushing into and splitting apart skulls is a sound that can never totally escape one's ears and memory. Spraying or dislodged brain tissue is anemically gray, or more nearly grayish-white and convoluted. And, lastly, I have stood helplessly by, while men's crimson life fluid has gushed from torn veins and arteries, while they themselves have watched it flow, passing from this world with paradoxical and even maddening equanimity - leaving my scarred soul emptied of feeling.

Yet, this comprises only one collective obscenity of the war our soldiers' witness. The other writhes in battle's aftermath - wounded men, lying on bloody ground by the hundreds in every state of mutilation in open-sky hospitals, in sun and rain, torturing heat and freezing cold, most to die and almost all with nothing to dull their pain nor give them comfort. They lie in their own clotted blood or bloody urine or the gagging corruption of their evacuated bowels. Horrible sights stun one's psyche - entrails piled around them, innards exposed to the heavens, hordes of flies tormenting their eyes and viscera, crawling up their noses or into their mouths and laying their white, elongated eggs in every wound and on all inflamed exposed tissue, except where their maggots gnaw and feast. Gangrene's overpowering stench, unforgettably putrid, never leaves one's nostrils. Surgeons' saws work day and night to the siren-like choruses of those non-anesthetized souls whose limbs they shear away - separated arms, legs, hands, and feet rotting in mounds alongside their makeshift operating tables or in heaps nearby, feeding ever more flies and maggots.

This, too, is our war and how it is to sacrifice for it. It is well that one disabuses himself of all illusions associated with the romance of spiffy uniforms and all forms of military pomp and martial music - unless doing otherwise means weeping with the Lord for the waste of it all. The singing that initially accompanied our soldiers everywhere they marched when the fighting began has long since echoed pitifully away, smothered by battle's soul-deadening cacophonies. Recoil from the reality of all this if you will, but know that your revulsion will change nothing unless the rational of both sides work together to demand of the war-makers...no more, no more.

In the meantime, where there are no lilies to beautify what man hath wrought, the sacrificing continues.

*   *   *

Bohemians

As I trudged through our regimental bivouac, I came upon a gaggle of nattily dressed so-called "correspondents" clustered 'round a tree. Weary but legitimate correspondents, who passed by toting knapsacks, blankets, canteens and writing files, unkempt and dirty after long days in the field, avoided them for solid, professional reasons.

The latter had my respect; the former my contempt, for I believe them to be alien to the responsibilities of the profession they claim to represent. They are embarrassing dandies despised by the Army - the kind who fancy themselves to be true "Bohemians" (as correspondents and reporters often are called), but who lollygag behind the lines away from the fighting - safe to write fanciful stories, much to the discredit of their profession, the Army and honor.

They studied me, noticing the journal case over my shoulder and my torn and worn-out garb. I do not know what they made of me, but they did not call me over, nor would I have accepted their invitation even if they had, for they knew their place. Never have I considered true journalists to be a club of their kind of "gentleman," though an obvious percentage of dandies do - those marked by sartorial splendor and telltale cleanliness. There is nothing "gentlemanly" about what dedicated professionals encounter, endure and do.

My blood heats at the sight of such "dandy" frauds. For I am convinced that, if forced to meet and face the Elephant head-on with our troops, they would soil their expensive britches to overflowing and run terrified to the shelter of the nearest drink. There, in order to ingratiate themselves with their adulating readerships, they would "bravely" write pure fiction or plagiarize the legitimate works of genuine professionals, thusly covering themselves with others' glory.

It is no wonder the Army's higher echelons seldom trust them to temper their reporting with restraint for the good of our troops and our war effort. Often, in their columns, they criminally reveal valuable intelligence the enemy would otherwise fail to collect - at the cost of our boys' blood. Accordingly, it should not be surprising that some have met with "rough" handling at the hands of our resentful troops.

Their reputations as irresponsible cavaliers make it hard for and sullies our entire corps of decent scribes, who seek no fame in dutifully reporting the war with absolute authority. Though these honorable servants of truth will receive little to no public recognition, even by default, they content themselves in having well-served their craft, earning their peers' hard-won and professional respect.

No honor could be higher.

Bless them. Our Army's trust in them is vital.

* * *

Suspicions

"You be a news-walker, ain'tcha," the sentry asked me, "'cause if'n you be, I'm told t'keep a close eye on you..."

No, I explained to the sentry, "I don't be a news-walker nor a thief, nor am I bonafide reporter. I just be following the Army keeping a journal."

"What be a journal?" he asked.

"It's like a book with blank pages, and I write on them about what I see and hear."

"Like a spy?"

"No, I ain't no spy," I clarified, somewhat perturbed. "I'm LIKE a newspaper reporter but I ain't workin' for a newspaper...I jest be workin' on my own!"

"Oh," he said, apparently satisfied, either that or mystified.

I shouldn't have been annoyed with him, since so many of our uneducated boys come from the isolated back-country and were never familiar with much of the world beyond the land they worked.

News-walkers have a tarnished reputation. Generally, they're independent news-gathers, like me, but light-fingered fellows as well, who will "lift" anything lying about that has either utility or monetary value. Some say they're especially fond of blankets or haversacks containing food, since they receive no regular Army rations. Neither do I, of course, but not often do our troops!

I'm told that usually, but not always, depending on the policies of individual commands, news-walkers are run-off or, at least, encouraged to news-gather elsewhere. One finds them attempting to sell their information to whatever newspapers and magazines chancing to buy it, though the accuracy of their work is suspect and their "news" sometimes manufactured. But, that detail hardly stops many hungry publishers these days. Common sentries, of course, hardly concern themselves with such trivia but do concern themselves with more practical issues - like theft, ergo that sentry's suspicions. Obviously an officer had to have briefed him on news-walkers' peculiar tendencies. I'm also told that, in many instances, news-walkers actually are welcomed by some commands. In this regard, I harbor my own suspicions.

Some officers, especially field grade and above, such as colonels and generals, who see political advantages in pampering what amount to personal publicists, will use news-walkers to enhance their images with the folks back home. Naturally, it rests with individual commands at very high levels to condone or prohibit such exploitation in lower commands. Fairness would mean also prohibiting it in higher commands, which for some ambitious officers - also for political reason - -might not be advantageous. So, no doubt, some prudently look the other way. But such are the realities of military culture.

Any officer of whatever rank who looks at me with exploitive eyes will find ME a very disappointing mark! The incorruptible men and boys of all ranks who have died in this war, or who have yet to die, would plead to have it no other way.

*　*　*

In the Beauty of the Lilies

Apology

I sometimes worry that, in my journal entries, I have given the impression that war is continual terror and that the men I write about face constant mental drudgery, depression, and physical tribulation. If so, I apologize, for reality is not always that.

Though no soldier commands his destiny, each finds occasional solace while also enduring endless hours of boredom, either on the march, in bivouac or on the drill field. Days and weeks often pass when the army remains inactive, especially in winter climes. Drilling becomes the persistent enemy at those times, as commanders fear that too much inactivity will dull the army's battlefield proficiency. Drilling, it is thought, wards off mental and physical rust and keeps the men finely edged while occupying time they might otherwise surrender to sloth and indolence.

You might ask - what makes drilling by definition different from drudgery?

The definition is that the drudgery of battle is a predominantly spiritual malaise born of the constant physical fear of wounding and death. There is not a fine line here between non-battle routine and those matters involving battle. Like water, wartime definitions seek their own level. And though men often bitterly complain about life and conditions when encamped for long periods, that grousing connotes a far different state of mind and, technically, a healthier one, than combat-related mind states.

I believe that Chaplains, who, at all times, receive on their doorsteps the full compendium of our men's problems, whatever their nature, will confirm what I've explained. True, they contend with solders' confessions and torments comprising all states of mental and spiritual distress over myriad concerns - most commonly about family and the terror of facing battle again. But, because the threat of combat is not immediate and, in fact, may be far off, there is far less stress involved with these concerns until they closely approach or evolve.

Actually, long encampments encourage men to think of, and concentrate on, imaginative ways to dispel the boredom of camp-life routine, such as producing song and dance and competitive games - from card-playing, gambling (not officially condoned), rough-house and winter snowball-fighting, all by the charity, and under the supervision, of their command leadership.

I can testify to all of the above, having experienced and survived with the Army for so very long and having witnessed all I've described. Yet, because I am not a rifle-carrying soldier, some may doubt my currency. Beyond what I've explained, I cannot prove my point, yet I'm certain that even then, fair consideration would grant my observation's weighty plausibility, if not total acceptance. For, despite the fact that I am not by definition a soldier, I have observed, experienced and felt, to the core of my being, all I've described.

And, one more observation: at no time does my pen guarantee me any more favor than does an enemy bullet or bursting shell.

*   *   *

Fields of Fire

Dark clouds threatened rain as General Hewitt led our sweating, mounted party to the place of his decomposing triumph, the buzz of a billion files sharp in our ears and rotting carrion burning our nostrils, gagging us. Two days earlier, his divisions had won on these fields. Now, haunted by conscience, he surveyed the human and equine wreckage he and arms had wrought.

A sensitive and religious man, he had brought me and his staff along so that we "might never forget the human costs of war." He need not have bothered with me, for I had seen it all too personally in Mexico and since this war's commencement. His young tentative staff, repulsed by the horror, had much to consider.

Offended as much as we were by putrefaction's overpowering stench, our horses grunted and pawed the earth, anxious to be away from it. Brought by a breeze, it was, nonetheless, as much a part of the army's trade as gunpowder and smoke. Nothing on Earth is more vile-smelling than rotting human flesh, for it clings to clothes and hair and never truly leaves one's nostrils. I, for one, will smell it for years more just as I smelled it after the war with Mexico.

"Taste it as well," the General bid his subordinates, "that you may never enjoy this business too much."

I had tied a kerchief in bandit-fashion over my face as had his staff, to which he had objected, "No, no, gentlemen, do not attempt to hide from it. Those men out there collecting the dead cannot and it is our work and the enemy's that they labor to put under." The rigid, bloated dead, he said, could not be blamed for the natural processes reducing them. Even as the burial teams struggled, other teams collected wagon loads of dropped, discarded and abandoned weapons and munitions, undamaged equipment and uniform apparel.

He explained that he had long ago made a pact with God promising that he would never be profligate with lives and would do all in his power to spare troops' injury and death in either victory or defeat. Though victory cannot always be achieved by such economy, he conceded, élan in battle should never be exploited or substituted for good military sense.

We rode through the battle's human and animal debris, war's material waste of every description polluting the scene as far as we could see - rifles, leather gear, caps, hats, paper, letters, body parts, cartridges, etc. - pausing here and there to survey mutilated bodies blackened in death and no longer resembling human form, many impossible to identify, horses by the score equally as rigid and expanded, some with their busted bellies expelling fly-infested viscera, their rigid legs like poles thrust skyward. Dead men, eyes horridly bulged and baked, lay with pants, shirts and jackets so stretched by bloating that we were certain they might explode, their mouths agape, their tongues protruding like swelled purple gut, their arms wide, fingers jaggedly crooked, legs hugely deformed, those, of course, still having limbs. And we watched the work of burial details all of whom were obviously tortured by the flaming sun.

The General wished to disgust and inconvenience his officers in every possible way. "Study and remember every detail, gentleman," he instructed with suppressed emotion. "Let nothing escape your memory of this." It was obvious he did not wish for them to take their responsibilities lightly nor, considering their elevated social status, hold themselves better than the enlisted dead. For that I admired him. He was no dandy pretender, as were so many of those given high rank by virtue of politics sans ability.

A large informal man, he, too, sweated profusely, hence his proclivity for riding in his shirt sleeves and encouraging his staff to do likewise. Bearded and wearing a common slouch hat, whose sweat-stained brim shaded his broad face, he hardly portrayed his rank - confiding to me that he abhorred restrictive uniform formalities, preferring comfort for himself and his rank and fils while encouraging his sickened staff to concentrate instead on efficiently performing their tasks.

"Continue this way," he motioned, skillfully guiding his horse around and through the heaviest concentrations of dead, theirs and ours. "Here is where the fighting was the most fierce. You will notice that in death, our men and theirs bear few distinctions. And why should they not have born only one?" he added with subtly sardonic empathy? "Were they not all Americans?"

Indeed, in many cases, their uniforms were too savaged to be distinguishable. Many, theirs and ours, had been victims of close-range canister fire - those small iron balls fired shotgun-like from artillery - the fighting having raged to and fro over the same ground. Wasting beneath the now overcasting sun, dead by the hundreds and horses by the score lay in wheat and corn fields, across fences, in meadows and on gentle slopes, their maggot-infested carcasses fully exposed or under heaps of killed. Flies by the legion lunched on this cornucopia of corruption as burial details invested it all in eternity, hauling it in and on horse-drawn wagons and sleds and dumping it into shallow pits of anonymity - human and equine waste being separated. Across the landscape, nearly all workers had tied kerchiefs or rags over their faces in futile attempts to escape the stench.

The General explained: "War's unwritten law dictates that the enemy's dead are buried last, time and circumstances permitting, though on occasions, such as now, it cannot be so precisely done."

I could see that our foes were being laid aside wherever possible to be heaped together in common sites not to be mixed with ours.

"Concerning your civilian readership," said the General to me, "do you think the printed word can do justice to these scenes?"

"No, not by words alone, General," I vouched, "and not even by my sketch work. I could do all but reproduce the smell of this, but without the smell the true impact would be lost."

"Indeed, it would," he mused.

The General impressed on me that he mystically believed the Lord's angels hovered over the dead to assist their souls in their transitions through the "shadow of the valley" and on "across the river." "When I was a private in the federal army during the Blackhawk Wars," he recollected, "we gathered and buried our dead ourselves - no dedicated burial parties such as these - every survivor to the task with bayonets, knives, powder barrel lids and ammunition boxes, hatchets, and our bare hands, every survivor with his musket at the ready. And while we dug, a padre, if one was available, or a religious man, would say prayers over the dead as we laid them in. In the Mexican War, as you know Mr. Chapman, we did much the same - not always but often - for we were always swiftly on the march after a fight. As a major there, I oversaw much burial work - that work of the damned. That is why I sympathize with these burial teams. In this war, they do our penance for us."

Halting, he turned to his staff: "This is your profession, gentleman, for this war's duration. Should we miraculously win this argument, and you come along in your post-war careers as a result but begin to think too highly of yourselves - and when the notion strikes you that you are somehow elevated far above the enlisted men you command - I want you to smell this day. Remember that not all the dead you see here are enlisted. There are officers among them whose flesh, like yours, is rotting as well. Remember that if you fall in in this war as they have fallen, your carrion will dissolve no less oppressively. And whether or not you remain in military service, you will remember this aroma even if you happen upon a dead bird or rabbit. Record it well. If in the military you remain, it is this smell you must first embrace if it is glory you seek or are tasked with achieving."

Though his officers discreetly contained their revulsion, the youngest lieutenant battled his churning gizzard. His face had turned sickly pale, his every inhalation tortuous. Only approaching rain promised to mask the fields' wafting miseries. His eyes pleaded, "Rain, come quick!" Minutes later, it did, on the cusp of gently grumbling thunder, softly and sparsely at first, then in a deluge. Burial teams paused to rejoice in its relief. The stench greatly lessened. We threaded our way back as we had come, wary of lightning's proximity, our horses needing no encouragement. In anointing the dead, the downpour appeared to moderate their grotesque postures, cleansing dirt from their deteriorating faces and glazing their stricken features.

I would not forget this burdened General's disguised pain nor how profoundly these scenes affected him despite his seeming nonchalance. I surmised that despite his elevated authority, he was a spiritually damaged man. No one responsible for so many Southern lives lost, not only in this battle but in others, as well, could have survived with his soul unscathed unless his conscience were made of stone. The irony is that if war is to be propagated, the consciences of many generals and approving politicians must be constructed of granite. But to be fair, I must reveal that I have seen some generals brought to their knees before God beneath such intolerable burdens. And I supposed that this man had so humbled himself on many occasions and would do so privately often in times to come. But a question remained; how long could he hold himself together before his conscience ate through his thinning veneer of compulsory senior grade composure?

As we hunkered against the deluge, he caught my eye: "Have you ever wondered why it so often rains after vicious fighting?" he asked. "Sometimes, I think it is God reminding us that He has promised to wash away our sins if we would but repent. But how could He truly cleanse these?"

It struck me that here was a lonely man craving to speak with someone, to confess his gnawing misgivings. Chaplains would not suffice. He desperately wished to communicate to someone also singed by the fire, who would understand. It could well have been me.

"It might be that God cannot," I ventured, carelessly letting my cynicism slip out. I saw it impact the General, who blanched, then looked away, as if I had inadvertently confirmed his worst fears for his questionable salvation.

As we passed a burial team, and in deference to the General, its workers removed their hats, pulled down their rags and kerchiefs and stood to attention, their faces haggard with fatigue. Rain poured from their exposed heads and now muddy apparel. Touched by their respect and humility, the General reined in his horse and paused there for several seconds, affectionately studying each man. Then, returning their tribute to him, and above those blood-wetted fields of fire, he raised his hand in a long salute.

"God bless you," he told them, his kinship with them apparent, "God bless your humbleness and decency."

Then, as we moved away again, he surrendered to his soul's pain - and wept.

*   *   *

A Comment by Dr. Joseph Simpson

Former Surgeon

Confederate Army of Northern Virginia

1863-1865

"My view of the war has left me with terrible and haunting impressions of suffering unimaginable by those who were not there. The wartime surgeons' experiences were not much written about, owing, undoubtedly, to their distasteful nature. Though Royal Chapman reported neither for newspapers nor magazines, he has honestly written for all of us, surgeons and soldiers, sparing neither poignancy nor truth. His imagery is as indelibly singed upon our consciences as the war was impressed upon our souls. And though humbled by defeat, we are yet stirred by his humanity and left uplifted by his record of our veterans and our fallen's valor. It is a tragedy that we cannot bring him home to thank him."

*   *   *

What War Be

"If'n y'wanna know what war be, it be what's on the field afta the fightin'…the cryin' and screamin', the wailin' and the pleadin'…pleadin't for wata, t'God fer mercy 'er death 'er all three…and the stink of it…the sulfur in the air from all the gun power smoke that burns yer eyes red…and the trash and bodies and parts a'bodies a'layin' all ova Creation…and the grovelin' and squirmin' wounded sufferin' the agonies a'Hell…and them's what's still foreva and the gaggin' stench a'blood and urine and feces and innards and guts a'spilled out eva'where…and maybe yer feelin' sorry fer it and yer conscience be achin' some 'cause ya put a lotta men down that day…a lotta 'em writhin' and thrashin' out there that minute…and maybe some what's layin' with others is the one's you put an end ta t'day. Yer body's a'tremblin' and yer tongue bein' as dry as old wood…and y'cain't think n'more and yer mouth and face be smeared with black power from bitin' into yer cartridges and loaded minie-balls and yer ears be a'ringin' and hurtin' and you feelin' like ya might go deef… and yer soul a'dead inside ya and feelin' like stone all cold and hard…and somma yer friends gone from around ya fer eva damned more that oughtn't t'be. So ya wanted t'know what the war, huh? Well, suh …that be jest a little part of it. So, if'n y'ain't gotta belly fulla it yet, well you jest come ahead and join right in cause there be plenta a'room fer ya…jest kick that dead man's guts and slimy liva outta the way and stand ova' here in this lake a'clottin' blood right here b'me!"

* * *

All a Man Could Do

There be spells 'tween fightin' that weighs heavy on a man. Oh, some tries t'disguise their thinkin' of the next fight and couch their fears, as they always do, in many ways, but they neva fool old vetrans lookin' on. Fear battles with pride and, most often, pride carries the most convincin' face, but onla to observas who don't know no betta. Some men sing and laugh and joke as if God's told 'em personal that they're gonna s'vive ever fight for the whole duration and see their loved ones agin. But othas - and here's sadness of it -well, they curl up inside theirselves and stay that a'way. Somes quiet and sleep all they can a'tryin' to escape the demons hauntin' their painful wakefulness. And some go off by theirselves a lot and stay quiet. And vetrans know betta that t'disturb their privacy, cause nothin' anotha man can do or say can change ana'thin'. They jest have t'git through it alone t'face the Devil when he come, as he come t'all on these fields a'terrible tribulation and death. Me? I'm always as skeerd as the rest, but I make m'peace with the Lord and put it all in His hands. If'n I'm kilt, then I'm kilt. If'n I ain't, then I ain't. In b'tween I bide. Is all a man can do."

Sergeant Lester Weems
Infantry

*   *   *

Diminished Majesty

When I view this poignant product of destructive human arrogance, my conscience shames me.

The shattered remains of a once magnificent oak stands where we fought. I suspect it has not only seen the Revolution but the Pilgrim's progress as well. Now slashed and shorn, it leans against the dying day, its vandalized stateliness the victim of careless artillery fire and blizzards of errant bullets.

How many generations will pass before its boughs will regenerate and its terrible scars heal? Or will it ever?

We hadn't any right to violate it so. We hadn't any right to detract from its God-given majesty. Silhouetted against His sun's golden demise, it was an example of His supreme Work and Word. Now, its damage mirrors our blasphemy. How, I wonder, will He reward us - and when?

I sulk before the oak, guilty. Here is the collective soul of both sides, shot through by their rebellious will. Here is our generation's conflicted image. And here, of our own making, is our repugnant self-portrait, yet how many soldiers will notice, understand or even care?

Exhausted troops trudge by but ignore it. Mounted officers look on, stooped-shouldered and bent with exhaustion. Generals, preoccupied with their material losses, feel no compunction about it. War dulls men's sensitivities and callouses their souls. How could anyone have expected less today?

We're abandoning the oak to its fate - while never seeing our perversity in its diminished majesty. We're moving on, too battle-weary to think, too beleaguered to care.

If only we had apologized to it or prayed for its forgiveness. If only we had managed, in the name of decency, a single syllable of contrition, perhaps God might yet have forgiven us and resurrected it with the magic touch of His Healing Hand.

RKC

Perspectives of Chaplain Robert P. Warran

Confederate States Army

**From a Sermon to his Regiment
on the eve of Pickett's Charge
Gettysburg - July 3, 1863**

The Mystery

"What does war teach?"

"That every man is given a preordained season, its duration Providentially specified.

"He cannot escape its details. His triumphs and failures, his ecstasies and sufferings are written, and he lives out his acts unaware that his life has been Divinely scripted.

"I cannot say why some soldiers live and others die; why a shell explodes next to a man who walks away unaffected, while next to him, others perish. Perhaps, it all can be explained by natural circumstances. But I doubt it.

"I have seen young men die and much older men live, who cannot reason why or for what purpose they have been spared but the younger men not, since their lives have seemed meaningless. But who can say, without knowing why the cards fall in their fashion, how a man's Earthly presence has affected others involved and set their direction in this great celestial play? Our natural tendency is to look for dramatic events to support this, when, in actuality, it may well be the simplest or most subtle acts or nuances that precipitate such outcomes.

"Every man's existence affects every other man's, even others unseen and unknown to him, so vast, interwoven and complex is this mysterious matrix called life and death. And who is to say that the curtain truly falls on existence in this vast Creation when the body serves out its time on this physical stage? And what if the curtain does not? What if there is a matrix beyond the physical even more stunning and complex?

"We cannot deny that, upon birth, men give themselves up to the Mystery. They direct their existences only within Divinely conceived parameters beyond which they have no control and which remain the Divine's Province. We are blessed only with limited senses. In this regard, even much of the animal kingdom is more highly evolved, it and we living out a measure of finite time.

"Perhaps, men at war sense this. Perhaps, only in war are or can these intuitions be acutely stimulated - and why soldiers turn inward and fatalistic without being able to put themselves into words, some knowing their time approaches its preordained expiration.

"And, perhaps, the greatest paradox of all will be that only afterwards, in a peace and contentment beyond understanding, will we understand. If so, we must bide even now and accept the Mystery's course. Isn't this, after all, Faith's mandate?"

*   *   *

He Wished

Written by Captain Terrence O'Sullivan
(a seminarian before the war and just before his death and Royal Chapman's
disappearance at the Battle of Franklin Tennessee in November, 1864, after Chapman
apparently confided to him that he believed he, Chapman, would not survive the day)

Before I lead my company into the fighting this very hour, with Royal Chapman beside us, I jot these thoughts, lest circumstances in this day's work defeat my attempts to record his last thoughts to me, should his premonition prove true. I, too, have experienced the same, and war has taught me never do doubt such insight. Even now our brigade is assembling, but strangely, I fear the moment not, and he has gone to gather his journals.

"Chapman wished there had been time to write good-byes to loved ones, but there never is time when one senses that his hour has come. Most soldiers seek but seldom find such opportunities, and they must leave all and everything behind to anticipate not good-byes but reunions somewhere in the Beyond.

"He confided to me that angels had spoken to him in his troubled slumber last night, bidding him, "Abandon your questioning and release all fear," and promised to guide him to Eternity after his last mortal breath. He confessed to me his supernatural weariness, since his body and soul, savaged by three years of war, had grown weak and dissipated. And he conceded that it was time to allow them their due. "How quickly my years have passed," he lamented. "Only recently was I a child. That being so, why do I feel so inspired that this day will be transforming?"

"I am certain that he leaves unresolved his ongoing dilemma - his inability to reconcile our Merciful God with the battlefield's horrors and man's obsession with war. I trust, as he trusted, that for all who meet in Eternity this day, the matter will resolve itself and they will at last find peace and spiritual tranquility where, he said, "with transcending beauty, the lilies eternally bloom."

"He and I prayed that if his time was now, it would be so."

A Reflection

"I have returned to peacefully bucolic fields and distant hills and woods bordering what otherwise appears to be an infinite expanse - to stand where they stood...the wind whispering, saying, 'they still are here,' those who came not home, where all now is green again where the crimson past lies beneath, still nourishing the thirsty loam...those numberless who stood with me."

Anonymous

The Tale Begins

The Recovered Works
of Royal K. Chapman

You and I were not there.
We did not see. We did not hear.
We could not feel what they felt
nor could we know, and yet it
haunts us still and we are
prisoners of its times.

R. A. Busse

In the Beauty of the Lilies

**The Wartime Journals
of Confederate Correspondent
Royal K. Chapman
1862-1864**

Journal One

Contents

*   *   *

A Thought

Crimson are the tides that toss nations
in violent discontent.

Our Poor Man's Fight

It is not for the rich man that our poor man fights, nor essentially to preserve any institution - social, political, or economic. He fights to repel invasion and to preserve his home and hearth and to be left to solve his society's problems in ways least disruptive to his state.

He fights to stave off the ruination and destitution of his family by brute federal power, all the while recognizing his society's injustices and imperfections. For it is upon the poor man that the enemy's hammer falls most destructively and whose predations have made moot the issue of secession but paramount his survival.

He is too proud not to resist - nor risk lying a coward in his grave.

He knows the war may not be won, for every day he sees the odds against him increase and his Army's strength diminish. But satisfied that he has made his point, he will die in these fields, as his kin and comrades have died in others, justified in his protest and in defense of his soil.

Slavery, a pox that would have perished of its own dead weight, was never our enemy's overriding concern. They made it, and not truly secession, their excuse to devastate our land, eliminate its economic competition and lay it low for a century. Our people have always feared and predicted such mendacity. Its costs to us are and have been unconscionable and wholly the product of the enemy's opportunism.

For the root of this war is economics, a negotiable matter. If only they and we, then tenuously united, had given ourselves to reason, and the matter to time. It is still a negotiable matter, but now that our enemies have tasted our blood, they will not squander their opportunity to devour our carcass, to once and for all free themselves from our threat to invite ever-increasing European trade and eliminate trade impediments.

And so, our poor man fights by the hundreds of thousands - who has never owned nor wished to own a single slave - many farmers like him whipped and shackled by the dire perversities of life itself and very hard fortune. It is not for the slave master that he defends his states, nor does he stand in this defense upon the black man's back. He does not sacrifice for the perpetuation of the plantation's owner's interests and the high price of cotton. It is for the poor man's parched acre and for his progeny that he defends his Confederacy against the tyranny of an all-powerful central authority - and lays down his life to oppose a Federal President who has assumed Caesar-like powers unto himself never countenanced by the Constitution. It was not the South that invaded the North after our Fort Sumter demonstration. It was Lincoln who mandated the invasion of the South. Yet, it is Lincoln who is being held up to sainthood and worshiped when, in truth, all he should be remembered for to date is his tenure's first and only great accomplishment - the needless deaths of hundreds of thousands of Americans. What supernaturally imaginative intellect he must have summoned to take that constructive course and achieve that hallowed distinction.

Today, I was asked by a captured enemy officer if we fight to preserve slavery. I replied, as I have replied to other captured Federal officers, "And how many of YOUR society's evils do YOU fight us to preserve?"

Perhaps, I explained, as a matter of fair sportsmanship, he would now consider permitting hundreds of thousands of OUR brethren to visit HIS country to liberate HIS citizens from themselves and THEIR evils - or would his people prefer to be left alone to cleanse THEIR house in time, as OURS would prefer to have been left alone in like manner?"

He did not answer.

*   *   *

In the Beginning

The day I began these journals I remembered our enemy's Battle Hymn, the one concerning the beautiful lilies that saw our Savior's birth. But the lilies in the pond we came to an hour later were not beautiful - and Christ remained absent across the sea, far from our affairs that day.

Bodies floated among those crimson-tinted blossoms and along the pond's banks while those who craved relief laid back in misery or bathed their faces in the cool waters now fetid with human corruption. Elsewhere, hundreds of parched lips tortured the surface, while scores of survivors soaked their bloody limbs or dipped their hands between the blossoms to flush festering wounds.

Packed all around, enemies of only hours ago moaned in unison, cried out or wept, sharing again, in their mutual agonies, common citizenship. Many, knowing they were doomed, stoically awaited death. Yet, on came ever more from the fighting yonder, homing by instinct on that liquid island of final resort.

Again, I was reminded of our enemy's stirring battle hymn. Ironic that it should have glorified such human wreckage. Nothing glorious breathed among the lilies I saw. I watched men of both sides - bent all that day on savaging each other - now, with grace and gentleness, tend each others' wounds. All were again members of the same family stung by war's madness - as if their opposing uniforms had ever truly meant anything worthy of their shared miseries. Yet, they could condemn only themselves for it.

I wondered how many abided their sufferings with aching consciences and how many regretted the day they had heeded the selfish calls of their feuding governments? How many now resented the firebrands who sit today in safety and comfort, some even in elegance, far from the catastrophe they have encouraged and sustained?

I resolved thereafter to write about "soldiers" as members of the same star-crossed multitude, not as opponents in a tragedy into which they have been naively seduced. Instead, I would write without regard to flags or uniforms, leaving all such distinctions to historians.

I hope that if anyone reads these journals long from now, they will be of future generations, whose forebears in this contest went innocently for soldier, only to abide the ages - in the elusive "Beauty of the Lilies."

* * *

The Lilies - First Impression & Comment

Across meadows and fields before me thousands of men on both sides deploy in mile-long lines, facing each other in precise formations soon to dissolve. So this is the nature of war in the 1860s. The numbers involved exceed those I knew in Mexico fifteen years earlier, representing a more ferocious reality than what Americans experienced in that campaign.

In Mexico, we faced a different people and a foreign culture. Our objectives were impersonal. We fought to go home again. But, now, in Virginia, as I watch the lilies soon to wither, form in those fated fields, the combatants are of the same blood and at home, Americans on American soil, ready to destroy each other with all the might inspired by their mutual bitterness.

I shudder, as artillery on both sides opens with thundering crescendos, clouding meadows and fields with pungent smoke. All along contending ranks, men fall by the score, drenched in each others' rifle fire. Gaps appear where shells take down bodies in clusters. In some places, the bloody lines, theirs and ours, merge.

I turn to a general officer standing nearby: "Is this what it will be?" I shout above the din, "This ferocity for only God knows how long?"

"I trust not," he replies. "All is in God's hands now."

Artillery shells explode fiery-orange above and along the now distorting lines, leaving boiling white smoke suspended in the sulfurous tendrils. Even in my dimming memory, the carnage of those distant Mexican battlefields remains graphic. Yet, now, I see the same agonies ripping through struggling infantry regiments on both sides. What manner of devotion steels men to mutilation and death, I wonder? Why do they not run from it? Indeed, why did we not run in Mexico long ago? Why didn't I? Will my seceded nation weather this storm and will its flesh and bone withstand these torrents of iron and lead, perhaps for years to come? On what side does God stand? Will I survive to learn the answers?

These are a few of my initial impressions. I am determined that in my journal entries, with few exceptions, I will not mentioned units, locations or battles, but index them elsewhere. My purpose will be to reflect upon the soldiers and civilians immersed in this war while refraining from cluttering my entries with military details readers will hardly remember. Besides, such minutiae will not matter since I will not be writing a pure military history or another record of great battles. Instead, I will devote myself to the common men and women enduring the fratricide, and reconciling themselves to wartime conditions.

Though many of the images herein will offend the naïve, I cannot sweeten the truth to spare them painful discomfort. If the reading becomes too harsh, they must set it aside. Only then can they escape the realities it illuminates.

Many in this struggle will lose their faith, but just as many will be graced by a generous Providence, their Faith enhanced and their characters mystically strengthened. I saw it happen in the war with Mexico. The whys of it remain beyond my understanding. Their weaknesses will be a testimony to human frailty and God's patience. Yet, neither side should forgive this holocaust, lest future generations repeat its folly.

I view this war with mixed feelings, having never conceded that it was necessary. Nor did I want it. But events build their own inevitable inertia, and like an earthen ball careening downhill, gathering mass, they become unstoppable.

Now the South is in it. They whys and wherefores of it are being rendered moot out there in those reddening fields. Either it will succeed in the defense of its soil or suffer a retribution that it has long suspected its Northern brethren of wishing to inflict upon it. Out of sheer economic ruthlessness, masked by patriotic vitriol and manipulated opinion, the North will devote every resource to putting us down for generations.

Throughout the course of events to follow, Lincoln will be advised by myriad self-interests to burn us to the ground and grind us to dust. If he succeeds, Northern historians will rationalize his methods as having been vital, his intent noble and his minions' efforts glorious. If he triumphs, we shall be hostage to his mercy. We must find a way to peace, even if not through battle, but we must not succumb. Otherwise, our progeny will suffer lifetimes of scorn and our culture insidious prejudice.

This conflict will see a new nation born or stillborn upon a bier of scarlet lilies. But, in song and myth, those ignorant of its tortured gestation will foolishly laud its birthing's false glory, those who were not here to see upon each petal the faces of the known and unknown, whose blood will nourish every bloom. I offer these grim reflections as testimonies to war's nature that they might be taken to heart. Whether we become two nations or remain as one, may our now disparate peoples henceforth devote themselves to negotiations in all contentious matters, but never again to arms.

*   *   *

No Longer the Same

Soldiers will tell you that, in war, a man watches and feels himself being changed by all he witnesses, by emotions he has never experienced but must contend with daily. And when, in quiet and private moments, he beholds great natural vistas that mellow and calm his soul, he looks inward and wonders who he's become. He stands apart from himself and dispassionately attempts to understand the new mortal he sees.

A soldier functions daily on many levels, the most profound belonging to a diminishing personal identity. If he is a good man, he fears that this peacetime being, so long subdued by war, has atrophied. And though he craves to commune with it again, as a lost man seeking to reestablish his true bearings, wartime conditions bend him to their will and callous-over whatever sensitivities he now cherishes in memory.

He knows his existence requires reconnection with the mental and spiritual nutrition peace provided it. For, without it, he fears the total loss of himself. And though he struggles to preserve his soul, it often remains beyond his reach. Day to day, he feels himself slipping farther away, as might a drowning man from a raft at sea.

The process of feeling one's self slipping away is painful and lonely, sometimes turning a man desperate. Many shall survive this conflict with visible scars, but all, in some way, will have been disabled. Most will struggle subtly for years or the rest of their lives to find themselves again. I cannot imagine how they will compensate or be compensated, except through the ministrations of other insightful souls endowed by God with compassionate Grace.

If I survive this endeavor, I, too, will need such souls as I have always needed them - for the Mexican gorgon is ever with me.

*   *   *

Red Ink

Critics who have examined my journal excerpts complain that I am apt to write too much "in blood." The accusation is understandable. This is war, after all, and I describe war. War mixes both blood and poignancy, and to truthfully record it, the observer must dip his pen in both.

Today we retreated. Things did not go well from the fighting's start. And though our stubborn boys gave ground grudgingly, they could not compete with the enemy's numbers. In the past few months, such has been the case everywhere we have resisted him. His resources and manpower increase every day, while ours dissipate like water from a holed canteen.

I stood atop a hill well behind the battlefield, sketching the retreat in charcoal. Wounded streamed by, some barely able to climb the gentle incline. "Have you no decency, sir?" a wounded officer on horseback bellowed as he rode by. "I beg of you, leave these poor souls to their privacy." Privacy...in the midst of an army...

In deference to his feelings, I lowered my sketch pad. He urged his mount onward, ignoring the blood seeping from its many wounds. More than prose, sketching produces history's most graphic accountings, but I understood his concerns. Officers, generally, measure newsmen with contempt, and he had naturally assumed I was contemptuous. Many so-called journalists feed on scenes like these to bolster their standing with the public and their editors, but hardly out of a true desire to accurately bring the war home to readers. They consistently fail to sincerely elicit concern for the maimed and compassion for the dying.

Slowly moving up the hill toward the rear, dejected troops trudged by singly, in pairs, in groups and gaggles. Some nursed bullet holes and bayonet punctures, knife slashes, shrapnel tears and hemorrhaging. Some, blinded by powder burns, clung to others. Still others suffered hideous wounds to the face and body. All filed back in every state of distress, disillusionment etched in their powder-smeared expressions, their blank eyes staring for miles into nothingness. The fortunate, whom fate had spared for reasons unknown, retreated unscathed. To a man, they offered verbal encouragement to their tormented brethren.

Their altruism was that of closely knit family members saddened by their kins' misfortunes. I worried that my meager artistic talents would fail to convey that essence, thus my alternate reliance on prose. Talent, I long-ago discovered, is a razor that cuts well only when used with humility - or to the user's bone when carelessly represented. To my regret, I bear many such inadvertent scars.

Powder smoke drifted from the battlefield and across the hill, embracing all sufferers in their special humiliation. One could see, in their slouched shoulders and downcast eyes, that the Army's confidence was gone. In the war's early days and winning times, even our gravely wounded conducted themselves with a reconstituting élan. But, today, its right flank had dissolved and the enemy had rolled-up its lines. Now, in confusion, its panicked survivors sought sanctuaries in the rolling countryside away from the killing.

"Watcha makin' there?" a bent and hobbling soldier asked me as I sketched, his wounds grievous.

Young and hatless, he looked on, his jacket bloody and torn, his trembling right hand clutching his broken rifle. His other hand and arm dangled at his side, shattered. His drawn and starkly ashen face indicated that he had nearly bled out. I stared, unable to comprehend the willpower that sustained him and kept him standing. But his innocent curiosity touched me, as if, in the last minutes of his life, he had returned to childhood. A shaft of sunlight shimmered in his dusty hair. Blood drained and dripped from his wounded arm and side.

"Is ya drawin' somethin' 'bout us?" he asked, "somethin' like them artist-fellers draw? Sure like art n'stuff. Ain't never had no 'edjacation in it, but I take to it ana'ways."

I marveled that he appeared so impervious to pain. How could he converse about something so removed from his ordeal? I explained that I was not truly an artist but merely a sketcher, though not a good one.

"Sure like art n'stuff," he repeated, haltingly this time. "Ain't never had no 'edjacation in it, but I take to it anaways..."

He began to totter and weave: "Gettin' kinda hazy and cold, isn't it?" he said. "Cain't be cold this time a year, can it? Jest cain't be. Mamma wouldn't b'lieve how cold it's gettin' t'be...mamma... mamma..."

He fell like a statue at my feet, his face in the dust, his hand still gripping his rifle, his ankles crossed in death's most telltale posture. Passing troops trudged by, their dazed eyes absorbing the tragedy, their expressions appearing to say..."This IS a day of death, after all. What matters one more soldier? Most of us also are young."

What mattered was that it mattered to me - that and the haunting conviction that, unlike the romantic sentiment in our enemy's vaunted Battle Hymn, we would find no beauty in the lilies across this bloody sea.

* * *

Simple Dignity

It has not been false modesty that has prompted me to ask men in every command I've marched with not to consider me during battle - and never to risk themselves in any way for my welfare, the risks I accept being entirely mine.

I wished them to ignore me, for I have taken every chance, fully aware of the consequences. But they have been continually perplexed by my attitude and have not fathomed why I chance so much to chronicle circumstances they would rather have forgotten.

I have appreciated their concerns but have explained that as they have had their missions to fulfill, I have had mine. Theirs has been the most arduous. Mine by comparison have been simple - to record what I see and, when personally significant, what I feel.

In their own eyes, I've been a curiosity - to their officers, an unknown factor. Politics lurk in this. Ambitious officers, sensitive about their careers and chances for promotion, have not always been able to determine if I would be a boon to them or a threat - for they have understood the power of the pen to be one or the other. Around me, they have been generally circumspect, neither too friendly nor too austere, until able to divine my non-hostile attitudes toward them and my sympathetic motives.

One officer, speaking frankly, told me, "I have found journalists to be snakes - passive until they bite." Although I could not discount his experiences with others, I could only vouch the following to him - that I have no political agenda other than to embarrass our government when its embarrassment will better serve our deprived forces and the men who have sacrificed in its service. In that regard, its failures have been, and remain, regrettable. I adopted this objective only after witnessing some of the most tragic.

This, then, has been the foundation of my work. What I've recorded, for good or ill, will speak for itself. My premonition is that I will not survive this war, but I think nothing greater of myself than any common soldier in ranks thinks of himself. I have observed that life and death are the province of a Supreme Will beyond our understanding - and have left it at that - as they are forced to do daily.

If I've found beauty in the lilies at all, it has been in the simple dignity of the men with whom I've marched - and the love I feel for their devotion to Cause and duty. To a man, they have been more noble than I could ever have been. If anything, I've attempted to illuminate the mystery of their devotion, accepting that humanity's "perfection" will forever glow as a distant light upon an unreachable hill.

* * *

The Gorgon

I have watched men panic under fire - even veterans for whom the pressures of death versus life and the imminent threat of oblivion overpowers all control, compelling them to act upon their most base instincts.

These pressures, for most veterans, are cumulative and a long time coming. No single event inspires such behavior. "Running" is the culmination of many emotional and mental factors, and many men fear it more than facing the enemy's iron and lead.

Running tears a man down, degrades him in his own eyes, forever fills him with the fear of repetition, because he trusts himself no longer. More importantly, running ruins him in the eyes of his compatriots. The gorgon therefore has two faces - one of physical terror, the other of cowardice, a greater terror.

Only a razor's edge separates cowardice from bravery. Given that a man's spiritual balance is unsure, he can fall to either side. Imbalance is assured when friends, whose moral strength he depends and leans upon, also begin to waiver. At that moment, the dominoes begin to fall, taking all others of compunction with them.

In combat, soldiers are so interdependent that the weakness of one can become the weakness of all. Panic feeds on panic. Beyond combat's concealing smoke, the enemy's ill-perceived mass becomes every man's personal demon, its size and ferocity magnified by the unknown, the unknown feeding upon panic - its portent made deadlier by heated imaginations. In this confused hell, made more hellish by the wounded's gore and screaming, men crack. One by one, they drop their rifles and race rearward, even through the ranks behind them. With animal focus, they opt for certain survival, forgetting who and what they were - each ever more terrified by that invisible beast whose cloven hoofs beat and shake the earth just behind them - that gigantic, bloody-clawed and fiery-eyed behemoth that each man knows is pursuing HIM and him alone!

How do I know all this? Because - I have run that very gauntlet with them.

No, never have I claimed to be brave or heroic. I have pledged only to do my best, suffer my worst, and then try to redeem myself.

* * *

Campfires

I probably would not be believed if I were to proffer that a man can spend hours staring into a campfire's flames without speaking a word. Yet, singly, in pairs or by the score, the men of this company and regiment do so at almost every opportunity.

To the casual observer unfamiliar with war, it may comprise a mystery. But to one all too acquainted with war, it is part and parcel of war's effects upon the heart, soul and conscience.

Campfires create a mesmerizing hold upon the minds of battle-weary and physically exhausted soldiers. Be a fire large or small, or merely the flickering remainders of a near-conflagration, its entrancing radiance reaches out to touch the watcher's most contemplative nature, captivating him, his thoughts his own, as if he has left his body to drift elsewhere, perhaps to loved ones far away, his shell frozen in the position of the moment and abandoned.

I, too, can testify to a campfire's mystical powers. Ironically, being charmed by one is akin to the effects sea and surf stimulate in a watcher. We are drawn out of ourselves and carried away. Besides being supernaturally restful, the contentment campfires engender are deep, soothing and profoundly satisfying, even if a man's mind is rendered blank as he stares into the dancing light. Thus, he escapes the world of war he knows only too painfully well for passage into limitless expanses wherein he is no longer trapped within tactile circumstances. No other experience compares, this one remaining singular in every respect. A campfire's gentle crackling adds a soporific spell to the sweet alchemy, further enhancing his sojourn. But there, within his eyes, the flame's reflections reveal secret stories and poignant tales of want and loneliness.

I attempt to divine and translate however man I can, trusting that my efforts amount to more than errant speculation. For every tale I record represents a portion of the collective experience of every soldier who has seen the gorgon, survived its hot breath, and wondered if he will ever see home again.

* * *

Fields of Mist

It is dusk. We sit watching mists rise from autumn fields beyond our bivouac. Perhaps fifty soldiers lounge here, lost in thought and mesmerized by the quiet evening serenade that accompanies deep shadows moving everywhere across the land.

We are lost in this scene. I cannot remember a more personal time. War magnifies the significance of small things because they represent life, and small things are what soldiers cling to and savor, knowing how cheaply they are spent on the battlefield.

Though I am not a soldier, I share their lives. They accept me as an alter ego who has chanced bullet and shell to go with them into harm's way, that his written reflections might accurately reflect their ordeals.

Clinging to the horizon in the last of the sun's light, rising mists assume a ghostly aura, merging into a luminescent sheet that grows and rises. The countryside's scent is sweet with the magical fragrances of wild grasses mixed with the pungent aromas of burning wood from crackling campfires in bivouacs all around. Company by company, it is their time for hot chicory and herbal brews in tin cups and cans and for whatever rations we have collected in our haversacks. Meager meals before sleep - common fare to tease half-filled bellies on which to dream or endure sleepless nights.

We would give our souls to wander into those forming mists and the mystical kingdoms they secret - and lose ourselves in whatever contentment they harbor.

*   *   *

They Will Never Know

When I study the men I march with in this regiment, especially those of simple heritage and simple faith, I see beneath their homespun dialects and rough edges a brash but almost childlike innocence. Most are farm or back-woods boys who come from hard lives. They know few social graces. Their hygiene, like most soldiers', is minimal at best, but, to be fair, they, also like most of our soldiers, have little access to hygienic facilities, let alone opportunity. Most are uneducated. They cannot read nor write. And most speak variations of colloquial English that would mortify sophisticates of higher learning. But, Lord, do they fight, even when they know their efforts to be futile.

They're naturally ornery, argumentative and stubborn, but I truly believe it is their innocent trust in our leaders and love of the Confederacy's independence that compels them to so fiercely resist the invading Federals - that and their seemingly innate sense of justice, as they conceive of it.

There is nothing equivocal about their opinions or their attitudes. They assert that there is right or there is wrong with little shading between, and they expect you to understand that men either do good or they do bad, also with little ground between. They're predictable in their fighting abilities but unpredictable in their behavior away from it, yet they are not brawlers.

Away from the battlefield, they live for the moment. They drink, gamble and enjoy swearing as much as they delight in subverting Army regulations, which they consider spiritually restrictive. Most are raucous by nature but deeply religious and respectful of religious piety. And though, when pressed, they will yield to wartime authority, they hate supervision and bridle to the point of rebellion at what they perceive to be overbearing martinets and other strict disciplinarians. Our officers have learned to be scrupulously fair in dealing with them, whatever the circumstances, simply because their fighting qualities and the inspiration those qualities bring to our forces are so vitally needed. But, to browbeat one of them is to very quickly invite the ire of all, yet, if one of theirs is wrong, they acknowledge it.

They consider slave-owners to be a class of fools and would generally accept a black man as one of their own upon the merits of his character. Having done backbreaking toil upon their farms for most if not all of their lives, they appreciate the black field hands' plight. They stay to themselves, remaining suspicious of outsiders and anyone not of their ilk, but if they accept you into their circle and make you a friend, you become a friend for life, and they will stand behind you as one of their own unless and until you betray their trust and goodwill.

All in all, to our enemy, they are and will remain an enigma. Northerners will never know their hearts, nor why they are as they are, nor their values nor culture, which dates to the earliest

European migrations. Many have come from communities isolated in the back country for generations. Still, most know the Bible well and are humbly loyal to God. But their wrath knows only supernatural bounds when they are teased about their people being incestuous. Many a man who's been careless enough to imply it has known severe discomfort afterwards, having spent much reflective time nursing a broken jaw, cracked ribs or a parted skull.

A day or two ago, one Private Elijah Weeks of Tennessee was hardly shy about expressing his political opinions concerning the war's origins. But when the subject turned to Lincoln, he grew angry and animated. Given his humble circumstances, I was amazed that he had apparently accumulated information enough, however slanted, to have cogently presented such views - which confirmed to me that although uneducated, his people are not slow: "Lincoln done hoodwinked them yahoos over there in Charleston to fire on Sumta! And he done it jest so he could give hisself excuses ta put down the South fer his big-money Yankee mastas up there in New England. No, Sumta ain't why ner where this here disagreement b'gun, no, siree! It b'gun when that ole' sona Satan in Warshinton sent his armies onta Southern soil, that's wen it b'gun. Harsh words ken be spoke fer a hunerd year and cannon ken raise all kind a hell, but wars don't be a'startin' lessen armies move - and any dead goose knows that - and this here begun when he done jest that with his. He don't give a plug a'chaw fer black skin no more than he do yern - and the onla thing he done trula emancipated's been the souls a'more white folks on both sides then a herd a'curs got fleas, what never had nothin' agin' each otha t'begin with! Reckon up North these days that make a man a great hero! Well, it don't t'the Lord. And down here, it jest make him a Pontious Pilate and a damnable dog that'd eat outta dirty hands full anuff t'feed it."

Indeed, Week's people do not endeavor to gild this war's lilies, neither in bivouac nor on the battlefield.

* * *

Doubts

A Letter from Infantry Lieutenant Miles Sidley
to his Brother, James

"November: It is cold and raining. Bone-chilling dampness spreads to all and everything, defying all attempts to defeat it. We are in winter quarters, now. We and the regiment's enlisted live in a city of log huts, yet they are anything but health-inducing, and we long to abandon them for the bright, open air in the worshipful warmth of God's Autumn sunshine. Unfortunately, there is none. We, like all other log hut residents, conserve our firewood by tolerating as little heat as is necessary to sustain life.

"Due to the general paucity of firewood, we must use our supply very sparingly. Consequently, the firewood in our makeshift stone hearth burns low all day long. In this cabin, including me, there are four officers, and we must move to and fro wrapped in blankets much of time. Our food is meager and tasteless - rancid Army salt pork, beans, and hominy with occasional dried vegetables donated to our regiment by local farmers and Samaritans. Yet, we've accustomed ourselves to these conditions. We play cards or read the same books, pamphlets and ragged newspapers we've already read a dozen times, hoping we might catch something we've missed before. Or we catch lice or stare from our doorway which we only partially open to freshen the air inside, only to find gloomy boredom staring us back.

"I do little but think and sleep between making my rounds of our company. We take turns doing so to see to the men's comforts as much as possible and to watch for sickness and melancholy. Yet, even in my sleep, I am unable to turn down my agitated brain, so bored am I with sleeping. My dreams are confused reviews of the conflict I've seen thus far, and I most often dread closing my eyes again and seeing the same horrors. Our senior officers neglect us juniors and usually leave us to our devices, but they cannot be blamed as they, too, are weary and as spiritually depleted and mentally exhausted as the rest of us.

"Though winter has yet to begin, our troops ache for liberation from this hellhole. As you are aware, I thought long and deeply about this war before joining-up, having tolerated severe criticism by neighbors at home for having waited as long as I did - some calling me a coward, slacker and worse. But, as you also know, I could not see the sense of it and still cannot, which makes my position all the more perverse and hypocritical to me, though I ultimately joined to save the family name from further degradation and abuse. Still, I will do my duty though my conscience berates me for it and tortures me over the horrible carnage and waste I've witnessed due to battle and disease. What might these men and boys of both sides have given to our then still undivided nation had not so many firebrands been so anxious to settle their regional differences with shot and powder.

"Not that I am unsympathetic to all you have given to the Cause, James. I wish you to always stay safe and to safeguard your family with care and diligence. That you have lost a leg in this war and are now home is a blessing in disguise when I think that you might have been lost to us forever, lying anonymous beneath the sod of a forgotten field somewhere. In a sense, I am an invalid, as well, though, like you, not a self-pitying one, as are so many others. Doubters like me must always stand without crutches to bear the weight of their consciences, but I understood this before I accepted my burden. I rationalized that my leadership might save lives that would otherwise be lost to families and sweethearts. Such thinking drives my daily energies.

"You would be surprised at the number of boys in our company who miss their families with almost debilitating homesickness but who must not be allowed to depend too willingly on us junior officers for solace and comforting guidance. We must be appreciative of their plight but firm in our leadership because sooner or later they must learn to stand on their own.

"So, with nothing more to do save for letter-writing, I cannot be excused for not contacting you often. Will await your reply with great anticipation and all the news of home and family affairs you can manage to include in it. If you can, send steaks, fruits of all descriptions, summer sunshine and balmy climes. If possible, also send us Davis and Lincoln, that we might enthusiastically persuade them to end this unnecessary war."

Miles Sidley fell in a skirmish two days later. This letter was found on his person and delivered to me. I thought its sentiments important enough to record. If I have tread upon decency, forgive me.

RKC

Board of Tears

Though I cannot recall the name of the town we marched through, our weary column paused there to rest after having trekked all morning. In its center, on a lovely green, stood a public notice board. Many small towns feature them. Yet, no longer was this a board of small concerns and petty joys. The war had made it a board of tears and sorrow.

Relaxing and supine in the middle of the street, hundreds of us watched, as word of the parish's wounded and dead coincidentally arrived by courier. Up went the "dead-lists" to the board, amid throngs who, for weeks, had awaited news of their loved ones in uniform. Then came screams of anguish, emotional devastation, and spiritual testing. Our sympathetic boys looked on, helplessly.

We witnessed horrified mothers, wives, and sweethearts suddenly clutch the coats sleeves of old men next to them, or bury their faces in the shoulders of friends and relatives - some collapsing where they stood. Here was one of the war's most unpublicized tragedies - its seldom-counted civilian casualties bleeding for The Cause just as mightily within.

We observed them stumble away on other's supporting arms, back to their buggies. I witnessed their tears fall into the dust of the street - and beheld the future.

Notice boards - who would ever have thought, before the guns commenced firing, that they would so humble our nation? Who would have thought they would become our national reservoirs of excruciating pathos?

The sun was hot that day. But shortly, as if to cleanse away the town's sadness, rain diluted the tears still spotting the dust - yet the sadness remained - as denizens recalled youthful faces that only yesterday had filled their world with energy and hope - that now, pathetically, were attached to the dead-lists.

Our soaked but pensive regiments filed into the countryside before sunset, wondering if the town, too, would eventually die. So many names, so many futures sacrificed, as if the dead had never existed, except in their survivor's imaginations, the promise of a generation - lost. Death of any sort is cruel, even sadistic, defying reason and contemptuous of mercy. Its challenging lesson is always hard...that, often, perhaps all TOO often, faith alone is not enough.

*   *   *

In the Beauty of the Lilies

**The Wartime Journals
of Confederate Correspondent
Royal K. Chapman
1862-1864**

Journal Two

Contents

*   *   *

A Thought

Battlefields are filled with life
released to higher purposes.

For Every Man

For every man there is a singular season - for the men of our Army, a season of trial. For many, that season is now. For many others, their season has passed, and they now lie beneath the earth or somewhere in the septic silence of hospitals, suffering agonies untold, or without limbs and on crutches, returning home to loved ones, but also to problem-filled futures.

Concerning the wounded and the recovering, our society has provided no compensations for them. They have served, but paid terrible prices for their valor and now go home to their own devices, to subsist or starve, languish or persevere according to circumstances and the strength of their characters. But who will assist them, beyond their families, with other than love and care? What of the practicalities? Families must be fed and provided for and men must work to support them, especially amputees and those with grievous disabilities earned on the march and on the battlefield that include chronic diseases, most of which are beyond our medicines to affect. What of these men? Who will hire them? What will our government do to assist them?

I envision a nation filled with disabled men and boys who will wander and beg their ways through life for years to come should we win this war or lose it. Given the meager means our government has established for the care of the maimed, it cannot be otherwise. For the sakes of our people, I wish it could be. We cannot abide this situation. If we win, our people must demand from the Richmond government a program of assistance. They must not permit their politicians to escape this responsibility. If we lose, with our government dissolved, we must do what we can, give what we can, to ease the veteran's burdens, even with the enemy's boot on our necks for a generation.

In defeat, our nation will be as a puzzle of a thousand spilled pieces that must be reassembled one by one, requiring fortitude and patience in an abundance we have never before summoned. If victorious we shall patiently heal our wounds, disenthrall ourselves and live out the dreams of the Founders. During that arduous process, the flush of victory will pale soon enough.

*   *   *

Distant Rumblings

In a small hamlet, miles from the battlefield, I watched a preacher step into his pulpit to address his small Sunday congregation.

Beyond the church's windows, a balmy autumn breeze graced the day. Wagon and buggy-harnessed horses patiently awaited their masters' return. Pawing the earth, they strained beneath flurries of fiery-hued leaves released by the breeze from overhead boughs. In surrounding fields, deer listened. Rabbits paused. Even foxes sniffed the air, confused by the rumblings of an unnatural storm of artillery fire carried on the breeze.

Seated inside the church, farmers, merchants, blacksmiths and housewives pensively watched the preacher prepare his notes, their faces firm. The storms' troubling thunder weighed heavily on their souls. Children squirmed. Mothers restrained them or tenderly scolded. Old veterans looked to the windows, remembering.

The preacher donned his spectacles and, with great deliberation, opened his Bible. Scanning the pages upon which he had planned to comment, he hesitated. Then, unsettled, he put his sermon aside. On this day, he said, with so many grave events occurring only miles away, preaching about right and wrong - in the context of King David's immoralities - would be untimely. He said his parishioners knew right from wrong well enough, and they would be correct to expect more from him today, something appropriate to their concerns - perhaps something from his heart. I commenced my shorthand...

"I know what lays heavily upon your minds;" he began. "It is on mine, as well. God is HERE, within our small gathering, making our surroundings tranquil and beautiful. Yet, why, you wonder, is He not THERE, where humanity suffers that terrible thunder - where, contrary to the hymn, there is NO beauty in the lilies this day?

"This is a time of leaves, when the earth prepares for slumber, and good people, like all of you here, ready themselves - in a poignant sense - for slumber of a kind. Yours will not be a physical slumber, but a reprieve from your toils in your fields and their constant influences. Your hard labors of spring and summer and your fall harvesting will have run their courses. You will live life for many months to come closely in each other's company, free of your former cares.

"In a leisurely manner, you will make adjustments, some of them difficult, and be prey to impatience and temptations. Yet, your families will sustain you. The Lord foresaw that you would endure such doldrums and gave you the strength in your hands and hearts to overcome. And He gave you His Book and His Word and the bounties of your fields to nourish you, body and soul, in such times.

"Our world of calm and peacefulness is of God's design. Because we follow His Word, and live as He would have us live, He rewards us with calm and tranquility. But although He protects us not from ALL crises, He has taught us to suffer the bad through faith in Him AND his Word, that a plan far beyond our ken might be fulfilled. And, He has promised us that He will give us spiritual sustenance and His loyalty, that we might endure all things and survive even Earthly mortality.

"The thunder you hear beyond our valley is not of His making. Nor is it of His sufferance. It is of MAN'S free will run amok, the free will He gave man to choose between His Word OR man's. That, I imagine, is why He makes no peace there. That is why He allows man to indulge himself and suffer - in this instance - the terrible consequences of such folly, that eventually, men might learn from it and evolve.

"I truly believe - and it is my sincerest conviction - that none of the issues being so brutally disputed there this very day are not now, nor ever were, worthy of war between countrymen. Through patience and prayer, and the solicitation of Divine Grace, I believe they would have found ultimate resolution. Yet, as that thunder indicates, impatient men did not trust the Lord to intercede - nor His Word - and rejected prayers for His intercession. Those who forced the firing of the first shots - and those who countered with invasion of our lands - must share the sacrilege and the guilt."

The distant rumblings intensified. In the church's modest pews, veterans of past wars knew the source. Some had marched into the same thunder in Mexico nearly two decades earlier, as had I, and images of those times raced through their memories, conjuring the horrors of battle and the plight of wounded. They recalled tables beneath foreign trees, where able-bodied soldiers held down wounded comrades while surgeons sawed through mangled muscle and bone. And they saw again the holes into which the dead were commonly and coldly cast.

Understanding little of battle, wives held their grandchildren close, knowing only that armies took away their innocent offspring and destroyed them.

The preacher closed his Bible and removed his spectacles: "I am sorry. Truthfully, by shutting these pages, I feel, on one hand, that I am shirking my true responsibilities to you. On the other, I have little more to say. Perhaps, it would be more appropriate if we all, myself included, listened within to God's preaching today, not without to mine. Perhaps, if you closely examined your hearts, you would find, in that quietude, more profound meaning than my sermonizing could impart today. As it is, God speaks more eloquently through hearts and consciences than through spoken sentiments.

"I can only add, that we cannot always escape other men's follies any more than we can escape our own. Of course, YOU know this. Whatever is occurring yonder will proceed despite us. And, I am certain the thunder we now hear will eventually touch us and soon - uniquely and, indeed, poignantly. Armies seek places to bring and shelter their wounded - and doubtless, one army or the other will seek our lodgings and assistance. I cannot tell you what to do with your own homes. You must search your consciences and pray for guidance. This church, of course, this humble structure, is always at humanity's disposal. But our duty is to God, our truest shelter and, through Him, to His service. And as troubling it will no doubt be for many of you, I propose that, if called upon, you will close your eyes to the colors of uniforms, be they blue or gray, and open them and your hearts and your doors to His Service. Being a veteran, and having left a leg in Mexico, I admit to a certain painful prejudice in this matter.

"Please, now, go to your homes and search your hearts. I feel that your time for decision is near. I must go to the fighting to see how I might minister to those in need. Understand that I might not return in time enough to be with you should the armies seek your help. But, by then, I trust you will have determined what to do. I have thought much about this and will say good-bye to you at this time. For, at this hour, you do not need me as much as you need each other. But, I am certain that you, in your modesty, have always understood this. Pray. Be Strong and love the Lord."

The preacher stepped from the pulpit, as the thoughtful congregation indecisively rose to file out, following the thumping footsteps of his wooden leg. A few parishioners wished him God-Speed. The undecided held back. I watched him go, knowing the first army he would meet on the road would be ours. I had attended church that day for the first time in months and left it shortly thereafter, believing the day had been well invested, for I had met and heard an extraordinary man.

Many hours later, with the roll of man-made thunder continuous upon the woods and meadows where two armies grappled, the mounted preacher made his way. The army he came upon first was not that of children's fantasies nor of women's expectations - neither of pomp nor pageantry nor of elegant men ceremonially garbed, nor of plumed automatons in precise ranks festooned in colorful regalia. Instead, he encountered gaggles of ragged wounded in every state of pain and mutilation - the afflicted helping the more tragically afflicted - dirty, bloody, whimpering and mumbling men by the hundreds struggling toward succor away from the fighting, toward water and solace and, perhaps, sleep. That they were of his own land gave him no less pause.

As he told me later, his visions return him to Mexico and to the surgeons tents there still filled in his memory with crying and screaming men being relieved of their shattered limbs - to piles of feet, hands, arms, and legs being carted off by orderlies and infantrymen to quickly dug pits. Yes, he had witnessed such spectacles before, and now it appeared to him that time had not progressed far from those terrible days of his youth, and which now returned to him - to requisitioned timbers laid upon two wooden horses where he had surrendered HIS leg, while four exhausted soldiers held him down and hostage to the septic imprecision of a drunken surgeon's saw.

"Lord," the Preacher prayed, remembering..."steer my course."

*   *   *

The Dappled Woods

I have not yet mentioned my fascination with play of light and shadows through the trees and on the earth when we trek through woods on sun-filled days - the way sunlight ponds and pools in undergrowth beneath while dappling the leaves on the boughs it seeps through.

Such effects often are overlooked by exhausted souls during a march's monotony. Besides gracing the land with loveliness, the dappling intimates a message that says to me, "Despite your war-making, another world awaits you in climes beyond human understanding - where the lilies thrive with supernatural beauty."

It is all too common for a soldier to lose touch with spiritual issues not associated with war, since during the stress of aggressive campaigning, every hour of his waking life is consumed by material matters - bullets, shells, canister, rations and more, together with wounds, foraging and constant hardship. All dull his sensitivities to non-material perceptions vital to his spiritual sustenance. The soldier who appreciates the relief such sensitivity brings him must drink in these dappled wonders, lest he deprive his thirsty soul of nourishment. So, I mention such things.

I am certain the Lord weeps over our transgressions of his Word and world. Yet, it is difficult for soldiers to acknowledge His charity when troubled with war's perplexities. Soldiers must remind themselves not to ignore His gifts even when preoccupied via letters from home with troubling domestic matters they can little affect. "Drink," He patiently entreats them from the dappling light, "and be sustained."

Try as I might, I cannot reconcile the disparity between the Lord's heart and man's intent. By warring at all, we violate every moral precedent of our Faith, yet both sides pray for salvation to the same Deity, as if both expect Him to choose sides, thereby manifesting their hypocrisy. We ask for salvation while dedicated to denying Him. How loving of us He must be. And though I am merely a "chronicler" of events, I sometimes believe I should have turned my efforts to protesting our tragic ignorance rather than exposing its anatomy. Perhaps, if I had, I would have better served God and country.

The woods are dappled again today, and once again, I satiate my thirst. Tomorrow, I will thirst once more.

* * *

Dusk Into Darkness

As the oppressiveness of this hot summer afternoon wears on, I forsake the choking confines of our trudging ranks to walk alongside the column, that I might observe events behind and beyond.

Dust rises from thousands of shuffling feet and shoes, giving a phantom-like pallor to the column's slow-moving undulations. Coughing is everywhere. A golden tide of sunlight inundates the countryside. The sun itself slips toward the horizon, approaching ever-nearer that point when dusk will shed its longed-for coolness upon our sweating infantryman.

I marvel at the column's serpentine length that winds into the sunset through fields and hills. Its glinting rifles capture the light like deadly sequins amidst the gray and butternut mosaic of the serpent's skin.

Soon, the sun's baking heat relents. Blazing light fades into dimmer shades and hues. The heat ebbs and cool air cascades from surrounding hills. Our men drink it up as if it were chilled wine.

The quieting panoply amplifies the column's metallic rhythms - a serenade of clinking tin cups and cooking ware and all other metal-on-metal. Far away, a dark blue column of the same American blood moves in like manner toward a point at which both will converge. That convergence haunts all. It will determine the fate of hundreds whose sore and blistered feet stir the dusts this day.

History lives in the gaunt, stubbled faces of those next to me, who route-step toward the unknown. If only I could sketch their expressions, that hide beneath caked dust and crisscrossing sweat trails, marking the mental exhaustion of men too much exposed to war. Some faces cry "enough." Longing eyes look homeward.

I watch God's handiwork take form. The sun declines beneath cloudy brush strokes of azure, pink and golds. Charcoal hues settle upon the hills ahead even as blue shadows and purple mists form specters around us. Some men take no notice. They crave rest and sleep's spiritual relief before resuming their pilgrimage to battle when the sun rises tomorrow. But once in bivouac, most will drink cool water and eat. Many will write letters home, lest they never see another night. Some will soothe themselves with sentimental songs. Others will salve their bleeding feet. Many will read their Bibles or reread letters from home or the tattered remnants of newspapers and periodicals they have carried and reread a hundred times for weeks. Some will watch the stars while still more will ponder mortality and its meaning. And beneath nighttime's chill, they will huddle together by campfires, each man to his own thoughts and sleepers to their dreams - teased by demons that taunted, "You are sleeping your last."

I am haunted FOR them, watching the uncaring gods turn dusk into darkness.

*   *   *

Homecoming

Private Jonas Burke had not heard from his wife in months. He explained that, though illiterate, she had always enlisted the help of literate neighbors nearby to write letters to him in her stead.

I did not know Private Burke well, since I had joined his company only a week earlier, but he came to my attention soon enough.

Two days after I arrived, our brigade was thrown into the fight at Fredericksburg. Having positioned myself at the wall overlooking the city from Marye's Heights, where a strong portion of our Army awaited the enemy's assault, he stood next to me. During the assault, he fought with a tenacity, as did our entire brigade, the enemy's tactics being not only bewildering but suicidal.

I cannot begin to convey the fight's intensity. That the enemy persisted the entire day long in sending wave after wave to their impossible task - that of taking the Heights away from us without regard to cost or the benefit of cover - beggared our comprehension. A veteran of many battles, Burke, like so many of our soldiers, grew angry and frustrated with the enemy's profligacy, repulsed by the necessity of having to shoot down so many and expressing same with a heart-felt sadness and tearful compassion for their counterparts "across the way" that only a soldier can appreciate.

It was not a battle but a slaughter, in which our boys, early on, sickened of the killing. I must credit the enemy's courage. His people fell by droves, crushed by our musketry and artillery fire that literally tore his advancing ranks to pieces. Yet, on he came in those doomed waves. We held all the tactical advantages, while he enjoyed none.

It was the next day after the fighting that Burke came to me, having remembered that I was keeping a journal-account of the war. Because his writing and reading abilities were barely adequate, he asked me to compose a letter to his wife. Obviously agitated, he was desperate to hear from her. We spent an hour refining his sentiments. I wrote the letter that night, and read it back to him the next morning for his approval, then mailed it via our regimental post office, hoping our country's struggling mail system would send it through with dispatch. Only miles from his home, he was not permitted a furlough to visit his wife. Ironically, and again, as fate would have it, on the march days later, the Army passed by his farm. Burke's anticipation increased to such a degree as we neared it we could barely restrain him. Providentially, so we initially thought, the Army halted for rest along the road bordering the farm.

Burke raced forward to our company commander to ask for permission to leave the column to see to his family. As it was, hundreds of men were using the roadside and the woods and fields beyond to relieve themselves. With permission granted, he ran the hundreds of yards to the gate fronting his small house, shouting for his wife. Then came, minutes later, another of the million poignant moments I've witnessed in this war.

Burke did not return before the column resumed its march. Worried that he might be punished for it, we anxiously looked for him.

"He'll catch up," his friend next to me guessed, who did know him well. "If I hadn'ta seen 'er heerd from my family as long as him, I'd be a'tarryin, too, as long as I could."

But, as our company, somewhere in mid-column, passed the gate, we saw Burke in his yard, desperately weeping, prostrate across three graves.

"Oh, Lord, that'd be his wife and two youngin's," the friend glumly revealed, devastation starkly in his eyes and expression, "his little girl, Rose, and his little boy, Bo, 'bout three and four, I'm thinkin'. Lord, Lord, that be hard...that be very hard. Who'da thought...who'da thought!"

Indeed...who'da thought?

We supposed the fever took all three, since it had ravaged many families across the countryside. Saying nothing, our officers looked on as Burke suffered. Mercy commanded that they not demand his rapid return to ranks. Feeling nakedly helpless, the men of our route-stepping company prayed for Burke, reciting the Lord's Prayer - Catholics, Protestants, Quakers, et al.

It was hot that day. The dust of the road caked on our forms and faces. But, as we prayed, a cooling breeze gently caressed us all as if offered by God to ease our grief and discomfort. And, as our sympathetic appeals spilled from our dry lips, I was convinced that we were being favored by a special Grace, the same Grace I hoped would mercifully liberate Burke.

We left him there, his absence forgiven. He never returned.

*   *   *

Wonderland

I paused today in the quiet of the Providential artistry created by snow and wind last night.

Across the countryside, the frigid world lay beneath a whiteness that decorated every feature--pines bowed with heavy mantles--every bush adorned with tufted majesty--tree trunks blasted with cottony fluff--the ground's brilliant blanket flawless and undisturbed. No mortal artist could have matched the effect. And none could have imparted the depth and significance of the quiet that descended in the wake of the wind.

For many minutes, I forgot the cold that laced my bones, so engrossed was I in this canvas that included me in its frame. Far behind me, campfires blazed, men ate, and the brigade prepared for another day of monotony. Smoke rose from the chimneys of our log-hut city called Winter Camp. I thought of sketching all that I observed, but the cold had stiffened my hands. Still, I committed the sight to memory and resolved to speak of it with charcoal when I returned to the hut I shared with three other men--all of whom are devoted to sleep at all hours. The hut, devoid of comforts, provides a small hearth, a little table, crude beds, a door and two windows and is cramped. Unhealthy in all other respects, it, at least, is warm, and warmth for our Army in winter is worshipped.

For a moment, the quiet suspended me in wonder. My mind freed itself of all concerns, save for the quiet's depth and mystery. Feeling neither cold nor fear, I thought I had entered an enchanted kingdom not of Earth. All tactile contact with Earth vanished. My usual senses slept. Mesmerized, I did not move, nor did I want to. I had become part of the wonderland and it had become a part of me. It was a feeling of freedom and belonging I cannot describe.

Then, my growling stomach urged me to quit my romance with winter. I had collected little to eat in the past week, but I would return to the hut to boil tea and savor the heat from our makeshift hearth. Still, I would remember that moment when the world I'd known became another. Perhaps, the two had melded and I had wandered into that intersection. If I could have lost myself in it, I gladly would have relinquished my claim to existence in the present one.

Creation is more than we know.

* * *

Silent Sentry

I trudged into the winter wilderness around our camp this morning, feeling the cold creep beneath my coat. I had spied in the distance a lone sentry at his post. And thinking that he must be not only chilled but weary after hours there, I meant to speak to him.

Rife with suffering, sentry duty in winter's worst is duty most harsh. Our boys' footwear and clothing hardly retain body heat, so we lend them our heaviest clothing, since the majority of our troops shield themselves in warm huts or in tents, each accommodating several men.

Frozen hands and feet plague the Army's existence, and sentries are the most numerous victims. We often are reminded of old Valley Forge paintings that portray Washington's soldiers with their feet heavily wrapped in cloth. So it is with many of our sentries. When venturing outside, I, too, wrap my feet with the remnants of a ragged woolen blanket. This bitter morning, biting winds whipped loose snow across the landscape.

The sentry appeared to be gazing across a field toward a tree line a quarter-mile away. Perhaps, I thought, he had spied something suspicious there. He leaned on his rifle, its butt in the snow, his blanket-wrapped body bent over it. Surely, I thought, he studied something in that tree line I could not yet see.

"Hello, there," I called to him as I approached, not wishing to frighten him by coming too close before extending my greeting. Either he ignored me or did not hear. There had to have been something interesting occurring beyond to have held his interest so intensely. I paused to study the tree line, feeling that I, too, had spotted movement there. Yet, I could not be certain that my eyes weren't deceiving me. Whipping snow danced in the meadows between my position and tree line, teasing me with possibilities.

"Hello, there," I called again as I closely approached the sentry. Only then did I see his bluish face and frost-encrusted nose and brow. No longer human, he had become crystalline memento of a living soul, his dilated eyes glazed.

The wind toyed with his blanket and snow-caked hair.

"God bless you, soldier," I mumbled, staring, as my shock abated. "God bless you."

I turned to trudge back to camp, empty within, numbly resigned to poignant tragedy.

* * *

Speak No More

Yesterday, I trekked with our column after our brigade's hard fight near a crossroads in its section of our Army's line. The contest had lasted all morning. The enemy, having withdrawn, had moved away. Our Army pursued.

Our ambulatory wounded shuffled along one side of the road we followed, with ambulances interspersed among them. The other side was given to passing artillery, caissons, and occasional cavalry. It was a wearying procession, with many wounded falling out and being attended by comrades. We needed water. Hundreds of our men sucked on empty canteens, desperately trying to trap their last drops.

The company I marched in occupied the column's mid-point. That we were not going to encamp after the fight signaled tremendous hardships for the walking wounded. They would have no time to attend to themselves, nor seek medical attention.

I felt deeply grieved for them, many of whom would walk themselves to death. Some, afoot with profusely bleeding wounds, should have been in the hospital. They trudged along on willpower alone, and though I had only been an observer, the fighting's emotional toll had been great enough on me that I craved sleep. All during that fighting, I had run ammunition to our lines and had helped evacuate the wounded to ambulances.

I could not say how many score collapsed along the road or sought rest and refuge in the bordering woods - there to either recover in time or perish. I, too, sought refuge, if only to drain my canteen in peace and unload my heavy journal case from my shoulder, its strap having dug deeply into my flesh.

Intent on finding a place of temporary rest, I wandered off the road among the trees. Many yards into the woods, I was halted by what I thought was a mewing kitten. I turned. The sound came from behind a large pine. I proceeded to it cautiously and peered around it, hoping to find a little ball of fur. What greeted me left me petrified.

Crouching against the tree's other side, a hapless soldier violently trembled. Strange noises came from his throat's exposed interior in masses of pinkish bubbles that sprayed onto his blood-soaked jacket. His entire lower jaw had been shot away, leaving a huge gaping maw! Never had I observed a wound so hideous. When he spied me, he stood, tottering. His panicky eyes darted this way and that, as if seeking escape. Cat-like sounds came from his maw. He reached out to me with a shaking hand, as if trying to hold me off. Gone was his tongue. Only the roof of his mouth and the remains of his upper teeth stuck out, giving him a monster's appearance.

His pitiful eyes stared, tears streaming. God, what must have been his pain? I stupidly stared back. His eyes pleaded...but what could I do? What could anyone have done? He was doomed and knew it. Even if he survived, what then - to what kind of life would he be condemned? His eyes acknowledged that he had been destroyed in the service of his country.

His trembling hand pointed to the pistol I had found earlier on the road and had shoved into my belt. He then pointed to himself. Realizing what he wanted, I silently prayed, "Oh, Lord, what shall I do?"

Only with great effort did he maintain his balance. He leaned against the tree, blood seeping from his maw. Again, he pointed to the pistol, stumbling toward me at the same time and making noises that passed for speech. But he would speak no more. Grunting, and stabbing his finger toward the pistol with greater desperation, he demonstrated that he would take the weapon and put its barrel to his head. The implications of complying with his demands terrified me. Because he was without his rifle, the pistol would be his only escape from a now impossible existence that should have mercifully ended on the battlefield.

"Lord," I prayed again, "tell me what to do!"

For three years, I had seen men suffer hellish agonies and die only because they wore different uniforms. I had watched them dumped into mass graves, or their bodily wreckage sent home in leaking boxes, others left on pitiful crutches or in contorted states of paralysis resembling nothing of their former selves. I even had witnessed emaciated dogs dig into graves and pull out body parts, or hogs drag away and devour whole corpses, as battle-numbed soldiers looked on. All of the dead had suffered for the glory of the Cause. Here was another for whom glory would have no more meaning - whose patriotism fate had sadistically rewarded. Even if he survived, he would remain a physical pariah - and a thing of personal and public revulsion - with no thanks nor scant regard from anyone for his sacrifice - let alone from his government. How would he eat? Who would feed him, care for or speak for him? How would he communicate? What woman would have him? What wife could still love him? Undoubtedly, he had considered his choices and instantly realized he had none. Only God would accept him, and it was to God that he wished to speed.

Considering his choices, my revulsion ebbed, overwhelmed by simple compassion. Had I been him, I would have seen matters the same way, begged for the same pistol and sought the same alternative, unable to envision any other.

Slowly, I reached for the pistol. His thankful eyes fixed on it, as a thirsty man would fixate on a full canteen. He nodded his approval and reached for it, but his hand trembled uncontrollably. He staggered, both hands to his maw, agony erupting from his throat in a spray of bloody lather and animal-like sounds. I turned away, not wanting him to feel like a circus spectacle. How could he bleed so much and still stand? No, if he was willing to die, not even God could blame him.

His eyes remained fixed on the pistol. Reaching for it again, he communicated that he could no longer tolerate his pain - and that the sooner I passed it to him, the sooner he would mercifully avoid more torturing spasms.

I worried in my heart, that if I did as he wished, I might surely spend my days trying to absolve myself of moral responsibility. But, that moment persuaded me that a higher code mattered to which neither right NOR wrong applied - involving the honor of soldiers - one to another - and a measure of humanity unique to these times and conditions that only soldiers could appreciate. In my fashion, I, too, was a soldier, and, as a humane reflection of that code, this man deserved a soldier's mercy. To Hell with my worried soul.

I put a restraining hand on his just as he was about to take the weapon. He stared at me, his eyes wide with sudden fear. Was I reneging? Was I abandoning him to hopelessness? No. I was refusing to allow him to humiliate himself by dying desperately in front of me. I wanted to leave him with his honor intact. I could do that by recognizing him for his sacrifice - as we did our battlefield dead - with a modicum of ceremony, his physical death being but a detail.

He appeared to understand. Though he trembled severely and grew weaker, his eyes mellowed. At that moment, he was no longer repugnant. Now, I understand why Christ had loved the lepers. With tears in my eyes, I saluted this star-crossed soldier and slowly handed him his salvation. He weakly returned my salute, covering his maw with his other hand - and took the weapon. Then, he bowed his head with relief. When next he lifted his eyes, they said, "Now, please, leave me to my task."

I asked if he had kin he would want me to notify. He shook his head, no. Then, I asked if he possessed identification, so he would not be buried anonymously. With his free hand, he shakily pointed to a blood-encrusted jacket pocket. I reached in and retrieved a piece of paper. On it was his printed name, Private Edwin Symes, his regiment and company.

"I will personally see to this," I promised him.

He nodded – a thank you - then painfully cringed.

I placed a reassuring hand on his shoulder, turned and walked away. Pausing only once, I saw him slide to a sitting position down the side of the tree away from me and nearly out of my sight. Then, I saw his elbow rise.

On the road, passing caissons pulled by lathered horses at a full gallop raised a distracting commotion. The rain that had advanced from the horizon all morning now fell softly - a balm to the suffering gripped by the fever of wounds and the heat of pain - a gift from God like that of precious oils to cleanse and purify the human flesh defiled by man that day. Assaulted by the powerful grumble of thunder, I barely heard the pistol's report. I saw the soldier's arm drop, pistol in hand, just beyond the tree trunk's rim. It was finished.

When we bivouacked that night, I fell asleep without regret, remembering Private Edwin Symes, seeing not the ruined face of a tortured soul - but a soul now restored and free in a new dimension of merciful Grace.

*   *   *

Rhapsody

Today, our regiment, to its surprise and delight, found itself entertained by a children's choir from a church near where the Army has bivouacked.

I cannot describe how, like magnets, the children drew our troops to them, many of our men being fathers who have not seen their families in months, some in more than a year, a few in more than two years.

As unkempt as they were, their dirty, bearded veterans' faces radiated the tender love and concern they would have expressed in the presence of their own children. Here were seasoned veterans, steeled to war's privations and horrors, mellowed by the angelic voices and cherubic countenances of youngin's between four and eight years. I, too, was swept away by their charm and their profoundly touching innocence that warmed and appealed to every observing heart.

The children sang hymns and Stephen Foster medleys, bringing tears of both nostalgia and home sickness to our troops' affectionate gaze. I cannot say how the children and their singing affected our men's morale, whether, each man came away inspired or saddened or both.

When the children finished, our men roundly cheered and applauded them. I saw some men weeping. They mixed freely with the children afterwards, that privilege bringing a resuscitating light to their eyes and mellow expressions that had long since abandoned them. The tenderness they displayed toward the children left me gratified and humbled. In a sense, for that time being, they were home again, and I could not help sympathizing.

When the children's shepherds gathered their little flock and returned them to the wagons and buggies that had brought them, our men stood like statues, watching them go, the lights in their eyes slowly diminishing minute by minute. And, as the last vehicle vanished over the rise in the dusty trail leading back to the church, only blank and regretful expressions remained. Not a man moved until many seconds later, as if once more seeing the joys of their civilian lives vanish, too. Doubtless, thoughts and images of home haunted their hearts, as if each comprised the ending notes of a fading rhapsody.

I opened my journals to write this reflection, noticing that as our men returned to their tents and campfires, they remained contemplative. So much war awaited them, and with it so much uncertainty. I could almost hear them thinking..."Will we survive to hold our children again?"

Standing nearby, the regiment's commanding officer, looking on, called me to him: "Perhaps, you will agree," he said, "but I do not believe we should allow such a thing again. This has been too much for these men. We meant to uplift them. Instead, we've left them disconsolate."

Perhaps, the truth lay between. No doubt, it had been a sweet-sour experience, especially for the married men. For others, as well, it poignantly reminded them of the necessity for continuing their resistance to the destitution and ruin of their homes and families by Federal armies. But, as I expressed to the officer, I thought the singing had produced a reassuring revelation - that the war, in all of its naked revulsion, had not yet withered nor deadened our men's weary souls - nor, I trusted, our people's.

* * *

Redemption

I watched a diminutive soldier drag his wounded body into ranks. He fought his agonies with every tortured step, even as blood seeped from his ravaged legs and side. Battle raged only a hundred yards away.

How could it be that he had not sought medical aid? Never had I ever witnessed such an abused soul struggle to take his place beside others only minutes from advancing to the firing line... never.

I made my way to him through ranks of assembling units, where the men of the company he now joined shouldered their rifles and shuffled toward their destinies. Missiles whizzed and whined by us, thumping into flesh and bone here and there, bludgeoning men to the ground. Occasional round-shot and iron bolts plowed through our ranks, tearing men apart in showers of blood, gore, entrails, limbs, and bone. Undeterred, the soldier persisted. Trudging beside him I shouted into the overpowering din, "Why are you not in the hospital, Private? You have every honorable reason to be."

He stared at me, extreme pain etched across his face, his eyes reddened with deeper suffering emanating not entirely from his body: "Cain't," he weakly replied into my ear, his breath short. "I runned once't, after I got these wounds. I runned 'til I 'bout died. Neva' was so skerd in all m'life. The boys stayed, but I runned. Some's prob'ly in Glory now 'cause I runned. So, I come'd back t'make up fer it. Lord, forgive m'shame...but I come'd back."

And so, he "went in" with the company. I watched him struggle to keep up, recalling his chalk-white and sweating face, bluing lips and the fatal pallor of his skin. He had no more blood to give. Perhaps, honor compelled him to enter Paradise conscience-free and spiritually clean. He may well have run before, but the gut-courage of his return now expunged that original sin.

Later, I was told he accounted well for himself and yielded not a single yard. In fact, he became the rock around which the company rallied and survived.

This war has taught me never to underestimate any man, regardless of his size and disposition, for the best of a man's mettle can lie hidden, even unto himself, remaining unexposed and unrevealed until it is tested. Twenty in his company perished that day. And when they buried him with the others, they did so ruefully - but not because he had died, for he had died well and to his credit - but rather because no one had known his name. So, they gave him one...Private St. Michael - Joshua St. Michael, befitting his warrior's spirit - and buried him with honors.

We hoped he was gratified.

* * *

His Last Day

The Private, a lover of poetry, confessed it was his last day.

"I can feel it," he said, as had countless others before him on THEIR last days. The feeling, he said, came from both intuition and the gut...an indescribable surety that paradoxically brings with it a Providential peace of mind.

I discovered him as I wandered the company's bivouac in the darkness, unable to sleep. It was nearly sunrise, and he wrote eloquently in his diary by candlelight, sitting against a tree. Odd, he said, that he did not fear this day but welcomed it, for the feeling had been his daily pursuer and he knew the time it foretold would inevitably find him.

Hundreds around him still slept.

He interrupted his reveries to watch the new day's dawning, as the glimmering horizon brightened. Birds welcomed the dawn with excited chatter, heralding Eternity, which, he said, he believed he had known before, perhaps in another lifetime.

He said he could not precisely predict how he would perish this day, but he sensed the moment's gravity. Self-consciously, he also confessed his comfort in knowing that he would not perish alone. He said that in his dream last night, he envisioned another dawn and long columns of weary, disheveled soldiers - ours and theirs - shuffling toward it. Thousands comprised those common ranks, he said, and beyond them, in enchanted landscapes whose beauty defied description, tranquility awaited them, where their souls would live forever free and where goodness and mercy would follow them all the days of their new lives.

He said one of those soldiers had been a former enemy, yet a kind soul whose face glowed with joy, and who, turning to him, said, "Come with us. Your place is here."

"No, not yet," he replied, the words prophetically spilling from his mouth, "I have but one day more."

"Then, we will save a place for you," the soldier promised, "in yonder land."

"Then, I awoke," he said, "without fear - all of it put to flight, able to greet the dawn with composure."

He revealed without self-consciousness that he hears celestial music in the crackling of the dwindling campfires around him. I watch him marvel at the intricacies of his hands as he listens to his heart's rhythmic cadence, awed by the genius in its life force. He said he notices as never before the soaring grace of morning birds, feeling preciousness in and of all things…"The trees around me appear supremely noble. I understand now that they are silent sentinels secreting the answers to all of Creation's mysteries. See how their boughs are lifted skyward in prayer?"

"I fill my eyes with Nature," he had written his diary, "knowing that, from a vantage point beyond my understanding, I will soon appreciate the fullness of its meaning - and am reassured. Even now, I feel I am dwelling in the last vapors of earthly memory. If only I could truly explain…"

He admitted that he should have been terrified to hear the bugles that would call him to battle this day, but that his calm extends even to that inevitability.

"I feel a compensating love for this Earth that has been my inn along the road of my terrestrial journey," he had written. "Now I comprehend the message in the eyes of so many before me who also knew their time had come - like those in those long columns. They were seeing through the veil and, like them, I will make my peace with my mortality and witness the candle extinguished, my labors done. I know that for me, as for all, there will be a new tomorrow, where all who have gone before me in this war now await me."

"Something greater than me tells me so," he confided to me, "and so I now leave the wearying matters of Earth to its tired humanity."

Hardly a simple man, I truly believe he had seen beyond, where the lilies thrive in eternal beauty. His final compassionate gesture was to will his diary to me.

His name was Private Willis Reed. His soul is now known to God.

* * *

In the Beauty of the Lilies

**The Wartime Journals
of Confederate Correspondent
Royal K. Chapman
1862-1864**

Journal Three

Contents

* * *

A Thought

Why do drums stir men's hearts
yet numb their reason?

Remembered

No man will ever outlive the images he carries from this war.

Even now, when I close my eyes, I see the dead in the bloody fields I've trod; the sacrificed - theirs and ours - lying in death's inglorious postures - the contorted dead, stiff and mutilated - those reaching out or upwards in frozen, dirty, bearded pathos - those in the mud, in woods or hidden in tall grasses, their eyes staring and those without eyes or even limbs - some headless, their innards spread or spilling out - others unmarked and appearing only asleep and untouched - some in fetal positions in childlike innocence, and those with bones smashed in the wake of artillery's thunder - or the skeletal remains moldering with all other rotting and rusting residue of battles months old.

I also see living faces - grim and gaunt, with eyes hollow and staring far into weariness and exhaustion. And, once more, my heart will go out to each one, as I lose myself in painful nostalgia, upon which not even a woman's love could successfully intrude. All these will be tattoos upon my soul and invisible decorations upon my breast.

I will remember laughter and conversations and the men and boys who gave them life. And should I not survive this tribulation, then I hope what I have written, if found, will contribute in its small way to their monument. Otherwise, it risks being of little worth to the merely curious - or avoided by the scarred who fought but wish only to forget.

This morning, an officer asked me, "Why do you persevere in your endeavor?" I asked in reply, "Why do you?"

He stared at me quizzically, and then nodded his head, saying nothing more. What more COULD be said?

As I write this, a breeze wafts across the countryside as the sun dashes behind passing clouds. It is part of a celestial game we have witnessed hundreds of times since war's beginning, yet one at which we continually marvel. Nature remains supreme. Before the war, we would have ignored such things. Now, such things too poignantly remind us of life's fragility - and how much we now value them and all such natural treasures. War has taught us to appreciate these little things, which, when taken together, comprise a wondrous tapestry. And we lament that we are too transitory a part of it - and we are greatly humbled.

* * *

Thoughts in the Rain

Rain soporifically falls again today, the sky as gray as our chances for victory.

I sit in a small dugout, away from the wet but not the damp, writing by lantern light, so dim is this interior. Around me, six men sleep. Sleep is their salvation, their escape from our world of grim realities. I cannot escape. My mind works too much. I look inside myself, wonder about myself, reproach myself. Rain encloses me within a cocoon of introspection, submerging me in, and embarrassing me with, self-absorption. I am not depressed, simply reflective. I ask myself, "What will come for us? What is the South's destiny? What will become of these men who rest as if they will wake without care to a world without war?"

It is impossible to know what future generations will make of our terrible times. But it is possible to fantasize about ironies. Indeed, I often wonder what would happen if, in the midst of our natural fratricide, a foreign enemy would capitalize upon our present disunity by invading both side's Atlantic shores, as Federal armies have violated the South's? Would we then, bitter enemies that we've become, give hiatus to our hatreds and, side by side, struggle to repel the invader, perhaps, in that effort, rediscovering and once more cherishing our former unity and common heritage? And would that effort make moot our violent dissensions? Who can say?

Speculation, though intriguing, remains only that. But as the rain this day deluges our positions, and the skies remain charcoal-hued and hang suffocatingly low, I think of such things. By also doing so, soldiers exaggerate their desperate hopes to the point of the fantastic, that this war will end before more killing and destruction ensue, since both sides are too prideful to acknowledge their common predations upon the Almighty's Scriptural entries of peace. I fear that only He possesses the power to end this misery. For with every face I see upon our battlefields, chalky-white or mutilated in the rigors of their reluctant slumber, I am humbled to ask, "Why? For what?" Far beyond the cosmetic principles for which both sides fight, these questions remain essential and paramount.

In those faces, I see not weighty issues of great idealism frozen with conviction, but common human blood and flesh. And I see an equally common humanity which, if stripped of uniforms, would lie in naked conformity to shared fundamental values - to the need for shelter, for sustenance, for family and for love.

These should have been the inviolate foundations underlying what should have been negotiations to avoid this conflict long before both sides resorted to the sword - these and Bibles carried in the hands of every negotiator for mutual reference. So, what, then, are we left with now? We are left with the sword in the absence of commanding and overpowering virtue. Both sides will sow what they reap and, as in every war, the innocent will suffer too much for the fanatical stubbornness of political zealots. And warriors, who might otherwise have refused to violently settle their differences, will realize too late that by willingly participating they perpetuated the madness, ignorantly victimizing their own kin and countless other families in a thousand tormenting ways - while, in the interim, a witnessing God, who has granted men free will, weeps into His hands that created them.

It is noteworthy that good men of both sides, who do nothing to end this slaughter, are as guilty of its endlessness as those who encourage it, for their moral sloth is the greatest encouragement. Yet, well-intentioned souls, who would interfere with patriotic fervor, risk much, not only societal scorn and banishment but, in the extreme, their very lives. The ultimate blame, human nature being what it is, is with leaders of both our warring societies, who should be the first to reject ever more destruction and, reasoning together, seek compromises that Christ Himself might advocate. But, I fear that the rain will sooner green the Earth's deserts than that men's natures will be thusly humbled, even by their own unforgivable errors and calamities.

And yet, here I am, not sacrificing via true conviction to protest the violence, but using my energies only to observe it and to write about it and, in doing so, to condone it, even if only inadvertently. Yet, does my inadvertence entitle me to less guilt for only indirectly condoning it while doing nothing material to deter it? Do I do nothing because I am mind-dulled by it all and bewildered by the unstoppable momentum of human weakness - or truly because I am a single grain of sand upon a dune-scaped beach, strained to consider how to discourage the tides of human perversity crashing over me? But let me not attempt to escape myself with alibis. No, I am a pure hypocrite without excuse and a betrayer of that sacred seed planted in all of us by the Creator at conception. Men diminish its majestic countenance and do Him an extreme disservice by calling it, merely...conscience.

Perhaps, by accident, my writing will, at the very least, partially compensate for my moral timidity and help, no matter how minutely, to cause conscientious souls on both sides to belatedly reflect upon this folly. And, perhaps, if my hope is not pure arrogance, what I've written may go at least a small way toward mercifully assuaging a portion of my nagging guilt.

*   *   *

That Haunting Music

I will hear it always - even in worlds to come - the music battle makes - that curious whining, whirring, buzzing, shrieking rhapsody of iron and lead that invisibly parts the air in search of bone and flesh to mangle.

Like bees, minié-balls zip past one's head. Passing shot, shell, and canister assault one's ears in a concussive windstorm. A man leans into it, as if by doing so he can avoid a destiny solely determined by fate and physics.

He may as well walk naked through a blizzard, his vulnerability akin to an infant's upon entering the world. He becomes a reborn child longing for the safe harbor of his mother's bosom -he weeps with fear and helplessness, even as his feet and legs advance to the cadences of rhythmic drums. He becomes two people - one who dwells in fear apart from his body - and the other, a trembling soul trapped within a physical cage.

Discipline gained from experience is of little comfort, for when metal and flesh unite, his pitiful nakedness is either damned with agony or blessed with oblivion. Some men, when struck down, instantly detach themselves to witness their own destruction - to see their limbs torn away, their viscera splattered, or their bones shattered and tissues churned to reddish mist. In those moments, those not immediately destroyed begin tortured journeys to lifelong invalidism or to the gentler mercies of that better world God has promised.

A maimed survivor will always hear battle's malignant music when memories roll down his sweating brow or when his eyes fix again upon painful images only he can see. Even his wife's arms will fail to soothe and shield him or stem the tears that will flood his visions. Nor will they quell the tremors of his persistent memories. No, such men will never cease to serve "The Cause" nor will they ever truly come all the way home.

I fear the music, for it comes closer every time I hear it. And I cannot escape the premonition that it and I have made an inevitable appointment. Whenever that rendezvous comes, may our handshake be quick and final.

*   *   *

Humanity Revisited

We paused in a meadow today even as the sun beat down hotly upon us. As I looked about, great vistas of uniformed humanity lay around me by companies for hundreds of yards in all directions - a full brigade.

Men sucked deeply on their canteens and wiped their sweaty brows. Shade beckoned here and there in patches of woods carpeting the countryside and flanking the road from whence we came. In minutes, it would allow us our continued passage far into the distance.

Many drifted toward and into the trees, relieving themselves in whatever privacy offered therin. Others searched for a meandering stream or creek from which they hoped to refill their canteens or, perhaps, in which they hoped to quickly splash. I followed them, anxious to note any successes. But they found no water. Some men returned to the meadow to throw themselves down in its cooling grasses shaded by the woods. Others refreshed themselves in the wandering breeze.

The sound of swaying grasses, added to the rustle of leaves, lent tranquility to what had been an arduous forced march. Some men stripped themselves of rifles, haversacks, and bedrolls and languished there, letting their exhaustion ebb from their aching limbs. Many immediately dumped their shoes (those who possessed them), trying to extinguish the fire in their burning feet by rubbing them. Some doffed their jackets or stripped to the waist to pour their canteens' contents sparingly over their faces and bared chests. Most did so in relative silence, as their actions spoke to their individual miseries.

I joined them in the shade, where I abandoned my hat, boots, haversack, and journal case and laid in the grass. Huge cumulus paraded across the brilliant blue dome that looked down upon our war. As I luxuriated in the moment, feeling my fatigue pulsate in waves throughout my body, I heard a nearby voice indistinctly speaking to something that could not have been another person. Looking up, I spied a bare-headed soldier leaning against a young tree, holding a curiosity. Turning to watch, I realized he had discovered a little bird that he cupped to his lips.

Only I noticed. He spoke to it, assuring it that he would do it no harm. But its panicked parent bird fluttered from branch to branch in a nearby tree, angrily screaming and screeching and desperately attempting to distract the two-legged creature it perceived as menacing its offspring.

The soldier's bearded face, traced with rivulets of grimy sweat, glowed with affection. He gently petted the baby bird, rubbing a finger tenderly across its miniature crown while unwittingly sending its parent's into fits of heightened agitation.

So drastically did the soldier's attentions to his feathered discovery contrast with the brigade's general mood that I stared with wonder. Here, in the midst of war, among thousands of men hardened by privation and mutual sufferings, a single soldier's commiseration with a tiny bird renewed my hopes for the salvation of their tired souls. It appeared miraculous that a veteran of combat and killing, with such large and calloused hands, could so delicately handle a creature of such fragile vulnerability. Where jaded others might have ended its tiny existence with a crushing rifle butt, he cherished it as he might have a baby child.

Providence guided this good soldier's redemption. His humanity shown through all he had experienced in war unto that moment, renewing my faith that the same ember glowed within all. Perhaps, I thought, when the war ended, all might yet retire to peaceful pursuits as humble children of God, and be shed of war's debasing influences.

I rolled onto my back to watch the sky, thanking the angels for regenerating my spirit with hope and reconstituting my faith in a merciful Father. Then, my eyes closed as I sunk into a brief but refreshing oblivion.

Many minutes later, a strong hand shook me awake. A different soldier looked down at me. As I gathered my wits, a distant bugle trumpeted the resumption of the march. Reluctantly, I raised my aching carcass to my still protesting feet and glanced to where the kindly soldier had leaned against the young tree. He was gone. I would never know his name, but I would always remember his humanity. And then, a ray of sunlight pierced the wood's tangled canopy, falling upon the small tree. There, illuminated on its lowest bough, two feathered children of God - a mother and her dependent - observed their world's return to normalcy. More practical men might have wondered how and why that single ray of light had sought out parent and offspring at that instant and place. Perhaps, because, in small things, God reveals Himself. Minutes later, our column was away again, leaving the alien woods and meadows once more at peace - and the lilies, this time, gilded.

*   *   *

His Mysterious Ways

I stepped into a damaged church recently rent by accidental shell fire. The church had stood between contending lines during the day's fighting. That it hadn't burned in the wake of exploding missiles appeared to me miraculous. The pungent vapors of burnt gunpowder irritated my nose and eyes.

Some things were singed and Bibles, hymn books scattered about and some carpeting. Three windows had blown out and much plaster had fallen from walls and ceiling. But the altar with its religious objects had impossibly remained intact. Metal shards had holed the walls and ceiling here and there, and where shells had come through the walls, large holes now gaped. Pews and floor planking where at least four shells had impacted were mangled and splintered, large holes revealing the ground beneath. I wondered why the Lord had not protected this house of His unless, of course, such material shrines were of more significance to men than to Him and more of man's convenience than of His.

As I studied the damage, the church's pastor stepped from an ante chamber behind the alter. The following is an approximation of our conversation. I apologize for its stilted tone:

"I sensed someone's presence here," he said.

"Forgive my trespass," I apologized, introducing myself. "I was concerned that the church might be beyond salvaging, yet, I see this damage can be repaired."

"Yes, my congregation and I shall see to it," he calmly replied. "I am Rev. Walter Shance. I am also good with a saw and hammer. We of the Cloth, you see, are not above a little toil and sweat."

"I do not know whose artillery was responsible for this, Reverend," I explained. "But I'm sure whoever's shell's they were simply fell short, as often happens. I know our men would assist in the repair work, providing the Army does nor move on beforehand."

"That will not be necessary," the Reverend assured me. "The labor will help bring my people closer together, as the war has distressed and distracted so many. The women will cook and the men will fix and all will be spiritually rewarded. Perhaps, there was a hidden reason for those shells falling short."

"Perhaps so," I agreed, the Lord's ways often being inscrutable. "I have seen His ways on the battlefield."

"Undoubtedly," he responded, this war being His chastisement for our nations resorting to violence instead of prayer. Many think the war will continue until its waste is realized and the lesson driven home."

"And then forgotten a generation hence," I speculated. "Excuse my cynicism, Reverend, but I understand something of human psychology."

"And I of human spirituality," he countered. "I trust our civilization will never permit a catastrophe such as this ever again."

"I hope not," I replied with a modicum of exasperation, "I hope not."

"Perhaps, by then," he predicted, "the Millennium will have come."

"Perhaps," I responded, at a loss to say anything more.

The wind picked up, whining through the holes in the wall: "A desolate sound, isn't it?" I thought aloud.

"Yes," the Reverend replied, "but repairs will manage that, as we must manage the South when this war ends. We will have much to repair then and much healing to do of bodies AND souls. I see you are apparently an artist or journalist by virtue of the notebooks you carry. They protrude from your knapsack. Your burden must be heavy."

"Not as heavy as yours, Reverend," I earnestly replied, "and not nearly as heavy as yours WILL be." I had often speculated on the spiritual costs of the war after the guns ceased firing and its uniformed survivors returned to disrupted or destroyed homes and the embers of their once violence-free lives. Adjustments would be hard for many and impossible for others. For a vital time, only our churches might be able to place a calming and restraining hand upon the desperation of countless thousands.

"I will take my leave now, Reverend. If our side was responsible for this, we will be truly remorseful. We do not target churches, nor, I am certain, does our enemy. God be with you and yours..."

"And with you, my friend," he answered, raising his hand benevolently. "Do not reproach yourself. There are reasons for everything the Lord permits that are not always apparent. Be at peace."

Relieved to breathe fresh air again in dusk's bracing chill, I looked back only once, noting how sun's fading light glinted from the Cross atop the church's still pristine steeple. There shouldn't have been enough remaining sunlight to have glinted from anything.

* * *

Flights of Conscience

As our column shuffled through the afternoon, clouds darted before the sun, casting shadows across our brigades, regiments and companies. Birds took flight at our approach, arching high above us in celebration of autumn's arrival.

Our troops looked up, admiring the birds' freedom, for which they gladly would have traded their physical beings at that fated time and place on our approach to battle.

Warm breezes rustled trees and grasses along the road, a sure sign that the gods of seasons were trading places and preparing the Earth for change. Yet, there would be little change for the Army until cold and snow forced both warring sides into another winter camp. But winter's respite remained a violent season away.

Still, the birds' flight stimulated much speculation about crop yields at home at harvesting times - times our men would not see as long as the war lasted. And then, when all conversations diminished, quiet fell upon every head. Except for the clinking of the equipment and cooking utensils they carried, each man's silence announced his turning of mood. Now to worries about home and families left to tend the fields. Now to concerns about the punishing labors that would age wives and sap the energies of elderly parents forced to assist. Now to fretting about their children, who were straining bone and sinew to help. Now to remorse.

Each man's loneliness hung heavily over all. For patriotism's sake, or in answer to adventure's call, most had abandoned their families to fate and now, belatedly, to guilt. All turned sullen and melancholy, their weariness inherent in their route-stepping, matching the droop in their shoulders and the slouch in their backs.

Birds continued their skyward sweep, sometimes dipping low enough to tease the human serpent winding below through the autumnal panorama that only hours ago had been theirs alone. What must they have thought of us? And what must they have known of the fates the gods had destined for each of us?

I secretly asked them but was answered with silence.

*   *   *

Note from the Road

One cannot imagine the tedium of the march. Marches generally begin after dawn and often continue until long after sunset. Not only is the physical toll itself great, men additionally suffer from meager rations and poor nutrition.

That they find the energy to put one foot before the other is inspirational enough. But, it is a crime of this war that our government, which demands undying devotion from every one of its soldiers, disregards their needs and war's the medical necessities.

Logic dictates that our leaders and military brain trust could muster the ingenuity to provide for all - but they are not here in the dust and miseries of the road. Why the men around me persevere is a mystical contradiction bound in their devotion to Cause and to each other.

I am awed by the depth and poignancy of such sacrifice. Yet, pen and paper cannot impart such spirit - and to date, mine have failed.

*   *   *

Singing infected our entire column today. Company by company, a single tune, originating somewhere in its center, spread forward and rearward until it became a shouting match between units to keep the tune alive. Mind you, this in a driving rain devoid of wind and lightning, which refreshed all and prompted hundreds to strip to the waist and bathe on the move. Never have I seen so many troops voluntarily rejoice in their nakedness as they washed and horseplayed at the same time - rifles slung upside down over their shoulders to keep their barrels' insides dry, clothes hung over every rifle butt and shoes tied together, wrapped in oil cloth and hung through every trigger guard. Thank the Lord that we came upon none of the fairer sex along the road. The countryside's blush might have lingered for years and then remained fresh in the conversations of that gender generations hence.

*   *   *

Our column paused today near a trickling creek that attracted our footsore troops. My road-weary company stopped opposite its widest part, and the boys drifted toward it to fill their canteens, splash their faces and slake their thirst. Afterwards, many sat along its banks, submerging their swollen feet while mesmerized by the water's soporific patter.

I, too, found the sound inviting, as if it were urging me to lose myself in reveries. No one spoke. Only a few shifted positions, their gazes never leaving the bubbling waters. Water and fire - how hypnotically they affect men's consciousness. The hypnotized put their rifles beside them or leaned them against their shoulders and bided. I laid aside my journal case, wondering how I would impart this moment to paper. We sat there quietly for a half-hour.

Few of us desired to leave the creek. How good it was to vacate our minds of all burdens for that brief period and to lose ourselves in what we later realized had been a comforting sleep of sorts - a time away from war. I knew that in the weeks and months ahead I would fondly recall the creek's temptations, as I tried to ignore the war's human destruction.

*   *   *

A little five year-old vagabond appeared from a woods this morning to walk alongside us - barefooted and bare to the waist - dirty, his belly distended. He carried a tiny toy rifle carved from wood. Like so many dispossessed urchins these days, he belonged to someone but no one.

"He be an orphan, 'Um sayin'," the soldier next to me insisted..."cain't be nothin' else. They come from their wanderin's a'lookin' fer vittles and we give 'em what we got, but this here looks t'be a fed one - though none too good. Some ain't but britches on bones."

The little one's sunken eyes and pallid complexion confirmed that he hadn't eaten well.

"Where's you maw, little soldier?" I asked him, reaching out to muss his matted hair...

"He ain't a'gonna say even if'n he be havin' one," the man next to me advised. "They come a'beggin' in their own way, sometimes fer their maws - thems what got 'em - but most times fer theirselves. But he ain't a'gonna tell ya nothin', most likely cause he's a'fendin' fer hisself and don't be needin' fer ya t'think he's a'bein greedy. Jest give him a morsel and he'll be on his way."

I took a half-dozen pecans from my haversack and bundled them in a kerchief someone had tied around his neck. Other men around me added items of their own. When I looked again, the little fellow had skipped away and vanished into a meadow.

"The war's come t'that," the soldier next to me said, pointing. "Cain't feed ar'selves, cain't feed 'ar wives, cain't hardly feed 'ar youngins'."

Just another innocent victim of the war and the enemy's depredations, I thought. If men must make war, they should arrange to protect and care for all its innocents with the same vigor.

*   *   *

We buried a fine officer last night - Captain Willard Laurent, who died of battle wounds suffered a month ago, although he had returned to ranks after his wounding. It's said he finally collapsed from blood-loss and infection. Some say his superiors should never have permitted him to command his company so soon after returning from hospital - that he should have been discharged and sent home when he refused a furlough because he worried for his men. Duty compels the Laurents of this army to do much beyond themselves, even when they perceive the ultimate costs. So it was with this good man.

Services were conducted by lantern light. His company - about sixty-seven officers and men - attended. They bent against wind and storm and cracking lightning that stitched erratic patterns across the sodden universe. His burial detail laid his blanket-covered remains upon an old door carried by four men, and lowered him by ropes into his open grave volunteers had dug beneath it.

Chaplain Rose officiated, remarking that, "He was loved and respected by all. He will lay here known but to God as generations pass, long after this marker board we have hewn for him turns to dust. But he will be remembered to God, as will we all, when our dust reconstitutes the Earth and our souls are redeemed in the eternal world."

A soldier, having picked a bouquet of lilies from a nearby pond, laid them on the Captain's body. I saw only pathos in each one. Forever more, they would remind me of this night, when thunder echoed afar - and those attending wondered where Eternity awaited THEM.

Incidentals

There's a product referred to by some of our veterans as "Old Celebration." Although its suspicious pedigree is guarded and its ingredients cryptic, it produces all the paralytic effects religiously sought by those who indulge its pleasures - and suffer its consequences. Others call it "Sweet Jesus", the appellation applied with appropriate reverence, or, more accurately, "Stoneblind", besides other affectionate monikers.

It appeared in ranks yesterday as the column I marched with wound along its monotonous way. Some report that it originated in Company B just ahead of the outfit to which I had attached myself. The jugs containing it had been ingeniously smuggled from the ethers and, like altar wine, liberally dispensed, but in a sacred ritual of prestidigitation - and other sleight of hand. How, is a mystery, but no one cared.

By noontime, the jugs' contents nearly drained, "Old Celebration's" seductions were predictably obvious. Here and there, men stumbled along or had to be supported by comrades, who also stumbled along. Raucous singing destroyed well-known melodies, no doubt rousing the ghost of Stephen Foster, though, by that time, having partaken of a sample or two as it came my way, I could not remember if he were dead. In my defense, however, I must reveal that I imbibed only to the point of exaltation.

"Old Eagle Buttons," the brigade's commanding officer, a Colonel by someone's charity, eventually ended our frivolities by confiscating the jugs (many remaining at least a quarter filled) and whisking them away to the column's van, where he normally perched upon his dilapidated sorrel. Oddly, neither he nor his staff dealt punishments. Some theorized that his generosity and theirs could be traced to the leavings in each jug, the Colonel known to be a tender of the vine.

I now soberly concur with the evidence, since the column - with an uncommonly inspired Eagle Buttons leading the way - eventually took two wrong turns soon thereafter, forcing its already confused denizens to ramble back upon themselves and afterwords spending more tortuous time trying to find the right track again - one semi-delirious wag proffering that we were not lost, simply maneuvering under imaginative leadership - as we groped through brambles, briars, woods, and swamps - and other natural wonders having nothing in common with roads. I am certain a few men are still wandering somewhere out there, their heads expanded twice their normal size.

But, the hours were edifying. I heard known and never-before-heard swear words from the tangled ranks that would have swollen the pages of the largest known devil's dictionary.

Though our trek and general condition might have mortified the army's general staff, having violated all known regulations, policies, and protocols, I pray the Colonel will escape a court-marshal and his staff and rank and file punishment. Writing as a prejudiced civilian, I say no compassionate observer could have faulted those men for their excesses. The stresses of the war they had seen and experienced to date and the prospect of more, seemingly without end, plus the constancy of destruction's black-hooded angel hovering over all, had to have eventually found a therapeutic venting. And what occurred in the days ahead, to my thinking, would justify matters completely...

I was privileged to watch the sun rise that next morning. Fiery-orange, its light remained muted by mists lazing high over fields and woods all around. Others watched with me, their expressions radiating wonder, overpowering the sadness in their quiet demeanors. On this day, no more drink, no more celebrating. They would return to battle. Many would see the orb no more unless it also rose in realms beyond their ken. They felt as children alone in a hostile wilderness. Once more, young virgin troops trembled, though not from the morning chill, no doubt longing for the security of their mothers' protection. Their plight weighed heavily on my heart, but I could hardly alter their fate. And only a fool would have tried to reassure them that they would stand with me again the next morning to witness the orb's resurrection. I turned away, looking back only once to see them silhouetted against the dawn like shades already in the veiled world beyond...and I wanted to weep.

*   *   *

Fighting that afternoon was vicious. One who has not been to battle cannot appreciate what eyes and ears perceive in its midst. Our brigades had advanced - I with a company of regulars - upon the enemy's lines, as his artillery poured shell and canister into us. "Get out of here you damned fool," the men demanded of me above the din; "Yer a civilian and we ain't got no time t'care fer ya none!" But, I remained to witness such carnage as to sicken me as no physical upset I can recall. What iron and lead do to bone and tissue is horrendous. I witnessed so much decapitation, evisceration, and disemboweling - and so much splattered blood and bone - that I cannot reconcile why I did not perish with so many others.

For what purpose had the Lord spared me? Perhaps, he wanted me to continue my journals so that posterity would know of these bloody times. I watched shot and shell tear men to pieces and scatter their innards in every direction. I saw men covered with other's viscera, as still other's bone splinters pierced and impaled still more. So many have told me since, "You jest be plain lucky, friend, jest plain lucky." There were thirty others, from my company of fifty-six, whom Fate also saved for another day. They, too, at this hour, wonder why. We assaulted the position with our brigades - more than four thousand men - but were repulsed, losing more than six hundred dead and wounded. What waste!

I watched from the side of the road as a cavalcade of our torn and disheveled wounded streamed rearward, some so weakened from their mutilations that others less afflicted helped them along. A buggy drove between them and stopped. It's driver immediately hopped to the ground to steady its horse, while a priest rose from its seat. A timid zephyr teased his long cassock. He observed the flood of human tragedy to either side and looked toward the sounds of battle that boomed and rattled far up the road. Pungent powder smoke drifted by, its effects eye-watering. But the tears I saw trickling down his troubled face found their genesis in other sources. I had witnessed priests observe this sacred ritual before. Then, Christlike, he raised his hands over that suffering humanity and, in Latin, blessed them, asking God to be merciful and to grant them a painless peace. Passerbys looked up, some stopping to kneel in prayer, as countless others have done on similar occasions even as their bloody wounds also dripped corruption onto other wagon rutted roads. I turned away, once again too moved to observe any longer.

*   *   *

Mail Call

It is the saddest matter to witness men who have received news that they have lost family members at home.

Such an incident occurred late one afternoon in the company I marched with, as the Army readied itself for battle sure to come the next morning. In the rarest of events, mail actually arrived, and the company flocked to the sergeant detailed to deliver it to one man at a time. He stood upon a barrel, his hands filled with letters, while another man, his arms holding packages, stood on the ground next to him, ready to deliver them.

"Dolan," he eventually called out. A small, timid man stepped forward, his face aglow with anticipation. Some men had not received mail for months, and they hungrily awaited the slightest morsel of information about their families and sweethearts.

I focused on Dolan, since he appeared so enthusiastic. He opened the letter but, being unable to read, asked a fellow next to him to read it for him. Reluctantly, because he himself anxiously awaited mail, the good-natured fellow took the letter and examined it. His affable expression suddenly changed. Obviously crestfallen, I could see that he debated with himself about how to convey the news his eyes beheld?

A minute later, the devastated Dolan stood looking at the sky, tears streaming, even as the mail sergeant continued to call out names. Convulsed with grief, Dolan plunged his face into his hands and walked away through the scores thronging the area. The letter-reader, who noticed me looking on, confided to me..."Wife and little daughter - dead a'fever."

I had witnessed such tragedy before and now prophesied the worst for Dolan. Battle would become his perverse salvation. Unable to survive his grief - he would unnecessarily expose himself to the enemy's fire the next day and be shot down. Thusly accommodated, he would end his anguish.

And so it happened.

*   *   *

The Human Side

We took prisoners today, well-fed men overwhelmed in the rush of our regiment upon their lines. They appeared not the least bit discouraged, but chatted pleasantly with their captors. It occurred to me there and then that we were fighting the wrong people. They and we should have turned our bayonets on the profiteers of this war, who persist in their perverted passions.

* * *

Hearts go out to those in ranks who, on the march, cannot keep the pace - whose weary, malnourished bodies cease to answer valor's demands and simply give out. Such men often weep with frustration for having to fall to the sides of the road, no longer able to tolerate the pains of their blistered and bleeding feet, nor able to encourage their quivering leg muscles that, flushed of energy, can no longer support their torso's weight and collapse beneath them.

These mortified souls, for the sake of expediency, must be left to their own devices as we march on. More able-bodied comrades always lag behind to give them water and spare vittles. But nothing ensures that the exhausted will not languish there and be overlooked or forgotten. Some men pridefully push themselves beyond common human care and endurance and lay where they fall or where gentle hands pull them. We are left to pray that they will be received by physicians farther back in the column. Most find their way to the "invalid corps" that trails all columns at a lesser pace. These men are neither slackers nor stragglers but victims of their merciless master - the road.

Even good and strong men fall out. That they persist in later linking up with the column speaks to their loyalty and devotion. Lesser men have found such conditions excuse enough to abandon Cause and comrades with neither care nor remorse. Let no one say our invalids are lesser patriots than those with more tolerant constitutions. The majority return to march and fight again.

* * *

Melancholy diminishes me as I peruse our bivouacs at night, where I view a nation of patriots sleeping upon the dew-soaked earth in the undulating shadows cast by waning campfire light. And I wonder who among them will sleep forever by this hour tomorrow. I fear for each one. Would that I could call down angels to protect them and influence God on their behalf. If only all on our side and the other would declare the contest null and void and leave the self-serving and powerful to the bloody details of violent politics. If only I were elsewhere - where no more would my conscience compel me to say nor contemplate..."If only."

* * *

Two days ago, a young Private came to me with a request I was duty-bound to honor. We were paused on the march. He appeared out of the dust of the road, as horses pulling caissons and artillery came thundering by. He said he had searched for me in response to the advice of fellow soldiers who knew of me.

Timidly, he asked if I would write a letter to his father, now serving in Polk's Corps in the Army of the West, whom he had not seen since his enlistment a year ago. Neither he nor his father could write nor read, but he said other men in his father's unit could and would write back for him. The last letter he had received from his father had come two months ago. He worried that his father had come to a terrible end in the meantime in the heavy fighting occurring there.

It is common that men in ranks, who DO read and write, assist men who cannot. But held-up mail occasionally collects on the by-ways in great volume, and sometimes is delivered all at once. Many illiterate troops receive more than one letter at a time. Letters mailed between military units often are delivered at the whim of events. When they DO arrive, it becomes an embarrassing matter for recipients to find a patient-enough reader to catch them up on each one - and another task for them to find someone to reply. Reticent or bashful men, self-conscious about their illiteracy, often hold back, too embarrassed to ask for assistance, lest overwhelmed readers and writers reject them. So it had been with this young soldier, now greatly relieved that I had responded positively.

As he nervously directed his poignant thoughts to me, I realized he was not expressing himself well as nor as articulately as his true feelings demanded. I therefore engaged him in conversation before completing the letter, that I might divine his thinking on several matters. In the twenty or so minutes remaining to us before the march resumed, we discussed his father, home and family and other personal issues. It became obvious that some of his most heart-felt sentiments were being obscured by his understandable self-consciousness. In order to do justice to them, and because it was rumored that the Army might see action the next day, I asked that he come by at reveille the next morning after we bivouacked that night. It would allow me time to cogently present his thoughts to his father.

Before sunrise that morning, he sought me out. I had finished the letter and sleepily read it to him, hoping that my paraphrasing of his thoughts would suit him. He listened intently, tears in his eyes. When I finished, he wept. (Only then did he admit to being sixteen tender years young - though he appeared much older - and already a veteran!) I was taken with his reaction but could do little else than hold him as might his father. War ages the young by years.

I promised him I would post the letter and did so in the regimental mail a half-hour later. Yet, I could not rid myself of his situation's poignancy - of that moment when all the tribulations and horrors he had endured in the past year had come spilling out of him in a torrent of emotion - too many for one who had come to the Army so innocently young. He thanked me sincerely, calling me a "word magician" and marveling at how "magically" my written words had expressed what had been in his heart.

I sincerely trust that his father will receive the letter, for we did see action the next day at a place called Campion Hill, from which his son failed to return.

*　*　*

I have come off the battlefield at this hour as shaken and exhausted as the others of the company I followed into the fight. Though its commanding officer forbade me from going in with the first ranks, and confined me to the company's rear, I sneaked forward. The powder smoke was acrid, the rifle fire deafening. Minié-balls hum like bees when passing close by and thud when borrowing into flesh and smashing bone. Other's carrion clings to me. My clothes remain blood-spattered. Small bits of bone stick to the fabric of my coat. A splash of brain tissue dangles from one shoulder. I dare not detail the horrors in the deaths of those I saw perish. At a punishing cost, we drove the enemy from his positions. My fatigue comes from witnessing the destruction of so many good and decent men who, if left to civilian pursuits, might have contributed mightily to the welfare of their parishes and nation. Only God knows to what heights their accomplishments might have risen. Among our survivors, there is neither a sense of victory nor elation. Much of the fighting came to hand-to-hand, and we bring back many wounded enemy prisoners. These stained and disheveled souls appear as dejected and spiritually drained as our people. Their most grievously afflicted, in company with ours, have no care for anything save salvation and the easing of their agonies - causes and politics be damned. There is no relief for us today for winning this battle. It merely means that our survivors will face another fight soon. Conversely, our well-fed prisoners are relieved for being out of the war. Among both, there is a compelling need to slake their monstrous thirst - which many are doing by emptying canteens or draining ladles from water-filled buckets we give them - and to sleep for undisturbed centuries. Every day, our road grows longer. Every day, we trample out the grapes of wrath, finding them ever-more abundant and commonly bitter - and the lilies ever more crimson.

*　*　*

As much as rain can be a misery for troops on the march, it can also be a blessing. On hot summer days, when we are paused on muddy lanes, we inhale the sweet-smelling breezes it brings and relish their refreshing touch upon our faces. They lull our weary consciousness into a half-sleep of sweet dreams, becoming a balm and intoxicant and, for as long as they last, our passport to unsullied dimensions of blessed peace. We cherish their beneficence. Yet in winter we curse the ice they lay upon the road and our dispositions, and we decry their frigid discomforts and debilitating tremors they wreak. But, for now, our troops doze beneath their comforting grace this warm day, glad for the respite they bring to our aching bodies and constant concerns.

* * *

As I record in my journal, the fighting that has raged since morning now ebbs. Smoke and battle's din drift away. I spy an officer who has lost much of his company. Trance-like, he stares across the quieting fields, as if searching for something never more. Without embarrassment, he cups his face in his hands - and weeps. I can do no more for him than turn to leave him to his pain.

* * *

We passed a dead soldier in the road today, one of ours. He laid face-down, flies and maggots ravaging his body. Each man surveyed the remains, as the sordid odor of his decomposition assaulted our senses. Had he been a sniper's victim? Had his heart merely quit, as occasionally happens even to apparently healthy-looking soldiers every day? Who could say?

All hesitated to turn over his seeping body to examine it for identification. But our men would not let him lay in the middle of the road - to be mashed by horses, wagons, and speeding artillery and caissons.

His rifle, ammunition and personal affects were gone and his body partially stripped. Also missing were his shoes. We could see that he had worn them. His bluing feet, though blistered, were neither dirt-caked nor road-bruised. How pitiful was his contorted form. Perhaps he had been scavenged by locals or deserters or killed by thieves for his rifle and equipment. Perhaps he himself had been a deserter. Theories abounded. Undoubtedly he would remain unburied if our men did not do the decent thing, for everyone looking on saw himself there. Those who believed the war had hardened their natures and stripped them of humanity were sorely tested. They knew the soldier deserved better than to be humiliated by thousands of probing eyes. He had belonged to their brotherhood and they were bound to honor him - even though they risked punishment doing right by him.

A dozen forsook our standing orders against breaking from the column "except for the most urgent calls of nature." They pulled his body from the road and into a bordering meadow, leaving behind a trail of his corruption. Falling far behind their company, they hurriedly dug a shallow grave, parting the soft soil with their hands and bayonets.

I tied my kerchief round my nose to defray the stench and fell back with them. Having no blanket to wrap him in, and no marker for the grave, and though they feared to see his other side, they could not rightly bury him in face-down. Reluctantly, they turned him over. He had been shot in the chest and gutted. Two volunteers bravely searched him for identification but found none. He would rest in anonymity.

They put him in the grave, shrouding his decaying countenance with grasses and wild flowers, and then covered him with the soil they had dug out, mounding the excess. Those who remembered the Lord's Prayer recited it then, and all hurried back to their distant companies.

Passing troops applauded their daring, knowing the consequences they faced. But their decency invited the admiration of all. Officers who had witnessed their departure and return to ranks looked the other way - and "decently forgot."

* * *

Personal Reflections

I observed our General standing beneath the sky's autumnal brilliance, his head bowed in prayer, his heart heavy and body bent owing to the deaths of so many in his command. Silhouetted against the afternoon blue, with majestic cumulus parading slowly by, his inadvertent pose betrayed his emotional and spiritual exhaustion. Yet, he knew that before the day ended, he would be forced to sacrifice even more men to battle. Thus, he prayed with a deep and poignant earnestness for the Almighty's forgiveness. I pitied him as I pitied no other man.

* * *

Battle is a terrible cacophony. Its noise breaks some men, sending them like cringing primitives to cover. Some tremble uncontrollably. Some soil themselves. Others cup their ears to escape it. Ravaging reason, the fear it inspires freezes their will, devours their sanity. Yet ironically if men were deaf to it they might abide their work too casually, never knowing its true voice. Perhaps, it is well that the majority dread it. Without it, many might too freely crave the narcotic of battle's violence, destroying too willingly to ingest it.

* * *

It is a crime of this war that the young, barely into long britches, are admitted into ranks. Some are too young. Little drummer boys often march with the troops into harm's way, defiantly beating their snares with their man-sized sticks. The custom is inexcusable. Custom or not, Mrs. Theodore Renke rebelled. As she related to me...:"I stood watching the little ones march - eight of them at the head of their regiment, including mine - through the main street of our town. My heart cried out and I grew terrified for them. "No, no, no," my conscience protested, "Not war for MY son!" She ran forward and tore him from ranks. Though he kicked and screamed in protest, she would not relent. She had sacrificed his father to this accursed endeavor, but she would not give up her boy!

If, in 1861, all mothers on both sides had demonstrated her brand of courage, no matter their son's ages, perhaps, I would not now be recording my miniscule impressions of this titanic tragedy.

* * *

Though I have struggled in my journals to convey the nature of this war, I have never seen fighting so brutal as now. Years of ever more bitter conflict have distilled it into a venom that has poisoned the consciences of all concerned - even unto the highest offices. Opposing forces have become wolf packs set upon tearing each other to pieces. This has made the war fearful enough, but I fret more for the peace, if and when it comes. Pray that it comes quickly, lest both sides salvage no humanity at all but survive with dead souls to conduct the impossible task of reconciliation. Peace will require strong men of surviving decency and Providential Grace to salve both side's war's wounds. Every day it lasts, the more both sides crucify each other's motives upon Crosses of sorrow. Yet, should there be a winning side, it must deal with the other with exceptional forbearance and with a charity that will resist ferocious opposition. Lingering grievances will threaten untold tomorrows, unless God restrains both sides and mercifully softens their hearts.

* * *

I submit a poem - given to me by its author - Private George Pogue, who discovered to his relief that his soul was still able to feel:

> "Even now, birds reclaim the skies above us.
> Nature pursues the seasons,
> indifferent to we below
> who prick its flesh with iron,
> singe it with fire
> and nourish it with tears.
>
> "How contrary to it we must seem and insignificant,
> for it knows that although it shall ever be,
> we shall not;
> that we, an annoyance,
> shall dissolve with the ages,
> our times forgotten,
> our bones to molder beneath
> its majesty sculpted by Creation for all time
> in Eternity's rock.
>
> We, of noise and bluster,
> command only the moment in arrogant pretense
> that we are more than a passing oddity
> of value to the universe.
>
> "If not for this prideful illusion,
> what more might we be or have been,
> who foolishly turn crimson the days
> and darkest the nights."

Private Pogue now lies beneath that majesty - where the lilies grow.

* * *

A Certain Sincerity

Countless times, I've observed soldiers cooking their meals, but today I was struck by the demeanors of two men quietly cooking theirs over a small fire in bivouac.

Nothing appeared to rush their endeavors, as is so often the case with hungry soldiers. One smoked a cob pipe, the other, a small cigar. Together, they prepared their meager fare with a sophisticated ease worthy of notice. As the meal cooked, both sat back, the pipe-smoker with his arms folded on his chest, the other in a semi-reclining position. They conversed. In their small skillet, lard and hardtack sizzled. The relaxed manner of their conversation matched their general aura. Both looked scholarly and possessed a professional bearing. The cob-smoker, slight of build, and his heavier friend, appeared learned, though their tattered uniforms bespoke the rank and file's general plight.

Coffee perked in a kettle also over their fire, disseminating its aroma far afield and inspiring the envy of all within inhaling distance. It complimented their personas that they fixed coffee and not chicory, grass tea, or worse. I refrained from asking for a cup, since coffee is too valuable to be shared without invitation.

I learned that the cob-smoker had been a professor of history at a small Georgia college and the cigar-smoker a Virginia attorney. It was novel that such men had enlisted together as Privates in this North Carolina regiment, when each might have found himself a staff position well away from the fighting. Though both kept to themselves, I discovered it was not because they thought themselves superior to their fellow troops, but because other troops found their conversations too elevated and their language "too fancy."

When speaking with them later that evening, I was taken with their sincerity and candor and asked why they had joined the Army as Privates. Because, they confessed, they had thought it necessary to demonstrate that not all men of their callings and stations believed in class distinctions and special privilege.

Thank God for such principled souls. How ironic, that who and what they are engendered in ranks the very attitudes each had sought to discourage. What price altruism?

*   *   *

When the Grimness Sets In

In the beginning, I watched men come to war with enthusiasm and élan. Patriotic fervor motivated their every sentiment, as reflected by their songs and boasting. They were going to perform heroic acts and defeat the enemy in short order. Their deeds would inspire the nation and cause poets to proclaim their glory. But, then, as time tested their souls, the reality of the tragedy they were about slowly sapped their energies and flagged their morale.

As their fervor gave way to fatalism, I watched the "grimness" set in.

I saw their minds and bodies tire, and a look overcome them that said the shock of that reality had crumbled the underpinnings of their idealistic expectations. They had seen and known the "elephant" too intimately. Death and killing on unprecedented scales had become the bloody coin of their realm, spiritually costing them far more than what little they had anticipated or could afford.

Today, disillusionment stalks their bivouacs, trenches and sleep. In their stench-caked nostrils, they abide the results of the dead's rotting flesh and suffer their supreme testing as never before. For too long, they have looked the gorgon in its eyes and must once more endure its fiery breath. Many have broken upon the war's crosses without having suffered the slightest physical wounding, their mortal injuries being within. The majority battle spiritual exhaustion and numbing discontent, belatedly realizing that, in the beginning, they were children pulling the tail of a gargantuan beast that turned and lashed back. Now they are hardened souls long since naïve.

Every day, in the eyes of eighteen and nineteen year-olds, I perceive forty year-old men. I see youthful veterans no longer youthful and, even at seventeen, never to be boyish again. And I ask God, what have we done to a generation whose souls and spirits were entitled to gradual maturity in accordance with His Divine intentions? What have we changed them into and, when the fighting ends, what will they have become?

This morning, I watched a "boy" sharpshooter explode the head of an enemy soldier attempting to climb an abatis seventy yards away - and coldly smile.

Again I ask you Lord, what have we done?

* * *

In the Beauty of the Lilies

**The Wartime Journals
of Confederate Correspondent
Royal K. Chapman
1862-1864**

Journal Four

Contents

*   *   *

A Thought

There would be images that would
freeze time
and memories to confirm each one.

Graven Images

Today we watched a portly man, wearing a white coat and straw hat, struggle toward our positions. Obviously a civilian, he labored mightily through puddles and mud left by a morning deluge. Over one shoulder, he hefted a long-legged tripod attached to a large box. A black drape that dangled from one end of the box flapped in the breeze. A valise, strapped over his other shoulder, swayed awkwardly, containing what appeared to be heavy materials.

The company to which I had attached myself defended a hastily thrown-up wall of earth and branches. Seeking victims, minié-balls fired by concealed enemy sharpshooters two hundred yards away, whirred around us - with our men occasionally firing back. Our regiment had strung itself along equally hastily-erected earthworks, awaiting a possible enemy assault. Aside from the occasional rifle reports, an eerie stillness hung across the surrounding meadows and fields, as if the Earth anticipated the eruption of massive violence at any minute. Yet, on came the struggling civilian, slipping and sliding so badly, we thought he and his burdens would spill into the mud. Each time, he miraculously righted himself, displaying surprising coordination for such a weighty man.

Stopping on a relatively dry piece of higher ground, he set down his burdensome contraption, spread its legs and pointed the box in our direction. From the valise, he lifted a square object and shoved it into the box. Then, his head disappeared beneath the drape. A moment later, one hand reached around and removed what looked to be a cap from the side of the box facing us.

"Ain't that one of them there picture makin' contraptions?" a soldier asked.

"It were," another replied. "Seen one b'fore."

"I ain't never," the first soldier responded. "'Heeard of 'em, though. Guessed what it be."

"That feller' ain't too quick upstairs," a third man remarked. "'Bout got 'hisself t'where them hostiles 'cross the way's gonna pin their big red medals all over him."

No sooner had the third soldier spoken, than wood flew from the box, toppling it immediately and leaving the astonished civilian still bent over but staring into vacant air. A second minié-ball dispatched his straw hat. Though it caused him no injury, it inspired his stubby legs to bring him at remarkable speed splashing to the protection of our wall.

"Ain't see'd so much mud fly since the Lord made dirt," the third soldier remarked.

Puffing and huffing, his valise swinging wildly, the civilian finally reached us. With our assistance, he clambered over our makeshift defense, his face redder than roses. Unused to such exertion, he slowly caught his considerable breath, embarrassed about his failure. Then, as our dour bunch looked on, he apologized, saying he was a newspaper photographer "capturing images of the war."

"Well ya better hunker low," the first soldier said, "'er y'ull neva' git t'captcha' much more than a pile a'heaped dirt, if'n we get the time t'put cha under it."

The photographer, Thomas Graves, admitted he had much to learn about military matters, explaining that he had been "photographing" all morning, but was at a loss to know what he would do now that his device had been ruined. "I'm a freelancer," he said. "That camera was my own."

"You may be ig'nernt 'bout war," the second soldier said, "'but y'be the luckiest creature a'God I ever did see. How them fellers 'cross the way hit that there box a'yers but missed a target big as you ain't natural. 'Spect it be owed 'ta their kindly charity!"

I suspected the same. His presence now attracted a curious group of our ducking riflemen. Distraught over the loss of his device, Graves explained that his valise contained "exposed photographic plates made of glass," which he desperately needed to "develop," his terminology fascinating our boys. Only two admitted to ever having seen a photographer or knowing anything about its processes.

"What'd happen," another soldier asked, "if'n y'ud 'deevelop them things you was speakin' of and seen the Devil's face a'lookin' right back at cha?"

The nonplussed photographer replied: "I believe, sir, that I would quit the profession and become a devout churchgoer."

Our boys exploded with laughter. From that moment on, they took the star-crossed visitor to be a regular fellow.

The enemy assault never came, and we were marched off to new positions later that afternoon. The last we saw of Graves, he was defying harassing fire to retrieve the legs and broken parts of his mangled contraption. I then remembered that I had forgotten to ask him if he had recorded OUR images before its destruction. Even now, I wonder if, somewhere on one of his fragile glass plates, our images will stare into centuries hence.

* * *

Unintended Chivalry

Enemy sharpshooters harassed our company's bivouac today, persuading us to abandon our cooking to seek cover.

Having sneaked past our pickets, they sniped from the protective cover of the surrounding woods, their shots bouncing off the rocks ringing our cooking fires and ricocheting over our heads. Only after a minute of panic did we realize that they were "funnin'," aiming not at human targets but at one of our large pots of perking coffee suspended on spikes over our fire.

Owing to its rarity, we seldom enjoyed true coffee. Our cavalry had liberated sacks of it from an enemy supply train the day before, and we figured the theft had inspired the sniper's retribution. The brew's enticing aroma had seeped into the woods and likely into their nostrils as well. We counted three enemy snipers trying to hole the pot or knock it from its moorings, probably figuring that by ruining it, they'd get back at us by devastating our morale.

More minié-balls churned the fire beneath the pot, blasting other cookware. Though their shots scattered coals and ashes, not once did they strike the pot. We rationalized that their army's luxurious existence had offended the Lord, who, believing in fair play, now intervened on our behalf.

Our pickets entered the woods, flushing the snipers from their cover, whose fire slackened and ceased. Feeling once more secure, we slinked back to our campfire, sorry to see that the kettle heating now ash-strewn possum stew had been holed, but that our perking coffee pot had survived intact. Actually, the stew had partially salvaged itself. A large portion, including two misshapen minié-balls, had drained into another hot skillet, blending with lard, sizzling hardtack and a modicum of ash.

Because of their inept targeting, our enemies had proved unintentionally chivalrous, since they might well have deprived us of both our stew AND our coffee. We celebrated their flight as we sipped our nectar, gleefully imagining their remorse as they painfully fled through the wood's terrible brambles and briars.

Soon afterwords, we strained our gritty meal, washed it down with our delicious coffee and considered ourselves Providentially protected. The two mushroomed minié-balls, though well-sautéed, found no takers.

* * *

Escape into Nature

Summer has lapsed into early autumn this year, spreading its artist's pallet of exotic coloration across moody blue skies.

Late this afternoon, as our column bivouacked for the night, a balmy breeze transfixed the hour, giving us pause. I caught myself in an almost trance-like state, as the breeze caressed my face with its soft, feminine touch. Magnificent cloud formations paraded by. Many of us sensed that we had been caught up in a mysterious, unworldly experience.

I marveled at the sensation, feeling detached from the present. Hidden behind the clouds, the sun sent its rays to the edges of puffy cumulus, tinting their landscapes with supernatural golds, pinks, oranges, and turquoise. I would have sworn I had entered an enchanted dimension apart from our mortal climes.

We stood for many minutes, not wanting the moment to end, our wartime fears and apprehensions momentarily calmed and put to rest. I desired to lose myself in the moment, never to return. And, as dusk descended, compelling our men to resume their mundane duties, I felt great, haunting pangs of homesickness for this concluding spectacle.

Few men spoke, as I'm sure they contemplated the very same feelings. Although not a formally religious man, I sensed that God had reached down and imparted to us a Heavenly hint of immortality and the nature of the world beyond, which we all would eventually know, if not before war's end. I slept with great peace of mind that night and, in the morning, several men admitted to having slept as never since enlisting.

To this day, I am convinced the episode was the Lord reassuring us that He truly holds us in the palms of His hands - and that all His promises concerning His eternal Kingdom are valid. Also, to this hour, those impressions linger like comforting echoes, moderating our fears of death by strengthening our faith in Heaven's existence and Eternity's certainty. The experience has deeply affected every man I've spoken to who witnessed this afternoon's sky.

God DOES speak to man, our Chaplain assured us, if men, with their eyes in such moments, would but "listen."

* * *

Three Asides

Today, we dragged our exhausted bodies through a deer path in woods that restricted our column's right of way. Barely wide enough to accommodate the passage of two men, shoulder to shoulder, it forced us to sidle back to back through vicious thorn brambles that protected its flanks and overlapped the path itself. Though troops cut and hacked the underbrush wide enough to allow the passage of our supply wagons, artillery and caissons, all of it grueling work, the Army's monotonous passage required hours.

Our regiment emerged from the woods swearing and complaining, with jackets and pants ripped and legs bloodied. Why, our men demanded, had the column's commanding officer chosen THIS infernal route? Surely, there had to have been a better one.

As we later learned, there HAD been a better one. But, some of our more veteran boys speculated that by pursuing it, we might have wandered far afield and allowed the enemy to reach the best ground first and occupy the positions our general desired US to hold instead - tactically meaning that we would have put ourselves in a position to be out maneuvered. No doubt, our boys would have been much more resentful then. But the march produced some poignant moments.

Though our officers frown on their men keeping pets, our company's smallest soldier, whom we nicknamed "Tom Thumb," found a tiny baby squirrel in the grass along the road as we rested during our trek. The starved little critter put up no fuss as Tom took it gently into his hands, touching its tiny mouth with water from his canteen while feeding it tads of water-soaked corn meal. It grew to adore him, satisfied to live on his shoulder. In two fights with the enemy, Tom placed it in his haversack, where it survived, as did Tom. When I left the company a week later, it remained the company's mascot. The men had named it "General Thumb." Oddly, in comparing it to its master, some boys insisted that, except for its bushy tail, it bore him an intriguing resemblance!

*   *   *

We were halted last Sunday as our column passed a small white church, that our men might take inspiration from the singing emanating from its open windows. Our column of thousands soon was discovered.

The singing ceased, as the small, astonished congregation peered from the church's front doors. Confronting a sea of armed, rag-tag humanity extending far into the distance both ways along the adjoining road, the congregration and Pastor John Tate, gawked. He quickly called out his flock and, on the church's front steps, positioned its choir, and for our sakes, continued hymn-singing.

As fragrant breezes and the bright sun lent themselves to autumn's signature, our men removed their sweat-soaked and tattered head wear, joining in the vocal worshiping until the area resounded with hundreds of earnest voices. Never had I witnessed such profound expression of faith among our troops. Many sang those familiar devotionals with tears streaming in grimy rivulets down their dusty faces. I doubt the good and overwhelmed Pastor had ever imagined presiding over such a tremendous Sunday throng. It must have been an Epiphany for him and all concerned. On bended knees, our faith-starved troops outdid themselves, leaving the congregation's sympathetic ladies joyfully weeping. I am certain the Lord, in full spiritual regalia, was present that memorable day, and I shall never forget that scene's spiritual power. For more than an hour in the midst of war, I witnessed a devout humanity's finest essence, one of the few times in our ongoing human tragedy that I observed the lilies blossom with true beauty.

* * *

Looking Inward

Today, I spied our Captain in his tent - sobbing. Seated inconsolably on his cot, his face in both hands, he emoted as if crushed by an inconceivable force. Though my first instinct was to go to his aid, I paused. Emotional situations arise in war that cannot be eased even by the best intentions nor personal intercessions. This was one.

I later learned that he had received news that his wife and two small children had perished with fever. Lord, God, how devastating - how remorseful and helpless we all felt. At its most vicious, fate spares neither enlisted men nor officers. I was relieved that I had not intruded, there having been nothing anyone could have done at that moment but bide and pray for the restitution of his tortured soul - and his family's salvation in Heaven. Losses like his are maddeningly commonplace these days. Fever is everywhere.

I have seen such disasters drive men insane with soul-crushing grief. A soldier expects to die in war. He does not expect his family, upon which his spiritual stability and salvation stands, to perish at home in his stead.

* * *

In their nighttime moods, soldiers, illuminated by their campfire light and made surreal by the undulating shadows it casts, study the firmament. In the stars, they find both magic and mystery. Up there, their thoughts float above their private cares. I cannot fathom how they resist that persistent demon that constantly nags, "Battle Tomorrow - Battle Tomorrow."

Some cannot and dare not sleep, lest they fail to mentally compose their last wills and testament to life - or with invisible glasses raised - toast their final hours on Earth. Upon my shoulders, I sometimes feel the weight of their burdened souls. Just as often, I cannot look long upon their faces, knowing I might never see them alive again. Experience has taught me to recognize Eternity in the eyes of those whose nights will be their last. It is not a welcomed talent.

In such quiet and privacy, by such flickering fire light, I think of my wife and lament that I had not been more true to her, nor could I ever have been. These papers and pens I cherish have been my mistresses - demanding and selfish. It was to these, as a matter of equal honor, that I also, and long ago, pledged my fidelity. To these, I have been more faithful. Lord, help me, for I regret it not though it cost me the wife I fervently adored and loved.

*   *   *

This afternoon, the boys collected hats full of wild flowers and adorned their uniforms, shoes, and rifles. Such buffoonery compensates for the battlefield's ugliness. No lilies were among them, except for those tinted red and superimposed upon the fields of memory they sought to escape. Only too well do they know that crimson lilies adorn the days when God leaves men to the perversities of their violent free will.

*   *   *

I received a letter today from a fellow journalist, J.C. Richards, now traveling with the armies of our foes. How he managed to have it smuggled from there to here remains his secret. I must keep confidential all such communication with him, lest we both are erroneously accused of espionage.

His letter contained no information useful to our side, and he regretted none from me that the other side might desire. Its postmark arrived smudged and illegible.

He reports that he was wounded in the stomach while following a recent engagement and regrets that he may well be out of the war for its duration. He begged me to care for myself, lest all that I have done "be lost to posterity." Though it is on my mind, I can only hope that a modicum, at best, of whatever I have done will be of any value to posterity. I have written primarily to present generations. Posterity remains a larger concept and far away. Every day of this war has narrowed my view and taught me that there is only one tomorrow for men who battle the gorgon - tomorrow existing within the clouded realms of vaporous chance.

*   *   *

Infantry Tales

Cold. Rain. Yesterday and the day before, the same. I write these notes beneath my rubber sheet. Water and mist shroud the countryside. Autumn has too early given way to pre-winter chills. The bulk of our brigade hunkers in a meadow. The company I am with shelters in a grove of trees.

The sky is without lightning, so that danger does not exist, yet many of our men go without shielding of any kind. They shiver to their bones and endure their soaking tribulations huddled together. Their chattering teeth are plainly heard, as the wet and cold are unendurable. Because of the rain, we've been unable to prepare even meager meals. We pray for sun's reemergence. As I write, its anemic orb timidly hangs to the west behind darting clumps of gray and charcoal.

My journal suffers the intrusion of cold water drops that blur the ink, even as the rain obscures our footprints in the history of these violent times. But now, as we look westward, the sun's orb grows brighter. We might yet be spared the fevers that surely will come if it betrays our trust. May its merciful warmth come quickly.

Today, during the ongoing deluge, our column passed over railroad tracks near a vital crossroads. Trains were bringing in our wounded from the fighting we would be engaging in miles away. Booming reports from the battlefield echoed through the ethers as we trudged along. Our men focused on its bloody residue lying in every state of agony upon box and flat cars. Using litters, scores of enlisted men lifted the wounded into wagons and ambulances for transport to medical attention, the cold rain multiplying the wounded's miseries.

As our boys watched, I surmised their thinking; would they, in kind, eventually return to this place in and on these same cars?

They looked with empathy upon the wounded, seeing themselves there and wondering how bad the pain would be. And when some screaming wounded twitched and squirmed, having to be restrained lest they fall from their litters, our young replacements balked. Having not yet seen the Elephant, they came away terrified - too green to know that some long-time veterans consider death preferable to the surgeons' saws - like those blades cutting and gnawing in the hospital areas we trekked through, where pain-tortured patients pled with surgeons for mercy. I watched the spines of our virgin troop turn to ice. Some boys vomited.

"Them saws'll be busy all day," one of our veterans remarked, "but they ain't a'gonna get me. I'll end m'mis'ries m'self b'fore I let them meat-hackers t'lay hands on me."

Not a seasoned veteran among them contested his attitude. Their grim silence said they all had seen enough of those bloody saws.

*　*　*

Thus far, I have avoided describing combat's intimate details, for my impressions deserve only second-best consideration. Eventually, I will take the testimonies of our veterans and synthesize them into a general commentary descriptive of their common experiences, thereby lending credence to the subject. None but their words will do. Mine will continue to be those of an interloper - theirs being those of men who have confronted the "elephant," their derisive term for battle, and thus far survived. Their testimonies, not mine, deserve the most serious attention.

Still, it haunts me that, if human nature and history remain consistent, anonymity will claim the men with whom I have marched for lo these many months, if not their deeds. When this war ends, countless thousands of its survivors will remove themselves to civilian pursuits, hobbled by wounds to mind and body. So intimately have they shared marching and fighting and war's general miseries, that they have become a brotherhood - bearded, dirty, smelly, hungry, fatigued, malnourished, demoralized, spiritually drained but fiercely loyal to each other.

Without knowing it, and by dint of mutual sacrifice, they've sworn loyalty oaths to each other in the sun's heat and winter's cold, in the confusion of battle and amidst bee-like buzzing of minié-balls thickly around them - and in the pain and deaths of comrades in arms. I try to commit their faces and voices to memory, feeling sacrilegious when I cannot, for they are and have been an integral part of my mission. I cannot divine any future experience that could surpass the present. My past military experience, which has blurred in my memory, does not compare. If the Lord grants me the privilege of growing old, I hope He also allows me to remember these men as the shroud eventually is pulled across my withered form. I do not want their faces to also be as ships that pass in the night, though older veterans tell me I should know better because it is always so with men in war.

"We're close 'cause we need each other now," a wizened sergeant explained, "but once free of all this, most souls'll put it, and ever'thin' it was, behind 'em. The mind'll do that t'pertect itself, but you can neva' sep'rate friends in war FROM war. You know that - you was in Mexico."

Yes, I knew. I WAS in Mexico - with Winfield Scott - but I feared I WOULD forget. South and North, for a century to come, cannot AFFORD to forget.

*　*　*

A private named Hobbs showed me a tintype today. Next to his image was that of his fiancé, a plain but pleasant-looking girl of seventeen, to whom he had promised marriage before going for soldier. "Don't know what I'd do if'n I couldn't come back t'her - 'er if'n I'd come back maimed real bad. Scares me."

Two days later we sent the tintype home to her, having gotten her address from a letter we took from Hobb's jacket pocket. We wrote to her, that after the most recent fighting, he was sent to a field hospital and, with scores of other men, was later buried near a place where a large rock juts from an otherwise nondescript meadow. We hope, for his sake, that in years or decades hence, she will find it and honor his remains with her tears of continuing love.

*   *   *

On the march today, one of our Privates began to read out loud from the New Testament in his small Bible. Taken were we with his sonorous voice. It captivated everyone and lent great profundity to each verse. So impressed were we that we were hardly aware of the time nor our fatigue and aching feet. After the march, we asked him to read to us often, which he pledged to do. The men truly were touched by the experience. Many do not realize how richly the Bible is written nor how meaningful are its words until they are brought forth with such interpretive power. Some of our boys believe that Private Benton has been Divinely inspired. I hope not. War too habitually claims the good like him.

And speaking of good: This morning, I came upon a very young Private sobbing on a hillside near our bivouac. Hatless, his clothing filthy and his rifle missing, he was the epitome of desolation. I sensed his dilemma. Homesickness plagues even our older soldiers these days. How much less a boy?

As I approached, he self-consciously turned aside. "Do not be embarrassed," I said. "I too am homesick." Disarmed, he sobbed in earnest. I sat next to him to explain my homesickness and how dearly I missed the peace I knew when surrounded by family. He revealed that after seeing so many men die horribly in his first battle, he lived in daily terror of it. Mortified that he had soiled himself in the fighting, and ashamed that he had run, he could not face his comrades who had stayed and fought. He also felt that he had profaned himself for having lost his rifle.

Poignantly, he told of having trembled beneath a ruined wagon for two days and how much he wanted to run to his mother. Only now had he returned, too devastated by his cowardice to face his comrades, whose censure he feared.

"I will die inside if they chastise me," he said.

I was touched by his admissions but thoroughly disgusted with the Army for having accepted someone of his tender years. Although he looked much older than fourteen, nothing had justified his enlistment, nor should we have expected a fourteen year-old to act the part of a mature adult. I asked him to wait where he was while I searched for our regimental Chaplain, whom I discovered in his tent reading Scriptures. When I explained about the boy, he immediately determined that he should come with me to speak to him. But when we arrived at the hillside, the boy was gone. We searched the bivouacs of three companies but never located him. No one claimed to have seen him, nor has anyone since.

Only God knows his whereabouts - home, I pray. He is constantly on my mind. The Chaplain, Reverend O'Hara, promised to watch for him and pray for his safety. I trust he has done so. It is discouraging that hundreds of underage males populate the Army. And I fear what the Army will do to him if they catch him and accuse him of desertion? Desertion rates are climbing, and we are intimidated by too many political but compassionless officers anxious to make examples even of the very young. Their criminal stupidity plagues our Cause. What should a mere boy matter to them, now, when he should have mattered to them greatly before they permitted him to put his name to enlistment papers? The problem is Richmond's.

* * *

I have run out of pencils and ink, and must now make ink from berry juices. It is a laborious method practiced by our boys who write letters home. I and they spend much of our time berry-searching. When we find them, we crush their juices into whatever containers are practical. I use a small bottle I've salvaged for the purpose. My resulting finger-stains indelibly assure me that the "ink" will serve well. One non-writer in the company, watching me work, remarked dryly, "Is this what they call the fruit of one's labor." I think half his name was "Wit."

* * *

A man fell out of ranks this afternoon during a forced march. Down he went, suddenly and without a gasp. We supposed the poor soul's heart had given out, as he had been ailing for weeks. He died without a decent meal in his belly and left no word as to relatives nor next of kin.

Though he wore no ring, some insist he was married, since, in the past, they say, he received letters from home addressed to him by a woman's hand. But, he could not read and was too proud to ask for help. They insist that all his mail went unopened or was lost. A small man, his gauntly cherubic face remained composed and oddly serene as he lay abandoned along the road.

We left him there, unable to bury him - forbidden under threat of court-martial to betray our pace by breaking ranks without authorization (though we've done it before in such cases). But our superiors were in deadly earnest, the march being desperate and time the enemy.

He is on my mind even now - all those letters unanswered, let alone unread. How the writer must have pained for a response, a poignant but sadly unnecessary consequence. If only I had known. No, no beauty in the lilies today. Our boys deserve better than to be left to rot on desolate roadsides. The regiment deeply resents his abandonment, the necessities of war be damned.

* * *

Strange Visitor

"The Prophet" wandered into our camp tonight. Some men said he follows the Army everywhere. Many say they have seen and heard him before, but he remains a mystery.

Favoring a crooked staff, he astounded us, appearing out of the woods in the glow of our dwindling campfires. Many of our more superstitious boys take him very seriously, saying he has accurately predicted the war's course.

This night, he stood ominously among us, tall and barefooted, dressed in dirty robes of coarse burlap, his greasy hair long and unkempt, a length of rope tied around his waist. I had heard of him but had never met him face to face. Now, looking into his bearded countenance and penetrating eyes, I studied him closely. For a long while, he gazed at each of us, saying nothing, chilling our blood with his unnerving silence...then: "The kings who have entrenched themselves in two governments have blasphemed by this war and even now insult the Lord. This war is wrong. Such men have abused their privilege of making policy without the consent of the governed! They have become pagan powers unto themselves! They have absorbed themselves in scheming without regard for the Lord's intentions. Beware these men. They are not here to suffer with you because you are the fodder for their ambition! Beware, little sheep, lest YOU pay even more severely the butcher's bill for THEIR sins!"

He stared again, then turned abruptly, disappearing into the woods. For many moments, no one spoke, then..."Sure is a dour cuss;" one of the boys piped-up..."but right this minute, Um more bewarin' a'chiggers than a'kings."

* * *

Last Notes from the Road

My feet pain to the bone. The boys say my arches are falling. I feel that I walk on large, rounded stones beneath each shoe. Yet, the entire Army suffers foot plagues of every color and description. How our boys manage, I cannot say. If they ever succumb to eventual dissipation, the cause will lie between toe and heel. Foot soreness and related miseries have become another daily burden. We are a hobbling multitude that grows more crippled with every step. Much of our boys' issued footwear is trash. Scores have thrown theirs away, calling it "foot dung." Amen.

*　　*　　*

Today, I was hit and knocked down by an errant minié-ball that struck my journal case containing my writings. The ball, being well-spent and probably misshapen, penetrated the sack and paper only to an inch, but its impact was ferocious. Having seen men lifted off their feet and punched backward by torso strikes, I appreciate how it must feel to be struck by a ball at full velocity. Even now, the relic that sought me out remains buried in one of my volumes - and there it shall stay as a remainder of my brush with chance. Since being struck, even boys who cannot read have asked for copies of my "lucky" journals. Said one: "Figured we betta' ask y'now b'fore the next ball kisses ya up b'side the brain."

*　　*　　*

I am writing this in my head as we trudge along on this seemingly endless march. Will put it to paper later.

A bony dog follows our column. Though cautious of us, having undoubtedly been mistreated, it is obviously starved. It disappoints me that some of our boys consider it and its plight with such contempt. After all, no matter how humble, it is a creation of God's. I have fed it, petted it and loved on it. In gratitude, it has "waggingly" returned my affection, though it has not pursued me. I don't know why. Perhaps, it has been too scarred by us to be thoroughly trustful of man. Whatever the case, the very fact that it understands and reciprocates loves proves to me that it possesses a God-given soul. But men do not usually match nor generally reciprocate its kind's loyalty and devotion, begging the question, "In these matters, have these furry souls evolved to a greater degree than man?" Whatever their behavior, I believe they are a reflection of us in myriad ways - and perhaps, collectively, a mirror by which God gives us to see our glaring imperfections. Though this animal's ribs protrude, and though it slinks with head down alongside us in its shaggy countenance and desperately depends upon our largess for its salvation today, no one shall ever convince me that it is not more noble than our enemy nor as preciously innocent as a child.

May God preserve it, if only to reassure us in this holocaust we serve, that life, even that of a humble dog's, still has value.

*　*　*

A Bane to All

It comes by day and stalks the night, debilitating men by the score and leaving many without life who have suffered it too severely. Dysentery - it scourges our ranks, disabling whole companies and regiments. It forces the Army to set aside its planning and compels it to pause at crucial times when it can least afford the idling of a single man, since pausing permits our enemies the advantage of maneuver.

I cannot overemphasize the suffering dysentery causes. On the march, we have passed gaggles of men so weakened by it, they can never hope to catch up to their units now far in advance of them. I have witnessed men so convulsed with gut pains and dehydration that they languish in agony. Nutrition, generally, has gone by the wayside in the Army. So poor are our diets, so often spoiled are our rations, and so malnourished are our boys, that soldiering has become a contest of sheer willpower.

For reasons I cannot divine, I have been thus far been spared, while so many around me have been attacked. The condition often comes on suddenly with mortifying embarrassment, and men soil themselves to extents entirely beyond their control. Their discomforts afterwards beggar the mind, and it is common to see men searching in woods and fields for creeks or ponds to cleanse themselves before resuming the march. They sometimes fall miles behind. Some drop in ranks, convulsed by the agonies of hell. One man told me that his pains equaled, and then surpassed, the miseries of two gunshot wounds suffered in battle months ago. Modest men, feeling the urge, race to relieve themselves in the discreet cover of tall grasses or woods, the thought of publicly humiliating themselves being too much to bear.

Our hearts go out to these poor souls, many of whom have not survived nor will survive their conditions. Out of profound frustration, our physicians prescribe experimental remedies which frequently do more harm than good, aggravating already severe cases. It causes me to wonder why nations go to war so spontaneously, when their medicines and medical practices cannot contend with the resultant effects. I surmise it is because the zealots responsible - who abide safely away from all harm - do not do the suffering nor dying.

I cannot decide if it is good or not good that cultural proprieties shielded the public from war's terrible details. Had civilians been treated to war's sights and smells early-on, they might have quickly ended this disaster. Yet, in writing this, I risk censure for sounding unpatriotic. I hope my words will not be so interpreted, for my cares are with the flesh and blood I write about. May they be spared mutilation or death and be returned to their families as quickly as possible - whole and able to raise their children and embark once again upon productive lives - and that the babes in our ranks, youngsters of sixteen and fifteen years and less, criminally recruited by unscrupulous advantage-seekers, be returned to their mothers.

I desire no more than this - nor can I recall a single devoted veteran in ranks who has ever wished for less.

*   *   *

Last Testament

I returned today from an Army hospital convalescent ward, having volunteered my services to the staff. I was accompanied there by Regimental Chaplain Josiah Sidwell. The much overworked staff, overburdened with crucial responsibilities, worked diligently.

One cannot imagine the scope of its uncelebrated duties unless one has spent a day or two witnessing its work. It is beleaguered in every sense. Cold autumn inclemency has restricted the outside ventilation to the wards, so common in milder seasons. Now, the interiors are close and oppressive to patients AND staff.

Despite all, I had the honor of helping compose a letter home for a young lad shortly to enter Glory. Knowing that he was rapidly failing, and because of his much weakened condition, he had implored me to pen his final thoughts to his parents. His dissipated but virginal countenance pointed to how immoral it has been for our government to receive conscripts his age and to encourage their enlistments. All of us, having once been young, can attest to the military's lure for innocent youngsters beset by grandiose dreams of high adventure. It is evil that they are exposed to the terrors and horrors of the battlefield they can only escape in their mothers' arms. I speak of lads barely into their teen years.

He self-consciously told me his age was seventeen. Later, to my outrage, I discovered he had just turned fifteen. I now wonder how many his age have joined-up, owing to the unscrupulous persuasions of recruiters told by their superiors to overlook such age disparities. If it were in my power, I would locate and severely punish all such scoundrels, whose consciences know better than to so manipulate the fresh and naïve and expose them to war.

The lad had suffered a minié-ball strike that had done great destruction to his bowels. Infection had eaten way a large portion of his intestines and filled the entire cavity with lethal corruption. To little avail, surgeons had removed the ball and had applied maggots to the wound to consume its dead and gangrenous tissues that reeked and gagged me. Its powerful gases filled the ward. I cannot describe the repugnance of that experience. The stench had combined with that from a score of amputees' gangrenous stumps.

Powerless to alleviate such conditions, staff members wore and issued us masks saturated in clove oil and mint. But the wounded remained unprotected even from themselves, thus adding to their indignities. Appalled and sickened, the Reverend had excused himself during his prayerful rounds, taking refuge in the refreshing breezes outside along the hospital's muddy grounds. No one took umbrage. Even the strongest among the staff occasionally left the wards to reconstitute himself before returning to his duties.

A physician explained that the young patient could no longer evacuate and suffered waste poisoning throughout his system. Despite the lad's helplessness, his humility tempered his embarrassment and put us at some ease. But we could see that, although he constantly apologized for himself and his condition, his intense self-consciousness added to his sufferings. And so, for his sake and peace of mind, though each mask made the smells endurable, we attempted to ignore the worst when they seeped through. Still, in the midst of his deterioration, he desired that his parents know of his love and concerns for them.

Worried that his passing would cast a burdensome pall across the remainder of their lives, he beseeched them not to look upon his death as something final or akin to oblivion, but as a rebirth into the Lord's Kingdom - and to consider their reunion to come in that marvelous place when the Lord called THEM home. His stoicism and touching attitude tearfully inspired us all. His suffering appeared to have sharpened his perceptions and prompted me to look beyond his emaciated form to see a soul wiser and more mature than its years. I remember thinking that our hospitals were filled with such spent potential.

As the lad had grown exhausted and was greatly in need of sleep, I withdrew, planning to finish the letter later on. Tragically, he slipped away in the interim. Yes, I had lost a new-found friend. Reverend Sidwell returned to the ward only moments afterwards and immediately inquired if the lad was to be buried in hospital grounds. He was informed that the boy's parents had sent funds for their son's embalming and transportation home. Apparently, the attending physician had advised them to make the arrangements. What a devastating impact the doctor's letter must have made.

It is wrenching to see the young expire so. And I believe that, after the war, those responsible for promoting and encouraging the recruitment of mere youngsters should be persecuted and publicly humiliated - even if it means the ruination of military careers and political reputations. Blame should go to the guilty, whoever they are and wherever they reign, for surely, the practice is known even in the highest offices.

These youngsters rightly belong to the generations we will sorely need to shoulder the responsibilities of their fallen mentors' when peace comes. What now for those communities who will no longer have them - who will be forced to depend solely upon the middle-aged, old and infirm, circumstances for our people being so dire?

I admit to being conflicted by sadness and anger over losing the lad - and I doubt that time will improve my disposition nor calm the turbulence his passing has engendered in me. Reverend Sidwell feels just as intensely. I have begged him to use his influence in the Church to decry what we witnessed today. He has consented.

May he do so successfully - and may we never forget.

* * *

An Old Soldier's Story

Excerpted and Condensed from the Testimonies
of Corporal Josie Willoughby, Infantry

"Was too old t'join the Army agin', they said - but I did.

"From the beginnin', though, m'bones ached and m'feet went flat and m'knees n'joints went dry and m'heart tortured me in m'chest - but I been stay'in with the younga' men and doin' m'duty.

"'Course, they done laughed at me and chided me 'bout m'age, but mostla' with good huma', 'ccasionally askin' me how on earth an old codger like me'd been let t'join-up agin' - 'er if'n I come back in t'hide from somethin' - 'cause the Arma' be a 'perdy fair place t'hide fumblers' n'fugitives.

"I try t'splain to 'em that I weren't 'scapin' nothin' - 'cause I failed at business and needed the sign-up money - and that soldierin' weren't new t'me (I'd been in the Mexican War) and that it give'd me m'onla' remainin' chance t'earn a livin'. But 'somma the younger ones done thought m'reasonin' were selfish and greeda' and unpatriotic. That hurt me some, but I got ova' it - even 'cused me a'killin' fer money 'steada sacrificin' fer a noble cause. Well, I got 'em t'thinkin' 'bout that 'perdy damn quick.

"Y'see," I tell 'em, "killin's killin,' causes 'er not, noble 'er not, and sacrificin' 'er not - and jest b'participatin' in this war, we's all guilta' a'the killin' n'perpetuatin' it, whateva' the reasons fer joinin-up'. B'sides, killin' ain't neva been the Lord's way, ana'how! THAT stops 'em up short ever' time! Them's bein' s'young n'all - they'd neva' done no powa'ful' thinkin' bout nothin'!

"Afta' that, they lighten-up on me and 'take me with more r'spect. But, that's how it be with them young rabbits all filled with vinegar who ain't neva' used their brains 'fer much yet - b'sides havin' no 'sperience t'figure on. Am able t'show 'em a few tricks, too, 'bout soldierin' they never thoughta'. And they take kindly to it. Even had somma' our sergeants takin' heed, 'cause they know'd I be right.

"Ends up sometimes that I bury some the boys that laughed at me. Sad thing it be - sad thing. But I done buried young ones b'fore - in Mexico. That there little detail 'bout war neva' changes.
"Then, I got this here minié-ball through m'side and had to quit - still drainin' pus and hurtin' - and that be five month now. 'Tuk m'rifle away from me, they did, and made me an orderly.

158

Now, might as well be a'chasin' afta' officas' with chamba' pots! Sure been a humblin' come-down for an old dirt-eata' like me. Leastwise, I still be servin' - and they ain't buried me yet."

* * *

Chatterings

Mental notes jotted at the moment:

Birds chatter excitedly as we pass through woods on this Autumn day's monotonous march. They gather even as winter clouds threaten on distant horizons. Yet, the vibrancy of their calls reminds us not only of Nature's indifferent constancy but of its absolute disregard for our personal tribulations.

The realization is not lost on the men around me who, with regret in their strained expressions, study the trees. The chattering speaks to them of peace, and, painfully, of freedom - the ability to wing away from every hardship below and from all things threatening and disagreeable. Sadly, that same Nature has condemned them to the ground and offers them only the "freedom" to desert or the peace of the unmarked grave.

Even so, their Chaplains tell them they have not been thoroughly condemned and remain as the Lord intended - free to answer to themselves for the choices they make in whatever manner their consciences dictate. And so, they march on, the purity of the birds' voices constant in their ears - nagging and sweet - their consciences divided, saying "stay your earthbound course" or "kill no more." One can almost hear their instincts imploring them to seek His peace, while the gods of war urge them never to betray such earthy conventions as honor, loyalty and devotion to duty.

After fatigue drains their mental energies, quietude prevails, leaving them to ponder their situations well into their evening bivouacs. They have lost many friends of late, and though they have fought well, they have fought futilely. More and more, the war becomes a daily dirge, with ultimate victory slipping farther away. They sullenly stare into campfires as the chatterings echo in their thoughts. Many will sleep fitfully, with the faces of wives and children or sweethearts haunting their dreams.

Such dreaming will cause many to awaken shaken and exhausted, having seen those images disguised in mist and forever beyond their reach. I, too, hear the chatterings and dream such dreams.

Every day, our roads grow more difficult and our marches longer. Every day, we pine more within and endure more without. Every day, we eat our self-pity - and bide. And, yet, every day, our men refuse to quit.

* * *

In the Beauty of the Lilies

**The Wartime Journals
of Confederate Correspondent
Royal K. Chapman
1862-1864**

Journal Five

Contents

*   *   *

A Thought

They watched a general drop to his knees,
crushed by the weight of his dead.

Of an Evening's Walk

I walked along our regiment's perimeter this evening, as blazing campfires dotted a dozen company bivouacs. I sometimes do so when fresh evening breezes sweep away the stench of fighting. And since our regiment had participated in a grueling, all-day-long battle, I sought relief from the depressing auras overhanging each one.

T'was a solemn time for those in individual campsites. Men were taking stock of their much depleted ranks and remembering those who would not be answering to morning roll calls. Scores nursed wounds to both body and mind.

Miles yonder, our enemy's campfires blazed just as fiercely. No doubt their people, too, languished in the aftermath of death and their miseries. It would not be long after dawn that we would meet them again somewhere in the already reddened landscapes between, for the fighting thus far had been inconclusive, neither side having gained the advantage.

For a moment, I watched our enemy's glowing fires, then continued my walk, lured into the night by its rising mists. Far to the rear of our campsites, lighted lanterns bobbed in the darkness. I hesitated, knowing what they represented - shadowy pits, some deep, some shallow, some elongated, most running parallel to each other, lantern light dimly illuminating the human costs of two nations' hubris - all being quietly packed-down with battle's contorted carrion. Odors of putrefaction assaulted my senses, coming from pits dug for yesterday's dead, but not yet covered.

Colored folk and Army orderlies worked there diligently, kerchiefs across their faces, dumping dead bodies into each gaping maw, their unceremonious labors remaining distant from and unobserved by the day's sullen survivors. It struck me, that the Army's and society's lowliest were ridding the world of barely recognizable refuse that many hours before had been living tissue of meaning to someone dear - some young and not so young, some whose sightless eyes stared into nothingness - some faceless. Where had their souls gone, I wondered...to all the Lord had promised, I hoped.

I watched for a time before wondering why I stood staring at such horror, deciding that the scene's poignancy remained morbidly magnetic. Overcome, I left.

For the remainder of the night, I slept fitfully, as I experienced a recurring dream - of being at the bottom of a dark hole, watching shovels full of dirt being thrown onto my face. Dream or not, I thought I might go mad and awakened sweat-soaked and shaken.

* * *

The Next Morning

Hours into the next day, as new fighting raged, I followed an infantry company rushing to the battle line. On the way, I noticed more of our dead's bloody remains being pushed off overflowing wagons, dragged to pits dug the night before, and shoved into oblivion. My experience with the pits the previous night had caused me hours of fitful sleep.

But now, as new bodies bumped and bounced down the pit sides, twisting like rag dolls, my mind conjured what lay inside them, tangles of shattered bones and tissue in shredded uniforms, jumbles of vaguely human forms disguised by coagulating gore. Throughout the night, the poor orderlies and Negroes working there had dug more in preparation for the morning's bloodletting. How they must have despised their work, for surely, they understood how passionately all soldiers fear that the pits are cursed.

I know that, once again, I repeat and belabor these bloody points, but one must understand how intensely the pits overshadow our soldiers' lives and color their many fears, especially among these, anonymity. The pits guarantee it eternally to all interred there, every soul forever lost to sweethearts and progeny, never a tear to be shed over them, never flowers to be left to honor them nor tributes granted them nor prayers to be said above them for their souls' salvation. Yet, the diggers perform a ritual that will continue even after the guns cease firing today - if we are not forced to quit the field first. Otherwise, our dead will lie where they fall or remained stacked on wagons, unceremoniously abandoned - all labors halted - left to God's guardianship and the enemy's shovels, if interred at all.

I wondered how many times in how many places in all the eons of human war-making had this same pitiful ceremony been performed? In that span, how many countless millions had such pits consumed? Why, then, had not the Lord placed a restraining Hand upon mankind, wiped war from his nature and commenced an age of Divine enlightenment? Why?

As I trudged to the new fighting I remembered the sentiments of a chaplain who presided over a soldier's individual burial months ago:

"Dear, Lord - take these souls who have transgressed thy Word - forgive them their humanness, which did not understand Thee - and, as You would be merciful to errant children, grant them warm food and decent shoes. And dear Lord, though they in their free will have disappointed you, grant them all-merciful peace."

I watched the neutral sun, anemically wrapped in drifting smoke, indifferently observe our blood-letting, and thought: "Despite our mayhem, Nature will not be put off. When the guns cease their thunder, birds will again wing high. And, eventually, time will disguise the destruction our hubris wreaks here. The landscape will forgive all, and a century hence, it will heal and be as it always was. And, where thousands have expired, only the slightest depressions will mark each pit's location, where their mouldering contents nourished surrounding forests of stately pines all around."

I vowed to never again permit myself to be so incautiously lured into shadows by lantern light. Instead, I would pray for the interred anonymous, understanding that if such trespass were unavoidable, I would again suffer the spiritual consequences, perhaps slipping once more on the snakelike entrails twisting behind the walking wounded or oozing from the bloated dead.

My calling demands that I not turn away from anything confronting me. I record what our homefront should know no matter how repulsive. Yet, I considered my dream's warning - that before this war's finish, I might yet know the feel of shoveled dirt upon my face.

Lord, I begged, let not that dream be prophetic nor that it too soon come true.

*   *   *

Letters Found

Yesterday, I found three letters, each of several pages. Still in their envelopes and exposed amongst a cluster of our dead troops - victims of canister fire, those small iron balls packed into single shells that spread their contents, shotgun-like, with mangling effects. The men's torsos lay ripped apart, their limbs and innards spread like refuse.

The nature of their wounds made visual identification impossible. Blood rendered the letter-recipient's address on two envelopes illegible, but the contents of all three survived. I worried that reading them would violate the deceased's memory, but, I reasoned, for their families' sakes, it was important to attempt to learn the recipients' identities. I discovered all three letters belonged to the same soldier.

This, then, are those letters that eloquently comprise a chronicling of our national sufferings. I have changed all names for propriety's sake, but I leave it to the reader to judge whether I have, by revealing their private contents, morally erred.

Letter One

My dearest Husband Wilson,

I write you this long letter, lest we not be in communication again for many months. I gamble that our dilapidated mail service somehow delivers it to you. Only the Good Lord knows if and when that might be.

In your last letter, you pleaded with me to honestly describe conditions here at home - which I reluctantly do now, only because I accord you your wish, though I worry that the details I include will depress and demoralize you. But you insisted that I be candid and forthright.

Our children are fine, my darling, yet I am so frightened. The enemy's siege guns boom in the distance, sometimes sounding as thunder. They send over huge shells that explode with terrifying force even in our most peaceful neighborhoods - shaking the house, and rattling and breaking dishes, glassware, and windows here while destroying homes elsewhere and causing raging fires. God has spared our street of all but the slightest physical inconvenience by comparison, though the Johnson house at the end of the block has endured considerable damage from a near-miss. In our home, we have lost patches of plaster and all mirrors, save one.

Our poor Atlanta is being pounded and reduced to ashes. Most of our public buildings lie in ruins. Fires, smoke, and dust are everywhere. Scenes of devastation begin only one block away from our doorstep. Even the once gorgeous trees along our most handsome thoroughfares and have been damaged. Some have been ravaged for fuel. Others droop forlornly in smoky haze.

Our people are desperate for food and the barest necessities. Yet, the enemy is both merciless in his chastisements and criminally careless of our young and old's safety. Civilians are their targets, so deeply have their war aims deteriorated into a frenzy of mindless conquest.

When errant shells rush overhead to fall in adjoining neighborhoods, Colleen cringes and trembles uncontrollably. Jason tries to be brave and cares for her in every case. I am unable to fathom that they have grown so since your enlistment - or that Jason now is six and Colleen four. I comfort them to my utmost and assure them that all will be well. But even now, they hear the rumblings of the fearsome battle raging on the city's outskirts and are terrified that the enemy will come by to carry them off. I duly fear the fighting will move this way. What then will I do?

How terrible it must be for our men and boys engaged there. The rumblings are continuous. Enemy siege guns fire all night. Sleep is almost impossible. Could it be that you are there also, so close to us yet so far? I pray you are not - or, that if you are, you will survive to visit us here. I and the children miss you, so. It has been one year, four months and twenty-seven days since your last furlough. Because Jason and Colleen have grown so much in that time, I worry that you will hardly recognize them nor they you.

Some wives in our community are going - or already have gone - to the fighting to see if they can be of use as nurses. Several have received word that their husbands are there. How anguished those women must be for them. I suppose that going to them is far better than sitting back to await grim news. If it were not for the children's needs, I would go in search of YOU on the chance that fate would bring us together again at last.

We are scantily provided for here but are making do. I have been able to obtain and store a modicum of bulk food items and jarred preserves. Yet, we also have potatoes, carrots, and several yams. Our fruit cellar stocks are greatly diminished, but will be sufficient for our needs if we remain prudent at meal times and do not over-indulge ourselves - though I am diligent in ensuring that the children do not want for nourishment.

The entire community is planting heavily this spring and, with decent rains and proper maintenance, our gardens shall be full in time. As I write, many women work in their yards or in vacant lots planting a variety of vegetables. Occasionally, they pause to determine if the trajectories of arriving shells are menacing. They have become very brave and stoical about this, as if they were born to the danger. And they take every threat in stride.

All the community's women are scraping by with what little is left in their larders. Yet, even now, they are sharing food with each other's children. How good and charitable these kind souls are. Most of us have long ago depleted our stores of smoked meats, yet our cow, Pretty Girl, though emaciated from lack of abundant forage, still gives milk. And we still retain enough grain for flour and biscuit-making - which now is a delicacy.

They are shelling again. I will post this and write you more tomorrow.

Letter Two

Dearest Wilson,

Please do not fret. The bombardment that interrupted my last letter was severe, but, again, enemy shells fell short of our street. We are fine.

Two days ago, while baking a dozen biscuits, I indulged in a flight of fancy. I imagined myself once again teaching in my classroom in peaceful times, with my energetic pupils awaiting inspiration. Alas, the ongoing bombardment forced us to close the school one morning almost a fortnight ago.

Early that very afternoon, it was partially destroyed by a ranging shell. We are certain that only the Lord could have prompted our timely evacuation. But gone is the beautiful lily pond Mrs. Bacon and her pupils worked so hard to create last year. It had been the school's joy and pride. Many of the children beyond our neighborhood suffer from want of good meals and nutrition, yet we, on our street, have not enough to share with everyone. Still, we despair for those more hard-pressed than we, and give what we can.

Jason and Colleen are of great help to me. They clean and do little chores that release me to my planting and housework. They feed Pretty Girl and help in our biscuit-making by grinding grains, kneading dough and preparing our baking pans. Colleen is fascinated with my knitting. As you know, to make extra income, I have knitted and baked breads to order. But that money, which helped to sustain us before the bombardment began weeks ago, has nearly evaporated since - with customers no longer plentiful nor monied, and prices for everything incredibly inflated and growing more so every day. Now, owing to a general paucity of available grains, and for the children's sake, I no longer bake for the public, but I do continue to knit and use my products for barter.

The war's endless duration has made living so different. The cost of everything now is exorbitant and prohibitive. Profiteering runs rampant throughout the city. I am barely able to afford lamp oil and candle wax, since both have become rarities. The enemy has strangled our commerce. No longer can I buy many other basic items, and I must carefully husband and ration our remaining resources. Clothes are unaffordable, yet I make what I can from scraps and also mend what we would have discarded in better times. Situations permitting, I trade portions of my knitted stock for cloth that will make into passable apparel for Jason and Colleen, and for barter. And though my body aches at the thought, I now chop my own scarce fire wood, as do most of our community's women. Though I am now accustomed to heavier labors, I worry that you will not find me as desirable as before. Our remaining mirror daily disappoints me.

More and more, our women complain of their deteriorating physical conditions and their loss of femininity, especially those whose men have left them on farms, compelling them to do all heavy choring. Many of these women have fled to our city. And though such hard work has been physically and emotionally ruinous, they have had no choice except to carry on for the sakes of their families. Our whole society has been turned upside down. Nothing will ever be the same again. The family tranquility we knew before the war is but a melancholy memory. And even if we win, there will be little employment for our men to return to, so wasted has been our economy, unless they are able to earn a living by devoting themselves entirely to rebuilding. Our cities, farms, factories, railroads and bridges will require it. But nothing will be done unless there is money to finance reconstruction. The banks will all have been dissolved and few institutions will remain solvent enough to loan a penny - if, in fact, there will be money left to loan that is WORTH a cent. So much of it has gone into the war effort. What remains has also been obscenely inflated. For a generation to come our communities may be compelled to subsist on agriculture alone.

Must interrupt this letter to see to the children's meals. Again, I will post this one and continue on with another tomorrow.

Letter Three

Dearest Wilson,

Every hour of every day, I fear for you. We receive such conflicting information about the war and our Army's progress that we know not what to believe. But all appears to confirm that our embryonic nation cannot hold out much longer, though our brave men doggedly resist.

I ask myself what I will do if you never return. My practical nature assures me that I will raise our children regardless, though emotionally I will scream with grief and desperation. Spiritually, I will be desolate, and there will eternally remain a deep, black void within my heart that will never be filled again without you. We have always been so close and so sharing of each other's souls, that I will never be able to find another you - and I am not certain that I will ever want to, for I will love and cherish you everlastingly.

I know you appreciate how the war has scarred everyone here, but we pray for the Lord's forbearance and protection. The terrible fighting must end, that life here may proceed with some degree of normalcy for all our children's sakes - and that we might raise them decently and put our communities together again for THEM. Honor has been mightily served, and now it is time for people of goodwill on both sides to take command of their senses and belatedly conclude this unholy argument. Let them and us bring our warriors home.

Despite all that has occurred, nothing will ever alter the fact that we all are Americans, no matter where we stay. Someone should have remained and convinced all on both sides of that blessing long before the notion of war ever took root across both our lands. May the Lord help us all - and may He bless you, dearest Wilson, and bring you quickly and safely home to us. I am sorry to have burdened you with these long, complaining letters, but there was so much to convey. I and the children send you our ceaseless devotion. Please write when you can. I trust that your most recent letters to us have been delayed somewhere. All our governmental services are failing, but we hang on every sporadic mail delivery to our street, hoping the carrier will come to our doorstep with a message from you. The children long to hear from you, as do I.

Come home to us, dear Wilson. Come home.

Your loving wife always and true,

Idora

*   *   *

Contentments

Nature has presented our Army with a vibrant day filled with refreshing zephyrs that bring the scent of rain on the benign peals of distant thunder.

The sky is magnificently painted with gold-tinted cumulus harboring deep gorges and rolling canyons hidden in shades and shadows of gray and charcoal, all of it upon brilliant blue. Many of us stand in awe of God's handiwork. War is an obscenity beneath these vistas, and we consider our human plight futile against the visual message imparted to us from above - that there is a far greater work in progress than all of man's. Indeed, there is comfort in the beauty of this day's lilies.

* * *

Today, enemy rations arrived in a dozen captured wagons - all of it liberated by our marauding cavalry units. The rations cannot accommodate the regiment's hunger beyond a few days even if sparingly distributed, but are welcomed with cheering and celebration. They come in an hour of critical need, a deliverance that some of our boys believe is more significant than coincidence. Though I doubt that anything supernatural is involved, their religious faith has bolstered morale and confidence all around. So be it.

* * *

We have achieved a much-welcomed hiatus in military operations. Yet, such relief is not without cost, portending a week of leisure (and drilling), and reading or writing letters home (and drilling), and catching-up on much needed rest and sleep (and drilling). Constant drilling is a continuing mystery even to our hardened veterans, who look upon it as "nonsense" ordered by an old-guard command structure worried about allowing its ranks too much leisure - lest they lose their efficiency and fighting edge-an unlikely result. Various bugle calls are reviewed during drills so the troops will not forget their meaning. I already have forgotten most and never knew the rest. But I'm fascinated by the whistles used to effect maneuvers and how our troops mechanically respond. Truthfully, I would make a very confused soldier.

* * *

I watch men in bivouac write letters and read books, including the Bible. They appear content in these private hours, as private as men can be surrounded by scores of fellow soldiers. Yet they find privacy and space even when confined to what civilians would consider severe inconvenience. But men adjust.

I find my own escape, writing my journal entries, which I treat as if I am speaking to another person. They allow me to express insights that I think are significant.

Then, there are the sleepers and the perpetual sleepers who find no intellectual nor spiritual stimulation in anything BUT sleep. They usually sleep the moment they lay back anywhere, instantly fleeing their otherwise threatened existences. But those who cannot write nor read deserve our special consideration. They find meaning in other ways - in nature and their observations of nature, and in simple comradeship and discourse and even in cooking. Like water, men of every shade, description and capacity seek and find their own levels, having little choice. Always above their heads, the hanging sword of battle waits to fall. Ergo, every minute and hour of leisure time becomes cherished fare to be indulged and fully absorbed, lest time dies with them on a near or distant tomorrow. Would that we civilians were as prudent and economical with OUR existences. Would that we viewed the fragility of our lives - which are hardly so daily and intensely intimidated - with the same desperate appreciation.

*   *   *

Some of the boys this afternoon tried catching squirrels that dart about our bivouac - squirrels being generally considered a delicacy these days of meager vittles. Unfortunately, the bushy-tailed critters proved too intelligent for their pursuers, whose guile in setting ingenious traps was surpassed by their quarry's stubbornness. It appeared the critters, sensing their imminent danger, refused to desert the trees protecting them, instead peering down and chattering mockingly, the air turning blue with our boys' hilarious frustration.

*   *   *

A letter received by Private Henry Kerns today gave cause for celebration. It announced that his wife had delivered a baby daughter the previous month, thus ending the nervous Kern's concern. Although he said he had anticipated the birth, he had received no word of it until today. With the company commander's leave, the boys boiled-up an inspiring home brew consisting of various ingredients that produced a heady sort of semi-intoxicating punch. And though the grasses and herbs that went into it remain their secret, I can testify to the joyous effects. The brew's thickly sweet aroma and pleasant taste were enjoyed by all, with seconds and thirds eagerly sought by every celebrant.

All equally experienced the curious effects - happiness, bliss, and illusion consisting of flights of fancy and physical disorientation. Kerns fell into a peaceful hibernation early into the celebrations, his face a portrait of smiling contentment. Had we served our enemies the same brew, or had we invited them to our festivities, the war might have concluded there and then. Whatever its contents, the elixir-mixture produced never-to-be-forgotten goodwill. In fact, some of our boys speculated about its effects on the war, if jars of it were loaded into artillery and lovingly fired, with nondestructive powder loads, into enemy lines. Others proposed that gallons of it be sent to both sides' stubborn governments, that South and North might be spared further anguish. Lastly, it was concluded, after brief soul-searching, that we not risk its waste, but that in the name of prudence and economy, we drink it all right there. We did.

*   *   *

I joined with a trading party today that approached enemy lines to exchange our tobacco stuffs for their coffee. Their coffee and our tobacco are much sought after by the respective sides. I was taken by how much like us our enemies are. Though much better uniformed (our boys wear little formal garb, and mostly homespun), they received us without airs of superiority, and we received them cordially, as well. I forced myself to remember that we actually were at war with each other. There and then, I understood how much the conflict amounted to an unnecessary madness. The very next day, we were going to resume the business of trying to destroy each other. They and we sat for an hour or more, exchanging news and commentary, talking about our families and discussing hunting and fishing. We explored confidences that produced an aura of goodwill and relaxation. For fun, we also exchanged hats and caps. How amusing to see our boys wearing blue kepis and their boys wearing our dirty slouch hats. When we departed, handshakes and warm regards were exchanged by all. But the poignancy of that parting truly upset many. Why could they and we not have agreed at that point to represent the common men of both sides and seal a compact to lay down our arms for well and good? The irony of their sudden comradeship was enough to drive the sanest among us mad. If only both sides had resolved there and then to tell their generals, "Enough!" - if only, if only...

*   *   *

I was much impressed this evening by how intensely our men's snoring shatters the quiet of night with strange symphonics. And I am convinced that without being able to snore, the majority of men in our Army would find sleep as impossible as they make it for the rest of us.

*   *   *

The soporific effects of wind rustling through the trees today is a narcotic. It induces an almost trance-like state among our weary, resting troops that removes them from themselves and their cares. I have watched those effects upon resting men, who fall into staring states. Some admit that their minds become blanks. Even I find myself lulled, as if I am being taken by the sirens of nature into realms of unknown contentment. Their seductions are irresistible.

*   *   *

Snow today - gigantic flakes gently settle upon and quiet the earth. The stillness is magical. Cold never feels as bitter nor intrusive in such conditions and intrudes only within boundaries of tolerable discomfort. We cherish such moments, though many of our men go without warming protection. Even the crackling of our campfires mesmerizes the weary. It is then that tea, home-brewed from grasses, tastes and feels it's warmest and most comforting. Odd how nature conspires with men to encourage their faith in all-encompassing Power beyond understanding.

*   *   *

It is poignant to watch our men share what few vittles they possess. They do so almost reverently, touching, and exchanging eatables with the utmost care and respect. Even their voices quiet, as if they sit contentedly within an awesome cathedral of mutual consideration. How gracious the lilies can be.

*   *   *

Corporal Clarence Hazelton is dying of spent health, yet there is neither panic nor desperation in his countenance. His fever is beyond control and he well understands his situation. In lucid moments, when his delirium ebbs, he expresses concern for his fellows and says he awaits his passage into the next world with great expectations. I have never seen a dying man more contented. Wrapped in scarce blankets, he perspires heavily and without let-up, his face reddened, his mouth dry. As we give him sips of water from our canteens, he blesses us for it. I cannot look upon him any longer without fighting back emotion. Never have I witnessed a more touching scene nor known a more noble man.

*   *   *

Today, I observed an old wagon horse contentedly munching grass. My heart went out to the gentle creature that ate with only an occasional signal that it was aware of my admiration. Its protruding ribs revealed its dire need for rest and decent forage, yet it appeared to contentedly accept its subservience to warring man.

Though too much abused and their well-being neglected, these indispensable servants are to be cherished and loved. It is a crime that they are not. What we do to them in this war is appalling beyond words, transcending errant cruelty, but I have no doubt that the Lord, in His good time, will take just retribution upon us all.

*   *   *

I have written much about our enlisted men but have yet to mention our officers. Despite themselves, these much harried mortals must serve as guides, mentors, and pillars of courage in all situations - while remaining only mortal. If they are discontented with their lot, God knows they do not show it. Bless them, for few among us could claim mettle strong enough that we could successfully trade places.

*   *   *

Weather permitting, our men will seek baths today in all available streams ponds and creeks - for which all of down-wind creation will be supernaturally grateful.

*   *   *

Another Letter Found

Another letter found on the battlefield today was brought to me this evening. The private who brought it said it was not addressed, but was lying on the bloody grass not far from a cluster of dead, theirs and ours. Then again, it matters not to which side in this war these sentiments belong, for they might have been written by any lonely soldier to his wife, whom he undoubtedly had not seen in months nor, perhaps, years. This then is that letter, which contained only the writer's first name. I have changed it, lest its intended rudely learns of his passing only through this journal. Otherwise I have reproduced it exactly as written. It speaks for thousands of common soldiers.

My Dearest Wife,

The hour is late. Yet I writ by camp fire lite ta tell you of my luv fer you, and ta say my last thot of this day will be of you and are home. I risk much by writin ta you tanight. Ifn I be wrong in doin it, I might be a woryin and torment'n you inxusbly. Ifn I be rite, and I feel I am, I must do it now, lest I never see anuthr chance. Tamarra we fite. I feel a dred bout mornin. I seen such dred in othurs and I know it to be an oman. So, ifn you will, hold are youngins clos fer me. Hold em long and titely. Kiss ther litle heads fer me and tell em I am thinkin of em even now. Tell em I want em ta be good and obay you and honer you as I wud have em do. Care for em well and teech em the virtews of honusty and compashun. Let em do for and onto othurs what they'da had othurs do fer and unto thern, as the Lord intinded. Take em ta church ever Sunday that they mite now the Lord and his Word. Of yerself, deerest lady, I ain't got anuff paper nor hours to writ of my luv and hopes. Thees passed two yers been the lonleest of my life. I hav not seen you er are youngins nor loked inta yer lovin eyes fer to long. I have falled asleep with you in my hart and dreemd of you ever nite and waked up with yer name on my lips. In the butee of the most buteeful days, even in theese glorus days of spring, I have sent you, thru my eyes, that butee - that we mite shar it. And I have talked to you of it, praid fer yer well bein and the youngins and praid fer the war ta end, that we ken shar are lifes agin. I now in my sole that we will - ifn not on Erth, than in a betta place eventulee. I will wate for you thar. And from thar, I will watsh ova you and are youngins and stand by you and gard you from eval. I shall not berdenin you with my presense, but I shal linga in the back grund an asure you of the anser to lifs most mistereeus qeshtuns. Even at the end, ifn it comes tammara, I will be thinkin of you. This thing we call dutee is almost as mistereeus. Just think how it makes me and all the others stay here round this camp fire waitin fer what we now is comin, with all us sufferin this loneleest nite, when we mite jest as well wak up and be shed of this war so I ken come back ta you. Yet I stay. I look round me and see so many, many othurs as blesd with famly as me whos also stayin'. Why, when sanity ses othuwise. What be it bout dutee that takes from men such irashunel loylty? I do not now. I simplee do not. I onla now that I MUST stay, even at the risk of losin all. God help us all, frend AND enamy, who keep this irashunl contest goin by foursakin His genteel wishus fer all of us and are famlys. Pleas forgiv me, my luv, as I hope God will forgive me - and axept my luv this nite and my thots and bid me as I bid you - yet eternl devoshun."

Yer devotd huzband

John

*   *   *

Dusk but Dimly

I awoke late this afternoon, face-down, in a semi-conscious state, and sensed that the light of the old day had faded. Was darkness truly descending? I recalled only that something had impacted my skull during the fighting. Afterwards, there came only blackness. Now, a message vied for survival in a fog of competing impressions..."You are alive, Chapman...still alive!"

Mist had begun to rise from the fields over which thousands had fought when the sun had shown brightest. And though the guns had quieted, combat's echoes still haunted the living. In that stillness I heard my own labored breathing. I had followed our people into those cauldrons which only hours ago had boiled over where I now laid. And now I remained spiritually and physically drained. I reached up to the right side of my head and pulled back a blurred but bloody hand. Something had furrowed through my scalp, not deeply, but sufficiently to cause heavy bleeding.

I would discover my journal case stained with blood, and then I remember that I had helped carry wounded off the field. Some of that blood was theirs.

Practitioners of my calling habitually observe the war from afar. For reasons such as I now suffered, they demonstrate better sense than to risk the battlefield's life and death struggles, thereby forsaking the authority such risk might lend their writing. But, this day, my volunteering had carried me to the edge of life.

Echoes filtered into my numbed brain. Vague forms moved through shadows. Pools of lantern light sloshed here and there. I heard talking and crying and whimpers and pleas for water. Elsewhere, choruses of agony rose like voices from Hell. If dreams were real, I might have believed myself alive in an underworld into which a minié-ball or piece of bursting shell had vaulted me.

Full consciousness slowly returned. My vision soon cleared. My fingertips felt dew on the grasses beneath me. A foraging ant meandered in front of my eyes. Blood dripped from my wound. Cautiously, I rose to my knees, my head pounding and spinning. I felt the arms of two medical orderlies lift me to my feet and steady me, their lantern light paining my eyes. One tied a kerchief around my head to cover my wound. I dimly remember thanking them. They asked if they could guide me to a nearby ambulance. Self-consciously, I declined. "We thought you was kilt," declared our company runner, who bounded up to me. "Been a'lookin' fer ya. Powerful glad," he said, "glad you ain't. Ya tuk a humdinger of a thumpin' up there."

"How'd the fighting go?" I asked.

"They whupped us in the mornin', but we come back in the afternoon and run 'em off. But, Lordy, we lost people heavy. Them, too! Heard the General say that 'tween the two armies, thousands was engaged. Did ja eva' hear the likes?" His muffled words reassured me that I still lived, and I realized my ears still contained the cotton I had used to dull battle's deafening din.

I caught my balance, regained my composure and began searching for my straw hat, spying it three feet away. But bending to retrieve it racked my aching cranium with infernal pain.

"Does this here be yer'n, sir," a sergeant asked, handing it to me.

Unsteady on my feet, I took it and watched him vanish into the shadows, forgetting to thank him for it. Then, I noticed where metal had ripped through it. Powder smoke's pungent stench hung everywhere, and as if to punctuate the day's violence, thunder rumbled like distant artillery fire on a breeze carrying the scent of an approaching rainstorm. I relished the thought of cooling rain bringing my cranium desperate relief, wondering what prompted rain to so often arrive soon after combat as if to soothe the tortured Earth and the maimed's agonies.

Now, the mysteries of the darkness revealed themselves in dusk's last illuminations. Men moved about in every direction, carrying wounded and retrieving equipment. They picked among abandoned haversacks and packs, bayonets and broken bayonets - rifles and broken rifles, spent shot, papers and personal effects - shredded banners, caps, hats, shoes, and torn jackets. They searched the mute and grotesquely contorted bodies that laid singly or in pairs or heaped against each other by the dozens, examining still others sprawled everywhere. They circulated among the wounded who sat or squirmed, some horribly mutilated and some only stunned. As they passed by, the tormented cried out to them, moaned or begged for help, some pleading with them to mercifully speed them to a pain-free oblivion. Streams of wounded hobbled rearward supporting the more seriously afflicted. Many of the worst lay down to patiently await medical care - or to die, rejecting medical care. I had witnessed all of it before on other fields at other times and places. But only now did I feel initiated into our Army's vast brotherhood of misery. For until this hour, I had escaped the worst of the lilies's ugliness - untouched. Had my deliverance been chance or purposeful? How could a mortal ever know such things?

In the anemic half-light, the fields revealed a crimson tint. Minutes later, it began to rain.

Later

As I labored again to assist the wounded, my head merely throbbing now, honking geese winged southward in great, undulating formations, ignorant of the events still transpiring below them. Odd, I thought, that they often soared in growing darkness. I briefly watched them, my head protesting its angle. Beneath them, orderlies and their enlisted helpers continued to probe the carnage for wounded, even as burial teams searched for salvageable bodies. Neither would experience a fruitless night. Here and there, slightly wounded and exhausted survivors leaned on their rifles, surveying their day's triumphant labors. I watched a soldier recover a pair of sticks a drummer boy would never use again. Another man found a shattered pocket time piece nearby and still another lifted what he presumed to be a material object too badly mangled to be identified without close inspection, then realized it was a dead man's arm still in its bloody shirt sleeve. I had witnessed such abominations before.

Wagon and ambulance drivers, directed by a bleeding officer on horseback, maneuvered their horse teams to receive dead and wounded. They followed lantern-carrying guides who sought paths through human debris. Far to one side, the survivors of companies half shot to pieces assembled in ragged ranks to be counted and accounted for. I watched this ritual occur again and again. Lanterns assumed firefly-like proportions in the settling gloom. The odor of burnt gunpowder still overhung the world. And, rapidly closing on the scene - the storm. The cooling breeze carrying the rain's sweet scent refreshed irritated senses still capable of appreciating it, while thunder's rumble reminded all of Nature's indifference to man's violence.

Distant musketry crackled where enemy sharpshooters violated the moment's sanctity. Would not even decency permit the sun to peacefully set undisturbed by more killing?

All through the night, in a soaking downpour beneath crackling lightning, we brought the wounded out, setting them down in rows and loading the most serious into wagons for their jostling trips to the tortures of the surgeons' saws and scalpels. Some prayed to die first. Others died where they lay.

More turned their faces to the rain and drank, letting it flush corruption from their wounds and wash away their dried blood. Still others began to violently shake with chills, and many of these passed on before dawn, their dilated pupils open to the darkness. Before we reached a few helpless wounded, their faces down and unseen in deepening pools of rainwater, they drowned.

I cannot recall much between then and dawn, but somewhere in that interval, I dropped and slept, soaked through and spent - my journal case still strapped 'round my shoulder, its contents thankfully wrapped in oil skin and dry. A hand awakened me after dawn, holding a cup of steaming chicory, its vapors rising into a murky sky. The survivors of the company I had accompanied into battle had found me and carried me to their bivouac.

Beneath my soggy kerchief, my head painfully thumped with every heartbeat. Sipping my warm brew, and feeling at one with the men around me, I secretly rejoiced. My bloody decoration said that I had fulfilled my rite of passage and had finally earned my membership in their brotherhood of battle.

*   *   *

God's Presence

Today, I watched tides of misery surge upon fields formerly free of conflict, seeking their levels in every vacancy among tall grasses and flowers wild and colorful. Victims of battle fell there or set themselves down to tend to their wounds or to other's, that they might endure the unendurable in sympathetic eddies of common suffering.

I observed a preacher guiding his horse through that human debris, determined, I later learned, to locate the fighting's vortex, where a man of God's presence would steady those most seized by fear. It troubled him not that errant bullets zipped and snapped overhead and around him. He had placed his fate in God's Hands, and if it were God's Will that he be taken, so be it.

"Water, Parson, do you have water?" the parched wounded asked, spying his white collar and reaching up to grasp his legs or cling to his horse's bridle. "Please, sir, a little water only"... this from the mortally fated soul whose wide and terrified eyes bespoke his terror of inevitable death. Yet, he collapsed before the Reverend could assuage the soldier's thirst with the refreshing contents from one the two canteens he toted.

The wounded surrounded him, their groping hands petitioning for no more than elusive relief and momentary salvation. He calmly yielded-up his canteens to them and moved on.

Eventually, on the firing lines, he found the crucible he sought, where roaring musketry and exploding shells all but extinguished the commands of officers and sergeants and the maimed and dying's pleas for assistance. With hot shrapnel raining down, and his horse shying with every step, he entered sulfurous clouds of eye-burning powder smoke, searching for a place where God would inspire him to begin his ministry.

Men dropped from every rank, some squirming, some vehemently and profanely protesting their sudden fate, others screaming, their agonized contortions making religious devotions impossible. Yet, the Reverend dismounted, bent over them and prayed for them, as if his meager efforts could calm their damning pains. Some quit their writhing and lay still, released to God by the holy man's reassuring presence.

"Go to the rear, Chaplain," a bearded officer yelled; "this is not your place!"
"It is precisely my place," the Chaplain yelled back.

"But you cannot remain here, sir," the officer insisted, "civilians cannot be here!"

"But they ARE here," the Preacher replied; "what ARE they if not civilians? Some are from my parish!"

"Please, sir, I must ask you to take yourself to the rear and safety," the officer protested.

"I am here on the Lord's work," the Preacher proclaimed, "and here, sir, I must remain."

Defeated, the officer shook his head, turning into the smoke and disappeared.

The Preacher pressed on, until a hand grabbed his pant leg: "Where be God?" asked a voice from inside the smoke, "tell me...you gotta collar...where be God?...not HERE...not HERE!"

Looking down, he stared into a powder-smeared portrait and two tortured eyes that drilled themselves into this conscience. There, a hatless soldier, blood pumping from a gaping wound in his torso and mangled legs twisted beneath him, searched the Preacher's soul: "Um skerd t'face Him," the man sputtered, his panicky voice oddly audible in the din..."Gonna meet Him soon, ya know. Um dyin', can't cha see...Um dyin', I tell ya!"

Here, the Preacher knew, was where his ministry would begin. He knelt at the soldier's side: "The Lord is here," he assured him, "and even at this moment, He prepares a place for you in His Kingdom."

"He's a'comin' fer me...He actual is?" the soldier innocently asked, his manner childlike, his words gurgling through the blood seeping from his mouth..."He's a'comin' fer ME?"

"Yes, He is coming for you," the Preacher concurred, his voice also audible above the noise.

"Got little uns t'home," the wounded soul lamented; "whata they gonna do with me a goner?... what they gonna do?"

"How little are they, soldier?"

The soldier winced, his pain irresistible: "One be two...the otha' three...wife be dead four months now...feva'...little uns be with their meemaw...what they gonna do, Preacha...oh, Lord...Um 'skerd fer 'em!"

The soldier's head jerked awkwardly, his entire body convulsing...one hand still gripping the Preacher's pant leg, the other clawing the air, trembling... "m'letta... m'letta fer meemaw...where be it?" Frantically, with his clawing hand, he felt beneath his open shell jacket, searching his bloody shirt... "cain't find it...cain't find it!"

A crushed corner peeked from where a canister ball had ripped away part of the jacket and rib cage, while others had destroyed his legs. The preacher tugged it free: "It is here," he said, holding it front of the soldier's fading vision.

"That be it...that be it," the soldier cried, crushing the Preacher's hand in his; "oh, praise the Lord...praise the Lord."

He pulled the Preacher's hand to his lips, kissing the envelope, it's blood-soaked inscription only partially discernible: "All m'luv be in it...all that'll be left a'me, don'tcha see...post it fer me, dear man, I beg ya...post it fer me...but now, gimme some wata'...please gimme some wata?"

Reaching inside his coat pocket, the Preacher retrieved a small bottle containing a mixture of water and spirits, the very sort of concoction given to the badly wounded by surgeons in Mexico long ago. He knew water would do the man no good—would only pour from the cavity that once was his stomach. Gently lifting the soldier's head, he put the bottle to the man's mouth and dampened his lips: "Thank-ye," the soldier responded without taking a sip, his eyes and face suddenly calmed and at peace..."thank-ye, kindly..." he mumbled once more, before gently passing from Earth into gentler Hands.

Now, the fighting's roaring fury intruded as never before. Trumpets blew...battle lines surged forward in a cacophony of yelling, musketry, and shells exploding overhead. Laying the soldier's head down, the minister returned the bottle to his coat pocket and slipped the letter in behind it. Yes, he pledged to the dead man, he would post it. Then, he prayed: "This soul belongs again to you, oh, Lord. Receive him into your Kingdom. Put your Hands now tenderly upon his children and kin...and help this letter find its destination. And, now, Dear Lord...grant him peace."

And the man of God's day had only just begun.

*   *   *

Gloria

Far into nightfall and long after the fighting I witnessed a bare-headed priest at work in his cassock among the wounded, where thousands had battled in and around a now-shattered woods. A regimental chaplain, he struggled in the rain through mud and tangled vines and brush torn asunder by shell fire. Lighting split the darkness. Thunder rocked the earth as no man-made artillery had that day. Rain had followed both armies for days.

Offering comfort to the wounded who lay thickly in every deluged shadow, he knelt in prayer, silhouetted in the lightning's glare, working by touch and by feel in the anemic glow of lanterns shaded by orderlies - taking hands outstretched to him or, in that glare, respectfully praying over stilled breasts vacated of all human energies.

For each, he offered simple prayers, trusting that all would reach the ear of a sympathetic God in the sanctuary of a kinder world. Only afterwards, did he notice a gnawing pain in his shoulder where shrapnel had etched the bone. And only then did he feel the weakening effects of blood loss, as if the Lord, to that point, had spared him interruption. Then, he collapsed, lying exhausted, still reminding himself that his services were needed where more suffering abided.

Ever faithful to his duties, he revitalized himself and took himself to the pits, where, from wagons and ambulances, and by lantern light, the soaking dead were being irreverently cast and heaped one upon the other, or packed side by side in the mire of long, shallow trenches—where no markers would commemorate the fact that they had once existed. These were the pits where, in the lilies of distant memories, time would conceal men's transfiguration and guarantee their anonymity.

Some had been so young, their faces calm and placid - cleansed by the rain. Others, with clouded eyes, stared into nothingness, their bloody mouths agape, as if shocked by their sudden departure from life.

In the downpour, watching the priest pray for their collective souls, I recalled Mexico and friends whose lost remains still resided there. And, as he prayed, I grieved, as old emotional wounds painfully reopened.

Then, came the dawn, refracted through a universe of ebbing raindrops, sunlight spilling over the horizon in a golden tide routing the night. Darkness fled. The priest found himself on a litter lying next to moaning wounded who, by the hundreds, suffered in the open of an outdoor hospital - in the shade of trees or in the morning's sudden brilliance — many beyond care. Fearing the surgeons' saws more than death, others refused help.

His shoulder burned. Its fires reached deeply into his back and chest, immobilizing his wounded arm. Yet, he raised himself up and stood tottering until his equilibrium returned, his bloody cassock muddied. He walked unsteadily among the wounded, making the Sign of the Cross with his good hand. Many called to him, even though medical orderlies had removed his collar after tearing open his cassock and shirt to bind his shoulder.

He knew he could not go on, for he could ask no more of his weakened body. His vision had begun to blur. His legs wobbled and then he fell, but I caught him and guided him to the shade of a fallen tree and sat him down. I put my canteen before his face, knowing its cooling contents would renew him. Then, I sat next to him. Together, we drank from the canteen. He said he had never before met a journalist in the field. I explained that I was not a professional, just a citizen marching with the Army to record its soldiers' devotion.

An hour passed, and as we spoke, I beheld how his faith reenergized him. And though he suspected his painful wound might fester and turn gangrenous, he said he was satisfied to be at the Lord's "disposal" - a haunting choice of words. Reluctantly, he said good-bye, feeling an urgent need to return to his regiment. I apologized to him for not having a horse to loan him, since I, too, trekked with the infantry. He blessed me, then said, "God be with you in your quest. May he cloak you with His Grace."

I watched him tenuously navigate the rutted fields, his arm still stiff, the white of his bandaged shoulder exposed to Heaven. Minutes later, the new day's light dimmed. Charcoal-gray advanced once more across the land, returning with thunder. So did my weariness. Yet, I could not take my eyes from the priest. The mud through which he struggled had much in common with the mire of adversity he overcame each day. Then a thousand raindrops exploded in the pools and puddle ruts around me. Lulled by the deluge, my head aching, I surrendered to sleep, never noticing that the kerchief over the shrapnel-graze on my forehead had loosened and fallen away. As the rain fell in torrential veils, the priest's image vanished behind it.

I would never see him again.

* * *

Observations

A poignant moment today: I came across a clearing in which perhaps twenty dead men lay, some barely recognizable, so grievous were their wounds. Their silent comrades stood over them, rifles tightly gripped, their hats in their hands, faces grim, eyes dazed - no tears left to commemorate the lost lives at their feet. Their faces mirrored the emptiness on those of the dead. Emptied of emotion, they struggled to touch hands one last time with those souls who had been a part of their daily existences for so long and with whom they had shared their dependence - now gone as if they had never existed. One of the survivors glanced at me. His expression said, "They was good men...like brothers."

*   *   *

As we trudged through the countryside today, people appeared at roadside. Their eyes searched every face that passed them by, hoping to spy a familiar countenance that might inspire them to rejoice and cry out, "He's alive...alive" - a father, brother, son, uncle, grandfather..."alive, and thank, God!" But I saw no signs of recognition. There would be no reunions that day - only frustration. If only there had been a single familiar face - just one - we might all have taken comfort and been glad. How long would they search, I wondered...and how futilely?

*   *   *

I admire our people more today more than ever. They share great burdens and titanic adversities. Their lives have been ravaged, yet, most persist with dignity and resolve. They take food from their mouths to feed the children. They care for each other. They watch their civilization being torn asunder but they do not abandon each other - and already they think of rebuilding when the madness ends. They know that, even then, their personal wars will continue. But they will struggle all the harder to salvage what remains and to reconstitute their lives, their homes, and their honor. They have suffered as their armies have suffered - from want and privations. Yet, they remained strong of heart. Yes, they will survive someday and, if in spirit alone, they will triumph

*   *   *

We sloshed through the waters of placid stream today, our images being momentarily reflected on its surface before being washed away by the tides of our trespass. And when the waters calmed, they showed us gone, as if history's eddies have passed us by - as if saying to us that we and our tribulations had never been. It haunted me that existence traps us in an illusion that will inevitably claim us all. Strange what one's fatigued mind conjures on endless treks.

Exhausted, we slogged along asleep on our feet, lost in a half-world of reality, each of us blindly following the men ahead of us - our bodies accompanied by hunger and pains - our men helped by their stupors to escape the question nagging them all: "How soon will we all be forgotten?"

* * *

Marching with our column in route-step alongside a creek yesterday, I noticed the body of an enemy soldier floating face-down. I paused, struck by the scene's pathos. Who had he been, this lone soldier who had come so far to perish in this obscure place? From where had he come? Had he left behind a family that would never know he had fallen? What had been the circumstances of his death - and what had been his last hopes, cares, and thoughts? Of course, I would learn none of these things, not even enough to write him a fitting epitaph, save this feeble recollection. Yet, his situation is only too common and can be multiplied by thousands - for just as commonly, the uniforms observed are ours. Abandoned there, the creek would entomb his bones.

* * *

I followed a man in our column today who, for miles, carried his rifle across his shoulders - one arm over its stock, the other over its barrel. I marveled that his muscles and sinews had not locked with fatigue, yet his habit appeared to affect him as little as the passing clouds. When I remarked to him that his stamina amazed me, he looked at me askance: "Got no feelin' up there n'more," he said. "A ball in the back done took it all away a year bein'. Guess m'brain don't know if I be achin' up there 'er not n'more, and I ain't a'gonna tell it."

* * *

How is it Possible

Civilians ask me, "How is it possible to tolerate battle's bloodshed and gore and retain your sanity?"

I explain that war dulls one's sensibilities. Horror becomes a constantly assaulting enemy that kills feeling and atrophies emotion.

Men joke and converse lightly over dead bodies, as if the once-mortal beings were rocks. They cook amongst the dead, eat amongst the dead and relax amongst the dead. It is not that they have lost their humanity. They've merely learned to ignore that which would bring them low and spiritually destroy them. But soldiers are vessels with limited capacities.

What does not affect some drives others mad. I have witnessed soldiers who have appeared to absorb battle's terrors for months without apparent stress - and then, just as calmly, put their guns to their heads. Others run off, never to be seen again. Most endure, though war's sights and smells become the only world they know. For the fatalistic, death means escaping such things. Fatalism comes quickly to men too much exposed to hardship, forming a callousness that armors their souls. Only loyalty to comrades sustains them, even as they rest next to dead men whose innards pool and clot.

Waiting to die is a cancer that some men trust God to treat by whatever means. Haunted that they might not survive the duration, many simply give up their lives to Him and accept His will, thereby realizing a peace of mind that salves their terror and stands them stoically against enemy bullets and canister.

Two days ago, during the heat of an engagement with enemy infantry, I saw a man hit in the chest by a minié-ball. Bludgeoned to the ground and stunned, he lay there with his eyes wide but his diaphragm emptied of wind by the missile's impact. As he gasped and turned blue, he strained to manage three barely audible words..."Thank you, Lord," then succumbed to asphyxiation.

No, I cannot precisely say why I tolerate the carnage, except to guess that my vessel has not yet filled. Yet, I dare not suppose it will not.

* * *

Introspections

In bivouac today, I spoke with a married corporal whose concerns mirror those of countless troops. He told me he lives every day with panic and guilt - panic because he cannot remember the details of his wife's face - guilt because he cannot remember the essence of their love.

"I remember I loved her," he said, "but I cain't remember how it felt. Ain't seen her but a year ago."

He might have added, "And too much mind-numbing killing since."

Because war callouses feelings, thousands have lost touch with what was good about their pasts. Some have gone home on furlough to families they did not recognize - to wives aged by grueling work in their absences, and to youngins grown two or three years, who did not know them. War has made them strangers in their homes, as if their pasts belonged to someone and somewhere else.

There is no cure. They must grope for handholds between then and now and be patient with themselves, though some fear they can never go home again. Their suppressed pain is acute, for they have suffered a mental wounding as severe as anything physical - and war is responsible. Many who survive and return to their families will have to reacquaint themselves with their former world and relearn who they were. Some will abandon the past and their families, never to return, because war has turned their souls forever cold or made them strangers unto themselves.

It is not a matter of right nor wrong, good nor bad, morality nor immorality. It just is. Chastisement helps nothing. A better balm is prayer.

This war has altered the definition of "Casualty." Casualty now includes insults to minds and souls as well as bodies. Though medicine has yet to recognize the fact, correspondents closest to our troops witness it day and night. Why cannot physicians?

* * *

We sat idle today, listening to a storm brewing to the west and wondering if, for the rest of our lives, thunder would remind us of cannon and cannon of everything about this war we will wish to forget.

*   *   *

One of our literate soldiers came to me last week, crushed with worry. He said his letters home had not been answered in months.

Torn between loyalty to the Army and his need to know about his family, he asked if I thought he would be justified in going home - in deserting "only temporarily." He said he had spoken about it to our Chaplain, who advised him to pray for guidance.

"I have," he said, "but I ain't been answered. Cain't sleep 'ner eat."

It would do no good to ask for an emergency furlough, he said, guessing it would set too liberal a precedent for many men in the same predicament - and his commanding officer would surely deny it. I explained that I could not advise him to desert, even "temporarily" - for what good would it do him and his family if a positive letter from his wife arrived for him in the meantime and if - in the same meantime - he were caught and shot?

He proposed to wait another month. Relieved, I thanked God.

Two days later, four letters from home arrived in one mailing. Each had been held up somewhere along our dilapidated mail system, the most recent one having been posted only a month back.

Overjoyed, he sought me out to profusely thank me for my "advice"...if only he had known how tempted I had been to bless his "leave-taking."

*   *   *

Some soldiers grow morose thinking about their families and how they neglected them to go for soldier. They feel a deep and abiding shame they cannot reconcile, having left their wives and children to their own devices. Belatedly, they see everything they could and should have done for them before leaving, but did not. And, suddenly, they understand their wives as never before.

Some attempt restitution by praying to be spared rather than die with so much left at home undone and unsaid. Sometimes, it's too late, and they perish with regrets more painful than the traumas that kill them. Yet ironically regrets also pull some men through and force them to survive despite grievous wounds, that they might make those apologies and restitutions in person. In some cases, such incentives have been powerful enough to bring wounded men back almost literally from the dead.

*   *   *

"That smell be green," a veteran told a young soldier today, referring to the obnoxious stench from a gangrenous wound the youngin' hid beneath his ripped and bloody pant leg. Feverish, profusely sweating, but terrified of surgeons, the youth had refused treatment. Now, two days later, he stood to lose the leg - or die because of it. "Thought a lot about it," he told me in a weakened voice, "but I ain't a'goin' to them butchers. Rather die than put up with those knives and saws. No, sir, if'n the Lord sees fit t'take me home, I'll be a'leavin' whenever He wants." For many men, going to the surgeons is a greater dread than facing the enemy's hot iron and lead. I have watched them pull their shattered bodies into weeds or behind trees or beneath brushes to bleed out, knowing no remedy existed for their mutilated limbs and innards - except those surgeons' knives and saws, without benefit of anesthesia. I believe it is a soldier's right to decline treatment. The young man limped off, dragging his leg to a fate unknown.

* * *

Last Sunday, praying and worshipping under the sky, our boys wondered if God heard them. They asked for a sign but received none. And though they expected none, they still were disappointed. Instead, they turned to the silence of a lesser god – sleep - and were rewarded with hours of merciful oblivion.

* * *

Lighted candles: I have never seen so many as there are tonight. How such numbers have been procured and saved by our troops until now is a mystery. They appear to burn in every tent and everywhere our men have bedded down. Some men write by the light. Others read. It is a flickering sea - a jeweled firmament. If only we possessed the means to visually record it. I cannot begin to convey its mesmerizing quality. Odd that war can produce such disarming beauty - odd and strangely disquieting.

Thoughts upon Night

On still nights, crackling campfires encourage sleep in some, while restless souls stir and walk about. Some men seek sleep as respite from the day's work - others fear its prophetic terrors. They envision tomorrows when they will be again to battle.

I sit among these men in the darkness. Only faint light from their dwindling camp fires intrudes, as I ponder all that has brought them to this time and place.

It is an irony of war that one's love for his fellow man is nourished by the deaths and hardships of so many. War makes men small, humbles them to their cores and strips their souls naked before God. And for those destined to meet Him, eternity is reflected in their faces.

I, too, am humbled, for fate has absorbed me into their brotherhood, and I cannot leave it until this tribulation ends. God grant me the wisdom to do right by these citizen warriors and to honor their faithfulness with every stroke of my pen.

*   *   *

In the minds of our men, there is a village to which their thoughts flee as their dusty ranks march endless miles on bleeding feet and wearied bones.

It is a pristine place, an inner retreat where their souls find refuge and rest that they might reconstitute themselves for their return to war's daily realities. And though their private universes deny entrance to all others and remain their safe havens, their thoughts must surely be akin. For they endure with their thoughts in those places - each man understanding and allowing his fellows privacy.

Such generosity is profound yet unspoken.

*   *   *

When men go into battle, they must carry inside them an unshakable faith that After Life is true. For between them and the hot iron and lead that seek them out there remains nothing BUT faith to guarantee them a continuing existence in the Creator's Firmament. Today, I spoke on the eve of battle to a tall soldier who displayed extraordinary equilibrium. Drums were beating our ranks into the line with alarming cadences, summoning heroes and cowards to the same fate. He surveyed the contested fields beyond with supreme calm, his face solemn, his demeanor composed. Seemingly oblivious to the possible calamities awaiting the regiment, he leaned on his rifle and appeared to pray, his lips quivering with devotion. Was this a man prepared to survive or die without fear? What did he know that God had revealed to him?

Solid shot screamed overhead. Errant minié-balls dropped men up and down our lines. "I seen Glory," he said into my ear; "ain't nothin' t'fear t'day...nothin' a'tall. It be beautiful. Wish you could see it!"

Minutes later, he entered it.

* * *

"We will not falter," our Chaplain prayed. With heads bowed, our regiment knelt before him. We were "going in" and many would not return. "We know that if you call us home, dear Lord, we will not be afraid."

He was wrong. We WOULD be afraid. We were always afraid.

A shell loudly burst overhead, anointing our ranks with shrapnel. To our right, two men slipped to earth, each with a grunt and feeble cry, blood spurting from their iron-pierced heads.

"What is written cannot be erased," he continued; "we are Yours and in Your Hands, according to Your plan - to be done with as You wish. We accept our destiny."

He advanced with us into Perdition that day, and minutes later, in the company of many others, departed the reddened dimension beneath his feet. To this day, his confidence haunts me.

* * *

Today, I passed a long row of dead, many of whose shoeless feet stuck out from beneath the blankets covering their bloody bodies. It was all the dignity left to them - anonymity and feet. Had this been their worth? Was it a requiem the rest of us should have expected for ourselves - or did our war-makers owe us more? Few generals who die are treated so. I cannot digest the injustice of it. This war's perversities know few limits.

* * *

Occasionally, I sketch faces. Today I sketched our officers'. Each is a portrait of duty. The pains and aggravations behind each are secreted by a veil of responsibility that gives little hint of each man's vulnerabilities.

Such posturing is expected. Invulnerability in officers is what our men trust and respect. Enlisted men are allowed to quake and quiver before battle - even to hunker behind obstacles, too terrorized to speak or breathe. NOT so our officers. Their commissions are thought to steel them against such vagaries and, lest they savage their men's morale, they are obliged not to succumb to common fears.

Most act their parts well. They are special men who lead out front and are the first to face the Elephant's fury and the odds against us. Just as often, they are the first to fall. Thank Providence for them. I could never be one of them.

Tintype

Yesterday, I observed a wounded soldier remove a tintype from his sack coat pocket. With shaking hands, he held it close to his powder-burned eyes.

As battle raged in surrounding fields and smoke hung thickly over the thicket sheltering him, he studied the image. Then, noticing that I sat close by, he showed it to me. Its soft, feminine image contrasted supernaturally with the day's noise and horror. Afraid that passing soldiers might knock the image from his grasp, he had dragged himself to that refuge.

Over battle's din, he told me many things. He wanted to "remember" the image in peace - to reverentially put his memories of her in their hallowed place, unsullied by the bloodshed around him. Rubbing his eyes, he tried to concentrate away from his agonies. As if praying, he touched the image to his forehead and closed his eyes tightly, rocking back and forth in his mild delirium.

Other afflicted men also laid in the thicket - some moaning, some crying for water. Yet, they owned no tintypes to help them recall better times in pain-free places. They simply waited to die, without aid or sympathy.

He said her eyes pierced his soul with a doleful purity he cherished and that as he had pledged to her his love and faithfulness, so had she promised him hers. They were to be married when he returned home. He said, that for more than a year, he had thought of her day and night and that now, as never before, he felt alone and abandoned without her near him. Without her, he said, he endured a terrible emptiness. He confessed that their year-long separation had caused him to love her even more - that it had taught him much about devotion's joys and longing. He said a single uplifting hope had sustained him - that the hurt of their separation would pass the moment they were reunited.

He revealed that, since his wounding, he had reviewed their relationship's chronology - from their very first meeting to their last parting - along with every nuance of every treasured conversation in precise order - and that he craved such details, for they filled his emptiness, soothed his wounds and quelled his longings.

Around him, misery thrived in every hideaway, beneath every bush and behind every tree. Mutilated men instinctively gathered in twos and threes, half-dozens and by the scores. Some awaited medical treatment. Others rejected it, knowing it was useless. But their moaning and babble could not distract the young soldier, nor could their sufferings compete with his sweet memories. I witnessed their miseries while hearing him ominously confess, "My body's got no feelin', anymore."

His fiancé understood nothing of war, he said. War exceeded by a thousand times any violence she had ever imagined. And though she had admired his uniform - as did most girls her age - she could never have imagined nor envisioned the terrors it represented. "She be too sheltered and saintly for the kind of man this war's made a' me," he said. "She only understands marriage and family, bless her. Did I tell ya she wants t'teach school. I wanna farm. Writin' and readin' be her joys. I cain't do neither, but she promised t'teach me afta' the war...afta' the war..."

But the life they had guaranteed each other would no longer be possible.

Around him, men convulsed and coughed out their lives. "Guess I been betta' favored," he said. "The Lord's banished m'pain to let me recall her in peace." He looked away: "Our artillery fire's been lettin' up." In fact, it was not. Nearby, our batteries pounded away with increasing ferocity. The young soldier had begun his passage from the physical world. "I'm gonna always cherish this image of her and neva' let it go," he said. "It promises so much...and her eyes pierce clean through me." He said he feared the coming of night because darkness would hide them, and he fretted that he might never gaze upon their virginal innocence again. Then, his breathing grew shallow and his head drooped in merciful unconsciousness.

I left him there, with the hideous wound in his side pushing out blood in ever weakening pulses.

The next morning, they found him in the thicket, his cold hands tightly gripping the metallic image of the young woman whose name I never learned.

"Bled t'death," medical orderly conjectured, "like s'mana' always do...they jest crawls away somewheres, close their eyes and go t'sleep...poor fellers."

They buried the young soldier still clutching his fiancé's likeness. No lilies commemorated his passing.

*   *   *

In the Beauty of the Lilies

**The Wartime Journals
of Confederate Correspondent
Royal K. Chapman
1862-1864**

Journal Six

Contents

*   *   *

A Thought

With clarity do warriors see into their own souls
whose eyes are fixed with war's exhaustion.

Joy-Making

Perhaps, I have given the erroneous impression that war is without merriment - that the lilies are unfailingly browned and withered and that our soldiers live in continuous doldrums - that they never find light-hearted moments when the threat of their destruction ebbs as they are buoyed by welcomed distractions.

Ironically, war is NOT all fear and terror. At this moment, I am witnessing a carnival of joy-making around several campfires. Impromptu musicians have taken up banjos, fifes, mouth organs, cider jugs, washtubs, voice and dance to entertain themselves. Even the company's Commanding Officer and First Sergeant have joined-in.

Although I am familiar with the ballads of Stephen Foster, I have never heard them interpreted with such liberties. As the dancing increases in tempo and dizzy soldiers fall on their flat notes, Foster's songs become unrecognizable parodies. Great guffaws peal across our bivouacs, as weeks of fears and tensions find release. Other "cider" jugs appear from nowhere, filled with home-brewed inspiration - the same elixirs that find their way down the throats of scores of men going into battle. Yes, be it known that our troops often "fortify" their courage thusly. On occasion, I have fortified mine. Some men go into a fight barely able to stand. And, two days ago, we captured an enemy soldier so drunk, he staggered in a daze, chuckling and talking to himself. Our boys liked him immediately.

It is easy to imagine that our innovative Commanding Officer would permit such "inspiration" to be so liberally distributed among his troops tonight. Although he is devoted to regulations, he is more devoted to his men and is much loved. And, tonight, he has risked harsh censure from above so that sixty beleaguered souls might feel like men again and not like disposable beasts of the field. And since I'm keeping this journal entry confidential, I will confess that by out-innovating himself at this hour, he has earned his men's eternal respect, for what he has allowed them is of little moral but of great morale consequence, and I will pledge my pen to his defense should his superiors take official umbrage. It is no secret, that our nation's soldiers have been pushed to their limits for far too long.

Since following the Army through this war, I have come to view human nature's more benign commonalities with greater affection. Tonight is such a case. It feels well to be a part of this special commonwealth. Like the others at this hour I too will enthusiastically sing, imbibe, and take up the dance, my formerly conventional attitude having at last matured.

* * *

Eve of Battle

Today I stood with Regimental Chaplain Michael Findlay, as his unit waited quietly in ranks for word to advance. Its two hundred and nine souls, survivors of a dozen campaigns but only a shadow of their former numbers, stared ahead, their vision clouded by drifting smoke. I was afraid as never before.

More and more, I feel the Reaper stalking me. Today, I felt him at my shoulder. My blood chilled and, to my shame, I trembled. Having survived many engagements, I appreciated the terror that would confront the Reverend when we advanced. For the first time, my feet refused to move, for I feared the firmament of pinkish lights that would flare behind the smoke ahead of us and the sheets of minié balls that would whir and buzz through our ranks, smashing bone and tissue and obliterating heads - and the whirring rush of canister balls as they tore completely through us, decapitating, savaging limbs and turning torsos inside out in explosions of red spray and viscera.

I fought my compulsion to stand back as the others moved forward around me. Often, I have hesitated while sketching what I witnessed, but never have I used sketching as an excuse to HOLD back. Yet, today, as we advanced, I sickened with revulsion as never before upon seeing and hearing men die and smelling violent death.

A shell exploded close above our ranks twenty yards away, hammering to earth a half-dozen men below it, the heads and shoulders of three were crushed, halved or split by shrapnel, their brains splattering over those next to them. The others, stunned by concussion, dropped to their knees or collapsed, holding their tortured ears in abject pain. As life drained from one of the fatally stricken, he writhed like a stomped snake. Another shell exploded higher overhead farther down the line, killing and stunning more.

Using a frontal assault, the most expensive kind, we were going to try to force the enemy out of his positions behind walls of felled trees and piled earth. I felt the Reaper's breath on my neck, his voice saying, "You will live today, but I will bring you low and own your soul."

There and then, I sympathized with those who have run from battle. I, too, wanted to run. Yet, I admit that although I have yet to fire a shot in this war, my "Veteran's" cup is nearly filled. The Reaper DID bring me low but, thank the Lord, he failed to capture my soul. Only the Lord has done that.

I looked to Chaplain Findlay for support, but he lay a few yards away in fate's mocking lilies, staring up at me through dilated eyes - a minié-ball through his forehead.

And now, in the battle's aftermath, I sit on this bloody earth, my head aching, my mouth dry, my senses reeling, pondering his fate and my survival, asking "Why, why him, who was so much more able to serve and give to God and these men than I? Why not me instead?"

I love the Lord, but I swear I will never understand Him.

*   *   *

Jotted Things

Lost a man today, but not to battle. His heart gave out as he was peacefully sitting by a campfire playing his mouth harp. His sudden death dampened our spirits, and for the remainder of the day, we kept to ourselves in deafening silence.

*   *   *

The Reverend Rivers, our regimental Chaplain, is down with consumption - has been ailing for weeks and was taken to hospital yesterday. In this war, God spares even His servants no hardships.

*   *   *

This morning an owl sat in a low tree branch above our bivouac, gently hooting. No one remembers ever seeing an owl do so after sunrise. Corporal Henry Red Deer, a Cherokee, took it as a bad sign - said it was calling his name - meaning his days are at an end. He died in battle two days later.

*   *   *

Many packages arrived in the mail this morning. One, for Private Tomilson, contained six pairs of new socks, a comb, a likeness of his sweetheart, and hard candies. Honor compelled him to pass the candies among the rest of us - or suffer banishment. Our boys diplomatically offered no resistance and left Tomilson enough to satisfy his Palate.

*   *   *

Our pickets intercepted an enemy cavalry patrol this morning. A fight ensued when the cavalry dismounted and laid down fire with their Spencer carbines. But our company rushed to the noise and attacked the horseman from the flank, driving off many, killing seven and capturing eleven. Their carbines, ammunition and horses were a boon. We took their wounded and ours to hospital, buried their dead and our three and said prayers over their graves and ours. Only an hour before the fighting, one of our now badly wounded asked me to read - at my convenience - a letter he received this week from his wife. I did so later in the hospital. Of course, to avoid alarming his wife, I will write his cheerful reply containing no mention of his misfortune.

*   *   *

Could not sleep last night - bad tooth - no relief.

*   *   *

We lanced a boil on Sergeant Grimsley's posterior today. In doing so, he was gravely discomforted - to the snickering delight of men to whom he had assigned extra duty yesterday. The always ill-tempered Sergeant complained that he considered our medical methods "excessive."

*   *   *

Am down to the nubs of two pencils. Unless I can locate more, I'll be forced to use charcoal or tap a vein.

*   *   *

I volunteered today to help our boys dig latrine pits. In doing so, my credentials as a bona fide honorary infantryman, sans rifle, were greatly enhanced in the eyes of this company's fellow diggers. My blisters honor me.

*   *   *

Some of our boys sighted a strange object in the sky this afternoon. They said it glowed brightly as it slowly drifted across the western horizon before vanishing. All decided it was a falling star that did not fall. Their impressions were baffling, leaving many spooked.

*   *   *

We found a cache of eatable berries today and brought hatfuls into camp. It was the first fruit of any kind that we have enjoyed in weeks. All were deliciously sweet - a genuine luxury. We craved more, but found none.

*   *   *

The talk around our bivouac today was of women. They are sorely missed. Elaboration is unnecessary.

*　*　*

Private Morris found a baby squirrel this morning and brought it into camp. As hungry for meat as our men are, none could kill it. "Even if'n I did," Morris said, "I couldn'ta et it. Ain't sunk that low, yet." None of us have...yet.

*　*　*

Got skunked playing euchre today. These boys are merciless. I do not envy our enemies.

*　*　*

In the half-light just before sun-up, I watched a young soldier examine a dew-drenched wild flower. It was obvious he savored both its elegance and fragility. And though he had never received formal training, he exhibited an artist's soul, for he later borrowed a sheet of my sketch paper and reproduced the flower and dew drops to near-perfection. Lord, I prayed, save that boy, for the world needs the lilies he will make beautiful.

*　*　*

Sunlight dappled the countryside this morning and pooled beneath the trees that shaded our bivouac. I had never before noticed how mellow the sun's light becomes when filtered through leaves and boughs. The troops cleaning their rifles below welcomed the light, as it helped them to closely examine their work. Sad, I thought, that they did not appear to notice it for the wonder it was.

*　*　*

Late this morning, while behind our lines, I came across a young soldier in terrible agony upon a stretcher. His wounds, of a personal nature, bled heavily. The outdoor hospital receiving the maimed from the fighting two miles beyond spread across acres. Of the hundreds of men sprawled there awaiting treatment only God knew how many would be overlooked or would die before receiving care. Never would there be enough doctors or surgeons to serve all. Out of his patient's earshot, the physician attending the stretcher-borne soldier, explained, "We can only give him slight amounts of morphine because we must conserve our supply. But the poor boy is ruined. If he survives, he will never sire a family nor enjoy the private privileges of marriage." As it was, he bled-out and succumbed hours later. The thought of yet another young face moldering in the earth saddened me to my core.

*　*　*

Thinkin' Out Loud

The following are samplings of comments overheard in and out of ranks:

Enlisted: "I don't thinka' the fightin'. I jest git ready for it. Live 'er die - it don't make no diff'ernce. Got no control over it anyways. Ya jest goes out there and does yer duty. If'n ya come back, ya come back. If'n ya don't, it be the Lord's will."

Officer: "Gotta keep out front - no strayin' - straight at 'em - the men have t'see me leadin' them all the way. Cain't show 'em fear - gotta be a rock - always a rock."

Enlisted: "Led a foul and bogus life. Lord's gotta a book on me thick and wide - and I know it. He's gonna make me pay for it out there, sure. Got it comin', though - if only ya knew. Jesus, U'm skerd."

Officer: "Have to watch the virgins. They've never seen fightin' before and they'll break and run first - always do. Have to watch 'em close. First blood or gore the weak ones see, they'll be panickin' - I can always feel it."

Enlisted: "Shoulda' married her. Was a nice woman. Shoulda' give her my name. What she gonna do if I'm kilt...what? Shoulda married her. Lord, I'm sorry I didn't...dreadful sorry. Meemaw'll watch over her 'til I git back. Lord, please git me back to her so I ken do right by her. She be havin' my child."

Officer: "I don't know how much longer I can lead these men. A body can manage only so much fear and wounding before it refuses to risk itself any longer. So, I'm in a quandary! I cannot let my men think me a coward."

Enlisted: "M'youngins and m'wife's all U'm thinkin' 'bout. Should neva' gone fer soldier... shoulda' stayed home with 'em. Weren't fair a'me ta her...weren't fair a'tall."

Officer: "When you command men to advance into rifle and artillery fire, they put their souls in your hands and you're responsible for each. They give you their trust. They see you as special - a worker of magic - because you're an officer. Officers are supposed to know all things and possess supernatural insights - and even know what they're doing. Most times, we know no more than our men, but cannot say so. We deal with them as we would with children. We keep them ignorant. It's easier for men to die never knowing that we and they have been intentionally sacrificed in the name of poor tactics and poorer strategy."

Enlisted: "Need m'whiskey. Always do 'bout now. Never took a ball b'fore, but I 'spect I will t'day. Can feel it. Been gettin' away clean fer too long. Every'body's time comes around if'n ya wait long 'anuff. I fear I'm gonna take a ball right through the gut. Need that whiskey."

Officer: "I take comfort in small things - like a morning breeze that arrives gently on the new day and refreshes one's senses. I cherish times when I can set aside my duties to write home or simply to walk and be by myself away from the humanity I must shepherd everyday. These things sustain me. Otherwise, I might walk away from it all and never return."

Enlisted: "Know'd it come t'this sometime - had to. Know dyin's what soldiers be for, but I cain't stop m'knees from rattlin'. M'guts is all tied-up and a'quiverin'. Cain't let the boys see me a'sweatin' like this, me bein' their Sergeant n'all. Damnit, I seen what canister and minié-balls do t'flesh n'bone fer three year. Ain't perdy. Jest don't want the pain - kill me outright, but no pain. Lord, please, if I gotta go, let me go quick."

Officer: "Did you ever notice how the birds take flight when a battle is evident. They sense it and head out across the countryside and only return when it's finished. If only we were birds."

Enlisted: "Don't want no woundin' a second time. Pain were hell the first time. Don't wanna 'magine what it'd be like agin'. Still be sick from the first one in the side, here - damn wound jest keeps a'seepin' and bleedin' out puss. Don't think it'll ever heal in this lifetime. Cain't eat right - ball went through and tore up m'belly. Five months in hospital's what come of it. Rather lay in manure than go through that agin' and listen to all that moanin' and screamin' around me all day long in that place. No, suh...I be a'takin' Heaven b'fore another hospital."

Officer: "We cry, too - in private - when things get too much to hold in ana'more. We just never let on."

Enlisted: "They're always sayin' war makes men outta boys. It don't. It jest mostly ruins 'em."

*   *   *

Dare Call Him Coward

Last night, I witnessed a Captain jeopardize his commission by confessing to a "mortal sin."

He sat by candlelight, pen in hand, refusing to allow the patter of rain on his tent to lull him into postponing what honor told him he must do. A sudden breeze slipped through the tent's unsecured flap, turning the candle's flame into a sputtering demon that cast dancing shadows across the tent's interior.

Dipping his pen into his folding desk's small ink well, he prepared to write. Since he had confessed everything to me, I knew what his letter to higher command would contain. I am not a brave man, but I recognized that his act bespoke a valor few men commanded. I will not divulge his name, since he is more than owed this singular consideration:

"Dear Sirs,

"I hereby testify to the facts set down herein.

"During the Army's assault upon enemy positions yesterday, I led my company in our regiment's attack upon the enemy's left flank. I assumed this responsibility with the best of intentions, having fought in many campaigns in the past two years.

"Though our casualties were heavy, we routed and cleared the enemy from his trenches. It was at this time, as the regiment (and my company) pursued him, that I froze. I cannot explain why, but I could not encourage my body to move. Nor was I able to recall any details of my experience from that point unto the following morning. I still cannot.

"I am told that I had to be carried from field. Command of the company passed to my subordinate, Lieutenant Jordan Powell, who has led it admirably since. I have left him in charge, believing my deportment has cost me my command's faith and trust. It cannot be denied that I failed it at its most exposed and vulnerable hour.

"I have recovered, am now in full possession of my senses and will make myself available for whatever action you deem appropriate. I request that you receive this resignation of my commission and consider that I be remanded to the ranks to serve as a rifleman, since I believe such an action would set a positive example." The Captain did not mention that he had been wounded four times in two years, twice severely. Nor that he lives with excruciating pain in his shrunken right leg - and daily sips laudanum, as prescribed by his regimental physician.

He signed the letter, called for a courier, and sent it on its way.

"It's finished," he remarked, as he stared through the tent flap at distant lightning, listening to the rumble of approaching thunder.

Not being a drinking man, he would find no escape in alcohol. In assuming that he had betrayed and failed himself as much as his company, he was left more bewildered than depressed. And though he would spend a sleepless night searching his soul for answers, he would not admit to his humiliation. Pride would prevent him from acknowledging that he, like all officers, possessed human limitations - and that his cup of war had simply filled and spilled over.

He thanked me for listening to his story, excusing himself to make one last round of his company's encampment, though, technically, he no longer commanded it. I assured him that I would keep his name confidential. In gratitude, he raised his hand to my shoulder, then donned his hat and cape and limped into the rain - leaving me to ponder why he had confided his experience to me, since we had not been well acquainted. I surmised that my sympathetic presence had encouraged him to unburden his overwhelmed conscience.

I never saw him again.

I moved on the next morning, not having learned his fate, though I tried convincing myself that his overseers would preserve his commission and transfer him to a rear area post. Yes, officers have been court-martialed and broken for less, but what would have been the logic in devaluing the years in which he had devotedly shed his blood in his country's service? What, indeed?

Unfortunately, common sense in such matters does not always prevail in the highest realms of command.

Veterans, who have regularly confronted the gorgon, say that Fate has NO conscience, nor would a court-martial board. I therefore have added my prayers to those of others beseeching the Lord to mercifully intervene to deny the Captain further degradation.

* * *

Observer

Today I observed our batteries firing on enemy artillery exposed in a meadow our gunners said was a half-mile away. Our eight guns had been masked and well hidden from view on a hill, and we watched the enemy move HIS guns into position, ignorant of our presence. In the fields below, their forces and ours had locked in combat.

Standing, as I was, behind a cannon called a Rodman Rifle, I could hardly tolerate our batteries' din. So accurate was this Rodman's and our other pieces' fire, that, one after the other, they smashed the shocked enemy's artillery pieces and bowled over their gun crews. As our iron bolts did their devastating work, our gunners cheered wildly. Enemy ammunition caissons exploded into huge fiery-orange mushrooms and white smoke. Dismembered men and horses writhed; other horses panicked and bolted, some enemy gunners tossed like rag dolls as they frantically attempted to pull their pieces to the shelter of a nearby woods. They managed to turn four of their guns on us and returned fire, but so rapid was our gunner's response that their surviving crews fled.

Anticipating their direction of flight, our gunners led all who attempted to pull their remaining cannon to safety - forcing them to run a gauntlet of hurtling iron. I shuddered at what those poor devils were experiencing. Soul-rending was the slaughter of their numbers and horse teams. More caissons exploded, their contents of surviving shells cartwheeling skyward on wispy tendrils.

Though my eyes stung and watered in the clouds of sulfurous smoke produced by our artillery fire, I hurriedly jotted my notes, desperately turning my ears away from each gun's shattering report. Still, each one pounded my eardrums. Not being able to share our gunners' enthusiasm, I could not divorce myself from the terror and destruction befalling those fated souls yonder, though I dared not reveal my revulsion, lest I be harshly regarded each time our boys pulled a lanyard.

War is war, and if the enemy had found our guns first, our people would have suffered the same mindless destruction. But I could not deny that our enemies were of the same blood and flesh, and I pitied them, as I would have pitied ours.

"We're thumpin' 'em good," said an excited soldier running shells from one of our caissons to one of our guns.

Yes, I agreed, we were "thumpin 'em good." But, I wondered, were any of our boys dying, too - within?

* * *

Footsore

Like gray backs and mosquitoes, bunions and blisters are the bane of our days. The miseries they cause cannot be imagined unless one has endured the march in poorly made shoes - or suffered barefooted across terrain better traversed by hooved animals.

Brogans do not last long. Officers suffer least from footware disintegration, since many enjoy generally well-made boots. But they are just as afflicted by blisters and bunions, as socks degenerate quickly and are not readily replaced. Socks come at a premium and are "sorely" (pun intended) sought by officers and enlisted men. Occasionally, packages from home - usually months late - arrive with fresh pairs inside. The result is ecstasy. In the meantime, every sort of relief is sought for afflictions of the heel, sole and toe. Poultices, alcohol, whiskey, homemade salves and Indian recipes are applied - some semi-successfully. Infection is the greatest enemy, as blood poisoning or gangrene claim nearly as many feet as wounds.

Foot inspections are frequent, since prideful soldiers are loathe to report infections or serious bunion and blister problems. On rare occasions, such men are disciplined, for if an army cannot march and maneuver, it cannot fight. Hundreds of troops have been waylaid with foot problems, thereby collectively diminishing their units' effectiveness. I have seen raw meat pass for feet and men pour blood from their dilapidated brogans. In an attempt to stave off gangrene, physicians sometimes use maggots to eat away dead tissue on seriously infected feet. And because gangrene's stench is appalling, it is readily detected.

These are charms of Army life. I wish we could persuade the government to issue as many socks as bullets. Men who receive socks from home, or who are fortunate enough to purchase pairs from sutlers, often wear two pairs at once. Although the practice lessens the onset of blisters and bunions, it often causes severe foot-sweating with all attendant ills, including toenail deterioration and skin-peeling - what the men call foot-rot.

Seldom are foot problems appreciated until conditions go from bad to extreme. I have experienced my share, including the excruciating pain of raw and bloody heels. Even now, mine are swollen and sore. I wear failing boots six months old. Should they give out, I will have to go barefooted with so many others in this company. These are my second pair. Both the first and second were obtained for me early in the war by gracious officers on furlough, when shoes were not yet a dire problem for our Army. I would need to purchase a third pair soon - perhaps in Richmond, Savannah, or Atlanta - before leather supplies there evaporate, like so much else in our harried land of late. Yet, I would suffer untold embarrassment and even greater humiliation by receiving fresh boots while so many in ranks go barefooted and worse.

No, I will soldier-on with the leathers I'm now wearing thin. Even in their present condition, they will fit me much more comfortably than brightly polished hypocrisy.

The Gentler Sex

In hospitals, female nurses and civilian women are the angels who hover over the bulk of our sick and wounded. Yet, their tender ministrations sometime mortify their especially modest patients.

Helpless young soldiers often lie in their own waste. Their bodily functions must be attended and they must be cleaned and washed. Having no choice except to surrender to female care, they sometimes weep with embarrassment. Yet, the women appear unaffected and endure their unwholesome duties with dedication. Were I one of the wounded, my mortification would be unbearable.

Besides attending the wounded, the women continually boil bedding - sheets, pillows and pillow covers - out of doors in all weather - not to mention blankets, towels, cloths, bed pans, and utensils. Their work is Herculean and their hours long - sometimes from dawn to sunset. I cannot fathom the depths of their fatigue.

Many a reconstructed man who leaves our hospitals owes his health as much to these ladies as to our doctors. And many a man who leaves this Earth in relative comfort also owes them an eternal debt. I have met seventeen year-old nurses and spoken to others seventy and beyond - all angels in white. The older women generally supervise the younger, but their hours and labors, considering their ages, are punishing. Yet, to a person, all say that if the wounded can endure, so can they.

In a touching scene, one young nurse, age twenty, saw her severely wounded father brought in suffering grievous leg and abdominal wounds. Naturally, others attended to his needs. But doctors told me that although THEY might not have saved him, her presence miraculously brought him through.

These women deserve special plaudits, yet I fear our government overlooks them. These days, we are so very much a nation of desperation, that the deserving may never be recognized. Most will have to remain satisfied with the knowledge that they have served well and loyally. Yet, they will take with them the gratitude of countless men who will never forget them. In that respect each man will have guaranteed them Earthly immortality.

Beautiful are THESE lilies.

*   *   *

Pruitt's Plan for Peace

Politicians do not fulfill their wartime designs - soldiers do. Therefore, why should it not be assumed that common soldiers might not know best how to design the most practical plans for peace?

Private Randolph Pruitt offered his.

Sitting around a campfire last night, several enlisted men speculated on how best to end this war that they agreed was so cherished by politicians on both sides. Pruitt was the last of nine men to bid. He had sat back, puffing on his pipe, listening to the others' opinions. A three-year veteran, Pruitt was acknowledged by all as having led a charmed life. He had yet to suffer even the slightest wounding. Now, he produced a scheme to reduce casualties and frustrate all generals who, he said, were the politician's "handiest tools."

"Best thing," he said, "is to git with them boys on the otha' side. Easy done, 'cause we do it all the time when we trade 'em tabaccee' fer coffee. Then, we tell 'em this: let's we'uns and you'ins fire three times over each otha's heads when the big fightin' comes. This way, we satisfy honor. Then, we all come out and meet and sit down togetha' where wedda' been killin' eachotha' otha'wise, and sip down some fine whiskey. Then, we smoke some high-class 'ceegars, pass around some good chaw and jaw 'bout what we're gonna do when we go a'marchin' home - as we be entertainin' ourselves a'watchin' our confounded generals a'jumpin' up and down, a'yellin' and a'screamin' orders and a'shoutin and threatin' t'have us all shot. And 'whul we're doin' it, we ken be a'speculatin' on whetha' some of them rounds we done fired off flew clean t'Washington 'er Richmond and put more holes 'tween Lincoln's and Davis's war-lovin' cheeks than the Lord intended. Now, that be a practical suggestion, I b'lieve."

And so did the eight other speculators and all others "a'listenin'!" And so did I. In his way, Pruitt spoke for thousands.

*   *   *

Cruel Justice

Desecration comes in many forms. During a forced march one Sunday afternoon, on fields fought over a week earlier, it repulsed all of us.

Where the fighting had left hundreds of dead on both sides, the enemy had quit the field, abandoning his dead and wounded where they fell. Among his were many of ours, those of ours who had been wounded but overlooked now gone to Glory. We found several decomposing bodies sitting against trees.

After the fighting, our troops had buried as many of our dead as possible before pursuing the enemy. His were left to the mercies of the elements. Even a week later, the air stank of putrefaction and rotting remains. Worse, the creatures of the field, including stray dogs and hogs that had escaped a burnt-out farm, had scavenged on the dead's flesh and were still doing so.

So put off were our boys that they broke ranks to chase them off. But, so hungry were the dozen or so emaciated dogs that turned some on our boys to defend their finds. They were quickly dispatched, and so were twice that many stubborn hogs that had rooted through graves to drag out bodies and body parts. Partially eaten and decomposing arms, legs, skulls, and viscera laid everywhere. So incensed were our boys, that several beat the most stubborn animals to death with rifle butts or eviscerated them with homemade knives.

It was a horrible scene of bloody vengeance added to the already sickening carnage. The dogs' and hogs' howls and death squeals prompted many men in ranks to demand that the butchery quit...

"Them animal's onla doin' what Nature makes 'em," they hollered! "Quit, boys, quit! It ain't gonna bring none of our dead back!"

But the avengers could not be restrained and our officers didn't try. A man in ranks who suggested that we ought to cut-up the hogs and salt them or turn them over to our regimental commissary was heatedly shouted down. The sacrilegious notion of eating fatback and pork nourished on human flesh prompted a reaction that, for decency's sake, is best left unrecorded.

Our boys raged that leaving our dead countrymen to the element's and animal predation had been an unforgivable betrayal of the dead's supreme sacrifice and could never be justified. Yet for most the worst that could be admitted was that this intolerable desecration had resulted in justice of a kind, the guilty being ignorant animals that had suffered for their transgression. One wonders if justice triumphs when only one of two species involved understands it. And though the rest of us remained sympathetic, none of us were proud of it.

*   *   *

Red Legs

Our infantry column happened by this macabre scene shortly after our cavalry's fight today - twenty enemy parasites dangling in the wind beneath the branches of a massive pine. The ropes around their stretched necks creaked as each corpse gently swayed back and forth, twisting round and round, their red leggings adorning them from the knees to their boots.

What strange decorations these dead made on this bloody July 4th holiday. Seventeen others had been killed by our cavalry in the running fight without losses to our side. All of the mounted raiders had tried to flee, being too cowardly to fight. But they had paid for their raping and plundering of local parishes. Though they wore our enemy's uniform, their Red Legs marked them as being no more than pillaging parasites.

I suppose the enemy tolerated them for the intelligence they gathered about our Army. Hundreds roamed our lands, violently taking whatever they wanted. That we had caught this bunch was enough for a holiday of our own, for by destroying them, we had saved numbers of our people from misery - and worse. No prisoners were taken.

Those not hung had been shot dead or sabered-down.

We learned from one of our cavalrymen that most of the hanged had died poorly, crying and protesting that they should have been treated as prisoners of war. Some had invoked the Lord's name in their pleas for mercy. In contrasting silence, our troopers had gone about the grim business of restraining each, while looping nooses around their necks and tossing the ropes over the tree's lower branches. Each horseman had then tied his rope to his saddle horn. It had made little difference to our men that some of the youngest violators had pleaded the loudest, every urging having had gone for naught.

On signal, he said, the horsemen had backed their mounts. Up went each renegade, feet and legs kicking long before going stiff or limp. None had been hooded, their puffed faces turning deep crimson, their eyes bulging, their tongues swelling through their lips - the bowels and bladders of many evacuating in their britches. I cannot imagine their agonies.

Much later, as we watched, when their tongues and faces had blued and their necks had stretched, our horsemen had coaxed their mounts forward, lowering the bodies to the ground. Hanging knots were undone, ropes coiled and the reeking-hanged and those killed in the fighting laid side by side in a single row beneath the tree.

Our cavalry collected the Red Legs' mounts and weapons, grimly reassembled, and galloped off. On orders from his commanding officer, one trooper remained behind to hurriedly chalk a sign board and nail it to the tree, using his shotgun butt as a hammer. The sign said: "As for their Dance, the Fiddler has been paid."

Our infantry column then resumed its wearying trek. Secretly, my heart went out to some of the youngest victims of our side's bitterness. Some looked to have been barely sixteen. They should have been salvaged. It had been the older men among them only who should have been hung twice for having corrupted all the young now wilted lilies.

This war is a hard affair...

*   *   *

Damned Luxury

Sleeping accommodations in the field would appall pampered civilians. To see two grown men, some tall, crammed into two shelter halves pieced together in every inclemency - their feet sticking out - would provide little incentive to join the Cause. Yet, this is how a portion of our Army rests every night. The greater portion suffers in the open.

These small tents, barely large enough for two, and sometimes referred to as "Dog Houses," are of little protection against the fiercest elements. Some men sleep inside them head-first, their feet exposed, others with their heads just inside the openings - whatever arrangement agreed upon by both. Were both to sleep with heads and feet opposed, each would risk the other's hoofs in his nostrils all night - or worse.

Some men rig flaps over their tent openings to keep out wind and rain. Yet, these often prevent proper ventilation and are used only in the worst weather conditions. Body heat provides a measure of warmth inside during cold weather when flaps are closed. But those who spoon in the open - back-to-back for warmth in rain and cold - consider tents "damned luxuries." Yet tents of every description remain in short supply and are some of the first items searched for when our boys overrun enemy supply trains.

Officers sleep in larger tents, and commanding officers, when possible, rig even larger ones. These, of necessity, contain a cot or cots, writing desks and room for conferences, administrative items and map-study. Field grade officers, majors to colonels, usually carry more personal baggage - furniture, uniforms and such, some excessively so. I have found that the most affected officers of higher rank transport the greatest amount of personal items, much of it unused but a boon to their egos. Unfortunately, the burden of loading and unloading it all falls upon enlisted men, who must drag it to or from wagons which would be better used carrying wounded, supplies and food. The largest tents belong to General officers, whose staffs work alongside them.

Thus far I have slept in the open with the majority of my fellow sufferers, that I might experience their hardship. That my health sustains me surprises me, since so many of our exposed troops contract debilitating afflictions - consumption and rheumatism being the most prevalent - rheumatism being a scourge, consumption a death warrant. While it is proffered that tent-dwellers suffer fewer disabilities, soldiers will tell you that the secret to surviving in the open in bad weather - besides covering with oil cloth, rubberized sheets and rain capes - is clothing in layers - which like much of the aforementioned gear, for the bulk of our threadbare men, is but a notion. What there is of it is shared, as is much of everything else they use.

Our nation was never equipped to fight a long war. That we are doing so and HAVE done so for so long is both incredible and inspiring. I do not believe our enemy thought we could. Yet, we're certain he considers that if he can bleed us of everything for long enough, natural attrition will ruin us. Common sense sides with him. But our men agree that we will not have finished our righteous "statement" until long after that day dawns.

What our governors have never understood, is that, in time of war, our states must pool their resources for the good of all if we are to achieve victory. It only defeats our purpose if they maintain independence of action to religiously honor the principle of "States Rights," as well as that may be in peacetime. And it is equally self-defeating for governors to selfishly withhold and harbor supplies and equipment needed by our entire Army that represents all of our states, so that individual states might defend themselves and the expense of our entire war effort.

In these regards, I am constantly amazed by their bullheadedness. Our rank and file are convinced that our cause would be miraculously served, if such supplies and equipment - that they're positive are being hoarded in abundance by various governors - were generally distributed to both our Army of Northern Virginia and our Army of the West. We have suffered mightily, and continue to suffer from their stubbornness, the blood of many thousands of our Southern sons wetting their greedy hands.

It is only due to our military's supernatural patience, and its devotion to the defense of its homeland, that it has not long since marched on Richmond and certain state capitals to evict the national Congress and certain governors from THEIR capitals - that the trash amongst our leadership be disposed of, replaced with patriots and such dire problems ended, if need be at bayonet point.

* * *

In the Beauty of the Lilies

**The Wartime Journals
of Confederate Correspondent
Royal K. Chapman
1862-1864**

Journal Seven

Contents

*   *   *

A Thought

To dust will multitudes turn beneath
their earthen mounds,
while scarred survivors languish among the lilies
of crimson memories,
harkening painfully to the bugle's eternal call.

Cause to Wonder

We were once again reminded of man's puniness beneath Nature's awesome powers. To the west, untold miles from our brigade's encampment, a thunderstorm gathered strength. Fascinated, twenty or more of us watched its dramatic progress.

As clouds darkened and billowed, they rose into the blue dome above them. Deep, earth-vibrating thunder rumbled distantly. Soon, lightning stitched erratic patterns along their base. The rumblings grew louder, forcefully shaking the earth beneath us, giving us pause. Their vibrations reached deep into our innards. Here was God's artillery tearing across a charcoal firmament of its own making, artillery so strong and powerful, nothing of man-made origin could have equaled it nor any Earthly army withstood it. How simple it would have been for the Lord to have frightened our opposing armies into eternal peace. Merely by threatening to loose it against us, and in the space of a heartbeat, He might have ended this war.

Fascinated, we witnessed the storm's development, being quickly convinced of our human inadequacy, while underestimating the rate of its boiling advance across the verdant miles between its genesis and our encampment. Wind whipped before it, yet even as we rushed to our tents, sounding the alarm as we went, it increased with cyclonic force. The darkening sky turned black.

Lightning flashed and cracked directly overhead. Thunder shook the earth with hammer blows. Rain drove like bullets upon the scampering forms of our brigade's eight hundred men. Campfires blew across every bivouac, embers flaring in mid-air before drowning in the following deluge. Because the tempest came upon us with such ferocious suddenness, we thought our God sought to angrily obliterate every one of us. For the next half-hour, we believed He might even end the world.

Hail stripped trees. Wind blew away our tents and freshly washed uniforms, tipped over our wagons, tore away their coverings and stampeded trace horses, sending our desperate ranks racing to cover. Had it encompassed a battlefield, it would have silenced all combat and made fleeing allies of dedicated enemies.

"God, make all armies flee from You," I heard a religious soldier pray; "make your storms weapons of righteousness..." leaving me to wonder if a mere human soul possessed the power to influence a Deity or appeal to its conscience. No matter, we survived the storm, spent the day's remainder recovering and repairing our bivouac and quietly considering our pathetic human insignificance.

Tomorrow, we would resume the march - supernaturally humbled.

*   *   *

Sad Mission

It was along our line of march on a hot afternoon that we approached the house of Captain William Benet, the late commanding officer of the company in which I marched.

The Captain had been killed in battle a month past, and it devolved upon the company's new leader, Captain Thorne, to deliver the sad news to Benet's widow, small son and younger daughter.

Consequently, our brigade's commanding officer halted the column for that purpose. Upwards of seven-hundred men paused that day in the shade of woods bordering the road, the news of our sad mission having quickly spread through the ranks. All eyes focused upon Thorne as he and his aide opened the gate in the picket fence fronting the house and slowly advanced up the path to its front porch. In a valise, Thorne carried the dead officer's personal effects. Mrs. Benet, a tall, graceful woman, opened the door, her children at her side, and stepped onto the porch. Her steely demeanor signaled that she well-sensed the nature of the message being carried to her. Standing straight and proudly, her bearing was both brave and magnificent.

I watched from an open vantage point, since our company, fortunately, had paused directly opposite the house. Thorne and his aide removed their hats and bowed respectfully. We could hear their voices but could not discern their conversation. When Mrs. Benet stiffened and looked away, pressing her children tightly to her, we knew the officers had delivered the unfortunate news.

It was obvious the men around me were not only sympathetically viewing the drama but imagining someone delivering a similar message to THEIR loved ones about THEIR battlefield deaths. They looked on intently, their expressions filled with admiration for Mrs. Benet's courage. They knew she would not break down in front of them or in front of her children - not her kind of woman. In having so stoically met her moment of grief, she represented THEM, their cause and their country, her strength nourishing their resolve.

Thorne set down the valise, and after a few more moment's conversation, he and his aide stepped back and sympathetically saluted Mrs. Benet. She bowed her head. Turning slowly, they walked back through the gate and returned to the company. She remained on the porch with her children, still tightly holding them to her side. Minutes later, the column moved on, with our company respectfully doffing their head wear, her courage bringing tears to many eyes.

As we route-stepped away, no one in our company spoke. When I looked back, Mrs. Benet and her children still watched from the porch. A turn far down the road eventually hid them from view.

The mood in our exhausted ranks turned both introspective and reverential. All understood that with such womenfolk supporting them they were obliged to demonstrate the same mettle on the battlefield. Many, after so much war, wondered if they still possessed such fortitude.

"Brave woman," someone behind me said, as if his thoughts had unconsciously tumbled from his mouth.

No one responded. None needed to. His sentiment found confirmation in the dust of our pensive silence.

*   *   *

Sutler Meanings

The arrivals of sutlers in Army encampments are always occasioned by joy and an immediate surge in morale. They bring with them many distractions, besides the usual extra "necessaries" of Army life needed or sought by our troops. For me, they are sources of information of varying reliability. One has to sift facts from rumors and gossip, an art that has more to do with pessimism than skill.

On this day, with my supply of paper and pencils low, I was gratified to see even John Tate, a sutler of dubious ethics and tainted reputation. One has to watch one's change and inspect one's purchases carefully to ensure Tate's honesty, but there is no denying his affable manner. It isn't that he steals as much as that he snookers with a smile - or as one soldier put it: "Ole' John aint' never offered a bargain that were."

Around his tent that day, several men imbibed in the spirits he'd sold them. They discussed recent events - the war's progress, the enemy's movements and intentions, the Army's intentions, homefront news, the whereabouts of friends and the woundings or deaths of comrades - plus myriad other topics. Oh yes - and the fairer sex. Fortunately, Tate was well supplied with paper and pencils, a passel of which I purchased after persuading him to lower the price by a dollar. He takes nothing on credit and only grudgingly accepts currency, of course preferring gold, which few, if any, of us possess. Occasionally, he trades for something he can profit from later.

Because he knows many correspondents, I inquired about my good friend, Henry Willoughby, a photographer and writer who free-lances for several newspapers. Correspondents and sutlers often cross paths in their mutual wanderings, and Willoughby and I consider ourselves alter egos in our approach to war reporting.

"Prob'ly shot dead by bummers last month," Tate speculated. "They're havin' trouble with that thieve'n scum up country who be killin' a man fer his store-bought teeth, and that be no lie."

Bummers are the scourge of our parishes - enemy troops who range far and wide, "provisioning" themselves with whatever the land offers - from livestock to grain to personal possessions and food off the table - usually by theft at gunpoint, or by pure violence and murder.

"'Parently," Tate said, "Willoughby wouldn't give up his image-takin' device, was how I heard it. Caught him in his wagon somewheres and done him in."

I could not believe it. Willoughby had been too rough and ready a soul not to have fought back and taken down a bummer or two, probably first. Though a friend to many correspondents, and being a fine writer and excellent photographer, his work is not well-known, which I consider a crime. I've known his parents since my childhood and was best man at his wedding. His wife, Charlotte, would have been crushed had this news been true. They have no children.

"Can't hardly believe it," I mumbled.

"'Fraid so," Tate said. "A major of artillery told me so a day after he said it happened. Doubt he be wrong. Nice feller, that Willoughby. Always paid with good federal 'shiny.'"

Tate's revelation, if accurate, might have sunk me to a grim level. As it is, correspondents are not safe from either side's depredations, nor have they and their profession ever been respected, nor truly appreciated by either side. I decided there and then to eventually arm myself with pistols, even as I worried for my friend. But because his "rumored" death sounded so unreal, I refused to believe it. To have believed otherwise, I would have to have seen him die.

For the remainder of the day and afterwards, intuition told me that if anything untoward had actually occurred, Hank had survived it. I might have considered writing Charlotte for verification, but banished the notion. Without knowing for certain, how could I have mentioned anything to her?

It stormed that night. The rain's soporific patter on my tent lulled me into a fitful sleep. But recollections of my adventures with Hank rolled scroll-like before my closed eyes. I awoke throughout the night, troubled, having to know, but how? I reasoned that a chance meeting with other correspondents somewhere in the field might yet yield the truth because they comprised an informed network. But I knew of no other correspondents in the immediate area.

One uneasy week later to the day, with no further information to be had concerning Willoughby, our trudging column rounded a bend. A wagon pulled by a team of weary horses stood at roadside.
"Lookee there at that feller," the soldier next to me remarked. "He be liftin' that wagon by the axle with one hand, and managin' that wheel with the other. Don't reckon I'd ever be wantin' to git on the bad side of a feller like that!"

There, large as life, a familiar tousle-haired figure slipped that heavy spare wheel onto that wagon's heavier rear axle with apparent ease, amazing everyone in ranks. Henry Willoughby never looked stronger or healthier.

"Me, dead?" he laughed during our bear-hugging and back-pounding reunion..."the Lord wouldn't have me in Heaven and the Devil'd throw me outta Hell!"

The bummers? Oh, yes, there had been bummers, as his bandaged armed signified, the emphasis being on "had been." They had confronted the wrong man and HIS pistols - and Henry produced the photographic plates to prove it - three dead on a road - shot clean through their gizzards, their eyes still wide open.

"Winged me," Hank confessed, "but otherwise were incompetent shots. Put two holes in my wagon cover on their way to Perdition!"

As usual, Tate's information had been as genuine as his "bargains."

*   *   *

A Stopping Place

Today I stood outside a recently constructed field hospital that contained four wards and an administrative office. Three physicians attended more than a hundred wounded men and boys, aided by six female nurses and squads of male orderlies. I had stopped by to note its functions and speak to its personnel. Of all the meaningful places I had visited in my sojourns, this one touched me exceptionally deeply.

One could see that all staff members were overworked and the hospital hopelessly understaffed. Physicians showed signs of utter exhaustion, having performed operations all that morning with little or no sleep for days. I cannot understand the scant attention our government has paid to our wounded's care. Has it never once considered the consequences of sending a nation's manpower to war?

Men and boys - and I emphasize "boys" - lay in every state of mutilation, most of them amputees with bloody bandaged stumps where arms, legs, hands, or feet should have been - others with open and often gangrenous wounds seeping corruption or purposely filled with maggots to eat away dead tissue. Body waste lay in pans or soaked rags and towels that awaited washing or elimination in controlled fires outside. Kettles there were stoked by helpers, who boiled water, into which dirty linens were being submerged. Though most of the wards' personnel were male, brave civilian women volunteers of varying ages from nearby farms and settlements were assisting.

Outside, gentle breezes wafted away each ward's stench. Alcohol mixed with urine, blood, gangrene, putrefaction and diarrhea makes for an overpowering reason to avoid hospital visits. Yet, staff members and volunteers work in the smell all day long. In summer, as now, each ward's canvas sides can be raised to permit ventilation, thus easing the problem. In colder weather when the sides must remain down, the corrupted air cannot as readily escape.

I welcomed fresh air's unfettered sweetness under the open blue sky, thinking it unfitting that so much pain should flourish beneath such beauty. The faces of the wards' younger patients haunted me. Here were boys, barely into puberty, enduring their torments in lonely isolation, and men the age of their fathers and older brothers fighting agonies, homesick for all they had loved and known - the boys for their fathers' loving guidance and their mother's comforting arms, the older men for their wives or sweethearts' soothing attentions. More than anything else, it was the poignant injustice of youngsters suffering in such conditions that drove me into the open that day. I did not want the tears that clouded my vision embarrassing them. By all measures of common sense and decency, there should have been no boys their tender ages permitted to attend this war. What a crime!

The severely wounded's humility undid me. Most understood that they would not survive their ordeal. A special Grace befalls some at the end upon whom God sets a merciful hand. Their pain diminishes and their faces glow. They see beyond themselves, as if looking into the next world, and they assume a Providential tranquility that is absolutely incomprehensible, becoming souls apart from themselves. I was impressed that I stood before sainted company.

So it was for me, as I spoke to boys destined to die, and older men well on their way. A physician told me that nearly half of the wards' patients would not survive the week. And yet, golden sunlight poured in shafts through the wards' open sides, its warming rays falling upon many in their beds who slept like children - as if each ray were a shimmering pathway guiding passing souls high into the Lord's Kingdom.

Freed for minutes to reconstitute themselves in the fresh air, orderlies trembled with fatigue and mental strain. They were heroes, too. Frail and timid souls could not have managed such repugnant responsibilities.

One particular orderly caught my attention. Older and bearded and, unlike the others, seemingly more than stoically calm and detached, he puffed a pipe and pondered the world of his own thoughts. His eyes told me he had seen much that would have shrunken the willpower of younger orderlies. Yet, he abided with apparent equanimity. A hundred yards behind him, in the hospital's cemetery, open graves awaited the day's quota. Around them, rows upon rows of mounded earth marked only the partial cost of our fledgling nations' pride.

"Quite a few out there, ain't they?" he asked, seeing that I noticed. "'Bout three 'hunerd filled up so far, maybe more. Pity, ain't it?"

Yes, I agreed, a pity.

"That there whole meadow'll be filled up by the time this here war's over," he said. "Seems like ana'more, we jest be comforters for 'em 'tween this world and Glory - like they was jest stoppin' over a spell on their way. Reckon it's all we ken do."

All they could do...I hadn't perceived their work in that fashion. Perhaps, it WAS as much as they could do and what the Lord had intended for them to do...manage a stopping place on the appointeds' way into His tender care.

From a simple man - perhaps a simple truth.

*   *   *

Lifted Spirits

Soldiers find ways to bury their troubles in momentary bouts of gaiety. They often uplift themselves when campfires light the night and empty bellies remind them of loyalty's "benefits."

"Benefits?" a veteran asked; "they ain't much, but the Army's gives 'em to ya FREE fer nothin'!"

And so, they disguise their "benefits" with voices raised in song and with instruments scrounged from everywhere - Jew's harps, jugs, fifes, banjos, mouth-harps, and whatever else makes musical noises. With feet "a'stompin'," they endure one more night, that they might endure one more day.

Normally shy about intervening in their men's amusements, officers sometimes attend, unable to resist. Here and there, the Devil's brew is resurrected from realms unknown, passed around and liberally consumed. Officers not only look the other way, they sometimes "slyly" imbibe.

Hoedowns last for hours. When they end, the quiet that follows is deafening. It depresses the sober, now deprived of that musical narcotic that only moments ago filled their world with welcomed unreality. Over-imbibers feel no such pain and sleep where they fall. For others, slumber is fitful. Morning means a return to painin' bellies and war.

"Never known a man who could sleep good after a hoedown," the veteran said, "lessen' he be drunk, which is why we keep spirits up, if'n y'catch m'meanin'."

Yes, I caught it.

Our soldiers' lives are subject to daily extremes - the "benefits" of loyalty. If it were not for occasional foot-stompers, their war would be unendurable. They appear to sense when relief is necessary and act accordingly. In that regard, they are their own best physicians.

Incidentally, I slept very well after our last hoedown - very soundly, indeed. However, one of my morning "benefits" tortured my aching skull the entire day.

* * *

Chasin' Hogs

Our amusements take many forms. Some come on the march.

If one can imagine day and week-long treks in mud, down rutted roads, through tangled woods and briar-filled fields, and across miles of heat, damp cold and rain, one can imagine thousands of stone-bored and body-aching soldiers. Humorous situations, therefore, become appreciated diversions.

Our column paused near a well-tended farm, and from its house came two young maidens to greet our brave fellows. They brought candies and sugared bread to compliment their teasing eyes and coy smiles. Our youngest responded the most eagerly, as our older and more wily veterans lay in shaded grass to conserve their aching legs for the miles ahead.

"Damn fool youngins," one of the reclining veterans remarked; "wished I be that age agin'."

As I sketched the event, I was surprised to see that one of the girls had also brought along a little pig, apparently as a gift to ingratiate herself amongst our always hungry boys. It got away.

Squealing down the road, it must have sensed the delicate quality of its existence, for away went our boys after it, laughing and hooting with the glee of pupils released from school. Leaving their rifles, bedrolls and packs in the care of others, they tore after their squeamish quarry, but none could match its nimbleness. Most found themselves face-down in the road's yellow dust, their hands clutching air.

The critter ran an ingenious course, confusing and confounding its pursuers at every turn, until it vanished into the tall grasses of an adjoining meadow, only its triumphal grunts marking its flight.

Alas, whistles sounded, alerting all to the resumption of the march. Embarrassed, our hog-chasers slunk to their assigned places, upright again but defeated. The column reformed. Hogless, we marched away to the waving good wishes of the young ladies who had amused themselves (and us) at our young lads' expense. The boys, all of them in love, waved good-bye in turn, dust clouding from their sleeves, sad to leave.

"Damn fool youngins'," the exasperated veteran repeated. "That pig had more sense."

Oh, to have been that senseless again.

* * *

The "Book" Times Three

Contradictions occur in war that make little sense. When they involve faith, they leave men confused and afraid.

Our column of more than eleven thousand men had trekked more than twenty miles on an all-day march through wilderness. We had brought along our supply wagons, ambulances and artillery in an attempt to link up with the remainder of the Army. Several times, wagons had predictably broken down along severely rutted trails in barely passable wooded areas. Each incident resulted in prolonged blockages that forced the column to halt as many times.

During one such pause, some of our religious boys refrained from resting or reclining along the wooded roadside, as is common practice. Instead, they gathered in small clusters to individually read their Bibles or read them for the illiterate among them. A great many of our soldiers can neither read not write. I marvel at how our weary troops listen to the Bible's words. They shed their fatigue as they ponder each verse. On this day, even our exhausted horses stood quietly, snorting now and then but otherwise motionless, as slobber dripped from their thirsty mouths.

Three men in particular attracted my attention. They passed a small Bible between them, attempting to follow the words being read to them by another man from another Bible. I am amazed by how our weary troops avidly read or listened to the Bible's words with childlike curiosity, their apparent innocence being touching.

Moments later, the head of the left-most man of the trio erupted with blood and matter, followed almost instantly by a muffled rifle report from deep within the woods across the road. The stricken soldier pitched into the middle man, who reflexively held him, as the wilting body slid gently to the earth in instant death.

Splattered with the slain man's brain and skull fragments, the survivor and his remaining friend looked on in disbelief, as the rest of the company scampered for cover. I could not shed my shock at such execution. Minié balls produce devastating head wounds. That an enemy sniper, undoubtedly ignorant of what his target was about, had chosen this time in these circumstances to kill one of us, decimated my spirit. Some men quickly loaded their weapons and blindly fired back, unleashing their anger at what most soldiers consider the lowest form of military scum. Their fire's volume increased so mightily, that their commanding officer, Captain Bartholemew, rushed to restrain them. When it ceased, a great many, keeping low, gathered 'round the dead soldier's body - whose rigid hand clutched his Bible so tightly, it could not be removed.

When they were certain that the sniper had been driven off, our men decided to decently bury his victim. They covered his shattered head with a towel, crossed his arms over his chest and gently wrapped him in a blanket, with his Bible still in his hand. His funeral commenced almost immediately, as our column was set to resume its march.

A half-dozen soldiers quickly dug a shallow grave in a small clearing in the woods, using small picks, bayonets and their bare hands.

Because the news of the soldier's death by sniper fire had quickly spread through the column, the regimental Chaplain, the Reverend Charles McFee, rushed to the site, offering to preside over the burial. There would not be time to eulogize the man or review his commitment to our Cause or to remark at length about the wife and children he'd left behind.

Scores of soldiers stood ready to return fire, should the sniper chance another round.

With the grave finished, the diggers carefully laid in the shrouded body. The scene's poignancy affected all.

"How come God let that man be kilt that a'way?" a soldier asked, as the Reverend prepared to speak. We froze at his audacity, yet the question plagued us all: "Weren't he a'readin' from the Lord's very Word?"

The Reverend looked on, his expression grim. I prepared to use my shorthand: "I do not know," he said. "We are seldom ready to die, even those of us who are most religious - for we cling to life as birds cling to branches, afraid to let go lest we fall into the unknown below. But, we do not fall except into the Lord's embrace. Now this soldier KNOWS the Word. He is born into a new existence whose wonders exceed our greatest imaginations - where lilies perpetually bloom in the most wondrous profusion - and the tribulations of mortal life pass away. This simple, Private Adam Smith, now has entered that Kingdom. I do not suppose it matters when a man dies to Earth or by what means. It only matters that he does so in the Word, as Private Smith surely did a minute ago. It was his time, and the enemy who slew him being an instrument of a mystery beyond our ken. Let us therefore silently rejoice in his relief - and ask God to watch over the Private's wife and children and ease their burden. I am told, they awaited his impending furlough. Amen."

Many of those, intrigued by the Reverend's thoughts, had forgotten to remove their hats and caps. They did so now. Only a timid breeze disturbed the moment's silence.

We closed the grave. It occurred to me that Private Smith hardly considered, when arising that morning, that he would die not only that battle-free day, but reading a BIBLE!

Minutes later, we were on the road again - hoping it would not be to Perdition.

* * *

Compelled to Suffer

You cannot imagine the efficiency of the Reaper's scythe.

The battlefield horrors it leaves in the wake of its swath beggar the mind. You must see the contorted dead and writhing wounded to appreciate modern warfare. Nor can words convey a battlefield's stench nor truly make you hear the wounded's cries, shrieks, and pleadings.

Death's smell - a combination of acrid, eye-burning powder smoke, blood, and the contents of viscera - carries on the wind.

Imagine jumbled bodies, theirs and ours, carpeting acres - with entrails, limbs, and brain matter strewn about, and the wide eyes of the dead staring into where ever. Imagine body parts strewn among the dead who lie in every state of devastation, while, in bewildering contrast, other corpses appear untouched, as if their occupiers were only asleep - and skulls without eyes and bodies without skulls - and legless horse carcasses and mounts torn to pieces by canister balls - and the wounded, so many of whom endure their agonies without hope of relief.

Imagine litter of every description - letters never to be mailed, some not yet read, some still clutched by the now eyeless dead.

Printed words cannot impart the truth of it - the dead's frozen expressions, nor the wounded's grimacing faces - men and boys groaning and whimpering and clutching their wounds and each other - and tortured souls screaming where surgeons probe, dig, cut, and saw away shattered limbs. The numberless arms, feet, hands, and legs being carted off and dumped into pits - nor those shocked and mind-numbed souls who sit with their powder-smeared hands clasped despondently over their faces, the exhausted and horror-crazed weeping with spiritual desperation.

This is your war, my civilian brothers and sisters, and these are the sights and sounds that wear away the souls of decent men and might well drive YOU - if you were here - to desertion or into madness.

In these sordid realms, the color of uniforms ceases to matter when the firing quits. Enemies of only hours before lay side by side in eternal respite or in agony's common embrace, their animosities dissolved in their shared miseries and draining blood, the waste of man's free will now apparent to all. Yet, we should fear that when human nature once again commands the peace, too soon will the costs of its darker sides be forgotten.

The powerful who make war, should be compelled to suffer it, then be dared, under threat of obliteration, to make it again. But, the protective conventions they have created for themselves will always insulate them from such justice - and leave them safe to freely exploit the lives of the powerless and repeat their infamy.

What history will say of this American tragedy only God now knows. If I were to guess, I would say that, generations hence, young school students will know nothing of it, its echoes faded into time's distant corridors and inevitable amnesia.

*   *   *

Long, Long Rows

Yesterday, after days of fighting, I wandered in its backwaters gathering impressions. The enemy had begun to fall back from the woods and fields both sides had contested near and far, leaving their dead and wounded among ours. There, I ventured upon long, long rows of battle's deformed refuse.

Its extent halted me. Despite all ambient noise and confusion, the dead lay cocooned in silence. Wounded men, many supporting each other, streamed rearward from the still raging contest, oblivious to all but their pain. Eye-burning smoke hung thickly over everything, shrouding them and the dead in veils of dusty gray.

Being buried was the war's spent currency, its denominations colored in earth tones and crimson - always crimson - seeping, dripping, flowing, pooling, clotting. And still burial teams brought in more. Black laborers and white prisoners dug shallow trenches to accommodate all who would share Eternity in shattered indignity - the dead's sightless eyes staring at me, mouths agape, always as if surprised by their mortality - their hands and arms stiff, legs rigid, some souls mere bundles of unrecognizable gore in shredded clothing. Most had been young and some very young.

Unable to remove my gaze from those about to be interred, I lamented that their loved ones would never know where the earth covered them.

"Stand aside, there," an officer ordered me, as his fresh infantry company trudged by toward the carnage ahead - his voice a muffled echo in my ears.

Fading sunlight fought through the smoky haze, collecting beneath the trees in alternately bathing each row of dead in shadows and gold - the only anointing they would ever receive. Body by body, in each trench, they were laid side by side, no words said over them. Their sweating undertakers worked by the score, quickly covering them with dirt. Even then, some bodies would remain above ground when the Army moved away - circumstances precluding the investment of any more burying time. In weeks, only bones would remain.

That night, I followed the troops away from that place, as the Army maneuvered into new positions. Battle would resume at daylight, the day's sacrifices having resolved nothing. But my memory would not let go of those long, long rows, nor my senses the scent of blood and putrefaction. I could not sleep that night, for I could not rid my nostrils of it. It seeped deeply into my consciousness, making me fear that it would forever cling to my soul - like the nauseating smell of moldering lilies.

* * *

In One's Sights

After every fight, conscience-stricken newcomers to war go off by themselves to examine their motives for having shot enemy soldiers. Their exclusive introspections are not well tolerated by impatient veterans who have long-since suppressed their compunctions about killing and have little tolerance for those who have not.

Again and again, these wretched souls wrestle with the pathetic images of the men they've destroyed. Haunted by their victims' faces, and to escape their guilt, they seek justification. Yet, they cannot flee their spiritual nakedness and remain miserable.

It is better when men blindly fire through smoke and the haze of battle into masses of enemy troops, for they cannot always see their bullets strike home or know who or if they've killed. It is another thing to take careful aim over cold iron sights and see their bullets pulverize tissue and bone.

Many men, not wanting to know how or if they've killed, close their eyes before pulling triggers. And though they know in their hearts their bullets probably have struck their targets, not having seen them strike leaves them conscience-free to pretend they may or actually have missed.

I have witnessed those, who know they have killed and regret it, struggle with their consciences. Many seek a Chaplain's guidance. Yet, despite religious counseling, some cannot live with themselves. A few end their torments with their own weapons, having decided that by so balancing the scales, they will achieve redemption.

A Chaplain can never truly know if his guidance will be effective in reconstituting troubled souls and preventing their dissipation. Theirs is a marginal business at best.

Occasionally, I am approached by soldiers carrying such burdens. Most do not desire to discuss their problems, merely to vent their pain and thus to momentarily relieve it. But I am seldom asked for advice. Neither do they seek it nor would I offer it. Being patient while they unburden themselves is therapy enough for all.

On those occasions, I am glad I am not a soldier, for when I put myself in their places, I shudder. One might think that all hardened veterans are immune from self-reproach - not so. Some sicken of their work and ask for duty in non-combatant roles. Depending upon their states of mind, officers commanding their line units do not desire to deal with the infection such reluctance might spread among their troops. It has happened, that in the torments of a single soldier, others also have acknowledged guilt and have fallen to pieces.

I cannot say what my response will be if I am asked or am forced by circumstance to lift a rifle against the enemy. But I know I cannot sacrifice the lives of my countrymen to protect or placate my own conscience later. Men endure many wounds in war - souls being as vulnerable as flesh. It is a risk I assume every day that I share our troop's existence and follow them into their unknown.

*   *   *

Conscience

Today, a youth, sixteen years young, came to me saying he had killed his first man during our last major engagement. He hadn't cleansed his hands since and they remained darkly stained with the dead man's blood. A strapping lad, he was spiritually stricken. He had used a Bowie knife.

"I r'memba his eyes," he told me, "starin' inta' me like two burnin' coals - right inta' m'heart. I had his arms pinned b'hind him. He couldn't do nothin'. I had 'em cold. He weren't a whole lot older'n me. Didn't wanna' kill 'em, but I didn't want MY boys thinkin' me a sissy - so I stuck him, and stuck him agin'. I could feel him stiffen like a board at the pain. His blood come a'gushin' out all ova' me and he jest looked at me, his eyes wide, like he couldn't believe I done it. I couldn't believe I done it, eitha'. I shoulda jest drug him off to the rear, like a prisoner. But, no - I done him in 'cause I didn't wanna' be called a coward by the other men. I shouldn'ta done it, no siree . . . I jest shouldn'ta done it!"

The boy would struggle with his transgression for the remainder of his life. I could do nothing for him, except remind him that he and hundreds of others his age on both sides had killed that day. Most, if not all, were undoubtedly chastising themselves in the same manner. Still in mortal agony, he appeared only momentarily mollified. He thanked me and went his way. Eventually, he would either harden to killing or by God's Grace would somehow salvage his humanity and live at peace with himself. "My, God," I thought, "if he survives the war, what will it have made of him then? Will he still have a soul? Or, even if he lives, will it have died?"

"I seen his likes b'fore," a veteran told me. "I were like him once't. I hope he don't b'come like me - cold as stone."

I prayed he would not.

*   *   *

Doldrums

Light is failing. I must write swiftly.

There are times when an army is comparable to a ship at sea caught in the doldrums and idled by circumstance.

So it has been with our Army for nearly two weeks. We have not stirred, and our troops constantly drill, so loathe are its commanding officers to allow them to laze and rust.

Time weighs heavily on all, and some men crave action to relieve their boredom. Others remain satisfied to spend the rest of the war at peace with the gods. I for one have found this period ripe with opportunities to write and sketch.

An army becomes a different vessel at rest - akin to a ship of the line whose rigging and sails are down for repair and refitting, while the gentle waters of a safe harbor lap at its sides.

It astounds me that some of our crew spend their days sleeping and otherwise demonstrating no intellectual curiosity about anything. Others enjoy story-telling, reading or arguing politics and military strategy. Still others play cards, even chess. Of course, around every camp fire, a hardcore of would-be generals always complain that the Army has sold itself short by overlooking THEIR military genius - and that the enlisted man's unappreciated tactical instincts and leadership abilities are superior to the Army's brain trust. These dissatisfied souls believe they could lead us to victory in weeks. And after hearing them out, I'm persuaded that some of their theories may be sounder than those of our present leadership.

*　*　*

One cannot measure the extent of each company's comradeship until one has regularly roamed their bivouacs - listening and observing. Some men joined up together in their home parishes at the war's outset and have not been separated since - and many grew up together also in the same parishes. All are brothers in every sense except by blood. Each is concerned for the other's welfare - in the truest sense of kin and family. The loss of any one brings a deep and abiding sense of loss to all - and they fear battle for the sake of others as for themselves. Afterwards, they are quick to locate and account for every soul in their adopted families. It is this spirit that inspires their courage, because they fight to ensure each other's salvation - a unique virtue to witness as much as to experience. Its mystical essences are difficult to define, yet they exist everywhere in the Army. Some say this spirit is responsible for the dogged stands our boys take against superior numbers and their frequent refusal to give ground or accept defeat. Just as often, however, they would not have it differently. Their officers are frequently hard-pressed to restrain them in battle or to force them to retreat or give up untenable ground that would otherwise mean their destruction. They fight to make their point, and since the war's beginning, that point has never been lost on our enemies.

* * *

Card-playing is popular among our troops, though they are forbidden to gamble with money or use substitutes to incur debts. Fishing is equally attractive, as we are near a large stream that surrenders large cat and pan fish. Our boys have eaten better in the past two weeks than in the past two months. Many laze between drilling and inspections, but they've earned that right. They know that once the Army is on the road again, the rest and strength they garner in these doldrums will serve them well, for they will trek from dawn to dusk with little sleep and minimal rations, while fighting in the bargain.

* * *

Many boys watch me sketch. Some are interested in trying their hands - and some evince obvious talent. Using my pad, a Corporal did an excellent sketch of me - not that I was flattered by his interpretation of my looks as much as by his ability and attention to detail. Although I encouraged him to develop his skills, he saddened me when he told me, "Doubt I'll be makin' it through this here war, sir - so, no use getting' excited 'bout what'll prob'ly never be."

Such comments represent a fatalism that infects many men day to day. They know that planning for the future amounts to self-deception, since the war's uncertainties make such dreaming futile. Yet, other men dream continuously, if only to rescue themselves from such corrupting cynicism and oppressive boredom.

* * *

During times of leisure, hungry soldiers experiment with cooking wild grasses, herbs, flowers, and roots. The object is to find things eatable and nourishing and to note their effects. Failure results in stomach and gut aches, vomiting and "the trots," as well as dizziness, disorientation and states akin to drunkenness - and sometimes worse - to poisoning and unconsciousness. Our regimental surgeons complain that our men are "careless for their own welfare," but these authorities do little on their own to improve the situation. Hungry men remain hungry men. Having partaken of some of their more benevolent concoctions and survived, I cannot say that they should not experiment, even given the risks our government has failed to minimize by attention to their nutritional needs.

*   *   *

There are no signs at this hour that the Army will move any time soon, yet, events could alter overnight. Its movements are dependent upon the enemy's, since it long ago surrendered its momentum to him. Gone are its days of the initiative - and our men know it.

"Early on, we was always attackin'," a Sergeant said to me this morning, "but the Army ain't got the men it used ta' and we cain't tolerate the kinda losses we used ta'. Wasted our people back then, we did. I know'd it then, but a sergeant ain't got no more say ta generals than a tic ta' elephants."

*   *   *

A Private confided to me today that he had read a letter from his wife a dozen times. Said he was destined to be promoted to Corporal and that his wife was proud of him. "But I ain't so sure I know what a Corporal's 'sposed ta do," he said. "Private Hanks used ta tell me 'bout things like that. Older fellow, he were, but he got hisself kilt last fight. Died right next ta' me. Jest kinda sunk real slow ta' the ground a'lookin' right at me. That bullet done went right through his heart and out his back. Heard it hit him and leave. Kinda thudded in and sucked out. All I do's think 'bout him, now since we ain't got no better ta' do...jest lay around and think a'him a lookin' at me the way he done, like he were a'tryin' ta' say good-bye but couldn't. Was a hard fight that day - real hard. M'wife's gonna be deliverin' a babe soon, ya know - says so right here. Worry 'bout her, though. She be but a wisp of a thing and plain too fragile."

*   *   *

Campfire smoke settles like mist across the landscape at dusk on quiet evenings like this. When evening's coolness seeps into one's bones, hot beverages drive it off. I sit with troops and sketch them as they talk and carry on. As often happens, singing erupts here and there. When conversations are interesting, I jot down notes in shorthand but seldom participate, usually spending my time listening and interpreting their moods. To me, the Army is a single being composed of the thousands of individual cells called "personalities." Its organs are its companies, regiments, and brigades. Like any being, its moods change daily. Some say I write too impersonally - that I do not record enough names. My defense is that I actually write about a single being - the Army, itself.

And now, I must close my eyes, for they tire when I jot in low light. I look forward to visiting doldrums of my own tonight. Sleep awaits me on calm seas where MY ship drifts alone in soothing mists. On its decks, welcome solace mercifully awaits, beckoning to me.

*   *   *

In the Beauty of the Lilies

**The Wartime Journals
of Confederate Correspondent
Royal K. Chapman
1862-1864**

Journal Eight

Contents

*   *   *

A Thought

Many fought who would otherwise
have known only nurturing and
tranquility.

Serene Repose

This war's strangeness comes home to me every now and then with special poignancy.

All morning, our brigade fought to wrest crucial earthworks from the enemy. These works fronted a sprawling woods behind which a paralleling road wound south and north, affording the enemy a ready route for resupply and reinforcement. The vicious fighting lasted for hours. We lost heavily but routed the enemy and drove him back across the road into the fields beyond. We took many prisoners and captured forty wagonloads of rations and ammunition - a bountiful harvest for our hungry and munitions-starved troops.

Walking along the battlefield afterwards, I noticed that our medical teams were already searching for the wounded among the dead. Carefully turning over bodies, they hoped to find many survivors. All along the line of earthworks, their efforts succeeded, as they separated the wounded from the dead and called for litters to carry the maimed to waiting ambulances. As customary, they lifted out our wounded first, leaving the enemy's for later or where they fell.

As I passed one team, I noticed how they opened the dead's jackets and shirts or rifled through their trouser pockets, searching personal effects for identities. Some bodies defied them, so foul were their mutilations. Among the piles of flesh brought down by rifle fire, one attracted an orderly's attention - a slight and diminutive form belonging to what one might have thought had been a young lad. I watched the orderly open the body's jacket. Finding nothing to identify it, he opened its shirt. Then, pulling way his hand in shock, he bolted upright and stood staring at the corpse.

"What is the matter?" I asked, as I walked over to him.

"That ain't no soldier," he responded, "that there be a woman!"

I looked down. A bloody breast lay exposed to the sun. The woman had been struck several times by minié-balls, yet her face had remained unmarred and appeared serenely reposed, her hair having been cut as a man's. Incredulous, another soldier walked over to observe the corpse.

"I heard a'this b'fore," he said, "but I ain't never seen it 'til now. Now, I b'lieve it."

Once the men had regained their composure, they self-consciously renewed their search for whatever might yield the woman's name and unit, carefully avoiding indecency - but found nothing.

"Ain't right," the soldier said. "Women don't b'long in this here business. I din't join-up t'see womenfolk gettin' kilt in uniform like menfolk. It ain't right!"

How tragic, I thought, that pending identification by comrades in her company, she might otherwise suffer anonymity in an unmarked grave - or be heaped in a hole with scores of other anonymous souls. Her spirit and patriotism deserved to be better rewarded, and I knew it would not sit well with burial teams to put her in with dead men. They would want to give her an individual burial with words said over her, whether or not her name was learned. And so it happened.

News of her discovery quickly spread, and soon the area became crowded with onlookers. Ultimately, a name was found...Jeremiah Hartly, the appellation she'd gone by, having disguised her gender with a male's name in a man's world. The obvious question arose: hadn't she had to share toilet and bath with her comrades in creeks and streams? How, they wondered, had her gender escaped detection? I was never to learn, and the revelation remained shocking to those with whom she had served. Where she stayed was never learned. Neither were the names of her kin.

Our regimental Chaplain, Major Otis Teague, presided over her burial later that day. We would never learn her true name but comforted ourselves that Jeremiah was as good as any other - as we would all remember her.

Said the Chaplain over her: "I never imagined that I would be tasked with burying a woman soldier. I cannot say that I am comfortable doing so, for it transgresses upon all convention and my deepest sense of propriety. Yet, we cannot deny her courage and the patriotism that motivated her truly magnificent charade. God bless her and give her peace in His Kingdom. Her fate will be as it has been for so many thousands of others who have gone for soldier, never to return home. May the Lord also lay His comforting hands upon those who will wait in vain for her return. We are proud of you Private Jeremiah Hartly. You will forever be one of us - and with us."

Three hundred strong, our regiment stood by in absolute silence, hard-pressed to reconcile this unusual but haunting event. They wanted to do more to honor her - believing they should - yet their pensive silence served as temple and monument.

We speak often of her these days and wonder how many more like her grace our Army's ranks in fields of both honor and anonymity - no doubt hundreds.

*   *   *

Wool Gatherings

When I think back to how bravely and enthusiastically our men and boys went to war, I want to weep. Vague images and sounds filter back - of comradeship and laughter, gaiety and confidence. How naively the young marched off to war, as if they thought war would be akin to attending a shivaree or a partridge hunt. And then, reality...

* * *

It is raining now. Cold and damp pervade everything. We huddle next to anemic camp fires in this additional year of war, absorbing their fading warmth as men starved for faith. Many are sick. Our thoughts turn inward, as always, to homes and hearths and to those no longer with us. We wonder where they are. Their bodies are in the ground, but where are their souls? This regiment's numbers have dwindled to but a small percentage of its original strength - and its survivors wonder when they, too, will step into the other's unseen ranks that beckon ever more.

* * *

I have prayed to God to show these men His mercy...but no reply. So many continue to be lost. Who, then, DID I pray to?

* * *

I watch our men clean their rifles. They work in silence and with meticulous care. A pall has fallen over all. No longer are their spirits high. They exist because they must, pledged to never abandon their nation's endeavor. The sun darts behind clouds. Shadows pass across the land. It is as if our boys already believe they belong to, and will soon be claimed by, eternity.

* * *

Fifes and drums play today. We are on the march again for the first time in weeks, and our boys glumly step in cadence with the drums - bedraggled and hungry. Their purpose is to see their obligation through and confront their fears with each step along with all the unknowns that daily stalk them. And they do so with stunning dignity. Who could not admire them?

*   *   *

We watch birds in flight and think of liberation - to fly away from this interminable drama. If only we were birds.

*   *   *

Our men stare at something unseen and far away only they perceive. It is not a normal look. Blank and otherwise nondescript, their expressions match their eyes. I see the look more and more. It comes before and deepens after every battle. More and more in bivouac, they go off to cocoon themselves in isolation - and cannot be distracted. Sometimes, they wander, trancelike, but cannot remember why. They are weary - deeply and profoundly weary.

*   *   *

We are boiling tea today. We make it from herbs our foragers have taken from the fields. We cannot say it is nourishing, but we pretend it is. It tastes neither bad nor good, but it is warm and we are damp and cold.

*   *   *

Today, a few surviving men of this company shared a bonanza - six broiled rabbits. And then they slept - as if they had never slept in their lives - their bellies, if not satiated, satisfied for the first time in weeks. We live each day on God's simplest charities and chance's most humble crumbs.

*   *   *

I am helping men pen letters home today. It is such a little favor to each, yet they thank me as if I have saved them and their families from extinction. How important the written word is to those who can neither write nor read. I have become a chaplain of sorts in a daily quest to preserve their links to the peace of the past.

*   *   *

How tenderly our men admire beauty - the trees in fall, the land in the bluish shadows of dusk, the serenity of its quiet moods, the brilliant firmament and the visual poetry that compliments all. In these moments, they are children again. One can see and feel their surviving innocence shine through despite their hardened and bearded exteriors. They are once more filled with childlike wonder. If they could, they would reach up and pull down the stars in obedience to their innocent curiosities and would sleep again in the security of their mothers' arms. And, if it were possible, they would forever wander the revitalized realms of their still youthful imaginations - where beautiful lilies still bloom.

*   *   *

Today, we watched a young soldier - a boy, really - die. Neither bullet nor bayonet nor piece of hot iron had felled him this day, not truly. He perished in his private search for manhood among veterans - assisted by an old wound he never reported because it was small. It became gangrenous. Still, in the midst of his feverish delirium, he apologized: "Guess I were too proud," he said, "and it kilt me." I supposed I, too, would have been as proud in the midst of so many mature veterans, had I been only fifteen.

*   *   *

One of our corporals produced a fiddle in bivouac today and astounded everyone with his musical acumen. Ten minutes after he began to play, at least twenty men were doing Irish jigs to the applause of onlookers. For a time, our ad hoc merriment dispelled the gloom overhanging all. Bless Corporal Freemantle T. Samuels. He did more for our spirits and cheer than could all the nectar in a backwoods distillery. Of course, a little back woods "joy" would have added immeasurably to our appreciation of his sterling performance, if by then we could have remembered it.

*   *   *

Our men sleep none too well at night and often not at all. Many, with painful joints, labor to walk. The cold has settled into their bones. At times, it affects their jaws and teeth. Occasionally, their hands become too stiff and sore to handle their rifles. Several in our company have also been jaundiced for days. All are weak and skinny and hardly able to function. And almost all of our personnel are abused by ailments of varying descriptions, which I believe derive from malnutrition. I cannot understand how our men are expected to function, given their pathetic diets. Most have bleeding gums and anemia. Considering what they suffer, what they do and accomplish borders on the superhuman. Some have been forced to shave their considerable beards because of irritating rashes, skin sores, and lice beneath. Dysentery guts many. What drives them on, God only knows. Call it devotion.

*   *   *

Sun and warmth today. We luxuriate in it. It has come at a time most needed. Men awoke this morning expecting continuing rain and more ruinous dampness, but their spirits quickly improved as they realized they would see sunlight again - which has been absent for days. Its warmth has proved a tonic, having rejuvenated our ranks and given men hope that they will somehow survive their miseries great and small. For the time being, pessimists are transformed. Even now, scores of troops, bare to the waist, refresh themselves beneath the sunlight and dry out. It is a reconstituting sight - a good thing.

* * *

Ration wagons came by this morning, turning our encampments festive. Now, we have good salt pork, beans, lard, sorghum, and potatoes. Also yams and some wilted vegetables - most items procured from local farms - though I hope not at gunpoint. Some of our desperate troops have been as hard on our own citizens as our enemy - and have engendered our people's wrath. It is hunger that drives them - and contempt for our government's self-absorbed bureaucracy that cares nothing for their needs. Some men angrily speak of marching on Richmond and forcing the issue. I doubt they will, but who could blame them? If it were to happen, the retributions they would render would be harsh.

* * *

Our ammunition ran short today. Engaged as we were in a stiff exchange with enemy forces, who charged us repeatedly, our boys quickly depleted their cartridge boxes. Some, who had stuffed their pockets with spare cartridges, fared well, holding off the enemy with accurate shooting, but we were forced in the end to give ground - or throw rocks. We left upwards of a hundred dead and wounded on the field in our regiment's section of the line - our wounded left to our adversaries' mercies. We trust they will honor our dead and care for our maimed as well as they care for their own, usual priorities being accepted.

* * *

I found a Bible on the battlefield this morning. We had reclaimed all the ground we lost yesterday, but this Bible belonged to one of our enemy - Private James Talmadge from New Hampshire. Not knowing if he had died on the field, I arranged with our regimental commander to return the Bible to the other side. We sent out a messenger under a flag of truce, and, accompanied by our regimental padre, Chaplain Blaine, he took the Bible to enemy lines directly to our front. Both men hastened back, saying they had been well received and that Private Talmadge was alive and thankful for its return, the Good Book having belonged to his grandfather in the War of 1812. If only we could have just as easily arranged a cease-fire, we might all have met between the lines, put down our weapons and acted like common countrymen again - despite our generals.

* * *

Rain again. Began just after dawn. By noon, we were swimming in a continuing deluge. Not all our men were under tents, for there are not enough for everyone. But it was a warm rain. Curiously, our men have more regard for protecting their rifles from the wet than covering themselves. I sat in the open on a felled tree, my ankle-length rain cape soaked, water pouring from my broad-brimmed hat, my bulky journals beneath the cape. The rain's seductive patter submerged me in mesmerizing isolation, lulling me to sleep. If only I had dared to lie down on the wet earth to slumber for a century. How good it might have felt.

* * *

Out of fresh pencils. Have whittled mine down to the nub.

* * *

Chaplain Lawrence Oaks was wounded today. A major, he had come to the front line to bless the fallen but was struck in the left side of the head by a spent minié-ball. The ball took away a chunk of skull, and he is suffering severely. The surgeons say infection will doom him, as the brain is exposed, swollen, and festering. He is semiconscious and constantly babbles. We feel helpless to assist him. Though we pray for him, the good Chaplain will see Paradise by evening unless the Lord works a miracle. That He would take even one of His dedicated own has left our men seriously doubting that religious devotion will spare any of THEM!

* * *

It appears the war will never end. We are constantly on the move doing the enemy's bidding and fighting where HE chooses to fight. Our men feel powerless to change matters. Morale is low. Early on, we fought the war on OUR terms. But this is no good and nothing favorable can come of it. It is a formula for defeat - and our boys sense it.

* * *

Shoes - Lord, how our Army needs shoes. We are becoming a bare-footed legion. As a result, our movements are inhibited. We cannot maneuver over great distances with the speed necessary to gain advantages of time and ground. Shoeless men must move cautiously through woods and fields, often suffering excruciating lacerations and punctures. Scores fall out every hour. We call ourselves the "Hobbling Corps." On the march, many wrap their feet in rags, having no choice but to go into battle so adorned - those still able to walk. Losses to foot problems have depleted many companys' ranks, nearly exceeding their battle casualties. Once again, our government ignores our plight. Its neglect is unconscionable and, as always, its dedicated soldiers pay most dearly even while charitably praying for Richmond's enlightenment. Eventually, there must be a reckoning, whether it comes after victory or defeat. Yet, I fear that defeat will result in such a universal numbing of our ruined nation's soul, that the memory of all such hardships will simply merge and vanish into a vast sea of paralyzing regret and decades-long exhaustion.

* * *

Four ragamuffins wandered into our bivouac yesterday - from where I do not know - three boys and a little girl - all emaciated and gaunt. Our hearts went out to all. Lord, what have we done to our children? What have we caused them? Our men, who have youngins' at home, took them in with loving care. We gave them what vittles we had on hand, and they ate ravenously, save for one - the smallest, a little girl named Esther Humes, 4. She simply knelt down and stared at her fare. Her demeanor chilled us all. It was plain - she was rapidly diminishing and would not long survive. But we resolved that she would, and the fathers among us took her under their paternal wings. They boiled her tea and made her a bean broth with bits of fatback. Fortunately, they persuaded her to sip the tea and let them spoon-feed her the broth - and they prayed. She shivered mightily in her ravaged clothing that barely covered her tiny frame. We wrapped her in blankets during the night and ensured that she and her brothers slept near one of our largest campfires. Robed in her warm coverings, she awakened this morning hungry but in much better fettle. We have received our commanding officer's permission to keep the children with us until we march out. Our little Esther will not perish. We will leave her and her brothers, Hosea, 8, Custis, 7, and Andrew, 5, in the care of one of our Chaplains, Father Joseph Michaels. A local congregation will eventually look after them. The boys have told us they were orphaned a month ago and have been living off the land ever since. Their parents died, they said, of hunger and fever. But we know better - they died of this damned war.

* * *

A cavalry patrol came through camp this afternoon. The cavalrymen and their horses were a mud-covered sight. We fixed them up with food and drink - what little there was of it - and watered, curried, and blanketed their horses. They thanked us profusely and said they had been patrolling for three days and that their horses were spent, as was evident. They had sighted the enemy fifteen miles away and moving in our direction - tidings not well received. It means we will fight tomorrow. It haunts to watch men mentally prepare themselves to leave this Earth. This regiment and brigade have fallen silent as the word spreads. Hundreds will sleep little tonight, if at all. Hundreds more are at prayer.

* * *

Firebrands and Fools

Many of our men are sick.

Some can hardly stand, but they insist on remaining in ranks and refuse medical attention, such as it is - and it is not good. Our physicians are generally at a loss to account for illnesses, let alone cure them, and guess about much of what they prescribe.

Men drop, their strength gone. Some die. No day passes without our ranks being thinned by those carried to hospital or to graves. It's devastating to watch them being put under. Our boys believe it is one thing to die of wounds nobly suffered in battle - a sacrifice made for something - but a waste to perish of random maladies neither understood nor curable.

Being distrustful of often contemptuous of physicians, many hide their afflictions for as long as possible while trying to overcome them in time. But we often find them in their tents or off by themselves where they've gone privately to recuperate...or die. Once gripped by the fever and sweats or by deteriorating muscles and bones or by digestive tortures, they anticipate their fate.

Bad food, meager rations, malnutrition - all prepare a man for illness. Dysentery is the greatest killer. Striking without warning, it almost always assures one's death. Its mortifying effects ravage not only the body but its victims' sensibilities. Men appear fine one instant, then unexpectedly evacuate their bowels the next, wracked by excruciating intestinal spasms. Soldiers say the pain is sometimes greater than being shot.

I have witnessed diseased men pound the earth with embarrassment and seething frustration. Disease is an enemy from Perdition they cannot fight.

The pathetic state of our medicine and its capabilities is criminal. Hack and saw is what it does best, too often with fatal results. Infections stupefy our physicians. We have sacrificed thousands to the earth who suffered not from wounds but from medicine's incompetence - though I concede that our medical staff are capable of working only with what they know. It is their infant science, not their intent that defeats them. Our enemy's medicine is no better.

Both sides have yet to realize that governments should not commit their blood to battle without assuring it the means to effectively attend its needs. Until then, high crimes and misdemeanors will not be the sole province of traitors - but also of firebrands and fools safely away from the holocausts they ignite.

God pity them.

* * *

A Pause for Relief

Our column was halted to allow our troops to relieve themselves in the convenience of the woods. Leaving rifles, knapsacks, and bedrolls on the road, most repaired to the privacy of the trees, while others relieved themselves along the roadside.

I am always impressed by how casually men surrender all social graces in war. They become creatures of common habit and near absolute immodesty, all of them prisoners of circumstance. The shy and modest soon are forced to abandon civilian conventions and meld with the common seas of the new human conditions that submerge them. Choice assumes no free dominion - opportunity commands. Like minnows caught by tides, they are swept along by gigantic forces controlling all. And they must feed on opportunity, lest they suffer greater privation.

Despite all, privation is their reward. It comes in many physical forms, yet its spiritual dimensions are oft overlooked even by laymen journalists. These are subtle considerations of mind and soul colored by the bondage of uniforms, orders, and duty. Soldiers are netted spirits who cannot swim beyond their commitments to cause and country. They fear to try, lest they be condemned and punished. Such restraints also contribute to their premature aging and physical reduction.

No, war is not an easy business save for the most callous and insensitive. And, given time, it reduces many, even the well-meaning, to those states, as their consciences rebel, recriminate and chastise them, especially if they have killed. Such men sometimes put down their arms and walk forever away, as if told by angels that they must or perish within.

Yesterday, in skirting the grounds of an outdoor field hospital, I passed a shanty used by surgeons as an operating theater. Heaped outside its only window were amputated arms, legs, feet, and hands. Some had lain there for days. Swarms of flies and armies of maggots attacked every area of flesh. The stench gagged me. Amputees, many without one or more limbs, suffered nearby, lying on the ground or on mats in grotesque contortions, some back to back, others face to face, moaning and whimpering, some crying out in their delirium. Many of the ruined were very young, never to be normal again.

Some poor souls, as maimed within as without, reached out to me, their minds obviously confused. Feeling helpless, I gave them water. Some thanked me for it and lay back, some quietly, some babbling, some to wretchedly perish. Yet these conditions, as during our war with Mexico, were what I anticipated. Still, to have them come alive again in fact amounted to reliving all, a painful reality, dormant specters of all I had relegated to memory's backwaters come back to life. It was a hard day - a very hard day.

*   *   *

Contemplations

Rain persuades me to think, which one in war should never do. Today is case in point. Even now, the entire brigade shelters from the present downpour. I fight the rain's soporific seductions, afraid to let myself sleep, lest my ruinous fatigue prevents me from awakening. Instead, I observe the men around me and consider how unfair it is that all will eventually be lost to time - that all who sleep or busy themselves at this hour by the hundreds will one day be no more, whether they die in battle or in bed of old age - as if they never existed.

And what will have been the contribution of their lives to the world then? What use will they have been to the universe and what will their existences have meant? When one thinks in this manner, the world closes in, trapping one within an inescapable box. It is better to sleep and not to think at all - even if only for a week or two - even if one never awakens.

$$* \quad * \quad *$$

"It is cruel that those of meaning to us are taken away by death," said Regimental Chaplain Willard Cox to me yesterday, during our discussion about the lives the war has claimed thus far. "That we cannot keep those we love most, as these men would wish to keep them, appears unfair and unjust, for we could be viewed as pawns in a game not of our making and - in that sense - innocent victims. And yet, many, if not most on both sides volunteered, no matter their reasons. In so doing, they endorsed and perpetuated the very thing that might claim them and already has claimed thousands. The Lord gave them the free will to choose for themselves whether or not to do so, even wrongly. In THAT sense, none of us are innocent. And as difficult as it might have been to do so, all us us could have said no to the politicians - in the Lord's name, despite our enemy's sins,"

But what of the youngest among us, I asked, those who still were children and too young to have truly understood? Who initially spoke for and protected them? "Unfortunately," he admitted, "no one."

$$* \quad * \quad *$$

"We live only for the time given us by the nature of our bodies," said Chaplain Sean Donovan, during a Sunday field Mass. "All men's faces are clocks that record and tick away time's passage with only so many hours painted upon each. Some believe it is a shame that we cannot go with those we love into Eternity. But we CAN, you see - and we do, at our given times. Unfortunately, some men preempt their times, and go by their own hands, thinking it is the ONLY way, as did that poor private yesterday who received word that his wife and child had died of fever. In his case, I am certain the Lord will be merciful - that the soldier will not be punished."

*   *   *

"I am one who resents the natural order of things," Infantry Captain Terrance Bennett explained to me. "The war's made me resent the conditions of life on this Earth that insult one's intelligence with such perversity as does this war. I am a civilian surveyor, now in my country's service, but not a professional soldier. I fight because our enemies lay waste to our land, yet I resent that I am helpless to change things. And, although I cannot abide this historical injustice in God's apparent plan for America, I am without other choices. I should be disgusted with all the powers on both sides for choosing war as a means of settling their disputes, and myself, in concert with countless thousands, for enabling them, but one man's protesting voice can hardly silence the unthinking cannon of warring peoples or bind their bloody passions."

*   *   *

"The war's made me a Deist," confessed an Artillery officer and college graduate. "As much as I might assign God's nonintervention in this struggle to man's folly in denying Him, I fear that in His aloofness, He is a father estranged from his children and no longer compassionately drawn to them. I see no Divine love mercifully inhibiting this war - none in any comprehensible sense. Yet, it appears He is contravening His own Creed - unless it is His purpose for us to see a perverse reflection of ourselves by allowing us to struggle like fawns lost in a gator infested bayou. Please forgive my blasphemy. It's the war, and I am tired. Neither my life nor my education prepared me for dealing with all of the theological contradictions this war has illuminated for me. I now believe that life is a mere machine. Its Creator throws a lever, the machine functions, and He walks away - to let it run as He's willed it to while judging our means for coping with it. Perhaps, He has done so as well with other races throughout Creation, perpetuating only the fittest. Perhaps, throughout Creation, life after all is actually without theological foundation but is simply a function of soulless happenstance, though our coincidental but prideful intelligence refuses to accept it for what it is."

*   *   *

An overworked and malnourished horse nearby stands sleeping on its feet, as do half our men on this present march, looking just as rickety and God-forsaken. I feel endless compassion for it, and the purity of its innocence. It asks for nothing, begs for nothing and complains not. Its humility shames me, prompting me to wonder which, man or beast, is truly the most spiritually advanced?

*   *   *

Soldiers tell me that, more and more, their memories revert to their youth. They "recollect" as if those times had just occurred. I wonder if their apparent blurring of reality occurs because the war has forced them to grow so much older spiritually - or because their retrospectives are the mind's way of relieving the stress of their constant fear. Whatever the truth, they appear eager to reach out to the past, as if seeking sanctuary in old and familiar temples of peace, while at the same time cherishing those halcyon days of purity in thought and deed - when they innocently comprehended the world and existence. Sadly, too brief were those times - much to brief, when measured against their war-jaded maturity.

A Corporal said to me, "Ever' step I took since joinin' up's been a wanderer's journey to find a purpose t'my life. But I ain't found nothin' that's meant more to me than m'early days when ever'thin' meant most. How come only afterwards do yer youth haunt ya agin' in yer heart when there ain't a damn thing y'ken do about it 'cept regret that ya cain't?"

*   *   *

Today, a young soldier gave me a locket to keep for him lest he lose it in battle or, if he dies, that it be stolen by others and never recovered. In one half of it, a sympathetic rendering of his sweetheart gazes dolefully at the viewer. The inscription in the other half says, "Forget me not that I may never forget you." We go into battle later today. Pray God that I do not have to send it to her with word of his passing. I would give my all to prevent that. Both are, as yet, unsullied by life and fresh upon the world. I am not, not hardly.

*   *   *

Rain has just ended. I watch them bring back the dead this evening - the cold and stiffening dead. One face remains so incredibly serene and peaceful in its rigor, and so without scratch or blemish that I find it impossible to believe it belongs to a dead lad. Where is he now, I wonder - amongst us, invisibly looking on? Are they all here, staring at themselves while awaiting passage to Forever. I know not why I feel they are, but the sensation asserts itself and leaves me chilled, especially when I notice many footprints in the mud around me. This is odd, since I have only just freshly occupied this spot after the rain and haven't moved. The mystery obsesses me.

*   *   *

I passed by an officer's tent this morning and spied a mirror hanging on a pole outside the tent flap. The officer was absent but the mirror intrigued me. I had not seen one in months and had forgotten they existed. Despairing of coming too close, I feared I might discover that my image was not as I remembered it. Yet, I could not resist the temptation to see what the war had done to the countenance I used to possess. It was as I feared. A stranger stared back -bearded and sullen, its eyes sunken with fatigue, the lines around them etched deeply in grime, the beard needing trimming and care and harboring lint. And when the image removed its hat, I discovered a graying, thinning mane. Studying the image, whilst remembering who it used to be, I wondered if I truly knew it anymore. It could not have been me, but a ghostly imposter instead, for it had aged too thoroughly. Yet the truth remained indelibly obvious. But how would it appear by war's end? What would lie behind the eyes then - and who would I be? "Let me not see a mirror again," I pleaded with the Lord. "Let me live in blessed ignorance of myself."

* * *

Another young private came to me today with a request I was duty-bound to honor. Not surprisingly, he asked if I would write a letter home to his mother whom he had not seen since enlisting a year ago. His story mirrored those of countless others. He said that neither he nor she could read nor write, but that certain family members could and at least one of them would be moved to read the letter to his mother and reply for her. Despairing, he said he had received no word from her in months. For me, well, I cannot recall the number of times I have performed this service for the very same reasons.

As I have mentioned elsewhere, it is common that literate men in ranks read and write letters for those who cannot. And when mail arrives in volume after long intervals, many of our illiterate troops, feeling self-conscious about revealing their ignorance, simply stash their unanswered letters away where they accumulate for months. When the boy dictated his thoughts to me, I realized that he, like so many others, could not express himself as well as he deserved. I spoke at length with him about himself, his family, his mother, and his home. And, as is my custom, I asked him to return later, after I had collected his thoughts and written them down in appropriate order. Fortunately, we were bivouacked and not due for immediate action.

When he eventually returned, I cautiously read him what I had written. He listened intently, overwhelmed that his innermost sentiments had actually been put to paper. He proposed to repay me with a token of his "thanks" - his St. Christopher medallion. Though I diplomatically declined it, he begged me to honor him by taking it, which I did, reluctantly. I explained that is has never been my intention to "sell" my services. He said he did not see it that way. Only then did he admit to me, as have so many others, that he was underage – sixteen - and a veteran of two grueling campaigns - another sixteen year-old who looked thirty.

I posted the letter for him in our regimental mail an hour later. But, as usual, I could not rid myself of that former moment's poignancy, worried that battlefield horrors would eventually wash away his innocence and warp it with realties too brutal to be resisted. He had thanked me profusely, not having been the first boy-veteran to call me a "magician" - and stared at me through that same glowing ember of boyish incorruption. I, too, benefited from his letter, for it sustained me to know the purity of what still survived in his young soldier's heart. Pity his mother, though! Like so many others, he admitted, he, too, had sneaked away from home and her gentle care to join-up without her knowledge. How Hellish her days must have been and

remain. Again I cry - how, in God's name, did the Army ever permit the enlistment of one so young? Someone conscientiously in charge, justify it to me.

*   *   *

This afternoon, I happened upon the brigade's commanding Colonel. With his staff around him, he studied the terrain to the brigade's front and dictated notes to one of them. Anticipating an enemy assault, the Brigade labored to build strong earthworks. He saw me looking on and motioned me over. "Our friends out there will come through here," he said. "We've been ordered to hold this position. You will have a hot time to write about before sunset."

Indeed I would. We held, but barely. The air still reeks with pungent gunpowder smoke. The ground beyond the works is carpeted with their dead. The ground on this side is strewn with ours. Only hours ago, I had chicory in bivouac with several now dead. Now, I stand over their remains, mortified and empty. This is beyond tolerating. When, Lord, will it ever end?

*   *   *

Today, I watched in horror as soldier slithered back from the battlefield, his feet gone and bleeding heavily from his stumps. I offered to assist him but he refused, crying out that he aimed to die on his knees before God, seeking forgiveness for his wartime sins. He crawled a few more yards before settling on his stomach and expiring, his body having bled out, with his hand tightly clutching a pewter cross on a chain around his neck.

I could not take my eyes from him. His humbling death should have evoked strong emotions in me but did not. My soul's numbness makes me wonder who I've become.

*   *   *

Memory, of late, fails me. I do not know why. I put items away and forget them in the next instant. I cannot remember names. My mind craves ever more sleep, but I get little that is restful. I write but lose my thoughts. Details escape me and I can no longer look with a journalist's detachment upon war's hideous guises without my senses rebelling. My purpose has become repugnant to me, and I fear that on each new day I will discover other lapses of mind. Yet I have seen these impairments affect soldiers when war too brutally insults their spiritual cores. Perhaps it now has overwhelmed mine. When will mine cry, "Enough!"...and shut me down as the mind has shut down others and made them blanks. We will see. Repugnancy and soulful burdens aside, I must play my role as do these stoic souls around me, who have committed their daily lives to possible destruction. They manage. So must I.

*   *   *

It is well into Spring yet to the regiment's delight a heavy snow has fallen today. Hundreds have cast their personal burdens aside to engage in snowball-fighting. It has been sheer hilarity - slipping, sliding, falling, charging, attacking, and snow fort-building. Their laughter carries

263

across the landscape as they play with childhood abandon. No physician could have prescribed a better medicine. Even our commanding and company officers are fully engaged - and I am covered with snowball strikes in this amazing free-for-all. I have paused only to pencil-jot these notes, yet, I am being assaulted a third time. What joy! I am ten again! Contemplate that, my gloom-blotted journal! Today, the lilies are fresh and renewed.

* * *

Sympathetically

I sometimes wonder if there is anything more I can write about this war, save to minutely describe battle. So much of a soldier's life is boredom wrapped in routine and repetition. During battle, a soldier's senses heighten to their utmost. No matter how fatigued or hungry he might have been beforehand, he becomes a different animal when his heart races and pumps blood through his system at incredible rates, and his senses become supernaturally charged as tentacles of fire reach out to embrace and crush him. His life hangs on slender threads of fear.

It is after battle, if he survives unwounded, that he often collapses, drained of all energy. He craves water and sleep in prodigious amounts. His body becomes so heavy its weight is burdensome and he moves sluggishly, even aimlessly. Frequently the march to bivouac is a trek of the mindless. One foot instinctually falls before the other, as the brain demands to shut down, to escape in sleep the horror it remembers. Men arrive at bivouac and drop in clusters. It matters not where, for they believe they cannot go on. Even then, despite their exhaustion, an unfortunate few, who must suddenly summon new strength, are assigned to dreaded sentry or picket duty and must overcome or be punished.

This morning, though still spent, those who awakened prematurely watched dawn's rebirth. Some had prepared meager breakfasts. Several units, still half asleep, already were on the march, admiring a sky full of colors not usually associated with sunrises - pinks, golds, and silvers touched by turquoise. Yet, they would not only remember the sunrise, but also the strangely calming aura pervading that morning.

Because the brigade would recommit itself to battle before noon, the worshipful absorbed the sight, knowing they might never see another, let alone another so spectacular. I was struck by the kindness and sympathy with which they treated each other. And when the entire encampment had prepared for the day's work, that deference continued. Never had I experienced anything so generally poignant, as if all reverentially expected appointments with the Eternal.

Being especially courteous to and deferential with each other, they appeared to cast away all personal differences - overcome by a spiritual metamorphosis. From lieutenant to private, from veteran to virgin newcomer, the Lord appeared to have touched all. Never, I suppose, had they so profoundly sensed their collective mortality.

How prescient they were. That afternoon, forty-two of the ninety-six in that company went, everlastingly, Home.

* * *

265

Food for Thought

These days, "thought" is the closest our troops come to food.

Many times, my belly pains and groans along with theirs for want of even the most meager morsel, forcing me to seriously consider why they fight on when sanity dictates that they should go directly home and eat.

Of late we scratch for berries and anything that can be mixed with bits of lard and hardtack to make a mush of sorts. Occasionally, a rabbit is caught or a possum, squirrel or coon, making it a rare feast that must be shared among as many as possible. Even then, the individual soldier hardly consumes enough to allow for more than a few small bites. It is not uncommon for us to imbibe in "grass stew" and "teas" concocted from unnamed and often unfamiliar greenery.

We are constantly scavenging. Haversack patrols are sent out hourly in all directions in hopes of finding anything eatable. I scavenge for mine. Rations have long since ceased to be distributed because, says the Army, they no longer are regularly available, but few believe it. They suspect they're holed up on rail sidings somewhere, rotting in sun-baked boxcars because bureaucrats have got things in a terrible fix. So, we scrounge woods and farms, sometimes begging off farm folk and civilians in general. Some are forthcoming, some even generously so. Others are no better off than our boys.

Though our troop's physical conditions are appalling, those of the children hereabouts are worse.

We have bivouacked here for nearly a week. Many times, little ones come to us from the wilderness, their bellies distended, their faces gaunt with hunger, sunken eyes radiating desperation. We give them what we can. Many of our hungry go even hungrier in deference to these tiny beggars. Such sacrifice is valorous, for these souls fight tyrannical instincts when they deny themselves even meager rations for the children's sakes. If only our well-fed enemies knew HOW valorous.

Many of our troops are weak and sick from malnutrition. Sores and cankers have broken out on their faces, in their mouths and on their bodies. Some resort to boiling leather. When, it becomes soft enough to chew, it briefly fools their stomachs and abates their hunger. Others gnaw bark. Our enemies have so devastated the countryside that few crops have survived destruction. What they do not steal, they burn. However, from furrows on these sites, our men extract unburned or parched corn ears or kernels and chew or boil them. Corn's restorative powers are remarkable. Many soldiers, whose pockets hide corn, consider themselves well-off. Sometimes, enough can be salvaged to be generously shared.

Do not think that our officers eat better than their men. Often, they eat less, preferring to feed their men before themselves. Such officers are indescribably respected.

Soldiers have asked me why I stay with the Army - why I do not leave for civilian climes where good food and myriad human comforts still are available. I reply that although I am not an official and accredited reporter or journalist, what I do nonetheless demands that I, like my true brethren, remain, for how else are future times to be informed of this war's course? Yet in many cases we are despised by generals, who consider us traitors for allegedly being supreme egotists who seek personal aggrandizement and career enhancement at the military's expense. Unfortunately, it has been the case with others, leaving those of us who remain true to live down a Bohemian reputation that often does us a crippling disservice. All we can do is remain loyal to our convictions and thereby prove to all that our profession is not without honor.

In the meantime I, and those about whom I write, occupy idle hours by chasing lice and ticks off ourselves, and holding contests to see who can incarcerate the greatest numbers. We imagine ourselves to be hooting monkeys, picking the vermin out of each other's hair. The men call them "graybacks." Yet, even as grimly as I have described it, our food situation is still not so bad that we have considered making them a feast. Fruit is what we crave to stave off scurvy and the ulcerations that plague so many men, but again, there is little to be had. That so many underfed men are able to trek vast distances at all beggars the mind, though some fall out along the way and must be left behind.

This war has become a hardship beyond all predictions. If only those who wanted it were now in ranks. How absurd their bombastic hyperbole sounds to our veterans. No, they are safe at home behind their wives' many-layered skirts. It has fallen to the common men - the ordinary soldiers, that segment of our people who had the least to gain from it but the most to lose - to bear the brunt of their war-makers' "valor." But isn't it always thus in war?

We march again tomorrow morning - those who can.

* * *

Painin' Bellies - Our Scarecrow Army

Hunger's gnawing effects are unforgettable.

Our boys go for days without much to eat. They grow weak, sometimes too weak to stay awake and march. They must bring strength from deep within themselves to stay apace, to keep themselves from falling out on the march or collapsing in place. Because they strain with nothing substantial to nourish themselves, their legs respond unsurely. Sometimes, because they do not want to fall away and leave friends to assume their share, they drag themselves along with supernatural effort.

Loyal to each other to a fault, they seek no personal advantages, though they vehemently complain about conditions while often stopping self-consciously short of blaming the Army and government for their plight. But that changes when their situations do not improve over time. They suspect that no one cares - that the government, especially, is taking them and the entire Army for granted because the military is doing heroic things on empty bellies despite all. When conditions are cruel, which is most of the time, they see no reason for the Army's supply problems being as severe as reported - proffering that some of their parochial governors are as good as traitors for holding back all that is in their warehouses or rotting in idled rail cars.

More than once, I have seen men in battle, their energies gone, loading and firing their weapons as if sleepwalking. Some are so dissipated that they have difficulty lifting their rifles more than a half-dozen times. But they do their duty. Somewhere they find the will and resolve to persevere.

They share whatever meager vittles they collect. And when those are gone, they forage together and pass along whatever else they find. These veterans, who have seen the Elephant so many times, should be eternally honored.

It is hard for them to sleep with bellies "painin'" and gnawing at their backbones. Some double-up with spasms. Others chew on sticks or bark or leather or munch on grass or weed stalks or fill-up on water to fool their bellies. Some press their bellies - or cinch belts tightly around their middles - to suppress their pain. Others moan in their sleep, as if dreaming of home and food-laden tables. Many are afraid to awaken because there is nothing eatable to awaken to. Sleep salves their painin' bellies. Sometimes, they dream they've arrived in special land in which they soar like birds free of war, the Army and the world itself. They relate that people sometimes come to them there to speak about that place and what it means, and they awaken remembering that it was a sweet realm they could not bear to leave.

But the war goes on. And many become so emaciated they CANNOT go on - and they cry like babies when lifted onto litters for hospital because they believe they are deserting their friends and duty. They demand to fight to the end no matter how long the war lasts, but they cannot be kept in ranks. Our officers - some as sick as their troops - regret having to let only the sickest go, when so many others are nearly as unfit.

Yet, I have never heard of any officer who has sneaked food somewhere without sharing it with his men - or who has not contributed it to a general larder for rationing to all. Most are deeply respected for suffering with the rest. They desire that the worst of their cases to go home, especially the youngest, who should never have been recruited in the first place. For these are always the first to weaken, grow sick - and perish.

Our conditions are depressing even to our older veteran soldiers who constantly reflect on their children's possible destitution at home. And it is equally depressing for them to know that we are so outnumbered by an enemy who is well-fed and fat on everything he needs, including and increasingly on Southern bounty. But our boys hope for miracles and by and large remain stubbornly dedicated to their work. Our adversaries know it and prefer not to close with them more then necessary, for hunger breeds a bitter desperation that translates into a fighting fury. They also prefer to stay in their holes and trenches, hoping the war will end before more of their own must die. Every time they have tried to overrun our positions great numbers have failed to return to their lines.

Yet some of our boys, sick of the killing, have spiritually withered. When they fire, they close their eyes. Sometimes, I close mine and refuse to watch. Minié-balls do savage damage to tissue and bone and to souls on both sides.

We immediately relieve prisoners of whatever rations they possess - even before we "requisition" their shoes, clothing, weapons, and ammunition. Many enemy troops tote haversacks filled with abundant vittles, which enrage our boys against our government. The air sizzles as they curse our political leaders, generals, the President, and the entire system. Even some of our sickest boys protest by refusing hospital, declaring that if they can stand, they will fight. The enemy becomes the symbol of that high-level "treason" and the target of their suppressed rage.

Next to be "borrowed" are ointments or elixirs for treating torturing foot and body sores and mouth cankers caused by malnutrition. Fruit is highly prized, vitally needed and often carried by the enemy. Our boys are sorely tempted to immediately devour all they find but are restrained by their officers, even as bellies growl and churn into twisted knots. The fruit is then shared to its limits.

Many men have grown proficient in consuming insects, and detecting which are good and which are not. Ants and grasshoppers are standard fare. Some boys also hunt rats, which roast up well - if a man is hungry enough, and has the stomach for it. I do not yet. Some say the rodents are stringy. But more than one man has become deathly sick after eating rat meat and violently vomit out every last piece - an excruciating ordeal for bellies already tender and raw.

Some boys sit down whenever they can and fall right off to sleep, saving their remaining strength. It becomes an involuntarily ritual. All are scarecrows who grow more emaciated everyday. Yet, most still shoot and keep the enemy's heads down. These days, nearly the entire Army remains on the defensive. Sometimes, our troops are too weak to go on the attack - and we must spare our dwindling manpower reserves to every extent. All know that to do otherwise is a sure recipe for defeat.

Dogs are no longer safe, and there are no more mascots in our lines, though some terrible rows arise between those who have never eaten pets and those who think it right to "roast 'em up." I have witnessed dozens of discontented soldiers who, over this very sensitive issue, have nearly killed each other. Many have to be carted to hospital with damaged teeth, closed-up eyes, ears ripped, lips bashed, facial bones broken, noses smashed, skulls cracked and innards ruptured. It is shameful when hungry men turn their desperation on each other. Those, who refuse to eat mongrels that drift into our lines boil-up grasses or bug soup instead. It grows even more common for our troops to thieve from our civilian population (which, anymore, has little of its own to donate) - from smokehouses, fruit cellars, larders, and barnyards. Stolen are goats, chickens, pigs, even mules, which are hauled away to bivouacs, butchered, and roasted. Many civilians resist, firing on our poachers, equally desperate to maintain their families against all calamities. Such are the dregs into which our fortunes have sunk. I do not exaggerate, though I am not suggesting that the conditions of our entire army can be so described, for they cannot. One must consider individual regiments and brigades instead, and their peculiar situations. Yet, to one extent or the other, our Army suffers greatly.

Though I have resisted revealing these facts to date, I do so now only because they have become too much a part of our war to ignore. We have victimized our own people because our Army never deserved to be so deprived by its own government's inept and incompetent planning and organization. It went to war like a child whose suppertime eyes were bigger than his stomach. It is such deprivation that has forced individual units to resort to extremes. Who cannot appreciate the bewilderment of our civilians facing predation by both sides! Our men are furious with Richmond. Nothing has been more devastating to their pride and consciences. None of us will forget these hard times nor our "painin'" bellies, nor the nobility of our officers who have tried - with reason and restraint - to set examples of stoical courage by their refusal to submit to desperate conditions. These noble men, also reduced from privations as acute as their troop's, have governed themselves with dignity and treated their charges with unselfishness and diplomacy.

After this war, win or lose, there must come a reckoning with the powers that be. I should not wish to be a politician, nor a leader of whatever station, guilty of having deprived our troops in the field of vital necessities available all the while.

God help them and all such miscreants.

*   *   *

Poignant Matters

Held a doomed boy's hand today. He'd been wounded earlier in the week - a bullet to his guts - and he passed in hospital as I spoke to him.

He had asked me to tell him about the trees on the hospital grounds. I did so because he said he loved trees. Just before the end his delirium abated and he became momentarily lucid. He said, reaching out to me and looking at the ceiling; "See them big white beauties in that garden there... look like lilies, don't they? Ain't they be the most whitest you ever did see? A girl be there...she's a'wearin' a pretty white gown. It be a'flowin' 'round her, like a gentle breeze's blowin'...garden smells so pure...air's so bright - like there be light comin' from all around and from ever'thin'in it. Neva' see'd colors like it b'fore...no word for 'em. She's a'motionin' me to come ova' to her, now...so pretty, she be - like an angel. Never know'd an angel like her b'fore. Guess I'll be a'goin' now...she's a'tellin' me it be my time..."

And it was.

* * *

I watched some of our boys share tobacco today - chaws broken off from stick of rich burly. It amazes how they discuss the fine points of "chewin'" while cramming their mouths so full. Their speech alters and their lips leak brown juice. Squirrels with bulging mouthfuls of acorns have nothing on these fellows. I tried a chunk one day and got too sick to live. Yet these boys chewed and spit and chewed and spit 'til the light faded. Got an education listening to them explain the fine points of growing this kind of tobacco and that. I'm still unconvinced that tobacco's for anything but burning. And I'm still wondering whether they chew for the enjoyment of it - or the spittin'.

* * *

One of our youngest soldiers caught a rabbit today - actually, a bunny - a cute, furry little critter. Said he thought he'd make a pet of it. But when the older men started describing in bloody detail how they were going to cut it up alive and eat it raw, the boy couldn't stomach the thought, and let it go. "Was so small, I wouldn't a'know'd it was in m'belly ana'ways," an amused veteran chuckled. "Sure turned that youngin' 'round, didn't we?"

"No doubt there'll be a passel more of 'em ta pick from the next time we come through," said another, "if'n I know rabbits." Then, he laughed!

* * *

As I sat jotting notes, a corporal walked up to me and handed me a cup of steaming coffee. I know not how he obtained it or from where it was "procured." But when the gods smile on you and do you simple favors it's best to graciously accept their fare, which, in this case, I did without question. I hope I continue to be in their favor, for such luxuries these days are deeply rewarding and, despite appearances, not a bit excessive, leastwise, we don't think so. I speak for all.

* * *

In a discussion among a dozen men earlier today, the question of the state of our society was hotly debated. The consensus was that it will be inevitably altered, win the war or lose it. Defeat, they agreed, will hasten what had begun before Sumter - namely the disintegration of the plantation system and the rise of a more equal economy and more equal rights for all classes - with all races acquiring more equality in time - the present system finding no sympathy among them, nor with poor whites (which comprise the Army's common rank and file), who gain nothing from it. But all protested the principle of change via a Federal force and plunder - and all resented Washington's use of immigrants fresh off the boats to fill its army's ranks - men told to fight and kill for their citizenship - who can neither speak nor understand English, and who know nothing of the war's issues, yet are denied fair consideration of our side's positions. Victory, they agreed, would hasten industrialization and trade contact with the European nations - with our government eventually offering those Blacks who want it repatriation to Africa or voluntary resettlement in the Caribbean. Several boys, scratch farmers all, said our present economic system is no longer practical nor had they ever had any truck with it, having worked small subsistence farms all of their lives. One of them remarked, to laughter and applause: "Them folks b'lieve we're a'fightin to keep slave-owners in business. Hell, before them more virtuous folks from up yonder burned me out, I were a'slavin' on my own plantation - all five acres of it!" But all feared that if the enemy won, he would gut our nation and keep it ruined and subservient for a century to ensure that our people and our economy would never be competitive with theirs or even Europe's.

I am continually surprised and gratified by the acumen of common soldiers whose education and literacy levels hardly equal their common sense. But I fear that even if our side wins its independence the full liberalization of our society will require a virtual civil war among our Southern states. There are powerful forces among us whose ruling financial interests and subsequent resistance to change will be defeated only by the threat of a popular uprising or by force itself, unless King Cotton bows to mechanization. But should we return home victorious our legions' persuasive powers will be difficult to resist.

* * *

Our regiment skirmished with the enemy today. Few casualties - most of the fight amounting to harassing fire between sides. The men call it "pickin' at each other." Some of our boys said they were certain they clipped a few, but the distances were great - over four-hundred yards - and it was all "sport" - with much splintered tree bark and spent minié-balls to show for it. I watched from behind a wagon but saw no one hit, though our boys were enjoying the competition. "Thought I drilled a few trees dead-on," said Private Will Hoskins; "but I guess I jest winged 'em. None of 'ems fell ova' dead yet."

* * *

I know that my writing sometimes rambles and my grammar often fails and that I occasionally misspell. I have no excuse except that fatigue sometimes obviates proper editing. Often, I write by anemic firelight - and sometimes by feel. Mostly, I am too spent for precision, as is now the case - and, presently, I'm too weary to manufacture any other excuses.

* * *

I have yet to describe bivouacs. During prolonged intervals between marches and fighting, bivouacs are both organized and disorganized affairs, with tents aligned, marking company and regimental boundaries, but with laundry hanging from ropes strung between trees or poles or from shorn branches - with equipment strewn about and blankets and oil cloths laid out everywhere - with rifles stacked on their butts by files - and camp fires over which are hung cooking or coffee pots and other utensils - with sleeping or reclining troops everywhere, weary from constant drilling - and uniforms, or parts of them (or what passes for uniforms) hung from whatever is convenient - with men sitting about and discussing the war and personal matters or playing cards or reading (those who can) pamphlets, books, and old newspapers for the hundredth time - or sleeping...and so on.

Bivouacs are communal enterprises in every sense. All socializing occurs there. I walk through them, cocking my ears for bits and pieces of errant conversation that will give me a sense of a unit's mood - and I commit such scenes to memory. Many will be with me all of my life, for as much as war is battle it also is what transpires among troops between battles - the human side of an inhumane affair. I sit with these men and attempt to meld with them, but I'm not always accepted. Some tightly knit units, much as a closed fraternity, do not appreciate interlopers. Soldiers like these are often inscrutable, ill-tempered and best left alone.

* * *

As I sat at roadside this morning jotting notes, I was oblivious to activities immediately around me. A heavy rain had just ended, and the road had turned muddy and puddled. Only when I was inundated with slime and muddy water did I realize that I should have been more alert to galloping horse teams pulling caissons and artillery hastening to what was developing as a major engagement farther up the road. Soaked and filthy, I followed them on foot, reaching the action minutes later, where I watched gun crews laying devastating fire on the enemy advancing on our positions. He was turned back with heavy losses - a gruesome sight. Hundreds were mangled for nothing. They had been brave men foolishly led. Contrary to the mood of previous occasions, when our Army's gun crews had triumphed, the atmosphere around these batteries remained somber and without joyful reaction. "We didn't enjoy this day," a gunner said. "It wasn't a fight but a slaughter."

*   *   *

I have a boil on my backside. Our boys call me "Old Tender Bottom" and, with bayonets, rush to "relieve" my suffering. No thank-you. They are too gleefully willing while possessing no medical acumen.

*   *   *

I stood in an outdoor hospital today watching young soldiers suffering indescribable agonies. As I did so, two gut-shot and screaming boys passed from this world. I was shaken, like the medical staff, having been powerless to do anything save watch them die. How must our surgeons feel who lose patients by the score after every battle? Discouraged, I left. One boy had been seventeen, the other sixteen. And this is not wrong? I grieved for their mothers.

*   *   *

Cold. The men sleep huddled together around campfires. Many have no coats and live barefooted. Through the night they sleep with their feet toward the flames and rely on volunteers to tend the fires to ensure that all remain fueled and lighted. Some have salvaged bits of blankets and clothing to protect them from the cold and wind - the most they can do. Some violently shiver in their slumber. Many will come down with fever. Of those that do, many will never see next week. Aside from dysentery, chilling dampness is the greatest enemy to our health, especially when accompanied by fatigue and malnutrition. It brings the most miseries to muscle and bone. Yet we cannot escape it. And, it would seem, Richmond and the governors of our seceded states that should be collectively providing shoes and fresh uniforms and blankets and food and medicines and ammunition and, thusly, encouragement are solely devoted to themselves.

*   *   *

Some of our men have incurred large personal gambling debts - the result of card games and other venues. The command frowns on such and declares those debts null and void, since gambling is illegal. But those to whom the money is owed seldom forget. Occasionally, debtors come to grief when unable to pay. Though superficial investigations are conducted, culprits are seldom found. No one will talk, and there is little time to devote to other than soldiering. We have left many a soldier cold in his grave because of his unfulfilled financial "obligations."

Kinfolk will never know that their "heroes" died in other than heroic circumstances - if they ever know anything at all.

* * *

Our brigades marched all night through storms and mud to reach a bridge over a fast-flowing river we needed to cross. We came to it just before dawn, believing we had accomplished a miracle, having exhausted ourselves tramping through and surmounting every kind of physical impediment. We found the bridge impassable, burned to its pilings by our enemy. Our angry, footsore troops trekked another five miles downstream to a shallow ford. Crossing it took the army most of the next day, and fast currents cost us several men and horses and several more men to ambushing enemy skirmishes on the opposite bank. Our cavalry crossed upstream, flushed them out, chased them and captured many, who glumly accepted their lenient fate - helping to tow our stuck wagons out of the stream and burying the men they killed. Some of our commanding officers might have had them breathing the river's swift, clear waters instead. This war grows ever more bitter.

* * *

I'll Tell Ya That

And Private Josiah Henshaw did...

Because I am not a bonafide soldier, due to self-consciousness, I have hesitated to describe combat in detail. One should rightly hear about it FROM those like Private Henshaw. His typical perspective does justice to the subject far more absolutely than I could hope to do. This then is his perspective, via my homespun shorthand. I have honestly attempted to preserve his manner of expression. He testifies for thousands:

"My first fight? Can't say for ever'one, but goin' inta it fer the first time's a back-straightenin' event, I'll tell ya that!

"It be plain confusin', with orders ya ken hardly hear bein' shouted all over. But ya jest follow the others cause ya ain't hardly understood none of 'em - with noise a'thumpin' at yer ears and hurtin' 'em terrible and yer eyes a'burnin' from the powder smoke. Ya be shoulder t'shoulder with yer friends around ya and they and you's a'duckin' yer head and bendin' low this a'way and that t'git away from the wind a'lead and iron and the noise comin' at ya, like trustin' ya ken git' sheda' them swarmin' minié-balls that a'way, like it'd make a difference. But it don't help, and cain't. And mostly, when the smoke's so thick ya don't know what's goin' on, or where yer a'goin' ana'ways, and yet too skerd to speak, it be the mightiest aggravation upon yer soul you can ever imagine.

"Yer hands be a'sweatin', yer mouth's a dust bin and yer body's a'shakin' and yer a'thinkin' a minié-ball's gonna be a'comin' right through yer skull 'tween yer eyes as sure as sin...and men's a 'gruntin' and a'screamin' here and there and a'fallin' 'er grabbin' on ta ya as they're a'goin' down--with their eyes wide open in panic and a'starin' at ya fer help ya cain't give 'em - and all the while yer a'hearin' the thunkin' of minié-balls inta other men's bones and flesh - well, it jest digs itself right inta yer bein' and won't never heal-up. Best ya ken hope fer it ta do is scar over.

"We jest keep a'firin' inta the smoke, even if we cain't see nothing' plain, and the noise seems t'go away 'cause yer a'concentratin' so hard on doin' little things - like keepin' yer tremblin' fingers from droppin' yer cartridges 'er them little copper percussion caps that git littler and littler ever' time yer needin' one. And yer worryin' that yer amma'nition's runnin' out 'cause y'cain't remembe' how much ya been usin' up, 'er if'n ya fired the last time y'loaded and if'n ya been loadin' but ain't been a'firin' the last couple a'times, and maybe ya got a couple a'rounds rammed down yer rifle already, and if'n ya fire now yer a'goin' t'blow up the rifle and yer face n'hands with it! And then ever'body's movin' forward, but the lines is getting' confused and yer friends ain't next ta ya ana'more, and then ya drop yer ramrod accidental, and ya have t'go fishin' fer it, and jest as ya do, the man next ta ya takes a ball in the throat and goes down like a tree all a squirmmin' and a'chokin' and a'gurgglin' and a'drownin' in his own blood - and there ain't nothin' you ken do 'bout it 'cause he's already turnin' blue - and then the man on the other side a'ya takes one in the knee and goes a'screamin' off and a'jumpin' 'round on his good leg like a man possessed - and ya know sure as hell the surgeons' is gonna hack off that hurt leg - and the fightin' keeps a'goin' on fer only the Lord knows how long - and yer mind's been froze-up steady the whole time, until ya think yer gonna go plum mad - and then there's big boomin' way out in front of ya somewhere - the enemy's artillery - and a second lata, shells, 'er canister or iron shot comes a whooshing through ranks, and the shells is 'splodin' and throwin' dirt and shrapnel all over that cuts men down like hunerds a little whirling razors, and some men's hit directly by shot and blowed ta pieces with legs and arms and heads and guts and bone a'splatterin' all ova ya, and ever'one else around ya still standin', and then one man hollers like the wind's been plum knocked out of him sudden, and ya look at him and he's got nothing left in his middle 'ceptin' a big hole with alla his innards blasted out, and he jest c'lapses like a little rag doll inta a heap a bloody clothes and bones! And the canister balls buzz through ranks like big shotgun balls and men is spun and flipped over and smashed ta the ground with bloody mist and bone and caps and rifles and belts and pants and shits and jackets and innards flyin'! One ball pops right passed yer ear, and ya know it' cain't be a bullet 'cause it sounds to big, but it hits a man behind ya with a squashin' sound, and when ya turn around, he's a'standin' there with no head and another man's a'tryin' to catch his body as it falls back stiffa' than board.

Then, fer some reason yer thankful fer the noise, and shootin' begins t'die away a little, and ya hear yer boys a'shoutin' up front that the enemy's a'fallin' back, but ya cain't figure out why, but firin's a'slacken off. Then, there's cheerin' comin' from somewheres down yer lines, 'cause the smoke diftin' away over there, and they ken see what's a'goin' on, and their cheerin's tellin' ya it's gotta be true, and that maybe we won this whole thing, though ain't nobody knows why, since a passel of us ain't been seein' through the smoke to aim at nothin', let alone hit nothin' the whole time, and then all the shootin', 'ceptin' fer some sputterin' here and there, 'ventually stops - 'cause the enemy's leavin' the field in front of us - and yer lucky yer still alive and intact - and it's like ya been confirmed in church but bigger and betta' - like ya be a bird jest let go from yer cage! And ya done made it outta Hell and the Devil didn't even touch ya...and yer free and feelin' ya cain't be destroyed - like the Lord's put his arm around ya special...but you figure He ain't, yet -jest kinda teased ya a little, and ya worry He might neva.

And then, they a'marchin' prisoners off ta the rear, and there's bein' dead and wounded all over and ya try ta help soma the least hurt, if'n yer officers'll let ya, but they don't, cause they's a'reformin' yer company, and the regiment's a'movin' off, and ya gotta leave the wounded there all a'squirmin' and cryin' fer help and water - and yer heart's jest a'crackin' open for 'em, with them a'reachin' out to ya with their quiverin' hands - and ya see yerself there and be a'wonderin' if'n it'll be the same when ya get yers someday - but it's the war and the way things be, and ya cain't do a damn thing 'bout none of it! And then, God Almighty, yer tired - and it comes on ya like a tent weighin' a ton that drags ya down - but ya gotta keep a'going' cause ever'body else is - so YOU gotta, too!

Don't know where yer a'goin' agin, cause, damn, the fightin' AIN'T ova, and ya ken damn-well bet yer gonna see more of it - and it all be noise again' and a'rushin' and a'hurryin' at double-time, 'cause new battle's a'flarin; somewheres else - and yer guts is a'bouncin' in yer belly, and yer so thirsty ya could drink an ocean, but they won't let ya - and that means yer day ain't over yet, and ya could STILL end up like all those others back there ya left behind - and then ya git cold inside and lonely - like a little boy lost - cause ya really see how cold war is with nobody a'carin' 'bout ya, cause yer jest fresh meat fer the fire, and yer government and nobody gives a damn fer ya, personal, and neva' will.

"And then ya realize all yer friends is gone - they ain't up with ya no more and ya don't know what become of 'em - is they lost 'er hurt 'er dead? Ya cain't tell, and ya worry mightily and it gets t'eatin' on ya, but ya keep a'movin' and don't neva' look back no more if'n ya wanna keep yer wits. But then ya remember - them prisoners looked as humans as you and yer boys - and ya git ta thinkin' how foolish all this be - how much easier it'd be ta talk kindly ta men than shoot 'em - and then ya feel guilty as God ken make ya - and maybe tears come ta yer eyes fer feelin' sorry fer yerself - but ya cain't stop it - and ya hope the day gets over quick, cause ya ain't sure 'bout what yer feelin' no more - and ya cain't believe none of what's happenin'.

"Then, them whistles blow and the firin' out front gets loud agin', and damned if'n yer compan's called back inta line and it all starts agin', cause the enemy's a'comin' back fer a second try at cha hand ta hand - and it be gruesome awful, swingin' and a'clubbin' and a'gougin' and a'scratchin' and a'kickin' and a knife-fightin' and a'swearin' and a'cursin' and a'lookin' inta yer enemy's wild eyes all the time, him being as scared and terrified as you be, and not wantin' ta die either! And ya cain't b'live it, that yer a'fightin; fer yer lives 'cause someone's a'wantin' ya to but it ain't right but ya cain't stop and neither can he, and ya wanna scream out yer terrorfulness and anger that ever'thin's come ta this, and maybe ya do and maybe ya don't, 'cause yer usin' all yer might what's left to keep his knife blade from sinkin' inta yer throat, and he's a'doin' the same 'bout yers, and yer eyes meet close-up and ya know he's a thinkin' what you is, but at that second, his arms give way and yer blade cuts inta his shoulder, and he cries out and quits strugglin' and you quit tryin' ta kill him, 'cause you really don't want to and ya don't...and he's a lookin' up at ya terrified, 'cause he's a'thinkin' you might try t'finish him off, but he cain't do no more ta stop ya, but you back offin' him and his eyes say, thank-you, oh, Lord and God in Heaven, thank-you - and then it be ova, and yer still alive and so he be, and yer thankful ya did't let yer blade go deep inta him, and so is he, and in that second, ya both respect each other real suddenlike and feel close, 'cause it don't matta no more that you and him be be wearin' different color uniforms, 'cause you and him ain't real enemies no more, and never was, though ya cain't b'lieve it 'cause yer both livin', numbed-up corpses. Ya got no more feelin' in yer soul fer fightin', if'n ya eva had, and yer guts is a quiverin', and the whole thing 'mounts ta a big noise in yer skull, and ever'thin's confused and a'turnin' over and over, 'til ya cain't stand it no more and ya gotta git away from it, sleep bein' the best way - but yer detailed ta take more prisoners back, 'er carry off the wounded ta ambulances or ta hospital, 'cause orderlies be needin' the help, there bein' so many mangled souls - and the man ya jest stabbed's taken off and ya go t'work pickin' up the wounded and draggin' away the dead 'til ya git blood and gore all over yerself, but it don't matter now cause them wounded boys - theirs n' arn - be a'lookin' up at ya through skerd eyes and thankin' ya ever so humble without speakin' a word, though some do - and ya git so damn mad 'bout the whole thing, ya be a'cryin' like a baby - and yer heart goes out ta all of 'em - theirs and arn--and ya love 'em all cause they be just simple people like you, theirs n'arn - and ya realize yer jest one big family that oughtn't ta have got inta this here fight ever a'tall - and Lord, yer low - oh, so damn low.

Ever'body 'round ya looks like you - even the prisoners - with their mouths all black with gunpowder smears from bitin' off cartridges and from caked-up dust and sweat - and ya stink so bad ya cain't stand yerself - but ever'body else stinks jest as bad, too - 'cause there's a stink about bein' scared and dyin' that yull never fergit, and ya get ta noticin' pains and scratches and a little bleedin' all ova ya in places ya didn't know ya had, 'cause seein' as how ya was so distracted and tensed-up fightin' - and ya find other men's gore and blood splattered on ya and on yer face, but ya cain't remember who it come from or when, 'ceptin' that minié-balls was a'buzzin' awful close ta yer head and hittin' others in theirs. And ya begin to hurt all over, like ya was rolled down a mountain and din't know it - cause yer body n'soul's all drained-out.

"And then, somewheres, ya git some sleep and ya sleep like you was dead. Sometimes, ya dream and sometimes ya don't - but ya hope ya don't, 'cause ya don't wanna relive none of what you've seen 'er been through. Ya jest wanna sleep and never wake up fer a hun'erd years, 'cause y'don't wanna go through it all over agin'. It could rain and thunder, 'er snow and lightin' could strike ya ten times, but you'd never know it, cause that be how 'sausted ya be - and ya never wanna wake up, but they're a'gonna make you 'ventually, cause y'ARE gonna go through it agin' sometime soon, and maybe the same day - and ya almost would rather be as dead as yer friends maybe are than do that!

"Then, sure 'anuff, they wake ya up ana'way and, by God, they put you and what's left a'yer company back in the line, 'cause the fightin's broke out heavy again - and ya cain't believe yer there, but ya are - and yer fightin' fer yer life with more boys fallin' all around ya - and ya jest load and shoot, load and shoot, and kill, yer ears pained shut, even though ya cain't see nothin' plain through the smoke - and ya don't why yer officers put ya there or whose doin' the figurin' er nothin' bout strategies, and ya jest do yer work and be a'waitin' ta die, like so many is a'doin' that minute! And ya give up a'frettin', and ya put yer soul in the Lord's Hands and say..."Lord, do with me what ya will." Ya ain't got no say, ana'how. And once't ya pray that, things lift from yer shoulders a little, and ya don't much care no more. Live 'er die, it don't make no matter 'til the fightin' quits agin' - and then - if'n you was a virgin Private b'fore, you ain't no more. Yer a vet'ran inside and out - and ya feel a thousand years older, and sick deep ta yer innards - and tired again - so damn tired - and hungry - worse than ever before. And fer the rest of the war, you'll stay thata way - tired and hungry in yer belly, but tireder in yer soul ever' day thereafta'.

"And, after a while, ya get ta lookin' fer the boys ya know'd - yer friends - and a'worryin' 'bout those who ain't bein' back, yet 'er answerin' up ta muster - and ya be a'wonderin' who be kilt and who be mangled-up - and then ya find out a couple who been close ta ya like brothers ain't never a'comin' back no more - and ya feel all empty inside, like somehow ya cheated 'em 'cause yer still a'breathin' and a'feelin', but they ain't, 'cause you 'bandoned them, and that's why they got theirs and you din't. Ya git ta cryin' - and ya ask the Lord how come they ain't still alive and YOU be - and what fer? He don't answer nor eva' will - and you be stuck with that ta think on mightily fer the rest a'yer days, if'n ya live-out that day 'er the next, 'er the next, 'er the next, 'er the next afta' THAT...like it don't neva' end.

"And it don't neva' get ana' easier, none's so y'ud ever notice, vet'ran er not. Sleep's yer savior for all things practical, and ya worship it when ya can, and when ya can, it be yer Heaven on Earth...I'll tell ya THAT!

*   *   *

Oddities

Often, after battle, a strange silence befalls the land, as if time ceases and men move at half-pace, their senses overwhelmed. Veterans say the cause of this oddity lies in the ears, which, like the brain, are stunned by the ferocity of noise during the fighting. Perhaps. I say the cause is more mysterious - that violence has so rent Creation its makers are thrust between worlds.

*   *   *

Today, as we dug entrenchments, we watched honking geese wing overhead in great, undulating formations, as if each was ignorant of events transpiring below. Odd, we thought, that they were above in day's dimming light. How free they were - how blessedly free. We studied them with admiration and envy, wondering, as we always do, why God had not given US wings?

*   *   *

Late this afternoon, I watched orderlies and their helpers probe for wounded in the carnage of today's fight, even as burial teams searched for bodies. Once again, neither would experience a fruitless night. Once again, here and there, slightly wounded and exhausted survivors leaned on their rifles, surveying their day's triumphant labors. I witnessed a soldier recover a pair of sticks a drummer boy would never use again. Nearby, another soldier found a shattered pocket timepiece. Still another lifted up what he presumed to be a rifle partially wrapped in a shirt sleeve, only to discover it still gripped in the hand of a detached arm. I found a bent metal Cross - and prayed that the Lord would graciously receive its devout owner. I now take inspiration wearing it around my neck in the name of all those anonymous who have sacrificed for the South.

*   *   *

A trembling, skeletal dog meekly ventured into camp today. We sympathized with its starving plight, and instantly fed it what we could, taking it to our hearts. The love and attention our men gave it moved me deeply. Our boys had found an outlet for their pent-up humanity, refused expression by months of distracting war. I saw relief in the animal's eyes, and, perhaps, even gratitude. When it stared at us, it peered into our souls. Some of our religious boys said they believed it to be an angel God had sent to test our compassion and to reassure us that He cherishes mercy. I will always believe that every creature has a soul belonging to God that eventually goes to Him. We are keeping her as our company guardian and mascot, trusting that we were meant to. We call her "Angel."

*   *   *

Mail arrived today in two wagons, some of it months old. It was no less appreciated. Four enlisted men stood on each wagon (two at each end) to read aloud each addressee's name, as each piece or parcel was picked from sacks. I received no mail but expect none. I have no one to write to, nor anyone to write to me. It required an hour to distribute everything, with the usual results - joy, sadness, elation, and depression, as news from home always covers the gamut of possible domestic situations, some of which are too poignant to endure, even as a bystander.

*   *   *

Late this afternoon, I saw our brigade's commanding officer carry a folding stool from his tent and set it beneath a tree. There, for the next hour, as a balmly breeze caressed the countryside, and as the sun passed to the horizon, he sat reading his Bible. In that humbling setting, he appeared unlike a leader responsible for more than eight hundred men but more like a common layman just in from his fields at the end of a trying day. I watched him silently pray, amazed that before Sumter, this resourceful officer had, ironically, known nothing of war, having been a book printer.

How is it that men untutored in military matters, such as this former tradesman, swiftly become more militarily skillful than others schooled in military sciences? He received his commission on the battlefield, when having lost their commanding officers, he - then an enlisted man - took command and led his unit into a successful fight against superior odds. So impressed were the brigade's commanding officers with his tactical acumen that they advanced him quickly, until he was noticed by division authorities and advanced again two ranks. He has confessed to me, that when the war ends, he will be finished with uniforms and orders forever and become a printer again, a craft he said he loves. Incidentally, his handwriting and calligraphy are the finest I've ever encountered. Mine, by comparison, are mediocre - embarrassing, in fact.

*   *   *

Corn Theivin'

Last night, I was invited to accompany three soldiers on a foraging party into corn fields belonging to a farmer a half-mile away. The order to forage came from the company's commanding officer, Captain James.

Initially, I balked. Were not our people hard-pressed enough without our thieving from them, too? I was gratified when they assured me that we would taking nothing that the farmer would not allow. But what if he refused? The Captain told us straight out - "You will have to take it. Our boys are hungry." That was true. They hadn't eaten much in days.

Corn fields not already pillaged, picked over or burnt by our enemies are often raided by our own forces without invitation. Who eats and how many depends on the amount of ears "foraging" parties bring back - ideally, two ears per hungry soldier. At best, the practice amounts to a moral compromise, with ethics balanced against necessity. Other grains also are "borrowed," corn, however, being the favorite, and thus we find ourselves having much in common with Roman armies of old. They, too, marched on whole grains.

"Take this here batcha amm'anmition and this rifle," the corporal leading the raid told me, handing me both. "It be loaded and capped. Hope ya know how to use it. Ar' enemies might just be a'figurin on a raid of their own t'night, but they won't a'beggin the farmer fer favors."

We took along a dozen burlap sacks - three per man. An hour later, after carefully scouting the area and leaving me with the sacks, the three returned to say no enemy troops were about. After we knocked, the farmer, toting a shotgun, met us at the door of his small house. A single lantern lit the interior, where I spied his diminutive wife and two small, frightened children, a girl and boy. We explained our mission. He thought a moment: "How much you be a'needin?"

"We'll take a hun'erd ears at least...two hun'erd if'n you ken spare 'em."

"Got ana'thin' t'trade?"

"Amma'nition - minié balls mostly."

We were not carrying enough ammunition for the one round per ear he wanted. After haggling, he settled on seventy-five for a hundred ears. The four of us ponied-up the sum, which left each of us only a few precious rounds.

Picking a hundred stalks by feel in the dark is a problem. If our blue-clad friends had decided to visit the farm in the meantime, they undoubtedly would have waited for us to do their work for them, and then would have relieved us of our sacks, and possibly our lives. But, to keep faith with the farmer and his family, we lived up to our bargain and picked only a hundred ears.

Upon our return to camp, the men hailed us as conquerors. Afterwords, the entire company celebrated with a corn boil and roast. I only wish we could have honored them with a dozen ears per man. As it was, each treated his one ear as if it were a glorious peck.

My heart went out to the farmer and his family. I could not rid my mind of the image of his emaciated wife and children. All appeared overworked and ill, as if life had been, and remained, an exercise in desperate survival. He had told us that only a week earlier the enemy had nearly picked one field clean. Only stores he'd hidden in the woods would see his family through. Nor could I rid myself of the feeling that despite our trade of ammunition for corn we had taken advantage of their insecurity - that we shouldn't have had to depend on families like them for our sustenance - that our Army should have regularly issued us rations. Feeding its troops is an Army's and its sponsoring government's responsibility - Richmond's. If the enemy revisited the farm, the family would have little to nothing left, save hunger and destitution - and ammunition to resist its pillagers, the family's fate resting in the Lord's merciful Hands.

Why does war always force common people to bear the heaviest burdens and pay the most unjust costs? Why is there not a universal law which demands that politicians who make war must serve on its front lines no matter their age - for its duration?

*   *   *

In the Beauty of the Lilies

**The Wartime Journals
of Confederate Correspondent
Royal K. Chapman
1862-1864**

Journal Nine

Contents

* * *

A Thought

Hurt enemies who share their canteens
die enemies no more.

Upon These Fields

Fighting ended today. At dusk, I watched drivers directed by a bleeding officer on horseback maneuver their horse teams and ambulances through a wilderness of human wreckage to recover the maimed. Among a wounded man's greatest fears is that he will be trampled by horses or run over by wagons and caissons.

Even in the poor lighting, the drivers were deft in their horse-handling. The lead team followed lantern-carrying guides. The others cautiously plied the same route.

As far as I could see, survivors of decimated companies assembled in ragged ranks to be counted or accounted for as reformation rituals occurred again and again.

Lanterns assumed firefly-like proportions across the fields and meadows. As usual, the acrid pungency of stagnant powder smoke burned and watered eyes. Swiftly closing on the scene, a storm boiled and churned as if determined to cleanse the bloody earth of our iniquities, the rain's scent refreshing to the senses of those still capable of appreciating it.

Our numbed survivors looked akin to zombies, their mouths and faces powder-smeared from a brutal afternoon of biting into and loading cartridges into their rifle muzzles. Into this mix, the rumble of thunder reminded all of nature's supremacy over our puny powers. Here and there, the wounded who could not stand clung to the pant legs of those who could, afraid to let go, lest they fall back and perish. I gave water to many, until my canteen emptied. Distant rifle fire crackled, again violating that unwritten code of chivalry that says that at this time of day, warring sides should allow the sun to set, the wounded to be recovered and the dead collected—in peace.

Again throughout a long night in a soaking downpour, we brought out the wounded. All the while, cracking lightning and exploding thunder forced us to cower, fearing the brilliant energy would instantly broil us. But the wounded's appeals for mercy bound everyone to their tasks.

Rain, wind, and mud became our latest enemies. Conscious that we could not protect the hopelessly mangled from it nor speed them to medical care, we set them down in rows, loading the most salvageable wounded into wagons and ambulances at hand. All would be severely jostled in their trips to the surgeons' saws and scalpels. Yet, we did not deny those who begged us to leave them be rather than deliver them to the surgeons' tables.

In deference to them, we left many to take the Lord's Hand where they lay.

I saw hurting men turn their faces toward their heavens to drink while letting the rain also flush their wounds and wash way their blood. Others violently shook with chills from the damps and blood loss. Staring into the darkness, alone amongst hundreds, scores passed on before dawn. Tragically, as too often happens, we lost many who lay face-down in undetected puddles, and too weak to help themselves.

Before dawn, during a lull in our work, I dropped and slept, soaked through and spent. I dreamed of cloud-filled places of breathtaking glory and of long files of soldiers, theirs and ours, walking toward a source of golden light, their uniforms clean and pristine, their pleasant faces aglow with youth and enduring health. I wanted to go with them, but one turned to me with a restraining hand, saying "Your time has not yet come." I had heard of others having had such dreams. Then, well into morning, history repeated itself. A hand holding a cup of steaming chicory awakened me, leaving me surprised but grateful. That I was alive to watch its vapors rise into a new morning sky emptied of rain exhilarated me.

Sipping and again feeling one with the recuperating troops around me, I rejoiced in the hot brew's promise that my membership in that brotherhood of tribulation was once more assured. And again, though I saw no beauty in the lilies upon those fields that fresh day, I pondered the meaning of my haunting dream, as I luxuriated in my longed-for measure of blessed solace. "Lord," I asked, "was it truly only a dream?"

*　*　*

Fancy Pants

Our troops in baggy pants are called Zouaves. They belong to special regiments that wear baggy britches (sometimes striped), fancily braided vests over their shirts and long, tassel-tipped stocking caps that hang down their backs.

Our regular infantry finds great good-natured sport in jeering them, calling them "fancy pants," insulting them with jibes that often call the Zouaves' manhood into question. And though some of the infantry's excessive badgering has led to flailing fisticuffs - Zouaves often being in no mood for parrying insults - the sartorial gentleman are known for giving better than they get.

Of course, they reply that straight-legged trousers mark the regular infantry as uncouth and cloddish plebeians of inferior fighting abilities and cattle-like intelligence.

I have no opinion either way, but know only that our baggy-pants veterans are renowned for fighting well, and cannot be faulted for their conduct in battle. And I have been told that regular infantry units perform with greater confidence when Zouaves protect their flanks. Said an infantry veteran to me yesterday: "Ain't no ordinary foot soldier here who'd admit to it - without suckin' down stoneblind first - but them fancy fellers can support us ana'time they're a'wantin' to and with 'ar 'preciation - and that be in the attack or the dee'fense. Ain't no troops better with the bayonet, neither."

Be it known, however, that our enemy also boasts Zouave units that fight with equal valor. I have never seen theirs and ours meet in battle, but those who have describe it as witnessing the unholy.

Rivalries being what they are, battle often intensifies a unit's determination to triumph. I HAVE witnessed terrible casualties result when pride compels a unit to refuse to fall back in the face of overwhelming odds. Some even have continued suicidal assaults with no hope of success. I know, specifically, of two cases where scores of Zouaves had to be literally manhandled from the field by other units.

In the heat of battlefield passions, men reveal attitudes alien to "civilized" minds. Fear and pain vanish, even as ranks are torn by hot lead and iron that feeds a unit's insatiable lust for savage vengeance. Some men fight on with terrible wounds, loss of blood and shattered or severed limbs, their frenzied strength turning supernatural and their defiance terrifying.

We truly understand little to nothing of the human mind and its terrible will. Perhaps, if we did, we'd fear for our races' survival.

*   *   *

Dust

We live with it, eat it, breath it. It is our hourly plague on dry roads. It coats our faces, mouths, and hair. It burns our eyes, clogs our ears and parches our throats. Our teeth grind it. It infiltrates our packs and haversacks and creeps into our vittles. It is grit without nourishment. For many, it fills their lungs and leaves them too weak and debilitated to march anymore. Some men spit it up or fall by the wayside, retching it out. Others cough it up so violently they grip their sides in pain, their lungs afire. Looking like hordes of bandits, whole companies and regiments march with kerchiefs tied 'round their faces. Still, dust finds its way beneath.

Clouds of it mark our progress, rising smoke-like above our columns. Only the first company in every column's van escapes. The last in every column remain the most tormented. We pray for rain and flanking winds to relieve us. And though we trust that our prayers are heard, only occasionally are they answered. Long-term, dust adversely affects constantly marching armies. It kills some, their innards corroded with it, their lungs shut down. Without winds or rain to help, it can be avoided only when our course takes us across grassy fields or meadows or through woods or rain or dew-dampened by-ways. But unless the ground is thoroughly soaked, thousands of slogging boots, shoes and bare feet eventually tramp it dry again.

As one private complained, "It can be as close as a man ever comes t'eatin' plain dirt."

*   *   *

Contemplations Again

In the quiet of dusk, I sit alone in isolated places, marveling at the ways Nature's tints the Earth with subtle pastels, despite we who arrogantly scar it with our offenses.

I am reminded of my home's sweetness, of the stream I used to sit beside as a child, and the lazy hours I spent studying the sky - and my mother's call at suppertime and the rich aromas of her kitchen - and my father stirring the hearth - and cattle lowing in the fields as they came home at sunset - and the mesmerizing scents of summer grasses on the cusp of evening mists - and the rains that bathed and purified the air and land - and the waning sunlight magnified through a billion raindrops as storms moved away - and the stars of the cleansed and beckoning universe afterwards - and the thrill of being a youth in love with every day, when the world and everything in and about it was fresh and new.

All these things, and the natural grandeur of my parish, I shall always remember as treasured images of a long-ago paradise.

* * *

One must think of how it is for soldiers to daily contemplate Eternity and the probability that they will meet it before ever seeing home again.

I, too, struggle with this reality - though as a civilian I may remove myself from harm's way without suffering recriminations, except in my conscience. So, I MUST go with them, follow them and endure with them, or call myself a coward who betrayed the essence of his mission.

If the Reaper takes me, so be it.

* * *

I witnessed skirmishing again this morning, but in trying to sort its details later, they all ran together. I forced myself to return to study the site, hoping to recall and record the incident's salient events. The wounded were being recovered and the few dead were being removed. Yet, it was as if I were a stranger to it all - as if I had never been there. I cannot explain myself. I simply wanted to sleep for a thousand years.

* * *

Today, I attached myself to a company in a "virgin" regiment that has yet to see the Elephant. Even after years of chronicling the war, why men volunteer so willingly to go into harm's way remains a greater mystery to me than war, and here I am again, risking my life in this one. I shall never understand the human mind. The odds of this regiment standing against veteran enemy units is great, for the shock each man will experience seeing the slaughter in a full-fledged engagement will be swift and devastating. Even their officers are novices.

I study their faces, trying to find something of the élan that characterized our troops at the war's beginning, but I see none of it. Certainly, conviction has prompted a few to join up. Social obligations have motivated others. But none have come because they expect to see what they surely WILL see.

Concerning obligations: undoubtedly, those with relatives in the Army, having avoided service until now, could no longer tolerate the stigma of avoidance. Others, I'm sure, were caught-up in the draft. The alternative for all would be desertion, except that they, their families and children would suffer social damnation for it. And there is always that percentage who are not virgins at all, but "reconstructed" veterans who ran once, thought better of it and returned to fight under different names in different units. I suspect I have already seen one or two. Sensing my suspicions, they furtively glance at me, as if I might know their true identities or recognize the Elephant's indelible mark. But many "skedaddlers" have not nor will ever return. Why? - because even more intensely than the battle-field's horrors, they fear to meet and face comrades who stayed or the ghosts of those who died because THEY ran. I wonder who among us will run next time. Of late, I wonder if it will be me.

* * *

Today, I watched, fascinated, as a half-dozen men carved and whittled figures and dolls from firewood our boys had collected. All were family men, doing so, they said, for their children or for children they might encounter on the march. Already finished were not only animals, but absurdly proportioned generals (which spoke directly to their "love" of same) and delicate little gnomes their little imps would cherish. Their skill humbles me. There is no telling the amount of varying talent in our ranks. One simply cannot predict, by a man's looks, what skills his hands possess or what inventiveness his mind harbors. It pains me to realize that we are exposing this all to destruction, when we so badly need all we can muster and will doubly need it after this war.

I can only hope and pray the war ends soon. If it lasts much longer, even if we win, all we will have gained will be a hollow victory, the cream of our talented potential having been drained into the earth of a thousand bloody fields known and unknown. Failure will bring the same result.

But, as I look on today I wonder why one particular carver and the onlookers around him keep glancing at me and smiling. Now, it strikes me: the doll he's carving IS me - wearing a ridiculously exaggerated broad-brimmed hat that sits down around its ears and totes journals three times their actual size. It's a wonderful joke, yet, a sentimental one. Now, they realize I recognized the doll. Laughter erupts. The carver, Corporal James Gentry, is an artist, and the keepsake he's created for me is one more reason why this army has endeared itself to me. I trust that, in my writing about it, I will honor its rank and file as dutifully as their humble souls have honored me.

* * *

I've been devastated today by news I feared to hear.

The young commanding officer of the company to which I had attached myself, and who, a week ago, had accepted my presence with such grace and civility, perished along with half of his company this morning.

During the fighting, he had directed me to the safety of a tree. From there, I watched his company's destruction but did not see him fall. I hoped to see him again to thank him for sparing my life, but he is dead and I feel I've betrayed him. I know he would tell me I did not, but I cannot banish my nagging sense of guilt for having survived - for not having stood beside him as honorably as he stood against his fate. Lord, let me not remember that as he died, I stood safely behind a tree.

* * *

We carried wounded from the field today. My coat is blood-soaked -- so much so that passing officers instructed me to repair to our field hospital for treatment. Embarrassed for having not been scratched, I had to admit that the blood was not my own. Would that some of it could have been, so that I might have shared in the honor of being called "an anointed brother in arms."

* * *

In the vistas my eyes scan beyond our regiment's bivouac, I hear sweet music. It comes in the rustle of wind through the trees and along the fields and meadows all around. The music disguises a message, yet I cannot truly decipher it. But I sense it saying that something beyond our imaginations awaits us after physical obliteration - something good, where peace and solace abide eternally - something inevitable. The music gladdens me and puts me at peace with myself and the Earth, and I wonder if anyone else hears it. Yet, it also frightens me. Is this what all warring men hear when their time has come? How can I know? I cannot, and so I must bide to await what possibly is the inevitable...but for how long...how hellishly long?

* * *

Touching Things

Last night, I slept fitfully. Though I was fully clothed and wearing my heavy coat, cold night air crept into my bones as I lay beneath my blanket in the open. I was about to give up on sleep and sit myself down in front of a still burning campfire, when I heard a youngster whimpering.

I remembered a boy-soldier who had joined our ranks only days ago, having watched him bed down earlier only a few yards away. Looking in that direction, I saw movement in the fading glow cast by the nearest fire. Taking myself there and sitting beside the youngster, I found him in depression's depths. I spoke softly to him, so as not to awaken other sleeping soldiers, asking if he were homesick. Embarrassed, he said he could not control his crying and confessed he gravely missed his home and family, being terrified of dying before seeing them again.

Minutes later, as I suspected from my past experiences, he revealed that he was "under seventeen." Slightly built and sickly, he should never have been conscripted. As he spoke reverently of home, he wiped away his tears. The whole time, I remained stalked by images of him torn to pieces by canister fire on our next battlefield. Eventually comforted, he drifted to sleep, but I could not rid my conscience of his situation's injustice.

The next morning I spoke to our regimental Chaplain, the Reverend James Hollenbaugh, who took immediate umbrage at matters and repaired to the regiment's commanding officer. As a result, our young lad was discharged three days later and sent home on an Army supply train that would pass through his parish. If only we could reach all such youngsters caught-up in this accursed whirlwind. When I imagine his mother's eventual joy and relief, I ask God to reward the good Reverend with Heaven's highest honors. The boy, I later learned, was actually a mere fifteen.

*   *   *

They are trying to execute Private Ben Stiles. Ben has been accused of cowardice under fire. But the two-year veteran is NOT a coward. Having witnessed too much death and slaughter, his nerves, like those of other dedicated soldiers in our brigade and countless others in our Army, have shattered. Accordingly, but unconsciously, he had backed away from the line during our last combat, whereupon he fell to his knees and wept into his hands. No, he did not truly run, having always nobly served the Cause. Actually, he remained no more than ten yeads behind the battle line. Yet our brain trust, which insists on making examples of such "transgressors," had Stiles arrested and, if not opposed, will hastily convict him. Try as they might, they have yet to persuade a single man from our brigade to volunteer for his firing squad.

This has forced the brigade's humiliated commanding officer, a Colonel, who I shall not name now, to search for a squad (that will not know Stiles) from another brigade, since word of the "persecution" has spread throughout our brigade whose mood borders on rebellion. At this stage of the war, our men supernaturally resent such harsh measures.

The Colonel assembled the entire Brigade today to explain the "necessity" for killing Stiles, and said he will assemble it again to witness Stile's death. But regiment by regiment and company by company, our men responded by turning their backs on him. Livid, he threatened to court-martial every officer of every regiment and company for permitting such "insubordination." Nothing thus far has come of his theatrics, but feelings against him run deep. Word has gotten out that he may well order Stiles secretly executed and anonymously buried so that the grave will not become a martyr's site. But our men have sent headquarters word that they will not allow it.

It is being wagered that the Colonel's "got his foot in a bear trap" and will be relieved of command. Said veteran Corporal Henry Pritchett, "Our Army's tired old 'generals still ain't senile 'anuff to watch a whole Brigade walk off owin' ta the lunacy of one natural-born half-wit."

(NOTE: Word has filtered down that Stiles will be cleared and a new commanding officer appointed. Thank God.)

*   *   *

Some of our "half-starved" boys went fishing today in a nearby stream. Caught three large catfish and were rejoicing, when two small, emaciated youngins' appeared with their little poles - saying their mamma was sickly and that they had to find her something to eat. Well, our fellows followed the little boys home, fried-up the fish and prepared a meal for the family - after discovering that the little ones had three sisters plus an aging grandfather in the house, but no food! Our fellows returned to camp at dusk still hungry because there had not been enough fish for them after permitting the family to consume every morsel. Valor often reveals a mundane but Divine face. Honors await them in Heaven.

*   *   *

Considerations

When I consider that men go into battle despite every instinct warning them to avoid it or flee from it, I cringe.

What is it about man's nature that overpowers such natural reactions and enables him to march into such appalling violence? One who has never seen or experienced battle involving thousands cannot imagine its shattering confusion and abject terror.

I study the faces of men "going in," wondering why they dedicate themselves en mass to self-destruction, as did I in the War with Mexico that now seems a century past. I observe virgin troops trembling so intensely that they soil themselves or become catatonic - while others calmly advance, even as friends all around them are obliterated - or despite having seen undulating carpets or gangrenous human misery in hospitals far behind the lines where the mutilated lay beneath the sight of an apparently indifferent Providence. Is it "honor" that compels them not to run or the stigma of being called "coward," or are they supernaturally resigned to their fate? What compelled me? Lord, I cannot remember.

It has been suggested that the infantry is a brotherhood of fear - fear subdued only when its ranks either refuse to be known as quitters or decide that God has already written their epitaphs. Calm, it's said, overtakes many and they go into harm's way masters of themselves, or believing that they are surely in His Hands. Otherwise, they could not coerce themselves or be coerced into fighting at all. There is truth in this. A so-called noncombatant now, I have chosen to go with them that I might discern their motivations. All those years ago in Mexico, I never truly understood mine.

I am not a brave man, nor was I then, merely loyal to my mission. I remember an army Chaplain in Mexico telling me that in their heart of hearts, all soldiers harbor a secret cowardice that terrifies them as much or more so than the hot iron and lead they endure. In transcending their mortal fears and trusting their fate to Providence they transcend themselves. Thus is courage born.

There was cowardice in me then, and I admit that I feared it more than the enemy. But time and maturity have made it impossible for me to believe that I could have been a soldier then or now, let alone courageous. I simply went where those around me went and did what they did, for, despite my love of life, I loved honor more.

* * *

Battle's Own

I was up this morning before the sun crept over the hills to the east. I had not slept, but ventured instead upon the encampments of thousands still slumbering. Sentries patrolled their designated areas while invisible pickets kept watch in the dark or shadowed perimeters beyond.

Here and there, the sleepless warmed themselves around campfires, drawing hot sustenance from pots and cans over dancing flames, drinking in silence.

I believed I could hear their thoughts about the fighting to come later in the day, and I wondered which of them would be alive when dawn came at this time tomorrow.

Looking into the placid expressions of those still sleeping, I fantasized that if I could awaken them I might try to persuade them to quit the slaughter - to reason with the enemy, end the war and go home. Generals cannot fight battles without soldiers. But the whirlwinds loose upon the land would have swept away all such idealism, and I feared that, eventually, the war would change me as it was changing them.

Nearby, a haggard soldier sipped his hot broth. He appeared at peace with himself, and it was plain that war had not tarnished his appreciation of simple comforts. War intensifies the value men place on common wonders that go unnoticed or ignored in peacetime. In that sense, death's specter brings them closer to an understanding of Creation's essence.

As he later said to me: "War either takes a man's life - or defines it."

*   *   *

Soldiers

I am sitting on a fallen fence, watching our troops return from the battlefield. The struggle was savage today. I saw men by the hundreds cut down on both sides. Even now, my hands tremble as I attempt to write this. You cannot image battle's brutality.

They return to their company ranks exhausted and dirty, their faces smeared with gun powder. Some are hurt. Some are bloody. Many, no longer in ranks, either are dead or too maimed to return. Water buckets are passed between the survivors and they drink as if possessed. They have long since drained their canteens and many have gone for hours without a drop.

They spit, they cough or nervously pace in place. The energies conjured in battle have not abated and pour out in the stench of ebbing fear. Fear produces its own sweaty aroma, distinct, and alien. Many throw water into their faces and each other's. They rub their faces, necks, and heads with it. Some pour it over themselves. Others sit, too weak to stand. Some collapse and lay still, breathing heavily, their mouths gasping for air. Some cannot believe they remain alive. Survival, therefore, has been their day's supreme achievement. Many have done what hundreds have failed to do in those fields beyond - returned without physical wounds. I can only guess about the damage to their souls.

Much of the fighting was hand-to-hand, and many have killed face to face. For that reason, they have not come away unscarred. The screams of those they have killed still torture their hearing. And some, who have not fully returned, still hold their ears.

"Was you there?" a soldier asks me.

"Yes," I reply, "I was there."

He looks at me approvingly and puts his hand on my shoulder, then turns and shuffles away. It is as good as a medal for me from them. I do not deserve it.

They lean against trees, dropping their rifles at their sides.

"Whupped 'em," one of them remarks: "By thunder, we whupped 'em good!"

The enemy has retired from the field, leaving his wounded to us. Prisoners who can walk come dragging by, their faces and uniforms as dirty as our boys'. All appear dejected, as if they believe they are abject failures. Many are hurt and are being helped by comrades. They stare at our water-consuming troops, their eyes glazed with thirst.

One of our boys turns to one of theirs: "Looks t'be you're a'wantin' soma this here," he says, handing the enemy soldier a half-filled bucket.

"Be obliged to ya," an enemy sergeant replies. He and his comrades refresh themselves as intensely as our boys.

"Sure is sweet," he says, his relieved expression mirrored by others. The enemy is human, too.

"Move on there," says one of the boys who guards them. "They be more water up ahead."

"Thank ya,'" the enemy soldiers says to us, "thank ya kindly."

All prisoners appear much better fed than our boys. On the whole, they're heavier, not nearly as gaunt.

"Somma' their boys be awful strong," one of our corporals says. "Be farm boys like mosta' arn. 'Et better than us, though...that's fer sure."

It WAS for sure.

I'm from Ohio," said one of theirs, a young lad, to one of ours. "Where YOU from?"

"Alabama."

"Your boys fight pretty good."

"So do yern'."

"We grow corn and wheat up in Ohio...whatcha' ya grow down in Alabama?"

"Tabacca' and cotton mostly...sorghum, too."

"What's sorghum?"

"Makes jest the dandiest nectar you eva' tasted! Come on down afta' we've licked y'all and have some. But, next time, leave all yer rifles and cannons and all yer Yankee friends down here t'home!" (Our boys laugh.)

This lull after fighting is always surreal. Only an hour ago, I witnessed canister pulverize and tear great gaps in both sides' ranks, shatter bodies, rip away limbs and toss skulls skyward. What madness kept the survivors in place, I cannot say. At this moment, enemies are conversing now as if they lived just down the road from each other, when before they were bent on destroying each other. Only hours from now, our boys will be in bivouac, playing cards or sleeping or quietly contemplating tomorrow. But sleep will evade ME because I will have much to write that will disturb me. And even as dawn threatens a second day of battle, I will observe men spending their last morning on earth calmly resting or drinking hot broth they've made from grasses - all seemingly inured to the possibility that they might not survive Hell a second time. Truthfully, war has steeled them and calloused their sensibilities.

Tonight I will walk among lounging men for whom sleep will come late. I will ask them "How do you remain so composed when you know that tomorrow will offer you no respite?" And someone will reply, "Ain't much we ken do 'bout it now, is there? Our gin'rals jest move their little checkers 'round their little boards - we be the checkers. Like as not, war be a game to 'em, but none's 'eva been up front where we'uns go - and no-one's never gonna put theirselves up there, neitha', not like we'uns do."

Once again, their fatalism will give me pause.

I am told that too much war accustoms some soldiers to hopelessness. They say the quiet and contemplative are the most resigned to whatever Providence decrees, while the outgoing are not the most confident of survival. But all agree the most talkative are the most terrified of death. The most passive and withdrawn often sense their doom. I have seen such souls go off by themselves to stare at something far away, perhaps the world beyond.

I could never be a soldier, nor as stoical. Nor could I generate a confounding peace of mind. The regimental Chaplain tells me that many soldiers put their trust entirely into God's hands. Alas, Faith for me has never been as forthcoming and my emotions about it continue to be mixed. I suppose I have been too firmly attached to mortal life for such faith. Still, I pray God will forgive my weakness and suffer me my misgivings until I learn the secrets of His disciples' courage.

* * *

The Inevitable

I helped carry the wounded off the field today. Once again, my coat is blood-soaked, so much so that I was asked by officers to repair to our field hospital for treatment. Embarrassed once again, I had to admit that the blood was not mine. It was inevitable that this happened, that again I should have been mistaken for being wounded, for those looking on would not have been entirely in error. My wounds so often have been spiritual, yet if my soul were able to bleed the crimson essence of sadness and remorse for our wounded and dead I might have perished, indeed, long before now.

Once again, I walk now through vistas beyond our regiment's bivouac, listening to the rustle of wind through the trees and grasses along the fields and meadows all around. Once again, voices, not of our realm, speak there, and though I cannot decipher their meaning, they transcend our world and comfort me. I am told that others in ranks hear them, too - very often - and sense that they are not of our world but communicate mystically through our imaginations.

"Don'tcha try to figure 'em out," a veteran instructed me, rubbing his chin; "they be of the Lord. Jest be glad that they put cha' at peace with yerself." They did, but a notion frightened me. I asked the veteran, "Is that what soldiers hear when their times come?"

"Sometimes yes and sometimes no," he answered, as he looked away: "A man's jest got t'bide and see - jest bide and see and let it go at that."

The voices this time sounded too benevolent to have been a warning. And now, whenever the wind teases verdant trees, or breezes rustle the bounties of undulating boughs,

I listen, for we have yet, as a species, to understand the language of Nature and, through nature, the voice of God.

*　　*　　*

Abandoned Drum

In my wanderings across a recently contested field, I spied an abandoned drum.

Nearby, a young boy with drum sticks still clutched in his diminutive hands lay shredded by a shell. Even accustomed as I was to the dead's mutilated bodies, the boy's prostrate form radiated horrific poignancy. He had not been an ordinary soldier of soldiering age - merely a boy of, perhaps, ten tender years or less - and small.

Drummer boys are common to the Army, and many times I have witnessed their intense performances as they call troops into lines of battle. But I had not considered that they actually accompanied troops INTO battle. Perhaps, I should have guessed it early on, but only gradually has my naivete about many military matters in this war suffered attrition. My anger welled as my gaze would not part from the boy. What I beheld was not only immoral but an insufferable crime.

I wanted to know who or what had been responsible for his being in harm's way...tradition, stupidity, or criminal negligence? His poor mother - had she voluntarily given him up to this enterprise, or had he slipped away from her one day to pursue fantasies of adventure and glory? Even if so, who had put him in uniform - and who in uniform had allowed him near the fighting? Had he simply been overlooked, or, for drummer boys, was such close participation in the fighting common fare?

Had he been my son, I would have been emotionally gutted and my rage at the government boundless. And if I suspected that his body had been tossed into a hole with the rest of the anonymous dead, I would have sped to the Capital with a gun, and made for the Office of the Secretary of War.

To this day, the memory of the little drummer lying contorted and mangled disturbs me greatly. I have since learned that drummer boys OFTEN accompany troops into battle, beating energetic cadences to motivate them to greater efforts. The discovery has brought me low. That such a moral wrong is perpetrated against children without expense to the government's conscience speaks much of war-mongering gone amuck. I also learned that my contempt for the practice is more than matched by veteran soldiers, who often shield such youngsters or pack them safely to rear areas before battles. Thank God for such men.

I protested in a letter to the President but have yet to receive a reply. By going over the chain of command I have sometimes set generals against me. Yet they suffer me because they fear my pen.

And what of the politicians I have badgered and begged to legally prohibit children from the battlefield? I've heard from none. So many care nothing of the wartime savagery they loose upon the land, so busy are they nurturing their political fortunes. Would that they all were forced into the front lines of every battle to fight and to bury the dead afterwards.

I hope my efforts and those of others persuaded someone to observe at least one feeble, redeeming grace. The dead drummer boy was belatedly embalmed and sent home to his inconsolable mother, and there received a soulful internment - with a military honor guard present - for all the good it did either.

God help her...she found no beauty in the lilies that awful day.

*   *   *

Sentiments That Apply

This cold afternoon, I sat next to a campfire, watching it dwindle beneath a gentle rain. The dampness invaded my bones and infected my spirit with the same dull grayness that hung across the countryside.

Around me, sullen veterans huddled as close as possible to the fire's anemic embers. I could see that the dampness also coursed across their trembling limbs. Some wore oil cloths around their shoulders. Others wore no more protective clothing than their shirts and shell jackets. Most wore hats or caps of various descriptions. All suffered chills.

I felt privileged. My broad-brimmed hat and heavy canvas coat protected me enough to feel secure, but my conscience wore no such protection. A young veteran of no more than sixteen shivered mightily. Though he wore a hat, his unprotected cotton shirt had rapidly absorbed the cold rain and he was well on his way to fever. I removed my jacket and threw it around him, for beneath it I also wore a heavy wool jacket. On the whole, I was in much better health than he. He thanked me, his eyes and complexion sickly.

Steam rose gently from the fire's remains as our thoughts turned to homes, families, and grim futures. I had learned from previous conversations with these men that some wondered whether they should remain with the Army or go home. Their hard-pressed families faced financial ruin. Farms were in desperate need of maintenance. Somewhere in that proposition, desertion raised its ugly head. It left those, who fretted about sick wives or children, to wrestle with the Devil. Some drew distinctions between desertion and treason, saying that temporarily abandoning the war to save their homes and loved ones was justified. Others countered that they could never abandon their duty to their comrades who might suffer or die in their stead. Some neared decisions. Family cares tortured hundreds in their regiment.

I recalled when, as a corporal in the Federal army during the Mexican war, I had idealistically viewed my place in it. I wrote in an early journal entry: "We are on the march upon unnamed roads that are thoroughfares in name only, and along trails lost to ages. We trudge through sand and desert and arid plains given to wild flowers and scrub. A startled fox bolts at our trespass. Occasionally, we slog through rain and winds angered by our presence--but usally over parched hills or through baking valleys that even Satan is said to avoid. Yet, all are painted by the Divine Master's brush. In every dry place, we eat the dust of centuries, as our shuffling feet disturb time in its privelaged sanctuaries. We wonder when the war will end, that we might be shed of these wastelands and go home again to our families and verdant lands. Always, we feel battle's lurking eye and wonder if we or our enemies are right in this sordid enterprise. But, every day, what has become of our wives and children worry us more."

That was long ago. Yet, the sentiments again applied. This time, enemies who once were our comrades in those arid places awaited us--out there. Were they or we right--or were we both wrong? Could this war's contending issues have been better resolved? Some believe it is not too late for them and us to lay down our arms and reconsider. But I think this new tragedy is unstoppable, and that we have been cursed by Fate into seeing it through. Unto that end, I will devote myself until my purpose is fulfilled.

Sitting by that campfire that morning, I considered how the battlefield had tainted both side's idealism with the smell of putrefaction. As in Mexico, noble convictions and patriotic sentiments had melded into a single common slag of suffering and regret. Even now, our men persevere not from duty to country nor loyalty to principle, as much as to their devotion to each other. Win or lose, they will continue to nurture their memories, not on the epic consequences of heroic battles but on hardships shared and comrades lost.

In the rain later that morning, the Army honored another bloody appointment. Some of those with whom I had shared the fire's dwindling warmth that afternoon took the Lord's hand and—with hundreds of others—stepped into the Paradise each had faithfully anticipated.

The young soldier, to whom I had given my coat, went with them.

* * *

No Quarter

The enemy's handiwork was brought home to me the day the regiment I followed came to an isolated backwater.

Thirsty, sweating soldiers, dust-covered after an all-day march, made for it immediately, only to be held back by officers and sergeants, who sensed what I would not have seen had I gotten there first. At the water's far side, dead horses - some still in harness - lay half-submerged, their bloated carcasses having left a putrid-smelling leakage across the water's surface. Obviously, they had been there for more than a week.

So this was how the war had degenerated. No more chivalry, nor gentlemanly considerations. Total war, was how the enemy had phrased it - no quarter given, nor expected - sick and worn-out horses shot dead and dumped into waters he knew we might need among the sickly lilies.

Our troops, their canteens empty, swore and raged. The brigade's commanding officer fumed at the enemy's ruthlessness, feeling as betrayed as his troops. But why should he have expected a kindlier circumstance? The next water source lay two more hours of hard marching off the road through tangled wilderness. Yet, the sun had begun its fatal descent. Our parched troops could either bivouac now, or march the two hours to a fast-running tributary - which not even the enemy could have successfully contaminated.

Our brain trust chose to march.

Despite their sore feet and worsening dispositions, the brigade's dispirited ranks moved out again. My protesting feet, aching and blistered, bled through my last pair of socks, but I trailed along with many around me who trudged on in much worse condition. We arrived in near-dark two complaining hours later at a place off the beaten track. No enemy sharpshooters or ambushes awaited us there. After sentries and mounted pickets were posted, our men were given leave to indulge themselves by torchlight in the tributary's cooling currents. Campfires were set and cooking begun, though our men had little to eat.

By that torchlight, dusk having faded into night, I soaked my feet for an hour with others who tended bleeding blisters and cuts. Those among us who wore brogans were offset by an equal number who went shoeless, suffering maddening foot lacerations. I cannot see why a government that sends armies into the field cannot shoe them first - or at least make provisions to re-shoe those whose footwear fails. I counted two-score around me whose feet had been needlessly tormented by thorns and branches in the woods we had scraped through. I felt deeply for those men whose devotion to cause truly impressed me.

Most were simple scratch-farmers, craftsmen, or laborers, who, fearing for families and farms, had joined-up to save their farms and homes from the depredations imposed everywhere by the orders of now alien generals once their countrymen. Their stoicism transcended the issues responsible for the war, as they saw themselves fighting not for political causes but for the salvation of wives, youngins, and parents forced by the enemy into destitution. And, though many detested soldiering, they believed themselves right for resisting the violence brought by others to their doorsteps.

Also by torchlight, exhausted soldiers dug shallow latrines. Hundreds of others ate, rested, or bedded down. Officers wandered their company bivouacs, as sleepy pickets were "volunteered" to patrol the brigade's perimeters on foot. Soon activities moderated. Except for the soft singing of the homesick, and the soporific crackling of camp fires, nothing further prevented me from slumbering with the rest - save the haunting images of dead horses rotting in ponds among the lilies - that forced me to awaken from cherished dreams of home and peace.

*   *   *

In the Beauty of the Lilies

**The Wartime Journals
of Confederate Correspondent
Royal K. Chapman
1862-1864**

Journal Ten

Contents

*   *   *

A Thought

I watched a young lad pull a trigger
and perish inside forever more.

Necessary Evils

War creates convenient "moralities" that neither generals nor governments shrink from invoking - and about which civilians know little unless they, too, have been to war.

I followed the Army through a series of marches that led to a major encounter with the enemy. There, two of our brigades surprised and attacked the bivouacked enemy. The fight lasted an hour. Our people routed half of theirs, while the other half fought doggedly. Though brief, both side's casualties were heavy, theirs more than ours. The enemy quit the field with our cavalry in pursuit.

I visited the carnage while the battle raged and took position with one of our hotly engaged artillery batteries that had just come to pour shell and shot into enemy ranks a half-mile distant. Only haphazardly did enemy shells come our way from one of their few unlimbered guns. By chance, one fell before our Number Two gun, bursting with a flash and much smoke. Shrapnel cut down four of its nine-man gun crew and sliced away one man's legs. Three survivors suffered concussions.

The legless man writhed and screamed so horribly that his voice rose above the blasts of the remaining three guns that continued firing. Help for him was impossible and he quickly bled out his life. My ears rung as I watched him die. Never had I realized how much blood the human body contains. Later, I searched him for identification, found some in his jacket pocket and gave it to the battery's commanding officer. The artilleryman would not be buried anonymously.

When the fighting ended I examined its effects in the fields yonder. It is one thing to watch combat from a distance. Men appear to fall like tiny dolls, as if blown over by imaginary winds. From that perspective, death never appears as ugly as close inspection reveals it to be.

Returning to the gun battery, I watched a survivor from the decimated gun crew as he located the dead man's legs, calmly removed the brogans from each foot, and then forced them onto his own bare feet. As debased as that might have appeared to civilians, it represented a common wartime practice - salvaging useable items from the dead. War's culture dictated that his actions were of no more moral significance than a rain storm. An unspoken soldiers' code permits this kind of scavenging, which asks the dead to give up what they no longer need. But the action revolted the regiment's pious Chaplain, whose prime was lived out in more chivalrous times, and who declared that scavenging was an "affont to God."

But, a tired veteran disagreed: "Don'tcha see, Preacher? It don't be wrong to a livin' man with raw feet who ain't got no shoes. The dead man jest be plum generous. He give'd 'em up 'cause he be kindly r'membad' afta'wards in the livin's prayers. Shoes be necessary t'us poor folk, and he know'd that!"

The war has since obliterated many of the Chaplain's naïve notions, dictating its own rules - shame, in this instance, not being a restraining factor, or a relevant factor at all. He might now be accustomed to war's other evil necessities, such as removing the dead enemy's uniforms and equipment even as fighting rages. And perhaps he has grown more relenting since personally suffering from our Army's destitution.

Since our politicians have put personal considerations above the war effort, our boys have learned to fend for themselves. They harbor creature comforts wherever obtained, and share them with each other. I have seldom found a soldier who believes the shortages are ever as acute as the Army portrays them. Most are convinced that materials are being withheld by governors unable to grasp the necessity for all states to pool their resources for the nation's common good.

I would not wish to be those politicians if, and when, the Army returns home in victory to settle accounts. Yet, that I would dearly love to observe.

*　*　*

An Indifferent Nature

Along a line of march, Nature is an army's persistent companion. Weary soldiers, foot and leg-sore, observe its constantly changing panoramas, aware of its annoying indifference to their pains and sorrows.

War is not an exclusively human affair. Nature wages it against itself night and day, oblivious to man's fratricide. But soldiers know that even if they do not survive Nature will endure and perpetuate itself, even as their bones molder beneath it. It's a lonely thought and crueler fact that forces them to ponder their insignificance.

When they consider themselves through Nature's eyes, they see time as an endless river that sweeps all before it, making war a futile exercise. Its currents leave nothing behind save swirling memories that will submerge in time. Their reflections make plain that they have given themselves to no more than a moment in the river's passage - and to anonymity when each reflection clears. What then, they ask, has made their existence consequential? Some become so absorbed in such surprisingly probing questions they lose themselves in thought. Others, compelled by fatigue alone, with nothing on their minds save sleep, shut down and surrender to it, trudging along like zombies, asleep on their feet, each step mechanically inspired.

At other times soldiers feel spiritually allied to Nature. Some are remorseful when they watch both Army's bullets and shells tear trees and shred fields, and when their feet trample crops and meadows - and when their hubris ravages whole forests. Even hardened veterans often feel regret and guilt.

I share their misgivings. War is a sinister intoxicant. I ask myself: "Why else do men advance into sheets of hot iron and lead while friends around them are being reduced to carrion? Why else do journalists pursue such violent history? Why else do battle-numbed veterans stare into the dilated eyes of dead comrades without going mad? Otherwise, they would be superhuman if such behavior were not due to their incredible dedication to cause and country.

A Chaplain explained his theory to me. He said he believed that concealed within man's psyche is the knowledge that something better awaits every soul on the other side of life. Hidden within is the understanding - planted like a seed upon conception - that the Almighty has inserted us into a violent universe for our literal sufferance, that we might learn the humbling nature of pain and disappointment. And though it hardly seems so, giving up one's body, even involuntarily, amounts to a rite of passage whose rewards exceed all expectations. Thus, men go into battle unconsciously harboring that assurance, and like pupils in a classroom of Divine instruction, sacrifice themselves despite their natural fears. Otherwise, they would flee en masse.

For my part, I've long since abandoned any attempt to divine God's mind and purposes.

In the meantime, Nature goes its way and we ours. I wonder if it harbors a mystical intelligence greater than ours that understands these and myriad matters not apparent to man. I do not suppose we will ever know.

Tomorrow, our boys will march in rain and dust. Weighty considerations will surrender to empty bellies, bleeding feet and physical exhaustion. Their plodding footsteps will become a numbing cadence in their ears. And many will sleep on their feet, prodded along by friends around and behind them. They will move to the metallic motivations of clinking equipment and the occasional voice of a homesick private lamenting his lot in the words of an old folk song. And while the miles creep by, they will tolerate their aches and urge their bodies to do more than God ever intended. Their mysterious brotherhood will inspire their momentum. Every man in ranks, worried about his soul, will wonder about his fate and what he's become - and I will be among them.

Whatever they have become, these times will have made them so.

* * *

Peace Again

Soldiers are not killer-beasts some pundits make of them. I have seen and lived with them close up, and I can vouch with authority for their deepest longings, which are anything but bestial.

They are as much the victims of circumstances as fowl brought down by hunters. All are trapped within in a swamp of politics they cannot comprehend, and by social mandates they cannot escape - except by desertion. For the sake of family honor, many go to war, lest they be branded cowards. So great are these pressures, they reluctantly volunteer, well aware of the effects of disease, shells, and minié-balls upon flesh and bone. Others go for soldiers, woefully ignorant of war's costs.

Many mask their terrors by assuming postures of manliness and bravado, but die in battle doing foolish things. Some puff their chests and banter like roosters. In their ignorance they unwittingly act the part of fools indifferent or oblivious to the dangers they face - much to the annoyance of hardened veterans - lest they diminish themselves in the eyes of their fellows. But all of this is merely to hide their insecurities - a fact as obvious to veterans as feathers on a mule. Men who have seen the Elephant do not act so.

By contrast, veterans are cautious, not always forthcoming and not always battle's bravest. They go into harm's way as mentors to virgin troops, that their examples might save young lives that would otherwise be carelessly lost. No matter their true years veterans always appear older within and without, prematurely aged by their wartime experiences. Many times I have caught them alone as they reverentially consider those peacetime treasures they've left behind, never to reclaim; of home, families, and sweethearts now a universe away and untouchable, except by thought and reverie. Often, they reveal great humility, humbling me with their private confessions.

I have spoken to simple privates who confess they cannot see any point to the war - that everything being fought for could have been negotiated - that compromise and level heads would have precluded the prolonged slaughter now sapping the spirits of combatants on both sides. I have spoken to veterans who have wearied of killing and who now find it difficult to pull the trigger against human targets. Unfortunately, I also have found troops who revel in it. These are nervous action-cravers hardened by all they have seen and done. They too, are victims. If war has brutalized them, the fault lies with its makers. What might these victims have become - what good might they have done our society - had not the war so damaged their souls?

Often, I have been driven to my knees in prayer, seeking the meaning of it all - but God has never answered. He has given men free will to spend wisely or foolishly that it might be decided on Judgment Day whether their Earthly lives were well-spent or misbegotten.

Some, for their wartime sins, experience Hell within themselves owing to their introspective powers. Every day they live with guilt for submitting to and perpetuating this madness that will not release them. These are the troubled souls who seek the counsel of Chaplains lest they perish in the swamps of their moral confusion. They know that if they survive the contest unreconstructed, they might afterwards lose themselves upon the land, uncontrollably devoted to continuing violence. Yet in their heart of hearts, they desperately wish to honor goodness again - that they might truly be God's instruments of peace. There is hope for these souls. I am convinced that those beyond redemption are few.

Most of our men who survive this war will forget its ways and abide those of peace. If you could hear the soulful singing of the most homesick in camp you would understand their good hearts. Most await liberation, win or lose. In the meantime, they gather in religious services to pray for the guns to quit and for themselves and their estranged countrymen to come together - for peace again.

Only circumstances are bestial.

*   *   *

Oh, God, the Wounded

I must repeat these thoughts:

The horrors of fields littered with maimed and dead cannot be conveyed with printed words.

Neither can they truly make the reader experience battle's stench and the smell of death - of blood and acrid, eye-burning smoke - of intestines, viscera, and feces spewed about; nor can the make them see dead eyes staring into nothingness and skulls without eyes, nor limbs separated from bodies, nor parts of bodies, nor hear the wailing, screaming, and pleading of the mutilated enduring their agonies, nor witness their writhings. No, words and sentiments cannot portray the truth of it.

This is what sons, husbands, brothers, uncles, and fathers come to when clipped by the Reaper's scythe. It is the war home-bound civilians never see and cannot comprehend, unless they, too, have BEEN to war. I cannot impart the reality of hospitals in the open, where row upon row of men and boys, clutching grievous wounds, lay groaning and whimpering - nor can I make the reader see what I see in the sufferers' grimacing faces, nor smell what I smell. I cannot record the cries of those upon whom surgeons dig, probe, and saw - nor recreate the piles of discarded arms, hands, feet, and legs that must be carted off and dumped.

These are the matters that sicken the souls of weary soldiers and often break even the strongest among them.

After a battle, the color of uniforms becomes one, for pain's single hue drenches all. Enemies lay side by side in a common brotherhood, animosities dissolved in their shared miseries and draining blood...no beauty in the lilies there.

Yet it is not God who suffered this upon them, but their free will in contravention of His Holy Law. Too soon, I fear, will it all be forgotten, when guns cease firing and human nature once again commands the peace.

If only the powerful who made war were compelled to suffer it. But, I fear the self-shielding conventions they've created for themselves will forever insulate them from that justice, leaving them always safe to make war again and to compel the poor man to do the dying.

* * *

Prayers Now Tendered

Unsung is the work of Army chaplains devoted to their calling. Theirs is a conflicted mission - the blessing of souls in a blasphemous enterprise.

Dozens of times, I have observed them appealing to their warring flocks, attempting to persuade them to honor and accept the Word of God when all around them men defy it in the most egregious ways possible.

The best they can do is appeal to the Almighty to overlook the killing and destruction committed by souls in their care, mortals being weak and thereby sinful despite themselves. Though they are too politic to declare their flocks deceived or misdirected by politicians, I know they believe so. Often they offer their pleading prayers in near desperation, helpless to halt the whirling wheels of war that every day spin out of control, and whose overpowering momentum was long ago miscalculated by the forces that set them turning.

Would that God might ease their mission by reaching down His hand and scooping away the very tools that make war possible. But He is silent, perhaps in hopes that men will sicken of their folly and desert it at long last. My sympathy goes out to these Godly servants who attempt so unselfishly to make men faithful. I swear that at times I can hear them silently weeping in frustration and defeat. Yet how dearly they are needed and how devoutly our helpless men respond.

Threadbare and in every state of uniform and dress, the men kneel with hats and caps off and heads bowed low. Desperately they pray, knowing the Kingdom awaits them across the way in the barrels of the enemy's rifles and cannon. Sincerely, they seek to cleanse themselves before entering His merciful world, their eyes tightly closed as they mouth in unison the Lord's Prayer. In turn, Chaplains raise their arms above them - and the men are comforted, their fears and private terrors momentarily eased. Ironically, across the way, men in different uniforms pray just as ardently and just as sincerely, filled with identical fears and terror. Their chaplains, too, raise their hands over them and plead for the same salvation. To whom does God listen - to those of the most righteous cause or to all who simply are human? I trust it is the latter, for all, in this common tribulation, are one.

* * *

Baked Goods

It is not often that one is afforded the opportunity while on the march to partake of civilian amenities that remind one of home's blessings.

On a sun-drenched day - cool and refreshing - our sore-footed brigade, being the first in line, was given rest alongside the dusty road that was no more than a wagon track devoid of weeds and grasses. Not far away smoke seeped from the chimney of a modest home whose out-buildings told us it remained, or had been, a prosperous farm. It struck me that its owners were graced by the Lord, for the enemy had not yet transgressed on this parish nor pillaged its resources, as it had in so many others.

Flowers bloomed in the home's front yard, giving us to wonder if the war we had fought and whose destruction we had witnessed for so long had been no more than a cruel illusion.

Men took the pause to relieve themselves - at considerable distance in surrounding woods - keen that they did so in violation of social graces long suffocated by war; the farther from the home, the less modesty required. The Army had come more than twenty miles in the past twenty-four hours, having marched through the night. Exhaustion had taken its toll. Most men were spent, yet there remained another six miles before we reached our destination. This respite, therefore, would be prolonged, its duration dependent upon our General's discretion. The men were given leave to drop and rest, which they did enthusiastically.

Soon, wafting from the house's direction and teasing our palates, came the aromas of fresh-baked goods. How dearly did we instantly yearn for all those home-bound luxuries we dreamed of every day, now vividly brought to heart by such scents.

Minutes later, as our men lounged by companies, our attention was captured by the high-pitched entreaties of a woman's voice. Looking up, I spied a red apron-clad lady of generous proportions waving vigorously from her porch and bidding someone to come to her yard. She pointed to something suspiciously like a pie in one hand. Behind her, a white-haired man, apparently her husband, passively rocked in a chair. Our General and his staff in the column's van remained mounted on their tired nags, absorbed in the mysteries of a large map held by three officers. Upon hearing the woman the General said something to his aide, who looked about. Spying me, he piped-up, "You, there, Chapman...would you see to her, please. We're indulged at the moment."

I trudged the sixty or so yards to her fence. She then came forward, bubbling with enthusiasm: "Please, invite your people there to come by...I have some baked goods I'm sure they would enjoy."

"But ma'm," I cautioned, "there are hundreds of men in this brigade!"

"Well, the Lord fed thousands with a fish," she declared, "so I 'spose I could feed at least SOME of you with whatch yer smellin'! Pick a few boys!"

As matters evolved the General asked that I and two of his staff attend the woman and accept her generosity, with a third officer to join us directly. None were disposed to deny themselves the delights of what we discovered to be a home-baked bonanza.

But the baker, Mrs. Emma Florence, grew self-conscious when it appeared that the officers had misinterpreted the spirit of her invitation, which I had relayed word for word. When she had referred to "your people," she had not intended it to mean for officers only. After cordial introductions I detected subtle signs of discomfort in her expression, especially as she twice looked back to the column, seeming to suggest that she had anticipated sharing her kitchen bounties with many of our rank and file. Her husband, John, kept to his rocker and made no motion to greet us, gazing straight ahead as if seeing something we could not.

Her kitchen, heavenly-laden with pies and breads, conveyed the notion that she had anticipated the column's arrival, else why had she made so much? She revealed that word of our approach had preceded us by at least a half-day, the road out front being the only logical line of march an army would take. Her husband, she explained, a twice-wounded veteran of the Mexican War, had been the victim of a seizure two months earlier upon news that their only son, a sergeant in the militia, had been killed in recent fighting. Understandably, she could not now hide her emotion.

Before we seated ourselves I took aside Major Franks, the General's aide, suggesting to him that under the circumstances it might be appropriate to bring a representation of enlisted men to the table. He concurred, nobly surrendering his table seat to ask her if he might invite a few, to which the good Mrs. Florence readily replied, "Bring as many as my inventory will feed!"

But when Captain Wilson also volunteered to give up his place to our enlisted men, she balked, affably affirming that she had prepared enough to serve him and a "passel" too, providing that everyone received an equal share. Despite the most recent loss of her son she still manifested an outgoing disposition and monumental generosity - a brave woman.

She served at least thirty enlisted men that day, who, sitting on the porch and in the yard, eagerly partook of pies and sweets, the Major having instructed his company officers to ask for volunteers for a "special enterprise." To their overwhelming surprise they were marched to the house. As it was, Mrs. Florence had volunteered the farm's well to reconstitute the dwindling levels of water in our troops' canteens. Ranks of men, each carrying a score of their comrades' canteens strapped over their shoulders, were detailed to fill them.

Inside the kitchen, as I and the original three officers enjoyed our delicious fare, my mind wandered to the remaining troops in the column. How sad that their struggling nation had not the resources to adequately provide sustenance - and how bitterly disappointed would be the hundreds who would learn of their comrades' good fortune this day.

I cannot remember the course of our table conversation, as I found myself studying the demeanors of the Major and the younger Captains Wilson and French. I realized, with profound spiritual discomfort, that I was gazing into the stresses and tribulations of our entire Army's leadership at that very hour. Giving me sudden pause, the strains of weariness were graphically etched in their faces and drawn expressions.

Each in martial form had become a harried metaphor of his nation's plight - and perhaps because I had been so much with our enlisted men, who radiated a unique exhaustion of their own, did I only now appreciate the pathos in the officers' conditions, and how heavily their responsibilities weighed upon them. Their frayed and tattered uniforms only reinforced my impressions, though my civilian attire fared no better. Our enlisted men's coverings suffered even more. I, too, had no wardrobe from which to borrow fresh wear. And, like our men, I always waited, as did they, for a halt at a creek or stream to bathe and launder fully clothed. And though I had never expected better circumstances, I wondered if our officers had, in the war's early days so painfully long ago.

After nearly a half-hour, a trumpeter announced the column's reformation and preparations to move on. To his extreme mortification, French had fallen asleep at the table with a portion of pie still in his partially raised fork, so deep had been his fatigue. Far from being offended, the sympathetic Mrs. Florence bade us not to disturb him. I thought it extremely noteworthy that the General had refrained from joining us at the table, which he obviously could have done. Instead he had, also nobly, remained with the column in the shade of a tree, munching hardtack and drinking warm water from his personal canteen. Mrs. Florence also noted his restraint saying: "Take this to him," handing me a slice of warm apple pie. "Is he married?" Yes, we replied. "Then," she added, "ask him to pretend that it was brought from home."

Our officers, including the embarrassed French, rose from the table, each one taking her hand in theirs and kissing it gently, with the sleepy French profusely apologizing, adding, "We will never forget you and your kindness." Her eyes teared. She dared not reply, lest she break down.

"Sir," the Major said, putting his hand on John Florence's shoulder as we departed, "you have married a saint - and you, sir, have our soldiers' deepest admiration and respect." John looked on, his eyes moistening, one side of his nearly paralyzed face straining to smile.

As the column moved along the road past the Florence household, our men cheered the couple, taking off their head wear and waving it energetically. The General bowed deeply from horseback, his hat in hand, sweeping the air with the hat like a royal cavalier in a gesture of thanks. Mrs. Florence stood at her husband's side, wiping her eyes. Then, unexpectedly, her husband raised a feeble hand, saluting us.

Once again within the column I could not restrain MY emotions, and neither could the three reconstituted officers who had treasured, and would always recall, the gentle couples' endearing graciousness.

* * *

Writin' Home

It tears my heart to see the numbers of men who dearly wish to write loved ones at home, but who can neither write nor read. They have so much to say and sentiments to express. For many, Earthly time will expire before anyone at home will have known what truly is in their hearts.

I help as many as I can, since they often come to me, knowing that I am a journalist or as some have called me, "a man of letters." Most call me the "WRITIN' HOME" man!

They come in all ages, from those who cannot yet shave to grizzled veterans in their fifties and sixties, who consider written words to be magical markings, but who doubt they will ever - or CAN ever - learn to "unscramble 'em." Some look into books and newspapers and marvel at what to them are unintelligible jumbles of inky symbols that appear hopelessly confused. And when I transfer their words to paper, they pause to examine the "scribble" to see how it represents what they've truly said. Often, they simply shake their heads and continue their dictations, however grammatically flawed or mangled. I, of course, attempt to set things down in recognizable form and spelling. These men are universally grateful and usually go away with a sense of true accomplishment. Some are profoundly relieved knowing they have finally communicated what they've wanted to say for only God knows how long - and that it will eventually be "heard" by their loved ones so they can go to their Maker conscience-free.

Thus, in my small, my non-military ways, my presence has produced something good for someone, and though I carry no rifle, I am accepted as one of their own. I feel guilty that I do not, but their officers have forbidden me to do so, lest "I mistakenly shoot them all!" Military authorities do not consider that untrained civilians are military assets - liabilities more often than not. And many officers refuse to take responsibility for me. But, with some exceptions, this regiment's officers are very outgoing and we frequently converse. They often ask me how I see things and how I believe the war is going.

The "exceptions" have candidly admitted that they initially worried that I might have adversely named them in newspaper articles or criticized them for this or that. Most are surprised to learn that I am a private citizen, not a bonafide reporter, chronicling the war as I see and experience it. Yet, I sense that some of the more aloof among them, while remaining cordial enough, consider me of no use to the enhancement of their military careers. And, most assuredly, I will not be.

*   *   *

Mud & Misery

Without reservation, I speak for many when I say that mud among all the war's miseries will be what they remember in old age - rain, thaws and mud - cold, heat, exhaustion and mud - woods, wilderness, raging storms, lightning, freezing climes and ice and mud - slogging and struggling through that deep, sucking mire, that plague of legions.

I will never forget it nor will any of the men with whom I trekked; barefooted men and those fortunate to possess shoes, toting them strung together over their shoulders and covered with oil cloth lest mud and wet ruin them. More precious than gold, shoes are treasured.

A terror for both shod or barefooted men, cold mud is the worst, be it during fall winter or early spring, winter mud being nightmarish. It requires exhausting labor mile after mile to lift one foot before the other while both feet are submerged in icy sludge. Ooze's tentacle-like grip drains one's strength while accompanied by devilish chills that spike through leg muscles and bones and eventually into one's guts and very soul.

Yes, I've experienced these and more. I know what it means and what it does to soldiers. I've seen the fever it engenders later that ravages their bodies, already weakened by malnourishment, and dispatches them to God in sweat-soaked bundles of already filthy uniforms or what passes for uniforms, some of those men calling for wives, and mothers and other loved ones in their fated delirium or outright ravings - with powerless physicians sometimes standing by embarrassed, frustrated, and discouraged by their obvious medical ignorance.

Mud and misery...integral ingredients of war, but because they are neither experienced nor endured by the bulk of the politicians who encourage and make war, they are not persuaded to end it or find and cherish saner means to ameliorate this most destructive spiritual fever of our precious flesh and blood, our God-given free will run amok. How supernaturally vexing is this timeless human disease He couched within us yet left us to cure. I wonder what transcendent magnificence awaits our species, if through constant trial, as babes yearning to walk, we at long last succeed.

* * *

Incredible

I hesitate to describe battle in more detail, for I do not wish to further devastate the sensibilities of those dedicated to propriety or ignorant of its horrors. Yet, that the public remains so far removed from such ignorance offends our veteran soldiers who endure battle's worst.

Equally annoying to veterans are those naïve souls who think war is a game composed of pomp and frilly uniforms, especially those frivolous women who act so excited in the proximity of soldiers, and who swoon at their very mention. These airs and affectations are sure to alienate and disgust men on furlough recently involved in horrendous fighting. Ducklings that never wander far from their mother's protective wings cannot be expected to imagine how naked one stands in battle, stripped of all human value and feeling, akin to an expendable piece of meat. Terrified men and boys soil themselves, their flesh being at the mercy of mangling iron and lead. Feeling alone amongst many they are vulnerable and self-pitying. These things can affect even veteran troops pushed to the limits of their mental endurance by months or years of war. I have witnessed such soldiers drop their rifles, turn and walk away, their break-up masked by a strange equanimity. Others calmly face their fate, feeling already dead, pawns of God's will. For men like these, fear so long a close and faithful companion, has lost its currency.

I have seen men torn in half or obliterated by iron shot in splashes of blood and viscera, who only minutes before prayed with trembling intensity for their salvation. And I have seen men, paradoxically finished with religion survive savage missile storms, as if protected by a Divine shield or God Himself. I cannot fathom the contradiction. I am only led to wonder for what ultimate purpose we were born to Earth, and whether our kind's existence was designed, or whether we are merely a complicated coincidence of nature sharing the same happenstance credentials with weeds.

But war assures men of one dramatic lesson - that we, not God, are creators of our own Hell on Earth. For that, only we must answer and bear the responsibility. In this, our ongoing collapse of conscience, we Americans feed upon ourselves like cannibal-insects.

*   *   *

Fireflies

They come out at night, searching for life in fields of death.

I watched them last night, as disjointed lines of charcoal clouds lazed within the faded turquoise of the evening sky after dusk, soon overpowered by the pallid light of a new half-moon...the stench of powder smoke still heavy in the air.

They flitted here and there, like sparks engaged in a macabre dance. But as some neared me, they became lanterns emerging as from a crypt, and carried by orderlies to illuminate the ways for the stretcher teams they escorted.

Distant moaning and agonized cries seeped from the battlefield's moon-blanched darkness, cynically reassuring me that tortured life remained out there, invisibly costumed by rising mists clothed in the orb's ghostly sheen.

Upon those stretchers, the tortured squirmed, arms and legs kicking or flailing, those whose limbs had escaped destruction by canister fire and lead. Other wounded lay unconscious, the last of their draining blood dripping from massive torso wounds or severed arteries, their faces shadowed with a morbid pallor. Others lay without faces, the lanterns' soft glow mercifully muting that incredible horror. Still, life pulsed through what was left of many, for how long only the surgeons could say, those not too exhausted from hours of gory, soul-wrenching toil.

A stretcher team was about to pass me by, but the young soldier it carried reached out his hand to me. As I took it in mine, the team halted, the lantern revealing both his tender years and the bloody mess of his chest. He managed a strained smile. Too weak to speak, he whispered a labored message: "Tell my maw I love her, will ya? Tell her I love her...please."

Then, convulsed by paroxysms of sudden pain, he gripped my hand with the power of a bear trap. The more his suffering intensified, the tighter he held me, until my hand felt crushed. A moment later, with a sudden lurch, he sat up, turning toward me, staring, as if he were looking through me, perhaps into the next world..."Please?" he whispered again, almost inaudibly..."please?"

Falling back, he died gripping my hand, his eyes rolling back until only the white appeared in each. Try as the orderlies might they could not break me loose, until, failing at everything less drastic, they broke his thumb and two fingers.

I held my hand limply as they carried him away, thankful that he had avoided the surgeons' tender mercies. If he had not died before reaching their tents, then, undoubtedly, as well-meaning as they might have meant to be, they would have laid him aside to perish in agony or lost him beneath their knives without benefit of anesthesia, that rarest of mercies.

"Wait," I called to the team, "who WAS this soldier? Did he possess identification?"

"We looked, sir, but couldn't find none," one orderly confessed. "It be a shame. He shoulda knowed better than t'go inta a fight shed a'some."

Troubled, I trudged to our company's bivouac hoping to be offered a cup of hot ersatz tea, anything palatable being appreciated. But, how was I going to keep a promise the boy had thought I'd made him - and because of which he had passed from this life comforted? I resolved to spend the next day trying to find someone who knew him. How could I have done less?

The enemy's wounded would remain in the field until ours were recovered. Their dead would remain unburied. But if it was decided that the Army could afford no more time in the area, their wounded would be abandoned. War is like that, pity for their opposites indulged by either side only when convenient.

Thinking back to the young soldier, I could not drink all my tea, tainted as it was with my guilt for seeking a pleasure when he lay cold in a pit with so many others. I tossed it away - haunted.

*   *   *

Bloody Wheels

Today, fierce rains lashed our column as the Army retreated over muddy trails through a wilderness of tangled woods and virgin meadows. In places, paths vanished in lakes of ooze blocked by small, downed trees that had to be cleared to allow our passage.

Wind lashed the column for miles. Stinging droplets forced our slipping and sliding men to bow against them, their footing made treacherous by troughs gouged by the wheels of our ambulance and supply trains.

Our company slogged behind the last ambulance of the twenty in our part of the column. Walking wounded struggling alongside leaned against it for support. But sizzling lightning and cracking thunder could not drown the pitiful moans and cries from the wounded inside. Their rickety carrier had become a vehicle of jolting torture, with pitiful, pulling horses straining and grunting.

I trudged barefooted in our company's right-hand file directly behind the ambulance having tied my worn boots together, wrapped them in rubberized cloth and slung them over my shoulder, lest the rain ruin their remains. Yet I could not lift my eyes against the wind and wet. Instead, my concentration fell on the ambulance's right rear wheel as it slowly turned in labored revolutions that lifted clinging mud from the depths and dropped it back, the process endlessly repeating itself. But it remained the agonies of those inside that overpowered all other distractions.

At one point a fallen tree halted the column. Troops armed with axes labored forward to chop it away. It was then that a trembling hand emerged from beneath the ambulance's drenched canvas-covering. It death-gripped the sideboards over the wheel, then became a rigid arm reaching grotesquely outward, the hand's fingers clutching vacant air like talons fiercely gripping prey. The macabre vision shocked me as lightning illuminated hand and arm. A stream of red dripped from its talons onto the stationary wheel and slipped down its contours. Impulse urged me to cry for help - to attract the attention of surgeons to the plight of the convulsing soldier inside. Though booming thunder nearly discouraged me, I attempted to call for help, but an inhuman cry issued from the ambulance, freezing my voice.

The arm jerked upward, the talons snapping into a terror-wracked ball. Red in greater volume streamed from the source beneath the canvas, falling from the elbow onto the still stationary wheel. I watched the color ride the rain down the rim to form swirling red puddles in the ooze beneath. Then the arm collapsed, limply hanging over the sideboards, its clutched hand opening only slightly.

"He's gone," the soldier next to me shouted through the thunder's din. "Bless him; he be better off, now."

I could not take my gaze from the reddened wheel. I had witnessed another life pass from this Earth in the haunted theater of war, made even more gruesome by a hostile Nature infuriated at our trespass. And then the wheel turned again. The ambulance moved, and with every succeeding jolt the dancing limb dotted my face with stubborn crimson droplets that refused to be wiped away.

"Best y'not look ana'more," the soldier next to me advised. "It'll grab yer guts if'n y'do."

Think not of it, I told myself, but of pleasant prewar vistas...of fresh breezes filled with warming sunlight where no dampness infects bones and flesh. Remember the smile of that pretty woman who graced the most glorious day of your life when she took your ring. Think only of her gentleness, not of these hundred or more wagons in this accursed column of bleeding carrion. Think instead of peace.

I tried...but reality mocked me...and the wheel turned round and round...

* * *

In the Beauty of the Lilies

**The Wartime Journals
of Confederate Correspondent
Royal K. Chapman
1862-1864**

Journal Eleven

Contents

*   *   *

A Thought

Threadbare are the hearts of men
too long committed to battle's
tapestries and the indelible
stains they leave upon their
sleeves.

Visions

A Diary Entry of the Late Infantry Corporal
Clarence Pace, CSA,

Included in a letter from his wife to
family friend & Publisher
J.A. Fuller in 1885

"I live now in the West, but when I step onto the veranda of my comfortable home or walk through these arid spaces, they are not always the panoramas I see. Instead, I see Virginia, Maryland, and, yes, Pennsylvania.

"So long after the war, these visions haunt me still. I hear bugles and smell gunpowder in lush green fields, and hills shrouded in smoke. I hear the rattle of musketry and the cries and shrieks of wounded and dying souls, and all the brutal cacophonies of a terrible time remain forever fresh in my memory. And once again I am afraid. I sometimes shake and sweat and must get away for a while, lest my family see me this way and worry. My dear wife, bless her heart, has never understood, nor have my children - nor, now, do my grandchildren.

"And when I come across young men whose ages I was then, I wonder what happened to that boy who was me - who went to war a lamb and returned a scarred ram. We came home feeling that the idealism we'd fought for no longer justified the suffering we'd witnessed and contributed to - and for which we felt guilty and conscience-stricken. Now, I wonder if any part of that prewar youngster still exists beneath the rubble of subsequent decades. Some parts must. Why else could I reflect upon them and rekindle emotions I thought dampened and sealed by time?

"There are no green fields here and no one present who also remembers what once was my youthful optimism; just sand and cactus and barren buttes indifferent to my memories. My grizzled face and balding mane bear no resemblance to that youthful countenance I remember, but now could never prove existed. Decades of sun and wind have seen to that, as if a punishing God had vengefully etched upon my once virginal exterior the sins I committed in that war, and then filled my bones with rheumatism's purifying fires.

"After my discharge, I tried to escape and distract myself by coming here to seek a fortune in mining. I found it meaningless. My thoughts have always remained back there in those bloody Eastern fields, which beckon me to return to them, lest death take me before I can resolve my lingering conflicts, as if returning could wipe them away and grant me spiritual liberation there.

"No, I see dead comrades in desert visions - Jim Flannery, Thomas Day, Henry Sessions and Ezra Benson - all friends back then and buried somewhere there. Mirage-like, they beckon to me and smile at me from across the veil of their present existences. They tell me not to fear the future, for time is but a notion while their new world is ever-present. I wonder why I was spared and they were not - or why they were denied the bewilderments of further physical existence on this harsh and unforgiving planet - while I was not.

"It is as if the intervening years have been indistinct dreams relived in my sleep. The mirror above my washstand betrays the truth. In it I think I detect the specter of that eighteen- year-old disguised beneath the present image - and I ask it, "Are you a shade to ever-torment me?" The shade is that same face I studied in cracked mirrors on tent poles in bivouac after my first terrible combat those decades ago - tinted with lost innocence and battlefield horrors I had not expected to witness or ever considered possible. That first combat laid the pattern for this present face, indelibly exaggerating it after every succeeding battle until, at war's end, I appeared fifteen years older, perhaps more. And I've aged evermore rapidly ever since. This confused head of mine could be Methuselah's.

"Every line speaks of the mortal sins I committed then - of the lives I took at rifle's range and by my own hands. No, age brings no escape, just more secret regret. I am continually haunted by the faces of the men I killed. They accuse me. These past decades have been time served in quiet punishment for my blood-letting then. And now, I think of Samuel Walker of my company, who one day in the heat of vicious fighting simply threw his rifle to the ground, calmly saying, "Enough of offending God," and walked away, never to be seen or heard from again. I know now that through his Epiphany the Lord had spoken to all of us.

"I look at my hands and still see the blood of a man who died agonizingly on my bayonet, one hand gripping my sleeve. My gut still wrenches when I see him reach with his other into his jacket before he collapsed, his eyes wide with terror, and pull from it a tintype of his wife and child, feebly handing it to me, his killer, mumbling with faltering strength..."Tell them I died... tell them I love them."

"I hear him plainly now as I have always heard him, and I weep. The patriotism that justified that killing sounds so hollow now and in the end justified what? His face has always been the other I see in my mirror. He, too, haunts me, condemning me for retaining that tintype and never doing what he asked of me. Though I found in his jacket pocket his name and place of residence...Hosea Kinnert...of Vermont...I have never searched for his wife and child. What, oh, God, have I thusly put them through, what excruciating spiritual pain and mortal anguish - never knowing his fate, ever-futilely waiting for years upon years for him to walk through their door to reunite with them in love and devotion. Yes, yes, if I hadn't killed him first he no doubt would have been killed me...or would he have? Perhaps he would have been more merciful than I, and spared me. The quandary drives me to my knees. Perhaps, he had been a far better and more charitable man than I could ever have been.

"Some would argue that killing is war's imperative, and because of it, killing him was not mine or anyone's fault. Yet, I despise that logic. Time has washed that duty clean of its false trappings and left it naked. I was wrong to have killed him and all those nameless others those three long years of madness. Time has confirmed it.

"Yes, I am wealthy, but not within. I eat well, but my food digests poorly. I drink but futilely, for the spiritual pain drink lessens constantly returns. And now I sit on my veranda disappointed in myself and guilty for the wealth I've accumulated at the expense of so many dead men foolishly termed my enemies. Conscience does not spare me for my former youthful naivete. It bares an impartial razor's edge God deftly wields to part the souls of men who transgress His Word, causing them to think, his punishment diabolical.

"Yes, I look and admire the exotic sunsets of this beautiful land. I have never wanted to abandon them. The vast and unobstructed distances here make me feel safe from those sordid fields and meadows of the East. I could never return to them to reminisce as so many veterans have done, nostalgia for that time in my life being an obscenity. Nor could I do so without returning with the blood of that past on my boots. In one of those fields Hosea Kinnert died staring at me, his eyes wide with pain and fright that will forever render my conscience his captive. My tears of immediate regret shed that day could not wash my conscience clean, nor can they here. At least, in this enchated wilderness, I've found a measure of solace.

"These distant hills and mountains are my monastery in which I do my daily penance. Here, piece by piece, I lay my conscience before God and pray for Hosea Kinnert. It is as much as I can do. Yet though I cannot stand the thought of war, I have lived long enough and understand enough of man's inequities to know that we are addicted to it, no less so then an addict to opium. We crave it, yield to it, seek it. We are born warriors, that proclivity produced in our blood generation to generation and in constant conflict with the Divine seed of conscience planted in our animal natures by God, that we might wrest with our misgivings for owning that nature and strive to overcome it, lest we forever be condemned to this planet of eternal tribulation, having failed His spiritual testing, and unworthy of anything better.

"Forgive me, my diary, for these maudlin visions of depressing self-pity with which I've once more burdened you. But, you see, I am a weak man. By now you should understand that. Let me now tend my rose garden that you might hope for a sweeter entry the next time."

* * *

A Lucid Soul

Major Thomas Hartman passed into Glory this afternoon. Mortally wounded yesterday during the fierce combat, his legs and torso devastated by canister, he mysteriously clung to life when, as our brigade surgeons proffered, he should have bled out and perished minutes after being savaged.

Before the war Hartman had been a professor of English literature at a small Virginia college as well as a published poet. As with many officers new to the military and war, and whose commissions had come through the auspices of admiring politicians, he had nonetheless proved to be a superior leader. He was known to express himself with expansive language.

We carried him to his tent and laid him gently on his cot, his uniform blood-soaked and shredded, so much so that we could not help staring into his shattered bones and pulverized tissue. He thanked us kindly, his manner differential and unbelievably magnanimous given what must have been his horrendous pain. That he could still speak astonished us.

I have witnessed the deaths of countless men in this war, not only those killed outright on the battlefield, but those who lingered and died slowly. But never have I known a mutilated man to have been as mystically lucid as Hartman to his last breath. I cannot surmise the precise import of his testimony, though it was in no way a continuous rambling. He expressed himself cogently, if mysteriously, his observations fascinating, as if he were looking into the world beyond and describing it for us. Those practical men among us who also heard him, while conceding that his manner was controlled, nonetheless refused to believe what we heard was other than an unusual form of delirium. I, on the other hand, am persuaded that it was cryptically profound. The following, to the best of my shorthand, is what he said:

"There are voices on the wind. They speak to us of times past in that golden light of Autumn days at dusk. They whisper, 'do not forget us.' Can you feel their presence, those who have gone before us? We hear a distant bugle and they come to us and walk beside us saying, 'Tell our stories...caution the living, please, for our stories will then become our release from our anonymity.' They are coming for me now. I see them, so I will not have to tell you their stories. Promise me that YOU will tell them, so that the living might become vessels from which these times will pour forth to future generations. Tell the future what the deceased cannot forgive nor forget. Help them touch future hearts and open doors that will be hidden by time's mists. By doing so you will let them live again in times hence, that future generations will know that nothing truly dies, but that human folly remains constant. Tell me that you understand what I've said."

As a courtesy those attending offered the Major their assurances, but it was apparent in their expressions that they considered they were dealing with a dying man's babblings. To those who may read this testimony and believe it was only that, I offer no rebuttal, having merely been a recorder of that incident. Nor am I now being the originator of fiction. But I wonder...in passing over the edge of life who can say what new realities become clear to a man? Perhaps soldiers who have gone before, and desirous of ending the anonymity of their circumstances, WERE there pleading with him to end it as he described. He cashed in shortly thereafter and was buried with honors. Thus I have no more to report of matters except the following, appreciating that its subjectivity may disqualify it from consideration:

After his death his sentiments echoed in my conscience, leaving me chilled. Intuition persuaded me that he was saying that those who had passed on now sought to warn posterity that the seeds of our fratricidal contest would lie tenuously dormant in both nations' soil even long after the fighting ended, no matter who triumphed - that our differences would remain fertile and subject to reawakening by the nourishment of future internal antipathies? From their present vantage points were the deceased anxiously seeing far into the future, telling us that America would never be beyond risking such costs again? Were they telling us that even should the South lose this war and the nation reunite there would always exist the danger of another violent division - that, for whatever reasons or issue, the land would always be of two fires that must never again be permitted to converge?

Had these points been the essence of what Major Thomas Hartman had poetically attempted to convey - or are such conclusions merely the products of MY prejudice? Certainly, I would know only when I touched hands with those heroes on that bridge twixt now and then. In the meantime, we had not even a single lily to poignantly award him.

*   *   *

Three Things

I previously wrote that I received news I feared to hear. It concerned the young commanding officer of a company to which I had attached myself, and who had accepted my inconvenient presence with such civility but perished along with half his command this morning.

During the fighting, he directed me to the safety of a large tree, pledging me to remain there for the duration. From there I watched his company's destruction but did not see him fall. I hoped to see him again to thank him for being so caring for my life. But he is dead, and I feel I've betrayed him. He would tell me I did not, but I cannot banish my nagging guilt for not having stood beside him - for having survived instead. I would expect no one to understand my attitude, save those who have stumbled down similar paths. I have since learned his name: Lieutenant Corbin James from South Carolina.

* * *

Today, while helping to carry wounded from the field, my coat became soaked with their blood. Much to my embarrassment, those thinking I, too, had been wounded insisted that I seek medical aid. Would that I could have shared that honor, earned equality with the brave and claimed to being an undisputed "brother in arms."

* * *

If I have already written something akin to the following since Thomas Hartman's passing, I apologize. Hartman was a friend and fellow journalist. He passed, I'm told, from consumption while in the field with our Western armies. I walk now through vistas beyond our regiment's bivouac, listening to the wind rustle through the trees and grasses along the fields and meadows all around. Voices not of our realm speak there, yet I cannot decipher their meaning. Though they transcend my comprehension they comfort me as they comfort others in times of emotional distress. I am also told that others in ranks hear them too, very often, and also sense that they exist in a dimension beyond our world, being truly mystical.

"Don'tcha try t'figure 'em out," a veteran instructed me, rubbing his chin. "They be of the Lord. Jest be glad that they put'cha at peace with yerself and let it go."

They did put me at peace with myself, but posed a troubling question. I asked the veteran, "Is this what men hear when their times comes?"

"Sometimes, yep, but I guess jest as often often, no," he answered, as he pensively looked away, thinking. "A man's jest got t'bide and see...jest bide and see."

*   *   *

A Soldier's Justice

Men form bonds in war that are not broken while the fighting lasts. Attachments grow spiritually strong. Though initially strangers they become kindred spirits via the intense adversities they share.

Death does not necessarily part them, for in a poignant sense the dead remain alive and constant in the memories of their surviving comrades. It's as if the dead were on furlough, or wounded and only temporarily away. Their presence persists, often powerfully, their survivors remaining fiercely loyal. Woe to those who dare to interfere with their memories or detract from the dead's honored stature. I have witnessed the living's ire leveled upon the insensitive and flippant and others who lack an innate sense of decency in such circumstances.

Chastened was one such photographer:

I stumbled along the battlefield's convoluted terrain a full day after the fighting watching medical orderlies collect the remaining wounded and burial teams begin to remove the dead of both sides. Our side had won a pyrrhic victory at best, our losses having been crippling.

Perhaps a hundred yards away, his ankle-length white smock brilliant in the savagely hot sunlight, a hated photographer arranged his tripodded machine to capture the pitiful likeness of one of our killed soldiers. Then, much to my disgust, he dragged the body to sitting position against a large rock outcropping and stood the dead man's rifle against the rock alongside him, obviously preparing to use the body to stage a photograph.

I immediately set out to intercept him, my anger mounting, that such a sacrilege should be perpetrated upon a soldier who had honorably given his life for his country. Besides, honor should have dictated that for the sake of the dead man's family, public exposure of his body in its mutilated condition should not have been risked. A sketch may be altered to disguise a dead soldier's identity yet convey a scene's pathos and poignancy. A likeness however, though perhaps technically alterable, could be exploited for the fame and profit of the photographer with no consideration given to the victim's next of kin. And I sensed that this manipulator was without ethics, let alone principle.

As I trudged between bloating bodies and battlefield debris I was preceded by five of our soldiers who approached the photographer unnoticed by him. One of them grabbed his arm and whirled him around to face them. By that time, I, in turn, approached within hearing distance. The following is what I initially heard, as best as I can remember it:

"I reckon ya 'shud put that boy right back ova there liken y'found him, don'tcha 'gree?" the soldier menacingly commanded, pointing. "He be one of 'arn, and we don't cotton t'scum like you usin' him the way yer doin'."

"Why, I...I" the startled photographer stammered, "I have permission from the highest authority to photograph this battlefield."

"You ain't got nothin' but us'ns here right now and 'ar permissions," the soldier responded, "and right now, y'all got 'ars to put that boy back b'fore we use that contraption t'cap'cha the likeness a YER dead body!"

"You have no right to threaten me!" the photographer protested.

"Maybe not 'cordin' t'yer figurin', but we surela' got call." Turning to the others, "This here feller's pictcha' box looks t'be kinda delicate, don't it? Turr'ble if'n it got felled ova' and all its innards a'split out accidental."

"Your general will hear about this," the photographer declared, as he moved to protect his machine.

At that moment, I arrived on scene. One of the soldiers, wounded in the arm recognized me: "What do y'all think 'bout this here feller?" he asked me. "He be one a'yern, ain't he?"

"No," I assured him, "his kind ain't one of mine."

I told the photographer that his action was enough to get him run off the battlefield and his credentials revoked for the duration. Also, I stated that word would be put out on him, and that he would likely be considered a pariah whereever he went. He listened, but arrogantly doubted me. Grumbling and indignant, he began to grab up his machine, prepared to trudge off.

"I wager you've done something like this many times before," I told him.

"I do what I have to convey the costs of this war," he answered.

Though I wished not to sound self-righteous, and conceding that his conviction sounded honest enough, I insisted that his methods would do nothing to enhance his stature nor guarantee the cooperation of common Southern soldiers. He protested that he did not require their cooperation or their good faith - and turned to leave.

"You ain't goin' nowheres 'til ya put this boy back the way y'found him," the threatening soldier warned, his rifle leveled, "er s'help us God, we'uns'll put cha in the ground. Hell, maybe we'uns'll jest lay ya out for the buzzards, 'cause yer hide'd prob'ly poison maggots!" He cocked the rifle's hammer. I noticed, but the photographer did not, that the soldier had not put a percussion cap on the rifle's nipple beneath its hammer. It would not have fired without one. Indeed, his rifle might not even have been charged.

Cautiously, the picture-taker released his grip on his machine and reluctantly returned the dead soldier's body to its original position.

"Hope that satisfies you," he sneeringly remarked.

With that, the threatening soldier swung the rifle, and with the butt cracked the man across the head. The man fell unconscious and bleeding. It could well have been a killing blow, but the veteran soldier knew how little force to apply. He then proceeded to smash the picture machine. I could not stop him, nor did I want to. The offender had earned that reward. If repercussions came from it I would vouch for the soldier, the photographer's methods speaking to his guilt. Not even the division's General, a soldier's soldier, would deny the justice of what had occurred - a soldier's justice.

Indeed, though the photographer later protested to the general's staff, I vouched for the soldiers, who were ultimately exonerated and the photographer banished. I later learned that while he had laid unconscious, the five had buried their comrade precisely where he had fallen, also having respectfully tendered their prayers for his valorous soul.

*   *   *

The Lord be in Ever'thin'

Fatalists abound in the Army, especially men who have seen the Elephant many times during years of campaigning. They face each day with astonishing stoicism, their calm demeanors and ready acceptance of events good or bad a mystery to less tempered soldiers. And yet the underlying foundations of their equanimity do not always lie in fatalism, but in deep religious faith.

I have discussed the matter with many such men and am continually humbled by their devotion to Scripture, and what some term the "Faith of Their Fathers." They truly and profoundly believe that the "Lord's in everthin'," that all that occurs in their lives and in manmade events correspond to Divine instigation, the reasons being too complex for human comprehension but intended for mankind's ultimate perfection.

Rationalists might object, reasoning that humans slaughtering humans cannot possibly lead to perfection of any kind, except more efficient slaughtering. But the religious boys remain convinced that war is a human affliction that like a disease must run its course, and against which men will achieve eventual immunity.

"He be a'mouldin' us like clay ever-day," one such soldier explained to me. "If'n He be convinced that war's like a purifyin' fire a'purgin' us of 'ar iniquities, like the preachers say, then so be it. T'day, peoples a'betta' at fightin' than talkin'. Maybe, one day, when we're too weary a'fightin' and killin' each otha' t'solve 'ar disputes, we'll quit it and learn t'be betta' at talkin' than fightin' and'll talk things out instead when we're a'differin'. And if'n men gotta die in the meantime like we been doin' here fer betta' than three year, that be His way. Things fer soma 'ar boys at home be so hard and unfergivin' they ain't all that a'skerd a'dyin' 'cause the Lord done promised us the next world be a finer place. So, ya see, all we be a'doin' is givin' up one life fer a betta' one, if'n He wills it."

Nothing appears to shake these men's convictions, and their attitudes have compelled me to examine mine. I have spoken to chaplains who tell me that such intense spirituality humbles them, and often makes them sense that they are in the company of special angels. Yet it remains difficult for me to reconcile war and God. Perhaps I am too much the practical thinker. Such faith confuses me. I must sit down in quietude to think it through, but I wonder if I'm truly capable of understanding it.

Yesterday during a vicious firefight with enemy infantry attempting to turn our left flank, I found a young soldier, a boy of perhaps seventeen tender years, trembling beneath a partially overturned caisson. Passing troops on their way to reinforce the battle line, glanced at him accusingly, their disdain for what they assumed to be his "cowardice" plainly devastating. Cognizant of his supposed crime, but too ashamed to return to his unit, the boy prayed to his Rosary, choking on his tears as he asked the Virgin Mary to forgive his transgression and help him to redeem himself. I asked him, as the sounds of battle roared in the near distance, "Son, will you come with me? You must consult a chaplain I know, and you will find relief. Come...you are not alone in your fear."

I had seen many like him through the years and appreciated his situation. The Elephant had so terrified him that he soiled himself and ran, his youthful innocence unable to stand against the titanic fright even seasoned veterans encountered when faced with masses of charging enemy, bayonets glinting within acrid powder smoke anemically penetrated by a timid sun. The noise alone could turn a man catatonic. The boy lay terrified, his knees drawn up to his chin, his jacket splattered with another man's viscera, still miraculously clinging to his rifle, that piece of symbolic manhood he had refused to relinquish.

"Come," I encouraged him, my words emanating from somewhere beyond me, "take my hand. The Lord has directed me to see you to refuge."

By saying so I thought I was being dishonest, and yet I realized that I had not planned to come this way but by another on my route to the fighting. I remembered that only an impulse had prompted me to alter my course. Stunned, I reasoned that perhaps what I had blurted out had not actually been MY words after all.

After only slightly more persuasion the boy crept from beneath the caisson and took my hand. I guided him along until I found Father Lucius Farino administering to the wounded and performing Last Rites over the dying. He immediately grasped the situation and my intent, having also many times counseled the terrified young. He firmly held the boy by the arms and looked him directly in the eyes: "See these men," he asked him, "they have served God's purposes and are going home. You have yet to serve yours and that is why He spared you as He did. Serve me here today and from here on as my assistant, and you will have served Him."

The boy immediately sobered. I thanked the Father and left the boy in his keep, knowing he would find himself this day and reclaim his soul. "Indeed," I inadvertently mumbled to myself as I trekked toward the fighting, "the Lord be in ever'thin'"...and, perhaps, I thought as I contemplated the enigma of faith, within everyone.

Through the terror and horror of that day and that special circumstance, the lilies shown with muted luster.

* * *

Trenches & Fortifications

Petersburg, Virginia

Captain William DeVane, a friend who formerly commanded a section of our lines, wrote these poignant words while attending a ball in Petersburg the other evening - before he was killed here the next day. He willed me these reflections from his diary as he lay dying of a shell fragment wound to his chest, perishing as he did, in such mortal anguish. The following are entirely his expressions:

"Tonight, we are attending a ball given by the fair ladies of this beleaguered city. I did not wish to attend. I and many officers were commanded to attend for the sake of public morale. Yet even as an ensemble plays as if there were no war, and as a forced gaiety prevails in this vast mansion's ballroom and salons, my thoughts are not here, but with our Army's miserable troops a few miles distant (I have retreated to the privacy of the mansion's study, where pen and paper now compel me to write these sentiments. I hope my unlicensed use of our host's stationery does not constitute theft). It is raining this late Autumn night. Thunder peels on lightning's talons in our troops' direction - to remind and accuse me of my blasphemy - that I am not with them but should be.

"Their debris-corrupted and water-filled trenches and fouled bivouacs will fill with mire, and their already deprived existences will be further complicated by torturing miseries. Few warming campfires - save those beneath bombproofs - will survive the deluge, and the cold and damps will creep and slither into muscles and bones, and many will shiver with fever by morning's light, their constitutions already criminally weakened by hunger - and tomorrow or the next day we will spend hours burying them in watery holes, if the enemy does not give us battle first - and I will spend hours writing letters of sympathy to their wives and mothers. But I am certain the enemy will attack come dawn. If so, perhaps I will no longer exist to finish those letters and families will never know their loved ones' fates.

"No, it is not fair that we officers - ordered here for political reasons - should be dancing with, and be so pampered by, so many lovely ladies with their solicitous ministrations, including precious feasting and drinking, while our famished enlisted men huddle in mud and within wet tents, drenched sentry posts and sodden hovels, awaiting tomorrow. Even now, I long to be with my company and would gladly share its miseries at this moment to quiet my conscience, lest my men consider me false and a traitor to their loyalty and admiration.

"Yet and still the Reaper reserves his attentions for no individual soldier but accommodates all - and I look hauntingly upon the faces of our regiment's youngest officers here attending in their tattered finery, so gaily festive and seemingly bereft of cares - for I know that many on tomorrow's killing grounds will lie carrion in the mud alongside their men and contorted in death's embrace, forgotten to history. Our defiance of Lincoln comes expensively in this rebellion. But a man must leave the balancing of its fairness or justice to God - or dwell in hinterlands of creeping madness."

DeVane was very much my alter ego. His passing has set the day weeping upon a bier of crimson lilies.

*   *   *

Wind Chimes

Today, I found little tubes of hollow bamboo dangling from the end of a log supporting a parapet in the blessed shade of a dugout - sounding as small bells when teased even by the air's most gentle breath. I was told they are called "Wind Chimes."

They intrigued me, for here in these bloody trenches amidst so much spiritual desperation were things delicate and fine, transcending every condition of our human desolation. The men informed me that someone had purchased them from a sutler, who had obtained them from Chinese merchants in the West. Whatever their origins, they brought us comfort.

Men sat for many minutes at all hours of the day and night staring at and studying them by daylight or lantern flame, fascinated by their crystal-like tinkling, so seemingly out of place amidst the rifle-crackle and cannon thunder in this accursed place. In those tiny instruments they found links to peace.

If only you could have seen their expressions - how the deeply etched and grimy lines beneath their eyes appeared to soften when the chimes soothed them. If only you could have felt the depth of their silent emotions. If only...some wept - no shame in that, anymore, no shame at all.

Some leaned back against the parapet and closed their eyes. I closed mine. In that instant they and I were isolated from the battlefield, free to roam lands of mystical tranquility. So close, and yet so far - those verdant realms of imagination, where we wandered again with childhood abandon, seeing our loved ones' images materialize behind our heavy eyelids, once more feeling the warmth and graciousness of their smiles and laughter.

A few mesmerized men fell deeply to sleep as the little chimes bade them "Come to us and we will give you solace."

"The Lord's in them little things," an older veteran remarked. "It be His voice a'comin' in the wind and speakin' right through 'em."

So the men listened, and some slept, and some dreamed. How good it must have been - the angels of Grace calming them through those little musical wonders. I know not what melodies they played, but none that had been written by human consciousness. And even if their notes belonged to the universe, their sympathies belonged to us. Oh, how thankful we were for their tender therapies.

And now I lay me down to sleep - to try to sleep - though war seldom allows it. Sleep - how lovely it sounds. Would that I could, my mind being cluttered with a thousand conflicting thoughts that will not be stilled. I wonder, anymore, what true sleep truly is. And, as day becomes night and the stars look down upon these mole-like structures around me, I think about that night Captain DeVane wrote so self-effacingly, describing his exhausted men's plight, and the next day when I witnessed the Army fighting in this mud and slime for its new nation's life. Does DeVane now know sleep's meaning more profoundly than we who survive? More and more, I wonder about that, too.

*   *   *

For Every Man

For every man there is a singular season - for the men of our Army, a season of trial. For many that season is now. For many others their season has passed and they now lie beneath the earth, or somewhere in the septic silence of hospitals, suffering agonies untold, or without limbs and on crutches, returning home to loved ones, but also to problem-filled futures.

Concerning the wounded and the recovering, our society has provided no compensations for them. They have served, paid terrible prices for their valor, and now go home to their own devices, to subsist or starve, languish or persevere according to circumstances and the strength of their characters. But who will assist them beyond their families, with other than love and care? What of the practicalities? Families must be fed and provided for, and men must work to support them, especially the amputees and those with grievous disabilities earned on the march and the battlefield that include chronic diseases, most of which are beyond our medicines to affect. What of these men? Who will hire them? What will our government do to assist them?

I envision a nation filled with disabled men and boys who will wander and beg their ways through life for years to come should we win this war or lose it. Given the meager means our government has established for the care of the maimed, it cannot be otherwise. For the sakes of our people, I wish it could be. We cannot abide this situation. If we win our people must demand from the Richmond government a program of assistance. They must not permit their politicians to escape this responsibility. If we lose, with our government dissolved, we must do what we can, give what we can, to ease the veteran's burdens, even with the enemy's boot on our necks for a generation.

In defeat our nation will be as a puzzle of a thousand spilled pieces that must be reassembled one by one, requiring fortitude and patience in an abundance we have never before summoned. If victorious, we shall patiently heal our wounds and live out the dreams of the Founders. During that arduous process the flush of victory will pale soon enough.

*   *   *

Those Above Others

Leadership assumes many faces; nobility as well.

On the march in the dust of midday, a brigade of perhaps eight hundred men to which I had attached myself wound its monotonous way through Virginia panoramas flushed with brilliant verdancy. As it had not rained in many days our men's trudging footsteps had raised a tangible pall above every regiment. The usual coughing and dust-spitting could be heard and seen throughout the column. I had often wondered about the health effects of throats' and lungs' exposure to dust over extended periods. It was common for some men to develop a weakness in their breathing that forced them from the ranks to regain their strength. Other men throughout the Army have suffered permanent debilitations Army physicians have not been able to counter.

On this day the route-stepping men of the company I marched with grimly persevered, kerchiefs tied around their faces in bandit fashion, their exposed skin dust-caked. As is often the case, we knew not our destination. All of us hoped it would be to the mercy of tree-shaded meadows and tall, comfortable grasses near cool-water springs where gentle, refreshing breezes would lull us into slumbering oblivion throughout the coming night. Failing these surroundings we would welcome rest and sleep anywhere out of the sun.

Through the dust I perceived four men far ahead of the column, hobbling along on my side of the road. Since my company occupied the van of the column where the brigade's commanding officer and his staff rode on horseback, we would soon come upon them, and did. Each man bore grievous wounds yet they helped each other along, their filthy, bloody bandages sorely in need of replacement. One man suffered a head wound, another leg wounds, the next a wound to his side and the fourth damage to both arms.

They appeared to me as children, their faces poignantly conveying their general helplessness. Two things occurred to me immediately - that they were neither deserters nor malingerers. Had they been deserters they would not have taken to roads where the Army was obviously on the move, our brigade being only one of several using the road that day. Had they been malingerers, taking advantage of their conditions to feign worse than they actually were, they would have avoided the scrutiny of officers.

Since the column approached a portion of the road shaded by a grove of oaks, the brigade's commanding officer, Colonel Freeman, halted the column momentarily, a respite welcomed by all. He would resume the march in minutes, since we were hard-pressed to rendezvous with the Army's main body miles ahead. But looking down, he paused to study the wounded walkers.

"What's your name?" he asked the the head-wounded soldier.

"Billie, suh, Billie Goodbee."

"How old you be?"

"Nineteen, sur."

"And what's y'alls regiment?"

"We all be from differ'nt ones, suh," the side-wounded man responded, "from the big fightin' two day ago in the Wilderness up Manassas way. You woun't be havin' ana rations and wata, would ya, suh, fer the boys here?"

"How long y'all been a'walkin?"

"Two days, suh."

"How'd y'all b'come separated from your regiments?"

"That fightin' through them woods n'all were a might confusin', suh, and lotsa our boys got lost from ever'body else. And Hosie and Jeffrey here and Thomas...well, they was down fer a while and couldn't be let go of, so they had t'be tended to..."

"And you did the tendin', son?"

"Yes, suh," the soldier innocently answered.

"Where ya headed now?" the Colonel asked, obviously impressed by these boys and their good intentions.

"Well, we figgud t'hook up with somebody suh, if'm we stayed t'the road long anuf."

"You mean to return to duty?"

"Yes, suh, if'n they'd have us. Ya wouldn't be havin' ana vittles and wata, would ya, suh?"
The Colonel's smile conveyed deep respect: "We have a'nuff for y'all," he replied, "and I pray to Richmond and the Lord that we always will." He turned in his saddle: "Major Jenks, put the men with leg and arm wounds inta my wagon and have a physician attend him. You others there, can y'all ride?"

They stared at each other, quizzically: "Yes suh, the side-wounded man answered, "I spose so."

"Then, you will," the Colonel said, firmly. "Major Jenks, you and I will be enjoyin' a little physical exercise - good for the constitution, wouldn't ya say? Let's dismount so these dedicated souls may be given the honor they deserve."

His staff helped the wounded men into their saddles, and then Freeman ordered the column forward again. "Sometimes," he said, "I grow weary of being one of those above others."

The four hikers were given water and vittles enough to sustain them but not enough to sicken them, as often happens when parched and wounded men drink and eat too desperately.

Freeman and Jenks trekked the remainder of the way on foot that day, bivouacking when we rendezvoused with the Army's main body that night, as spent and foot-sore as the hundreds behind them. The four wounded were sped to hospital, all of them having been rescued from further deterioration by a man not above others - and as devoted to his infantry as the four he had mercifully honored had been to their countrymen.

* * *

Drudgery

Morning dawned today with a vengeful Georgia sun fiercely baking the fields on which so many perished yesterday and the day before. Hundreds of dead already have bloated. The stench of putrefaction saturates the air. Wounded still out there, theirs and ours, cry and moan and beg for water, their hands and faces already seared by yesterday's sun or worse, two day's worth. On both sides soldiers' lives have become pure physical and emotional drudgery.

Soldiers speculate that for their senseless slaughtering, God is repaying the struggling armies here by making their days too miserable for continued fighting. But even if that were true it would make no difference to generals on both sides who, from secure vantage points, will commit their people to battle again, until sheer force compels a decision.

In yet another inconclusive year of this War Between the States, it has long since become obvious to both nations that their civil contest will range even farther and last even longer. To the men doing the fighting and dying, the war's political issues no longer matter. They see it in much simpler terms, the prime one being survival. After that only the intellectuals among them argue its fine points. The common soldier on both sides hears only his side's propaganda - Northerners that their men are fighting to preserve their Union and end slavery - Southerners that they are resisting a powerful central government that has dared to invade their lands to crush the independence of action the South believes the Constitution guarantees them.

"Stop resisting and yield to your legitimate government in Washington," a federal soldier shouted from his trench last night, part of a trench system inching ever closer to ours.

"Take yer legitimate armies and go home," a southern soldier countered. "Leave us to settle our own affairs like the Founders intended."

"We are acting legitimately by putting down this illegal rebellion," the Federal argued.

"Yer exceedin' the Constitution and cain't no way justify yer invasion," the Southern officer protested.

"We're gonna do away with slavery," the Federal argued.

"I don't own no damned slaves and never have, you infernal fool!" the Southern officer responded.

Whatever the correct interpretations of the Constitution and its authority, both sides well know this argument will not be settled by reason, but by force of arms - a precedent history will honor, rightly or wrongly. In the meantime soldiers and civilians by the thousands will die or suffer this war's innumerable injustices.

The sun very early reaches into both side's lines and entrenched positions, spreading its fire indiscriminately. In Southern lines men await a Federal assault. The stink of blackening, rotting bodies broiling out there on those heating fields and wrecked fortifications will grow more intense hour by hour. Malnourished bodies, especially those of our Southern boys, deteriorate more swiftly than well-fed Yankee carcasses, and circling buzzards have become the targeted sport of both side's best marksmen. Unwritten laws of chivalry dictate that when some things (like scavenger buzzards, human or otherwise) transgress even upon both side's calloused sensibilities, both sides, for the sport of it, momentarily set aside their mutual grudges to wreak vengeance on offenders (human or otherwise).

Rifle reports issue here and there from both lines, these missiles only occasionally producing explosions of bloody feathers high overhead. When such explosions occur, cheering erupts from both sides as shattered bird remains cartwheel to earth, honor having been served, and the scavengers having been foiled from committing the greatest of all sacrileges upon our common dead.

Water - in our fetid positions even warm water remains more precious than gold. Buckets of it, raised from brackish wells, are passed down our lines, soothing parched throats dry since the previous evening. Some men drink sparingly knowing how vitally water must be conserved; overindulgence being a mortal sin that threatens to deprive others of their just due. None will satiate their thirst this morning, but most will pacify it.

"Remember, boys," a wizened sergeant now reminds his charges, "kill the privates when they come. Them people cain't fit their war without 'em, and they ain't gonna fit it jest with their officas!"

His men listen, showing no emotion. Most are long-time veterans of this never ending national disagreement, and need no instructions concerning killing. Yet, a sergeant must always BE a sergeant.

Every man in this trenchline moves slowly, deliberately, dried-out as they are by the heat. Some move listlessly, others lethargically, the drudgery of this battle and war weighing heavily upon their drooping shoulders. Indeed, it weighs on mine, yet as a civilian I am not compelled to confront the gorgon of battle as do they, but I do so with them because I must.

Their blood and my ink flow as one.

*　　*　　*

Teeth

One might wonder why I should devote an entire journal entry to teeth – because, like sore and failing feet, bad teeth plague our ranks.

Dental care is a concept alien to our rank and file. Yet, deep caries and terrible abcesses are bemoaned by scores of miserable soldiers.

Surgeons attempt to aid sufferers by recommending all sorts of relief methods, extraction being the extreme, but mint being commonly suggested, for which our troops diligently search. Usually, mint leaves are wetted and pressed against the affected tooth or gum. In extreme cases, soldiers seek anyone nearby who claims some expertise in teeth-pulling. Very often, maddened by pain, besotted sufferers use knives to dig out their own, thereafter soothing the damage with ever more whiskey. This knife business requires a gumption (as it were) I do not possess.

It is common to see soldiers with slings supporting their jaws and tied at the top of their skulls, perverse passerbys seeing humor in the sad conditions of poor souls' with grotesquely swollen faces. Whiskey is the preferred medication for all tooth and gum ailments, the sufferer holding a slug in his mouth - usually for the duration - on the affected or infected area. Seldom is such brew ever spat out, swallowing it being the preferred technique, the therapeutic slug then washed down with two or three more that often produce in the sufferer a more gracious disposition - and send him happily into delightful realms of welcomed oblivion.

Fortunately I have remained free of severe tooth or gum disorders, though three molars have broken off in the past year. But after a short, painful interlude, their nerves atrophied. Thus I have been spared the dubious skills of well-intended but ham-fisted Samaritans. The preferred tool used in extractions, of course, is the plier, a utensil as rare as buzzard fangs. But I've also seen frustrated victims use their fingers to grab hold of a bad tooth or teeth and pry or yank it or them free - mostly after liberal doses of other fermented elixirs, usually of mysteriously local origins.

After successful surgery, celebratory doses of said elixirs are generally distributed all around, thus making extractions highly anticipated and well-attended events often overlooked by patrolling officers who generally, in fealty to an unspoken code between officers and enlisted men and honored at such times, are persuaded to join-in. How reassuring it must be for the sufferer to be able to rely on so much moral support.

I have yet to discover what methods tooth or teeth-miserable officers employ to relieve their woes. No doubt they rely on a surgeon's tender mercies. Yet anesthetics are not always available even for them, save, of course, for those of mysteriously local origins, which, I am certain, they have privately (individually and as a class) secreted away.

*   *   *

Catchin' Much Needed

There are times when our regiments are pulled on line, only to stand for eternities without seeing immediate action.

Often before a fight they are held in reserve, where they can see the enemy maneuvering hundreds of yards ahead. Rather than keep their men standing, officers allow them to lie down to nap or rest to conserve energy - if only for minutes - or as some enlisted men term it, to be "catchin' what's much needed."

Ten or twenty winks can be sufficiently refreshing after long, hard marches. Even then errant enemy bullets, shot and shell make no allowances for vulnerable flesh. For standing men the danger posed by simple physics is increased, so it is prudent that troops not invite those "coincidental conjunctions," as this company's droll commanding officer puts it.

Our boys thirst for sleep at all times, even in small amounts. Veterans are more economical about it than nervous virgin troops yet to see the Elephant, who cannot close their eyes no matter how compelling their fatigue. I try to sketch men at rest since they assume many intriguing postures. Some of certain religious persuasions refuse to sleep in prone positions. Instead they sit in their sleep, saying they have done so since childhood, as have their parents and kin. They tell me they are taught that the Devil more easily enters a prone body than a sitting one. If they can lean their backs against trees or gentle slopes they are satisfied, but they insist it is always preferable that their backs remain upright in slumber.

I have no such compunctions. Sleep is sleep - prone, sitting or standing, no matter how long or brief. I have learned to march along in a stupor, as our troops do regularly, aware of being in two worlds at once - the one beneath my feet and the one of my dreaming.

Today, lying prone and in reserve in a dried creek bed, we watched our enemy form ranks and advance toward us. Yet he made only half-hearted attempts to challenge our Army's positions. Wild bullets from his timid firing buzzed harmlessly overhead before he turned and left the field. We did not return fire but could not divine his intentions, being relieved when told our continuing presence in line would not be required – meaning our boys could catch some "much needed" after all.

Incidentally, wild minie-balls are a unique hazard. During confused fighting one never knows whose they are. Being impartial, they care not what uniform colors they grace with red. Often, and sadly, in the blinding tumult of battle, ours sometimes carry away our own.

* * *

In the Beauty of the Lilies

**The Wartime Journals
of Confederate Correspondent
Royal K. Chapman
1862-1864**

Journal Twelve

Contents

*   *   *

A Thought

For some there will never be an ending,
their restlessness apparent to those
with special sight.

An Attempt at Verse

While others celebrated the beautiful summer night I watched a lonely soldier, a bard, saunter off to the edge of his company's bivouac, there to study the evening sky. While the glow of campfires danced along tree trunks and toyed with shadows he turned his attention to the stars and to clouds drifting lazily by, many still tinged with diminishing sunlight. As he later told me, his imagination soared among them as he wondered what they were and why.

From his jacket he pulled a notebook containing his most private thoughts gleaned from years of war. Of course, the growing darkness prohibited him from writing in the book, but he clutched it tightly as he explained it to me, deciding to permit the words to come from the night - words he would later put to paper inside the book's weathered yellow pages. He thought now of weighty things from his veteran's view in a stream of thoughtful consciousness:

Written On A Quiet Night

"I see naught in the stars but tears and sorrow though innocently they shine unaware of me. And through my weeping soul, I see the nobility in small men made large by events greater than all. In the storm far away - eternity's rumble, where lightning splinters across the face of a sleeping God. Obscure is war's meaning upon these courses, the need of its sacrifices a puzzlement made mysterious by a moon brightening by the minute and encrusted in sentiments veiled in duty, honor, and country, where simple hearts caught up in war's winds ever-long for home - passing clouds looking down unconcerned for us in flesh bound where no man knows and moved by powers apart from our wandering minds that seek simple serenity, confused in the meantime by warring causes no longer of meaning. The firmament will go its way and obey itself apart from us who comprehend it not. And, despite the whirlwind we've spawned the sun will set, the moon will nightly debut, and dark relief will again descend upon our weary heads. And dawn will come, illuminating both heaven's timelessness and our mortal insignificance below - then pass away once more without hearing our desperate cries, leaving us homeward gazing, faces gaunt, our reddened eyes sunken, staring into memories cherished and home fires constant made of domestic things as they were before this strife...of life as it was, of loved ones as we loved them before - hope being our blood, faith and bread - that we may yet survive and bide in peace, released from battle's terrible reunions, our heads to beds familiar and soft. Yet, haunted now we stand, a pittance beneath these stars, bidding for Heaven's mercy, our destinies clouded, our lives not ours but mortgaged to haunting unknowns, yet, into God's Hands entrusted should He awaken at last and sigh with pity enough to extend His hands over our lands, ending our long tribulation and commanding us gently home to salvation, no longer afraid, no longer stalked by fear our faithful tormentor, never more afraid but blessed, blissful sleep in the loving arms of loved ones cherished and longed-for."

The soldier, for a minute more, watched the sky and that distant lightning, wondering if he would see it tomorrow or ever again. For across the way, miles away, the enemy's tamed fires burned ever as brightly as ours. He would leave his notebook with me that very night after making his entry, certain - as only a soldier can be - that the words he would put into its pages by firelight before closing his eyes and releasing himself to fate would constitute his eulogy. But fate would spare him in the morning, while countless others dutifully went into that dreaded sleep of ages.

Thanking God, I returned his book to him when he staggered back from the battlefield, sweat-soaked and exhausted. He accepted it not only humbly but with ever more puzzlement, as if he could not fathom that fate had betrayed his intuition when so often in the past they had served each other as unfailing, if tenuous, allies.

* * *

Not for War

One might think that compassion is not for war, but it most passionately is. I often wonder what war would otherwise be for those who daily endure it, if it were not for small but spiritually redeeming and reconstituting things that rekindle the best in one's soul, as fresh air refires a hearth.

Many soldiers covet pets, and many secretly carry them, pets being generally forbidden, but often "overlooked" by officers. Yet pets are a soldier's most direct link to peace and escape from war. I have witnessed tenderness and compassion pour from hardened veterans who harbor little puppies or furry kittens, as if huge reservoirs of otherwise repressed humanness scream to be expressed and released, and must be, if a man is not to see his most innate and giving identity perish.

It is as if he must not only find such expression but that in finding it, it in turn nourishes and sustains his soul. I am reminded of felines and canines that are released to the out of doors that they might medicate themselves on grasses and other flora. So it appears to be spiritually with soldiers - pets being medication in the way of giving tenderness to other living creatures rather than death, thereby reestablishing contact with the sort of unique creativity war denies him - love, I believe it's called.

As I write I look up to see soldiers in this bivouac going about their mundane tasks - sewing, preparing their meager meals over campfires, cleaning their rifles, washing their threadbare uniforms or whatever passes for same - or sleeping, sleep being more preciously therapeutic than gold. Occasionally, a hidden kitten or puppy or bunny or tiny squirrel escapes, to the amusement and joy of all around - and I am reconstituted. For in their joy I find inspiration - that war has not fatally corroded their giving natures - that the hearth therein still glows - that something of the Divine still and also inspires them. And knowing this, I sleep much better and relieved.

* * *

Snake-Bit

I have often wondered if our war-making hubris angers the beasts and creatures of the fields whose domiciles we disturb and destroy. Does nature take umbridge as well? And why should it not?

During the enemy's retreat from the fighting this morning our boys probed for wounded in the high, untrampled grasses of bordering and uninvolved fields. They found many who had crawled there and many who had died after doing so, ours and the enemy's. It is common for the wounded to do this, many in mortal pain or otherwise delirious, their positions betrayed by their moaning or screaming. After every battle many wounded drag themselves into surviving cover both armies have fought through.

Recovering these men at such time can be a difficult and heart-rending exercise. Some do not wish to be touched, as every motion promotes paroxysms of unspeakable agony. Others attempt to treat themselves, resenting anyone's interference. Still others assume childlike demeanors, meekly and innocently wishing for a kind of parental care and consideration. Some are helped away to medical attention with only a modicum of supervision. At the other extreme, many have lost consciousness and must be littered away. Others are carried seated on rifles handled by able-bodied soldiers. Still more are virtually carried by two, the wounded man's arms over the two's shoulders. How the wounded are transported greatly depends of the nature of their afflictions, those with serious blood loss or with intestines dangling or organs or brain tissue exposed requiring individualized methods.

I accompanied a group of soldiers recovering the wounded in tall grasses alongside a woods. The distant, heart-wrenching screaming of a hurt man encouraged us to urgently pound through the turf in his direction. On the way we stumbled over dead men and found four wounded quietly suffering but nursing their torments. After marking their positions with bayoneted rifles we pushed on toward the desperately screaming man, hoping to ease his agonies or to attempt to in the name of mercy. We found him all right, but what we also discovered gives me trembling pause even as I write this, my spine chilling.

He was a writhing enemy soldier, kicking and convulsing, his hands gripping a three foot-long poisonous copperhead whose fangs had sunk deeply into his neck. His wide, terrified eyes peered without focus into our faces, our expressions conveying our disbelief. Two of our men promptly sat on his legs. Another two held down his torso while two more steadied his shoulders. Yet another soldier pulled a huge Bowie knife from his belt, placed the blade's sharp edge under the snake's head, and with a jerk decapitated it. Then, using the blade he pried out the fangs and tossed the head into the grass. But we could not break the wounded man's grip from the snake's body, whose severed end bled across him. It was obvious that the man had initially been pierced by a minié-ball that had severed a leg artery. His was doomed unless the torrent gushing from it could be stopped, but then only if he could survive the snake's venom, a tremendous volume of which the snake had emptied into this system.

The man who had killed the snake attempted to squeeze the venom from the fang wounds, but to no avail. The wounded soldier violently convulsed two more times then stiffened, his eyes dilating almost instantly, his face ghostly white, bubbly foam creeping from his nose and the sides of his mouth. Who was this man, I wondered, who had come down from the North to lay the South low? Had he believed in his mission or had he been conscripted? Had he accepted money to act as a substitute for another who shied from obligation or had he merely been an adventurer?

We rifled through his uniform for identification and found a soiled letter in his jacket pocket addressed to one Corporal William Jones of an Indiana regiment, its number illegible. We did not read the letter. It did not seem fitting, considering the circumstances of his death. Instead, we replaced it. Then thinking better of matters, I retrieved it, assuring the men that I would submit it to a chaplain who might then be able to forward it to enemy lines.

Then one of our group yelped and jumped aside, pointing downward. Another copperhead struck at him, just missing him, then another. We found ourselves in a mass of the menacing devils. They slithered through the grass around us from the wood's direction, as if determined to wreak vengeance on us for the damage both side's artillery had done to it and, possibly, to their dens. Each man found his own route of survival, jumping and hopping away from their striking heads. Panicked, we tore through the grass back the way we had come, having to leave the dead enemy soldier to moulder, still clenching the snake that had expedited his death.

As I retreated, I thanked my conscience for persuading me to preserve the man's letter. At least his fate chanced being known to his family who would otherwise have wondered for years if he would ever return home. And he needn't have worried in Heaven about having died anonymously on Earth. Seven Southern soldiers and an ordinary Southern citizen would not soon forget Yankee Corporal William Jones, who we no longer considered to have been our enemy.

*   *   *

The Wretch

(Soldier's Testimony from Hospital)
Written by the hand of
Royal K. Chapman
1863

I watched them bring the poor fellow forward - a whimpering, frightened wretch he was - frail, emaciated and obviously ill. But he had, in the face of the enemy, run for his life, and now his life was forfeit.

The powers in charge had thought to make him an example - to sit him down on a wooden box his size before a grave he himself had dug - where he would be shot by a firing squad of his peers before the entire assembled regiment.

The dismal drums beat a somber, deliberate, morbid cadence as shackled and barefoot, he stumbled through the mud of that cold, rainy morning toward an ignoble destiny, trembling uncontrollably, his uniform a ragged shade of his original issue - as were those of most troops watching in formation - his hair matted, his expression a portrait of abject bewilderment and fear.

Surrounded by guards who paced themselves by the drums, he stared this way and that at the regiment's rigid officers who looked on iron-faced. Our hearts went out to this lost soul, who was no less guilty of a crime than many in ranks who had suffered the war's course and bouts of sudden panic - who also had run but never had been caught, and most of whom had returned to their companies, ashamed yet chastised and chastened by their redeeming consciences to eventually become dedicated soldiers. None dared to condemn this fellow sinner for what had been his all too momentary weakness.

Resentment simmered in each of us - resentment for what was being done to him by those of superior rank who themselves had made mistakes which had unnecessarily cost lives, no less - mistakes for which no superior had levied a single punishment! What had this man's sin meant next to theirs? What had this frightened wretch done except run away from HIMSELF? And why was he being destroyed for it while guilty officers went free? For nothing - yet they were going to kill him for it just the same.

Justice? Where was it that day? Not THERE - only tears being shed by many a hardened veteran, not only for the wretch but for themselves - a long deserved expression of self-pity for themselves and every soul so victimized by such senseless object lessons. Battle was the greatest teacher of all. They needed no artificial lessons from superior officers for in combat they had learned all about human strengths and weaknesses. But this travesty was the ultimate high-ranking example of hierarchy's contempt for enlisted men - an insult and indignity we were being made to additionally endure, while that poor man suffered his unfair fate. Yet as ordered we timidly stood at attention, studying him while honoring the drums - seeing ourselves there, just as our senior officers had intended - rank upon rank, company upon company, silently raging - too disciplined to mutinously free our comrade as he should have been freed. No, WE, not HIM, were the cowards, the weaklings now permitting this hypocrisy and atrocity!

Then, ominously, the drums stopped. We knew what was coming next. STILL, we did nothing more save witness his mental torture as they seated him on his box. The regiment's executive officer then asked him if he wished to speak in his own behalf before the charges and judgment against him were read to the regiment. Some regiments varied this procedure. Ours did it this way.

Too distraught to reply, the wretch turned to study US, searching for mercy and salvation in OUR eyes! He found sympathy, even pain, but nothing more. Then, reading firmly and without emotion in the miserable drizzle, the presiding officer paused twice to divine the document's handwriting now blurred by raindrops and to wipe away the wet. Quaking and still whimpering - too terrified to be conscious of anything save his impending destruction - the condemned soul bit his lip. Death would come from the barrels of a dozen muskets aimed at his heart. A dozen minié-balls would tear life from his body.

"Again, in all decency," the officer remarked, "I ask you - do you have anything to say at this time? You will not be granted another opportunity..."

We expected the wretch to say nothing. Yet, to our astonishment, he looked up, rain dripping from his hair, his body soaked, his lips trembling - and stood. Helped by a guarding soldier too moved to deny him this kind assistance, he spoke in a timid, quavering voice - groping for the words that would comprise his last but futile defense while accurately expressing his ultimate sense of betrayal by a land and government he had faithfully served and for which he had, more than once, shed blood:

"I been in this here war fer two year," he began with great trepidation..."been in a dozen engagements...been wounded thrice - once't real bad...didn't mean t'run the other day - it jest got t'me's, all...I'da come back, I know I woulda'...YOU know I woulda'," he said, looking at us, plaintively insisting, "I'm a soldier...I ain't a coward..." Then, sensing the hopelessness of it all, he looked down, demoralized and beaten..."Don't understand why I need dyin' fer it," he lamented..."don't them two years a'good soldierin' account fer nothin'! Don't there be no heart 'er fairness to it?"

Visibly moved, the executive officer remained silent, unable to deny the condemned man's logic yet powerless to stop the proceedings without being party to mutiny himself.

The pause hung ominously in the air, the drizzle at that moment increasing, adding a touch of almost deliberate drama to the moment.

"Do you have anything ELSE to say?" the officer sympathetically asked.

The condemned man looked away agin, his eyes closed, his shackled hands pressed against his chest in prayer, then…"What else BE there t'say?" he softly questioned without opening his hands again. "If'n what I jest said's ain't of no worth, then nothin' on Earth COULD be." Then, turning his face up into the rain, pitifully beaten, a calmer countenance overtook him…"No…I reckon there ain't nothin' more…'ceptin' t'meet the Lord…"

The officer, moral consternation spreading across his brow, hesitated, his conscience visibly at work, its wheels grinding against his orders and duty, his humanity struggling to surmount and survive this clownish carnival with some vestige of honor intact. But duty prevailed - as we knew it would. He looked to one side, as if hoping that perhaps, just perhaps, he might yet hear mercy slip from the lips of regiment's commanding officer. But no mercy came - and we would never forget it.

The officer looked down: "I'm sorry…I truly am." Then, to the firing squad officer: "Carry out the sentence."

The drums recommenced. The guard who had helped the condemned man up now gently settled him again upon the box. I looked from side to side, seeing near despondency in some men's faces - grimness in others - all expressing disbelief that God had not touched the commanding officer's heart but had abandoned both!

The regimental chaplain came forward: "No," the man bade him, looking up defiantly, shocking us all…"I'll be a'seein' the Lord soon a'nuff no matter what'cha be sayin' here…ain't abidin' no perdy words that ain't a'gonna keep me alive…er preachers that cain't, eitha …yer all so fired up t'shoot me and have yer show, then SHOOT ME, GODAMMIT…go ahead and SHOOT ME!"

He stared at us - defiantly condemning us with eyes that said YOU'VE BETRAYED ME BUT YOU'VE BETRAYED YOURSELVES MORE - and we cringed. Then they blindfolded him.

He did not object. "Better," we thought. We did not want to see his FINAL expression…and perhaps he no longer wanted to see ours. Only God knew what that final look might have been. We had been his friends, his trusted comrades, yet we were doing nothing on his behalf…nor ANYTHING to ensure that justice prevailed! That was what his look said to us…NOTHING TO SAVE HIM NOR YOURSELVES! We were killing him, as surely as the army and his country were! But behind their anger and devastation his eyes also pleaded, leaving us weak-kneed and filled with self-disgust. Then, the blindfold blocked all further communication.

Authority would not be denied. It would HAVE its unstoppable way, as it always did. The "example" HAD to be set. Regulations and tradition DEMANDED it, and all knew how devoutly our higher-ups worshiped both. It was their INVIOLATE code, their measure of MAN'S power on Earth - and the gods had spoken.

I wondered what the poor man's thoughts were, what mine might have been. Certainly he was thinking about the pain - the pain of a dozen minié-balls pulverizing his chest. Would death be instantaneous - too quick for pain? Or would he linger even a second, and feel each of them - their impact and the aftermath? What would his family think? What stigma would his wife and children now bear? Why had he put their reputations in such jeopardy? What dishonor had he brought upon his name and how would it condemn their lives?

There and then I resolved to tell them of his bravery, of his past acts of kindness and consideration towards us; of the campaigns he had endured and the wounds he had suffered; of the sterling service he had given his country - things the army, in its self-centered selfishness, would never speak of. I would tell them how unfair this action was, and would forever be, and, if I survived the war, I would bring the army's disgrace to the attention of the government's highest authorities and fight to have his reputation reinstated!

All these things I now resolutely pledged as I stood so bravely by, feeling that somehow my resolution would excuse my cowardice, and though inspired by my newly-felt but belated righteousness, I knew not from where the man hailed, nor even his children's names - nor if I possessed the necessary influence to change anything. But I was determined to find out, and to encourage my comrades to join me in righting this terrible wrong. Would they? I was sure they would!

Those drums beat the haunting, death-dirge cadence...but we heard them not as much as the rain falling around us with soporific relief. And we took our eyes from the victim to look skyward to a brightening patch of clouds that threatened to dissolve into sunlight - as if God, Himself, might yet pour through to reach down and snatch up the condemned man's soul. But the inundating rain would not stop. Puddles grew deeper, the mud thicker, and we found sudden fascination in the way each raindrop exploded upon the other where ever water laid - seeing, in the tiny ripples that followed, our humiliating insignificance.

Rain would fall here long after our existences were forgotten. Of what shattering significance would this great lesson be to anyone then? I kept thinking: we are inconsequentially born and we inconsequentially die, no matter where, no matter when, for time makes all events moot. Beyond our grandchildren, who will remember us and what we've done, or care that we had lived at all? It may have been my imagination, but I was suddenly chilled...for in the rumbling of distant thunder, I sensed eternity's presence, as if it were opening its portals to the soul on the box, affectionately waiting to embrace him. Would it one day do so for me...for the rest of us?

It was time...

The executive officer nodded to the firing squad officer:

"READY..." We flinched. A dozen paces away from the condemned man, the squad brought its muskets to the ready position and cocked hammers...no turning back, now..."AIM..." we stiffened...it was going to happen after all, and we were going to LET it happen...we who would make hollow excuses to his wife and children, if, in the end, any of us even tried to do even THAT much...we who would be caught up in the war the very next day, its priorities obscuring all our best intentions and suspending even our most brave and sincere vows, perhaps, for many of us, eternally. We braced, some of us closing our eyes. NO, WE WEREN'T READY to bear the GUILT..."FIRE!"

A THUNDEROUS report...we recoiled...the ears of those nearest the sound painfully protesting! The noise echoed, carried by the rain over the countryside, scaring up huddling birds...resonating in our hearts and consciences...imprinting our brains with shame. The condemned man's head violently jerked...his body lifted with the missiles' impacts...his chest obliterated in red mist... lungs and heart exploding...spine and shoulder blades blasting through his back...penetrating minie-balls splintering the box's lid, splattering it with gore! His bloody body slammed down backwards on the lid, his quivering legs straightening...his twitching hands and feet dangling over the lid's edges...blood immediately pouring across it and cascading down the box's sides.

We stood transfixed, the report fading away across Creation, absorbed by the rain, with only the still soporific sound of falling raindrops mellowing the disquieting tranquility that followed. Only now did we feel the rain soaking through our already soaked uniforms. We were alive. The wretch was not. We still could feel...he could not. Only now did we realize how wet and miserable we actually were. Only now did we regret wearing our uniforms at all.

The rain mingled with the dead man's blood, trying to wash it away, yet the bright red flow overpowered every drop, endlessly escaping its host. What, we wondered, as the firing squad filed away, was the wretch's expression beneath that hideous fold? What HAD been his final thought?

How still he laid, so obviously shrunken and flat upon that lid, smashed ribs sticking up through that cavernous wound. Unable or not wanting to move, each of us sorted our impressions and filed them away. We had survived. While our consciences cowered, our animal instincts rejoiced.

Then it was time to leave, to return to our bivouacs and the blessed, warming fires being kept for us by those assigned to maintain them in our absence - before the cold turned our lungs to fire and drowned us in killing fluids - as always happened to some men were forced to endure cold rain like this - as would happen in the next few days, when two of the dead man's friends, who had watched him die, would pay for our sin by joining him in Paradise.

Company by Company they led us away from the death scene like a giant square serpent uncoiling itself, leaving the cooling body on the box to the mercies of a burial detail that would obliterate all signs of the grave and erect no identifying marker - thus heaping more revenge upon the leaking body inside by leaving it pathetically abandoned, even as God had abandoned him.

The chaplain stood by, now belatedly saying righteous and lofty things of no use to the wretch anymore...hollow and now meaningless-sounding platitudes. Lifting his draining corpse, they laid it in the box and nailed down the damaged lid. Manhandling the box, which immediately seeped blood, they slid it into the hole, leaving it at a cock-eyed angle, contemptuously heaping the final degradation upon the muted form inside. Then as we marched away they began shoveling dirt back into the hole. Most would have said it was over, but many suspected it was not and would never be.

Birds winged this way and that, concerned that the distant thunder warned of high winds and torrential downpours, but the storm veered away, leaving only cold drizzle in its wake. Thus in bivouac, we spent the remainder of daylight building more fires against the damp, or laid blanket-wrapped in our two-man tents, shivering while our soaked bodies fought off the insidious chill invading our bones - each of us listening to his conscience, the day's images indelibly alive in our brains - wondering if that poor man now sat at the Lord's side anointed in a special Grace his mortal kind had refused to grant him - and worried that the constant damp would claim us all.

As I feared, the damp is taking me - and death will soon relieve the fire in my lungs and the fever that has so quickly incinerated my entire system. Dehydrated, and fever-laden, I languish, awaiting the coma that I am told will speed me into the next world - there, perhaps, to reunite with the wretch on the box. Our chaplain assures me that I will. But at least they gave the man a box. Me, they'll dump into a water-filled pit with other carrion as fatally afflicted. In a sense his execution will also be mine - my sin against him justly balanced and punishment meted out. I simply hope the next world will be just as they promised - a place of peace, beauty, and rest.

When I am strong enough there, I will search for the soldier I watched die that awful day in the cold rain, and I will apologize to him for all those on Earth still at war. Someone else will have to make peace with his family. I pray that whoever does so, if they do so, will thoroughly express our sorrow and leave them feeling proud of their kin, and strengthen them to meet the tempest the nature of his passing might engender. And I hope, when I meet the man, he will forgive me and will already have forgiven...us.

Corporal Augustus Branch
Infantry-CSA

Sittin' Quiet

A Soldier's Testimony

"There was times when we'd sit quiet - a whole bunch of us - not sayin' nothin' t'no one - jest watchin' the clouds marchin' 'cross the sky, and thinkin' mostly 'bout home and the past - ever' man to himself.

"It'd be odd for someone watchin' US contemplatin' the way we'd be doin'. But it were 'anuff fer us t'listen t'the birds 'er feel a breeze and try t'link up with the Lord, as it were. Sometimes, y'could hear Him, I swear - not speakin' words, 'a course, but speakin' in the language of the calm and the colors and all them feelin's and impreshuns. Made ever'thin' 'bout the world and a man feel small and of little matter. I 'member those times 'cause there ain't never been nothin' like 'em b'fore 'er since - not fer me! Could never capture THEIR spirit ever agin', that's fer certain.

"Our yesterdays don't matter none now, and we figure we ain't got no 'tomarras, 'ceptin' what the Lord give us one b'one. Never know how many we have left, but that's what use t'make those quiet times so 'cherishable. Ain't the same no more, though - I mean times as quiet and meanin'ful in the same ways. Guess they never CAN be n'more...but maybe it's best. Ya see, if'n we had 'em 'agin, they'd jest spoil us fer sure. The war's diff'ernt now...ever'body bein' real serious 'bout killin' each other, n'all. B'fore, y'jest shot at that other feller 'cause he was there and that's what you was 'sposed t'do - nothin' was ever real personal 'bout it. Now, there's anuff bad feelins' and hate out there t'thrill the Devil.

"Guess we all come a long way since the beginnin' a' this thing. It's grim, now - has come down t'both sides takin' it out on each other for things draggin' on fer so long like they have. Time was we thought it'd all be over in a few months at most - soon as ever'body got some shootin' outta their blood and some coolin' off done. Sure never figured on all this. Jest gotta keep goin's all - gotta jest try t'survive 'til EVER-body gets tired a'this thing. We're all fixin' t'go home soon as THAT happens.

"Hell, nobody want's t'die the day b'fore it's over - not them and not us! We kinda made a deal with those fellers - kinda n'gotiated 'tween their lines and ours when we was tradin' coffee, 'tabacca and things. They don't shoot at us ana'more 'lessin' it's absolutely necessary - and we don't shoot at them - kind of a unwritten agreement 'tween us, ya know. Suits me. Might even be able t'git away with it right up 'til the end, them and us figure. Hope so. Never really ever hated them other fellers ana'way, them bein' Americans jest like me! Much rather of traded with 'em fer four years 'tween the lines than what we BEEN a'doin'. But I ain't no President. If'n I had been, there wouldn'ta been no war in the first place - maybe a fist fight 'er two - but killin'?

HELL, NO! But nobody ever asked ME nothin' 'er nobody else I ever knew in this here contest - jest told us t'go and fight. Some of us volunteered and some of us didn't - and thems what didn't is damn sorry - and thems what did is 'sorrier.

"We oughta' of gone back t'61, started this whole thing all over 'agin - and quit! That's what we OUGHTA' done! Then we 'oughta' sat down t'gether, watched the clouds 't'gether - with nobody sayin' nothing! Sittin' quiet's what we 'needed t'do on BOTH sides and what STILL needs doin'!...and that's what them history fellers is gonna say we oughta' of done right from the START...I jest know it... you'll see!"

*   *   *

Revisions in Passing

Once again I watched from the side of the road as an endless cavalcade of torn and disheveled wounded streamed rearward, so weakened from their hurts that others less afflicted helped them along. It was deja vu, as if I were recalling a night's dream. I watched, transfixed.

A buggy drove between them and stopped. Once again its driver jumped to the ground to steady its horse, while a priest rose from its seat. Once again a gentle zephyr teased his long cassock, as he observed the flood of human tragedy to either side, even as the sound of battle boomed and rattled far up the road. Once again eye-watering powder smoke drifted by, but the tears I saw trickling down his troubled face found their genesis in other sources. Then, once again, Christlike, he raised his hands over that suffering humanity and, in Latin, blessed them, asking God to be merciful and to grant them a painless peace. Again, passersbys looked up, some stopping to kneel in prayer, even as their wounds dripped corruption into the dust of the road. Again, I turned away, too moved to observe any longer, my own soulful tears too pervasive to allow me to see, my mind attempting to reconcile the past revisited.

*   *   *

Again, our General stood beneath the sky's autumnal brilliance, his head bowed in prayer, his body weary with care. I well knew that his heart was heavy with the deaths of so many in his command. Once again, silhouetted against the afternoon blue, with majestic cumulus parading slowly by, his pose would remain classical in my memory. That pose said he was emotionally spent and spiritually exhausted. Once again, he knew that before the day ended circumstances would force him to sacrifice even more men. Again, I pitied him as I pitied no other man. How many more times before the war's end would he place his soul into God's Hands?

*   *   *

A Repeating Sentiment

A portion from a letter found on the battlefield from Private Lester Osgood to an unknown recipient:

"Battle is a turble noize, Dear soul, jest so turble cause it braks some men and drivs some plum mad. Or sends them cringing like beests to cover jest a trembling with ther hands over ther ears and ther eyes full of tear. If men was deef to it, they mite be to willin to fite like animals all the time and like the slotter, cause it be the noize that skers you and keeps you afrade. Guess it be beter that men stays afrade of the noize. otherwiz, they mite get to likin war to much and that skers me."

A poem found on the battlefield - its author unknown:

We, upon our honor,
Turn crimson the day
And colorless the night
With fitful slumber.

From a letter written by Colonel George Pane to his wife, Jeanette:

"Melancholy follows me as I peruse our bivouacs at night and see on our dewy earth a nation asleep, and I wonder who will sleep forever by this hour tomorrow. Thus, I am stricken with helplessness and mortified by fear for each soul."

From a pre-battle inspirational by Chaplain Clarence Chase to the troops of his brigade:

"Honor is a strange master. It can create both saints and fanatics, cloud one's judgment or inspire it. Put your trust in the Lord and He will set your honor on its purest course."

From an address by pacifist Collin Cummings:

"It must be to a Divine purpose that God has granted defiant man the free will and ingenuity to make war. Otherwise, I cannot conceive of a single, compensating grace."

* * *

Haunting Thoughts

Warmth: I trust it is not irreligious to worship it, for truly, it is a miracle of worship, longed for in damps and winter cold, cherished and reverentially considered. In such conditions, we crave it. It sustains and rejuvenates and becomes a sanctuary unto itself. Even a tad of it is welcomed. You cannot comprehend what it means to the common soldier bereft with cold and wind-rejecting clothing. For us these days, that soldier is most of us. On future biting winter days in the cold of peacetime, if peace ever comes, and in the creeping dampness of autumn, we will never truly be warm again, for our bones and muscles are permanently impaired with diminished circulation, like those of all others with whom we endure these treacherous days. It is not odd to see men huddled together, arms wrapped 'round each other for warmth in their sleep lest they perish day or night in savage weather. Even meager campfires are cherished, well guarded and faithfully fueled by our wood-scavengers, who search out twigs and branches, chop-up small trees and burn ammunition boxes. Warmth - if we ever stand or sit before civilian stoves or hearths again, it will be with our souls wrapped in the memories of this war's cold miseries. Those who have not been here with us will never understand why we will return, haunted, to our homes, filled with such recollections, never again to be as we once were - before we succumbed to the fatal romance of distant bugles and seductive visions of elusive glory.

Defeat: A stigma. To abandon a battlefield to the enemy is to admit to the nullification of lives lost and sacrifices made. Humiliation is not word enough to describe its effects and aftermath. It consumes exhausted soldiers' souls until sleep wrests them away from earthly concerns. To wounded men, it is but one more agony for their consciences to endure. Recovery is a thing of bitter taste. And one always wonders if defeat will come again, or be repeated as common fare for the war's duration. Self-doubt can gut an army if not checked by leaders who allow it no fatal play. It is only an army of true professional bearing and strictest personal discipline that can survive it to fight again. In such circumstances, I have witnessed our Army raise itself to challenge its enemy repeatedly. But win or lose this war, my eyes will tear when I recall our veterans' élan and the tribulations they endured and overcame. I weep when I think of the many thousands yet to be put beneath our soil - their deeds unheralded - their names unknown. Wherever I wander upon our land after this war, if I survive it, I will wonder where the lilies lie and upon whose rest I trod.

Learning: To kill - yes, men in war learn to kill - or recall how to. And, yes, they soil the beauty of the lilies with other's blood and stain them with the cold tears of dead innocence. The consequences to their souls cannot truly be calculated. Men kill and boys learn to. One might ask - what makes them do so? Why do they not reject it? I could argue that they do so because those around him do so - that killing in war is glorified, prestigious, and rewarded, or that all do so because the stronger among them do. Or, I could surmise that by doing so they avoid the vilification that their societies and those who kill would heap upon them otherwise - the word "cowardice" haunting them more powerfully than the Word of God; that to contravene the herd's imperative that binds an army risks the herd's rejection. And yet killing is not in the nature of all men. For these souls the wartime road can be long and the journey devastating. Perhaps our tribal hunting skills, developed of necessity over the eons of our prehistory, have merely evolved into a more sophisticated and exciting challenge as our global tribes have enlarged. Yet to infer that to kill once makes killing thereafter more easily done, as I so often hear, is contradicted by fact. Some men, perhaps not THAT "evolved," sicken of it, their consciences destroyed by it, and either desert the Army or flee to Chaplains, seeking spiritual sanctuary, their guilt before God too crushing to bear. Others relish it and find it consistently therapeutic in a twisted sense that leaves their souls contorted. Many will become future miscreants who will prey upon society when this organized killing ends. Armies, like tribes, fight for survival above all else, knowing no more essential compulsion than that which motivated tribal competition before the evolution of compromise and negotiation. Perhaps the experiment that enclosed man's spiritual essence within a physical shell ensured that to contend with a predatory universe, killing would always be a necessity. Nonetheless, I wonder why I acquiesce to it; perhaps because its seed remains just as compelling in my most ancient blood, awaiting only the germinating nourishment of circumstance and opportunity. Perhaps our deepest natures still adhere to prehistory because - if the darkest secret of our animal ids was revealed - it might say, "Our most noble rationalizations for our aggressiveness are not only self-deluding, but disguise an inherent truth - that we still risk destruction to satiate our thirst for that which still binds men more closely than any other endeavor in our still primal brotherhood - the hunt."

The Hardness: Veterans say it comes inevitably to all, when war strips men of all dignity, compassion and humanity, leaving them shells that fatalistically endure each day, having lost hope for themselves and having given up on surviving the war's duration. Long gone is any regard for the enemy's humanity. All are merely targets to be shot down with cold indifference, as bottles on fence posts. I have met many such shooters. Each has had the identical look, a stare unique to his kind, distant and empty, never focusing on men nor anyone else, always looking away or to the ground, his words often mumbled, his sentences disjointed, his thoughts sometimes incoherent-sounding, his voice sometimes mean-sounding. He can no longer relate to others with friendship or ease. Apparently, he would rather be left to himself, as if he senses that he no longer belongs to the world of his brethren. Yet, in battle, he can be deliberate, cunning, and ruthless, the kind of soldier who is most efficient and effective, and the kind that virgin troops and even less affected veterans gravitate to, as they would to rock for cover. Yes, he is paradoxically the finest soldier, around whom armies rally and who stands like boulders to win battles. He is not so much reckless in his courage as unmoved by danger - hardened to it and careless of his fate. He is difficult to know but as valuable to companies, regiments, and brigades as artillery. Ironically, therefore, though he seldom mixes with other troops, he contradicts the moral disparagements I've described by being security to timid souls less inured to war.

*   *   *

Critters

Fleas, ticks, and lice are the most diabolical of all God's sinister creations. They fight us day and night in ambushes that never cease to curse our existences and draw our tired blood.

We call them "graybacks," demons. Unprintable appellations also apply. The naïve and uninformed merely call them "chiggers."

They are the torment of our lives on the march, in bivouac and in hospital. And they are unremitting in their daily discouragements. We capture them, burn them, pierce them, and smash them - but the bulk escape - and remedies old and new do not discourage them. Tars, gunpowder, lamp oil, alcohol - none ward off their legions long enough to give us prolonged relief. The cold waters of rushing streams do, but we seldom come to rushing streams - let alone bathe - and so they regroup, multiply, and attack us again and again.

I have witnessed men rush into the night, raging with frustration because they cannot rid themselves of the critters' maddening tortures. Some men hang their uniforms (or facsimiles) and undergarments over wood fires to smoke them out. This method is successful for only short periods. But in the cold and damp winter weather it is not practical, though some unnerved souls will suffer naked in the snow around roaring fires, sacrificing filthy clothing to wreak vengeance on as many creatures as possible.

The most practical among us have invented competitive games to make sport of our sufferings. They hold contests to see who can pick the most off each other's clothing and carcasses. Each picked critter is counted by judges and dropped into a can. The winner is accorded great laurels, and his fame is duly recorded and celebrated throughout our ranks. He also is accorded royal titles, such as "Chief Bug" or "King Kootie" and other monikers befitting the number of times he has triumphed over all contenders.

It is a cynical but amusing exercise that contributes to our spiritual survival. Though I have not yet won a title, I HAVE placed a close second, earning the right to become a Chief's or a King's counselor, with all the respect due members of his royal court. Officers have given us full rein to conduct contests and award titles - whenever such activities do not interfere with military routine. Not that our military gentry are immune from critter attacks. I suspect that any officer in the regiment could enter our contests, pick the little demons off his uniform, and give any one of the enlisted a very close run.

* * *

Nor Could I

Days ago I surrendered to the compulsion that drew me to the surgeons' tents. Was I being morbidly curious? Perhaps. Yet I felt I should not ignore them. What was it, I had to know, that motivated such vilified souls?

I have observed many surgeons, who having soberly worked endless hours to save lives, collapse afterwards with exhaustion. And I have seen others operate while so drunk they could neither stand nor intelligently speak.

Initially I thought the latter to be not only grossly irresponsible, but criminally negligent. And then, on that day when I spent hours witnessing the horror inside their tents, I was converted. Never would I criticize them again, for I realized that the majority are sustained only by supernatural courage and incredible willpower - a power I was born without.

Yet I both admired and pitied them. They work covered in the wounded's blood and gore, while enduring the screaming agonies of those they probe and saw. How much of that can any average man witness and bear without going mad? And I learned that it isn't incompetence that produces the haphazard results of their work, but the inadequacy of their training, due to the crude state of the medical arts they practice.

Words cannot do justice to such awful scenes - to the writhing victims whose crushed or mangled limbs condemn them to swift amputation - barely two minutes to remove an arm - three or less per leg - and generally with the victim receiving only a modicum of anesthesia or whiskey - while at other times, lacking both, no anesthesia at all.

Perhaps in peacetime arms and legs, and even lives, are saved because time is not an adversary, allowing surgeons the luxury of working carefully and diligently. But behind the battlefield, where hundreds of mutilated await critical treatment, never can there be enough time to devote to individual patients. Surgeons must rush their work on their improvised tables, many victims perishing of terror or loss of blood. Success is reduced to a vicious game of chance, and only the strongest patients survive.

"Next man...next man...next man..." I came away cursing those words, having seen how, in daylight or by nighttime lantern, surgeons cut into bone and tissue to remove bullets or shrapnel, or to saw off shattered limbs, suture stumps and treat burns - always instantly demanding, when finished..."next man."

For hours, exhausted and profusely sweating, with tables running with blood they hack, saw, probe, cut, and sew without respite - their directions to aides slurred by rampaging fatigue, their patients' howling and shrieking. Much that keeps them sane reposes in nearby bottles or jugs of spiritual relief, which they use to dull their patients' wits and their own. Using buckets of water after each surgery, aides slosh clotted tissue and corruption from each table, spiriting patients away on gore-drenched litters to outside convalescence beneath sun, stars, or rain. In come ever more litters, bearing moaning or semi-conscious victims. As these men are rolled onto the same tables, surgeons use separate buckets of bloody water to cleanse their hands and arms of gore. Outside their operating theaters - be they tents or sheds, barns or homes - piles of arms, hands, feet, and legs grow, until teams of orderlies remove them in wheel barrows for disposal in fly-covered, maggot-infested pits whose gagging stench cause passerbys to vomit.

I watch it all - young soldiers losing their limbs, older ones losing theirs - blood squirting from wounds or incisions or saw cuts and gushing over them, orderlies holding them down - victims' bowels and bladders evacuating uncontrollably, the smell of it all causing me to lose everything I've eaten that day, until I can tolerate it no longer. And yet the surgeons continue their work in an endless routine, as if made of iron and oblivious to the horror beneath their crimson hands - their sweat dripping into their victims' exposed wounds.

For the remainder of that day, in the resuscitating warmth of our bivouac's campfire, and by the fire's undulating light that night, I recalled and recorded what I saw and felt - as I sipped from a jug of slow relief brought to me by our company's generous denizens, who produced it - as they magically do - from nowhere, knowing where I'd been and what I'd witnessed and why my hand produced such erratic script.

"Never could I be a surgeon," I remarked to a pipe-puffing corporal, my tension severe, "even if the Lord Himself tried to persuade me."

"Nor could I," he replied, puffing vigorously, as he reclined against a tree, "no, siree - nor could I. Been up agin' canister fire and shell and rifle fire that'd cut men in half, but nary could I do THAT!"

We expect our all- too-human surgeons to possess the strength of gods when contending with war's inhuman consequences. Yet they are far too few, and most are not criminally negligent, but criminally overworked. That some work under whiskey's influence is a consequence of war, not of human failing, something under such circumstances to be expected lest all go insane and none remain to do what they can. We cannot expect perfection from them, nor more professionalism than their situations and training allow. Those who eventually break down should be mercifully removed to recuperate in mind and soul, not chastised and derided. Who else could we then expect to voluntarily do what THEY must do and ARE doing? Both sides' politicians, who daily encourage this civil tragedy, are to be blamed for the hellish scenes I've described. It is THEIR faces that should be thrust into the gore they themselves have produced, not the surgeons'.

When surgeons break down at their tables, they are helped away, replaced by colleagues who have often already worked twelve and more hours with minimal or no sleep, but who have no other professional choice. Yet, as a group, they are chastised and their reputations disparaged by our rank and file who misunderstand them, and by others who can neither do such work nor would want to.

I know I belabor the point, but this war is not of medicine's doing. Yet for as many as surgeons lose on their tables many more, incredibly, are saved. Still, I have yet to hear a surgeon praised. They know how harshly their troops regard them, but they persist in their craft. On rare occasions they are assaulted either for the loss of someone's friend or relative, or simply because they're surgeons. Why they persist, I cannot say, except that their dedication to medicine is near-religious. If some appear incompetent, it may be because they've simply been used up - or because the medical situations they encounter are beyond the powers of present-day medicine to remedy - AND equally beyond a surgeon's reserves of emotional restraint.

If, in some cases, ineptness cannot be excused, neither, generally, should our vainglorious politicians. If there are not enough surgeons to serve the Army's needs, it is because this war has gotten too huge, too bloody, and has lasted too insanely long. If the Lord's Heart were known, it might say the war should never have begun.

*   *   *

Parades

"None of us is FER 'em," a veteran told me: "They be a pain fer the 'musement a'ginerals and pol'ticians and ign'ernt folk who don't know betta." He was speaking of things that made war appear glorious, like parades.

I watched one such procession in Richmond, having gone there on a furlough of sorts. I wanted to gauge our civilians' reactions to the war, and judge how much they were aware of the Army's plight. It appeared to me by the discussions I engaged in and through observation, that they cared little for nor understood anything but their own wartime discomforts and material shortages.

The parade was passing through. Cheering crowds lined the streets. Bands played. Men whooped and hollered. Women and children waved flags. Already jammed walkways seethed with fresh throngs arriving to see and hear the war their fantasies had concocted.

A poignant scene thereafter held my attention, as I witnessed what apparently was a veteran hobble on crutches along a boardwalk paralleling one side of the street. He wore an infantryman's kepi and threadbare sack coat. One leg was gone above his knee. A peg supported what was left of the other.

A noisy band had just passed by and another was on the way, with tired, war-weary troops marching between, cavalry and horse-drawn caissons towing artillery, soldiers atop each, marchers being careful, lest they pass through mounds of horse-droppings.

The veteran furtively watched the crowds that bumped him but otherwise ignored him. Cheering and clapping erupted everywhere, but as the crowds greeted their marching heroes all along the way a boisterous merrymaker backed into the soldier's crutch, nearly causing him to collapse onto the boardwalk.

Ladies threw flowers at the passing marchers. Men doffed their head wear out of respect. But their joyousness told me, as it told the veteran, how ignorant they were of the truths behind the parade. Nor did they comprehend that those marching troops had not come from idyllic summer encampments. Only days ago they had been to battle, and except for the perceptions of unsmiling older men watching along the route, who by their demeanors were undoubtedly survivors of past wars, the civilian throngs could not have understood why their heroes' battle-scarred solemnity appeared to contrast so starkly with all the surrounding gaiety. The marching troops did not want to be there. They'd been ordered to be there. They would have wanted to spend the time sleeping, writing letters home or repairing their tattered uniforms.

I sympathized with what the veteran was undoubtedly thinking. The entire affair was a charade, a fantasy produced for the morale of revelers for whom he and thousands like him had given so much, but whose names they would never know. His expression confirmed it. I studied others in the crowd who watched without emotion, who were neither cheering nor displaying the slightest merriment. Their hard and wizened looked convinced me they had been recently discharged or were also on furlough. The arm of one appeared stiff and immobile.

Then to my horror two running youths collided with the crutch-borne soldier, spilling him and his sticks to the boardwalk, as though he were a doll knocked from a shelf. His head struck the boards. Around him civilians stared, but none offered help. Instead they withdrew, frightened by his disability, as if they too would be similarly afflicted if they touched him.

Men who appeared to be veterans rushed to his aid, hoisting him gently to his peg leg as they repositioned his crutches beneath his arms and recovered his kepi. He thanked them profusely and enthusiastically engaged them in conversation, obviously relieved that allies were about. Smiles went 'round, as I'm certain they exchanged information about their parts in the war - units, battles they had participated in and other military minutiae. The veterans stared-down sheepish onlookers, verbally chastising and shaming them for their lack of decency in doing nothing to assist the crippled soldier. Their courage gladdened me.

After a few minutes of conversation, with handshakes all around, they left him to his day and went about theirs, convinced, I assumed, that he would need no further assistance. Still dazed, he leaned against the building behind him, his head bent low. Other civilians passed him, eyed him but avoided him. I wondered - what would be his future? In truth, HE was the real parade - the personification of the real war they refused to consider or in their ignorance thought was such sport. He represented neither the jaunty music nor the bogus pomp nor the reviewing stand politicians, who were lapping up the ceremony's political potential like thirsty pack mules. But unlike the hundreds of troops brought this day from recent battlefields to amuse the populace, he had hobbled by only because his government had discarded him.

I was about to converse with him when a young lady approached him. She paused, smiled, and then greeted him. He instantly responded as if he would never have believed that as cultured a woman would have spared him the time. After chatting amicably with him, she pulled a flower from the small bouquet she carried, put it in his coat's lapel and took his hand. Leaning forward, she kissed him tenderly on the cheek, wishing him well before going her way. He could hardly have fought back his tears. Nor could I resist mine. I thanked God for her good soul, certain that neither she nor the soldier would forget each other. Nor would I.

I came away convinced by virtue of every civilian who ignored him afterwords or who stared at him as though he were a public nuisance that our men in the field belonged to a vast unknown.

The soldier gripped his crutches, turned, and made his tortuous way through the crowds, trapped by a thousand eyes that asked, "Who is this seedy, peg-legged derelict marring the occasion with his presence? Didn't such abominations deserve avoidance? And look how oddly his disgusting stump sways between his crutches!"

My anger turned to a suppressed rage. I greeted him and helped him along, returning him to a privately sponsored hostel for crippled soldiers.

Some onlookers had made him go around them. Others made way only reluctantly, some disgustedly. No, they would never understand. A half-hour later, the parade ended and the streets emptied, leaving me hoping that the soldier's life would never become as vacant, that somewhere a young lady, out of devotion, not pity, would brighten and resuscitate his life.

Parades? From then on, I, too, was no longer "fer 'em."

* * *

A Decent Service

I have seen much suffering in this war. Hunger is among the worst.

Its effects upon our troops are as uncompromising as they are stark, as are its ravages among our Southern people. It weakens bodies and will, causing sickness and driving some men to painful distraction. Yet for reasons beyond understanding, it does not break all men's fighting spirit, those who supernaturally endure to force Northern armies from Southern soil.

Tonight, the company to which I've attached myself lies on cold ground in late autumn, the bodies of its sleeping men either covered by tattered blankets or nothing at all. Many huddle together in fetal positions, depending upon each other for meager warmth. A bone-chilling mist has descended across the countryside, bringing with it the threat and reality of lung infections. Still these men suffer quietly, accepting whatever fate they believe God has willed for them.

Many shoeless lie with their bare feet close to campfires kept lighted by those on watch. Dry wood is scarce. It is an art practiced again and again by our fire-starters to ignite wet wood and keeps it burning, resulting in thick smoke hanging densely over our Army's entire encampment. Those who cannot sleep brew chicory. A few enjoy grass tea. Genuine tea is a rare commodity. Yet, warm drink helps combat the effects of the dampness that gnaws at muscles and bones and creeps into marrow. Nonetheless these troops, compelled by honor and a mystical sense of duty, stay the course.

To a man, hunger cramps their bellies. They've had nothing substantial to eat in three days. All suspect the supply column is nowhere near. Still they remain, sustained by hope and their stubborn pride. Some lay awake, too starved to rest. Their emaciated bodies refuse to produce or hold heat, and they tremble beneath repeated assaults of chills and related miseries. Minute to minute they are haunted by thoughts of home. They long to be with loved ones, to be warm and well-fed. The idea haunts their waking hours and dreams - in camp and on the march. Home is their sustaining religion and reason for being.

Originally a fashionable affectation, private journals have become catalysts to some men's sanity. This night in a tent, by the anemic flame of a single candle, our company's commanding officer - Captain Holt - writes in his journal. He bears time's wear and scars – an ink-blotted chronicle of his star-crossed unit's wartime history. Of late the company has fared badly. Battle and disease have reduced its strength to a shadow of its former number and capacities. Replacements to fill its depleted ranks no longer exist. Nor will its ragged denizens receive new shoes and fresh uniforms. Instead they'll suffer reduced ammunition allotments and food rations until fresh supplies arrive, if they arrive. Yet more fighting, a commodity never in short supply, will continue to be served-up in generous portions.

The Captain, seated at his small, portable writing desk, puts down his pen and lays his head on his arms. He weeps. He weeps for his men's destruction and his own frustration, unable to relieve their tribulations nor honor them even with the barest amenities of service life. Their poignant loyalty has touched him deeply, torturing his conscience. He has watched their ravaged bodies surmount grueling marches, build earthworks and fight the enemy while their souls battled spiritual demons. He has witnessed them repeatedly do the impossible with courage and strength summoned from unknown reservoirs not possessed by ordinary mortals. And he believes such men are too good for him to command – that they deserve a commander whose leadership is equal to their devotion and far more worthy of their lives.

His pleas to higher command for supplies have brought him only assurances that the entire Army suffers shortages just as intensely, but that God must intercede on our side by all that is right and just. Still, he has long since realized that peace will be the most practical of all intercessions.

He worries about his family and home. His letters of late have not been answered. Has this been due to the Army's beleaguered mail systems or has war come to his wife and children? Are they well, or have they been burned out like countless families? Will life for them ever be as it once was? Will he and they ever be able to put the war behind them? "God," he prays, "tell me what is happening to them?" Uncertainty has ground him under.

"'Scuse us, suh..." a voice says beyond the flap of the tent's entrance, breaking his reveries.

"Yes?" the Captain asks.

"It's about Private Wilikerson, suh," the voice says.

The Captain bids the voice come inside. A Corporal and Private enter, alternately illuminated and shadowed by the candle's flickering flame: "Private Wilkerson, suh," Sergeant Sparks reports, "passed in his sleep. This here's Private Ornsby, his friend. We want to know if'n he and some of the boys ken bury 'Ole Wilkie decent come dawn?"

"Wilkerson," Captain muses, hiding his face in his kerchief to hide his tears and now his regret. The two enlisted men are impressed, knowing Wilkerson's death has touched their Captain: "his leg amputations..."

"Din't go well," Sparks says; "too much gangrene."

"Well, we cain't wait 'til dawn," the Captain answers. "The brigade may be movin' at first light. You may bury him now, if'n you wish."

"Yes, suh."

"Have you a fittin' place?"

"Figured we'd put him under in the woods, suh," the Sergeant replies, "there bein' a restful place on higher ground."

"As you wish," Holt responds. "How long'd ya know him, Private?"

"Mosta m'life, suh . . . come from the same parish . . . grow'd up t'getha. Was m'brotha-in-law; married m'sista and I married his. Awful hard, suh, losin' him. He suffad hard 'til t'night. Passed peaceful at last."

"I see it's awful hard on you," Holt says.

"Yes, suh, but it's gonna be harder t'home."

"All right," Holt agrees, "y'all prepare things and I'll be there directly. I'll look for y'all's lantern lights."

"Preciate, suh," the Sergeant responds, but before disappearing into the night, he pauses: "Old Wilkie were a good man and a fine soldier, Captain. Wish you coulda know'd him up close."

It is a short but decent lantern light service. Holt recites the Lord's Prayer, offers personal remarks about Wilkerson's devotion to the company, and thanks those attending for the honor of being asked to officiate. They do not detect his sense of profound inadequacy. Ornsby has given up his only blanket to cover Wilkerson's body that his brother-in-law might be put under with dignity and, symbolically at least, be spared contact with the earth's corruption. After retiring to his tent, and moved by Ornsby sacrifice, Holt takes one of two blankets from his cot, calls in the Sergeant and instructs him to deliver the warming article, with his compliments, to the grieving Ornsby.

For the remainder of the night, a sleepless Holt lays on his cot, worried the brigade and his company will be called to battle in the morning, the enemy being close and spoiling for a fight. Would the Army challenge the enemy in open country or, in its weakened condition, would it fall back to prepared positions? He prays it will fall back, that he will never lose another man and that all will eventually return to their families. Only an hour or so before dawn does his restless mind submit. He sleeps soundly.

He dreams of his young wife and their two tots romping in their yard. He sees beautiful vistas and brilliantly green valleys and white birds in graceful flight - and a light so brightly white he dares not look at it, yet it does not hurt his eyes. Within it, he senses supreme peace and beyond it the home of his soul. Wilkerson is there, healthy and joyful.

"I be b'holdin' to ya, Captain," the soldier says, respectfully doffing his stained slouch hat, the blanket wrapped around him. "I always will."

The dream awakens him. A moment later, Sparks appears at the tent flap. Dawn has begun to illuminate the eastern horizon. We're moving, suh," he announces; "We're a'fallin' back."

Groggily, the disbelieving Captain rises to the edge of his cot, his face in his hands, his head bowed, his heart pounding: "Thank-ya, Lord," he prays, his body and spirit feeling energized and mysteriously strengthened, "thank-ya, sincerely."

I walk with him to his hungry company's assembly area, my belly growling. Smiling confidently, he inserts his journal into the case he carries over one shoulder: "It'll be a good day," he remarks, patting the case's side. "I've prayed for it, in here, so it must be true."

And so it was. Providentially, minutes later, wagons arrived with rations and, with redeeming beauty, the lilies bloomed once more. I could hardly believe it.

Report to a Friend

Royal Chapman wrote the following letter to fellow journalist, William Edgerton, in May, 1864.

The Wilderness – Virginia

Dear William,

I have campaigned with a single regiment for two months and can testify that they are bone-weary and nearly fought-out. They have participated in some of the hardest fighting of the war and their losses over time have been severe.

Having originally enlisted 546 men in late '61, their numbers are down to 222. Note that this figure includes recent replacements, whose exact numbers are unknown to me.

The proof of this regiment's exhaustion lies not so much in its numbers of dead and wounded as much as in the eyes and faces of its veteran survivors. Even then, considering how much action they have seen its desertion rates have been mercifully minuscule.

Once again engaged with the enemy – this time for days in deviously treacherous terrain hidden within miles of burning wooded wilderness – these veterans have become ever more grim and sullen. They were a dispirited lot when I linked up with them, but the last two months of campaigning have drained them almost completely. They fight without the dash and spirit that once marked our Army's character. Even the least experienced among the newcomers proceeds slowly and cautiously, reluctant to blindly stride into this tangled Hell. There was a time when these proud fighters would have done so. No more.

Everywhere, fires, ignited by combat, burn out of control, consuming the trapped able-bodied and wounded with equal frenzy. The screaming agonies of those burning to death panic even our most steadfast. Our troops and the enemy's collide by accident in the underbrush and smoke, each side's lines being entwined and out of sight of their own. Companies become detached from regiments, lost and blinded in the smokey confusion and unable to communicate.

This battle is very much a way of individuals and individual effort. Never have I witnessed such attrition. I'm told the struggle contravenes the most fundamental rules of tactics and organization, but convention hardly applies here. And we are suffering greatly for it. Officers have lost control. I regularly see men break down and weep with frustration and fear. Many refuse to move. Some menace their officers when ordered to do so – "To where?" they ask; "to what?" – to inevitable death or capture? Some have gone mad.

Officers, commissioned and non-commissioned, are no less affected. It is impossible for some to deliver cogent orders, let alone know the tactical situation, that they might properly direct their men – and many are gripped by an infectious mental paralysis that defies them to act.

But I fear something more debilitating is abroad in the ranks – a fatalism seen in all eyes and faces – an acceptance of inevitable destruction stemming from a nearly tangible belief that it will forever more liberate them from their constant terrors. Captured enemy troops suffer no less from it. Some, theirs and ours, become catatonic.

Many of our boys appear to wait for death and even to desire it. The waiting simmer quietly in their blank expressions. They stare soullessly into infinity and like lumps of stone passively resist orders – dumb and deaf. Many must be manhandled and carried by their comrades, or shaken until their stupors are broken. Either that or be consumed by the flames.

Men become separated into groups of twos and threes that must constantly maneuver to flee the fires with only a passing thought of the enemy, who is doing the same. Those who lose their bearings to hopelessness huddle in gaggles to await destruction – or surrender to death by their own hands. But the fighting's most contradictory nature comes when enemies, fleeing the fires, come face to face. At that moment, they either succumb to instinct and reflexively kill each other point-blank or after a moment's hesitation assert their common humanity by pulling each other's wounded, to safety – instantly reducing the war to absurdity – and just as instantly discovering the unity their politicians rejected before the first wartime shots were fired – or because pride and obstinacy pledged them to betray it. Those self-serving felons should be dragged here – today!

Fires burn day and night. No one sleeps. To sleep is to burn. Our boys pray for rain. Our generals and theirs are on their knees for it, asking that the flames might be quenched so their respective armies may be delivered from this nightmare – so that the killing might organized again!
How all the enemy's wounded and ours will be recovered without hundreds being consumed first I cannot guess. These wooded tangles are impossible and the smoke is self-defeating. I fear that most who die in the flames will perish undetected.

Though not a combatant and worth nothing to the Army, I, too, am as exhausted and fearful as those about whom I write. I've composed this letter over a three-day period in brief moments of respite, and in my head while on the move. Aside from the fire's dangers, the enemy will spare no minié-ball on me because I carry only pencils and notebooks. After a time in conditions like these killing becomes a thing of spiritual blindness. Stupefied soldiers do it by rote without conscience, never mind discretion. So-called "civilized" and "humane" rules of warfare blur and are lost to animal reactions. Killing becomes a reflexive exercise as terror overcomes even the most reticent and turns them into near-mindless machines. A "no prisoners" mentality spawns an insidious blood lust that turns men's souls into disintegrating metal. The wounded are sometimes shot down or shot dead where they lay.

This war will claim thousands William, long after the guns are stilled and the drums and banners put away. Even now, the seeds for that calamity are being sown. Posterity will reap the after-winds of these times in lost and mutilated hearts that will not soon heal. We cannot know what the inevitable or final costs will be, except to surmise that all will be great. And I fear that my chronicling of these times, if I survive them, will continue as their ripples fan into the distant future.

Let us hope that when it all ends, the decency and humanity robbed from our people by these events, will Providentially reassert themselves, and that passions will cool in time – so that good men on both sides might at last look to Higher Authority for guidance, as both should have done initially before taking up swords so long, long ago.

Your obedient servant,

Royal K.

In the Beauty of the Lilies

**The Wartime Journals
of Confederate Correspondent
Royal K. Chapman
1862-1864**

Journal Thirteen

Contents

A Thought

Men, after battle, drank into themselves
the beauties of tranquil hills, valleys
and skies under setting sunlight
and were calmed.

The Bloody March

"Look well to your feet, gentlemen," the surgeon warned the officers of the regiment to which I attached myself two years ago, when I began these journals. "They will determine your destiny as much as the enemy."

His words haunted me as I plod with the men of the regiment two years later. My feet bleed from the heels, worn raw and open from countless miles trod in recent months, my boots filled with blood.

I have long since become inured to the pain, but my condition appears mild to that of others around me, half of them barefooted, some having tied their footwear together and slung it over their shoulders to preserve the leather for combat.

We have all ready come nearly fifteen miles, leaving a trail of bloody footprints behind us. I cannot begin to imagine the agony in ranks because of it, nor the dedication and resolution of these countless sufferers who endure it for Cause and country. Lacerations, bleeding callouses, cuts, abrasions, scabs, broken toes, slashed soles, punctured heels – their afflictions of feet run the gamut. Yet, they march – or should I say, shuffle and slog.

Perhaps, had the Army initially issued them decent footwear, and regularly replaced it when necessary out of respect for the rank and file's sacrifices, the Army might now be able to travel faster and longer distances, changing the war's course to our strategic advantage. This is, of course, also being dependent upon the regular issuance of decent food in sufficient abundance, which seldom happens. I cannot calculate the hundreds of men whose savaged feet have forced them to drop out of ranks, many of whom have since constituted a hobbling invalid corps that trails miles and even days behind us. Some, of course, but not many, have used their suffering to malinger and some to desert, but these men find no sympathy among those who make honest efforts to return to their companies and regiments no matter how long it requires nor how difficult.

I watch men limping, some grimacing in quiet agony, some stoically refusing to yield to their pain while undoubtedly suffering greatly. The roads we travel often deteriorate into mere paths through woods and brambles, across fields and wild meadows, over jagged stone and rocks and piercing twigs and branches, thorns, and cutting underbrush. It is a relief to tread down well-worn surfaces and wagon tracks, dirt and sand being a comfort. Serious foot infections plague scores of harried troops, some eventually leading to gangrenous sores and wounds requiring amputation. Many men have died as a result of all these hazards.

When rest comes during a march, or eventually in bivouac, a sorry mass of humanity collapses to tenderly nurse its feet with water, salves, herbs, poultices, and whatever else the men believe might bring them relief. It is a luxury for them to find a flowing creek in which they might bathe their worries while relaxing along its banks or lying back to sleep. I yearn for such relief, and time to rid myself of the overwhelming fatigue that weighs on me like a coat of iron. But again, my woes are unequal to those of countless others who, of military necessity, also suffer otherwise debilitating physical ailments too long neglected. And then there are those whose past battle wounds have never been properly attended and grow aggravated from abuse.

Pain is everywhere, a constant tormentor.

A Face Too Young

Part One

I stood with a grizzled artillery sergeant, looking over the battlefield spread before us, the fighting just ended.

A calm and a stillness pervades the universe after a battle. I cannot accurately describe it, for it must be felt and otherwise experienced if its nature is to be fully appreciated. Suffice it to say it is born of relief mixed with bewilderment. The blood slowly drains of fear and supernatural tension. Nervous exhaustion and high excitement just as slowly evaporate, leaving men numbed with mind-dulling somnolence.

The Sergeant, a veteran of many campaigns, rubbed his face to energize himself and shook off his creeping stupor: "It be like this eva'time," he said. "Best thing is cold water on yer face and neck to bring ya back. Yer body says sleep, but you ain't got the time. There be too much t'do, like bringin' in the wounded, even if they be the enemy's. The gore be worse than the fightin'."

We surveyed the smoke-hazed panorama: "Lordy, Lordy," he mumbled, the interminable field littered with enemy mutilated and dead. "They come'd right into 'ar guns, they did. What pea-brained general a'theirs done made 'em do that? They know'd ar' position was too strong and double canister be their reward for it. Can't say we didn't give it to 'em...poured a loada' iron into 'em, we did. Look at the rest of 'em skedaddling back into them woods."

Hundreds of blue-clad survivors of what had been proudly aligned ranks were falling back in gaggles, many of the wounded helping each other while able-bodied survivors carried the desperately maimed.

"It ain't a good feelin' suckin' down a beatin' like we jest gived 'em," the Sergeant said. "I know cause I been on that end a'things a time er two. Most-wise cause the people ya loose been sacrificed fer nothin', and they been good people ya ain't never gittin' back. Mostly, it be a waste.""

No, he said, he didn't hate those "fellers across the way." Rather, he sympathized with them despite their being the enemy, as if blue and gray were all a part of a tragic human brotherhood, like a pot of mixed paint. Eventually, the last of the enemy survivors trudged dejectedly to the safety of their wooded starting lines, their flags and regimental banners drooping in defeat.

"There come a time in the fightin' when ya know'd ya jest beat yer enemy, and then ya gotta have shed a the killin'," the Sergeant explained, "cause it don't make no more sense, if'n it eva did. Ya gotta let 'em go the same way you'd want 'em to let YOU go in their place. It be soldiers grace to otha soldiers. Ain't no rules say ya got to, 'ceptin' those in here," he said, pointing to his chest. "I'd say God give'd the rules ta us, but I'd feel guilty 'bout associatin' Him with ana a'this."

Behind us, his battery's gunners swabbed and greased their cannons, while men brought up fresh ammunition from nearby caissons. Smoke drifted from the heaped remains of a furiously burning caisson far down the line, the victim of an errant spark that had set off its stored powder bags and vaporized or maimed a dozen men.

"Them boys that explosion kilt be better off that some of the lads it wounded," the Sergeant said. "They be alive, but that ain't no blessin' when ya see what it done to 'em. When my time come, I want it quick. No surgeon's saws and bloody hands diggin' inta MY guts. Don't want no burned flesh hangin' offin' my body 'er eyes blowed out 'er limbs severed off like them, no siree. Jest a minié-ball through the noggin'll be quick and good anuff. Wouldn't be perdy, but I'd neva know it."

He scratched his head: "Never see'd a canister-slaughter like this b'fore, and I seen plenty. They say them blue-boys got theirselves a new general that's a drunk half the time. Sure musta been, t'send all his good boys agin us here like he done. We done double-charged all our guns eva'time we fired, like shotguns agin wheat stalks. Brave men they was. Lordy, they was brave the way they jest kept a comin' on. A shame t'have t'kill any of 'em. I 'spect they was real young, mostly, Yes, sir, a damn shame."

The Sergeant rambled on, his thoughts tumbling out. All the while, I jotted down his comments in shorthand, though he didn't appear to mind. I don't believe it actually mattered to him. By expressing himself, he was bleeding off suppressed emotions, a good thing. I could see relief overtake his countenance bit by bit, his commanding presence of mind and intent returning. He hadn't earned his three stripes being a weak nor timid man.

I thought the conversation would end there, but an officer approached us: "You, sir, are a journalist?"

"Yes, I am," I replied, though I carried no professional credentials.

"Perhaps you would wish to go with the Sergeant here into the fields to view the result of the enemy's folly."

"I believe I've seen such before, Captain," I remarked.

"Then you must know," he insisted, "that to appreciate it fully, you must witness it close-up."

He could not have known that I truly was no stranger to battlefields and their aftermath. Yet not wishing to be impolitic, I agreed, with a reluctant "Thank you, sir," to go forth as he suggested, dreading what I knew I would find. I hadn't told the Sergeant how many fights and battlefields I had witnessed to date in this war and in my life, not wishing to influence any comments he might make. I wanted his expressions to be purely illustrative of his original thinking. Yet I knew I could not prevent him from guessing that because of my age, I, too, was a veteran, yet, of another war.

I judged the Sergeant's age to be about forty, but was surprised when he told me he was fifty, though I was not also surprised that he, like me, was a veteran of the Mexican War. We briefly exchanged observations about that war, and I found it almost too coincidental that he and I had fought at Churabusco, though at opposite ends of our lines.

"Grieves me t'think that some of them fellers we kilt t'day mighta been with us in Mexico," he said. "Shame we weren't on the same side no more. I was bout thirty-three in '46. Been in the Federal army twelve year. Were a sergeant then, too, which is what I reckon I were born t'be. Then come Sumter, and I resigned t'fight fer Virginia. Guess I done seen too mana young faces neva go home."

Battle smoke still hovered in the unmoving air, enemy dead and wounded carpeting the intervening meadows, the maimed crying for water.

"Private," the Sergeant called to one of our passing soldiers, "git some men t'go back fer as mana full canteens as they ken carry and start givin' these wounded here a drink. But give the belly-wounded jest a sip, lessin' too much'll kill 'em."

The Private hurried off.

"Cain't give 'em back to their mammas and sweet-hearts," the Sergeant said. "least we ken do is give 'em water."

A moaning chorus of wounded, whose uniform colors didn't much matter anymore, grew around us.

I find it difficult to reconcile the apparent existence of such a paradoxically strong sense of comradeship between both sides in these conditions but maddeningly, only when the killing claims a hiatus. Yet all are Americans, are they not, and in that sense of the same blood? Of course, not all Southern soldiers would answer yes, and neither would all Northerners. Regardless, on both sides on such occasions, a fundamentally common humanity survives. Despite the different color of his uniform it is hard to hate a mutilated, bleeding soul, as helpless as a child. Many times I have witnessed one of our soldiers or one of theirs cradle a man of opposite uniform who cried for his wife and children while writhing on Eternity's edge. And I've seen tears in those cradlers' eyes, suddenly conscience-stricken with the poignant tragedy of it all. If asked at that moment, he would undoubtedly have concurred that in both fraternities of common suffering, one's dying enemy countryman is kin.

We continued our morbid battlefield tour, the Sergeant organizing the bringing of water to wounded Federals along the way. Despite horrible injuries, some suffered quietly, while others cried out in mortal agony amidst viscera, body parts and decapitated skulls. Some men wept like children for their mothers. Still others attempted to drag themselves toward their lines, too delirious to understand their conditions. Those able to stand supported others who would otherwise have collapsed, calmly proceeding into their haven of captivity.

"Pathetic the way some of 'em try t'stand," the Sergeant remarked. "I feel sorry for 'em, I truly do. Always did, even in Mexico. If it was me, I'd jest lay there 'til someone come fer me – er I died."

"How we gonna care fer all these Fed'rals, Sergeant?" one of our soldiers asked. "Hell, we ain't got anuff of ffices' t'care fer our own."

"They'll be a trucin' soon fer an exchange, I 'spect," the Sergeant replied. "Jest be patient and do what yer ordered."

Medical orderlies in butternut and gray moved into the field, collecting the salvageable, while abandoning the hopeless. Then, just as the Sergeant predicted, under a white flag of truce and to our side's relief, enemy teams arrived on the field to remove their wounded to the care of their surgeons and makeshift medical facilities. We, however, retained as prisoners all mobile enemy wounded. I watched as both side's orderlies intermingled, some amicably chatting with each other, ours helping theirs place the immobile on litters for evacuation. Civilian observers might have thought it insane that both sides should demonstrate such humane cooperation after having savagely mauled each other only a short time before. But such is the odd culture of war, as if what both sides had competed in had simply been a noble athletic contest.

Across the battlefield that extended perhaps a quarter-mile to either side of its epicenter, that in turn occupied perhaps two hundred acres, the dead lay in small heaps where they were cut down by canister fire. Where slain by rifle fire, they lay in disjointed rows. Their wounded lay among all these configurations, some with bodies piled atop them, squirming beneath the accumulated weight. Many of the dead stared skyward, their eyes wide open, as if surprised that death had snapped them away too quickly. Contorted, others lay face-down or on their sides, entrails spilling out or otherwise exposed, some headless, many still clutching their weapons. Body parts scattered everywhere, the result of those small iron balls within each canister round that tore shotgun-like through enemy ranks with scything effect. I had seen it all before in this war and in Mexico. Except for the rifling of barrels, which had greatly extended the killing range and deadliness of rifle fire and more powerful artillery since then, the use of weapons as well as tactics hadn't much changed. But be advised that my attitude and mood as I surveyed this killing ground was not as clinical as these words make it sound.

"See that dead feller over there," the Sergeant said, pointing, "see how his uniform be all mussed-up? Looks like he were a'diggin' inta it tryin' t'stop his bleedin. How mana times did we see that in Mexico?"

"Too many," I answered.

"Poor young soul," the Sergeant added, "musta run outta blood b'fore he could stop it. His mamma'll never know what happened to him, 'cause I'm bettin' he ain't got a sticha idenifyin' writin' on him. Probably didn't know how to. He'll be goin' inta a big hole with a ton a others or to the buzzards."

We'd leave the burying of Federals to the enemy unless they withdrew form the area beforehand. And then we'd leave them to rot where they fell, there being no time for burying them all. The Sergeant looked down at the seemingly peaceful countenance that belied a bloody hole in the youth's stomach:

"He died a'sufferin' bad. Stomach wounds is the worst pain a body can feel. Jest look at him, though, so peaceful. The angels musta come for him and took him outta his agony. Sad, though. I sometimes wonder where the Lord be in this war. He sure weren't here t'day."

Part Two

Indignity spawns indignities.

In an attempt to identify their dead, Federal orderlies ransacked the dead's uniforms. Dead men's coats lay open, shirts mussed and pants and jacket pockets pulled inside out. It didn't seem right for them to so abuse the dead, but without identification, the dead would be consigned to anonymity in body-heaped graves, their kin never to know where they fell nor were buried. Of cold military necessity, we did the same with ours. Armies on the move cannot afford civilian-style luxuries, the mass burial of dead being time-consuming enough. But this day our forces were not moving from their positions just yet, since it appeared the enemy might chance another costly assault with greater numbers. We therefore looked on, watching the enemy's recovery rituals. We too, had lost men in the day's fighting and were collecting our wounded and burying our dead at that very moment. I had witnessed such burials far too often, and cared not to watch them again.

On the battlefield, rummagers, taking pity on horribly mangled corpses, covered them with torn jackets borrowed from the less repulsively damaged dead. Had their uniform colors been gray or butternut or plain homespun, they could have been our side taking pity on our own dead. The Sergeant and Officer had gone their ways to see to their duties, leaving me isolated amidst the human wreckage, and sorry I had agreed to examine the battlefield, since I needn't have done so to have appreciated its impact.

One of our defenders, a tall, lanky Tennessee soldier, thin almost to the point of dissipation, trudged by, inspecting our side's work: "Sure can see that canister got 'em close up," he remarked, shaking his head. He told me that three years of this war had hardened him to mutilation and death, but that the killing had gone too far for far too long, much farther than either side had intended, or that either side should have allowed. He said that until this day, he had thought the war had so jaded him that he would never feel sympathy for another human soul again. But not since Malvern Hill, when it had been our boys by the hundreds who had been slaughtered by Federal canister fire, had he seen this kind of stomach-turning destruction. He said that at one time the suffering of the wounded had "slid easy off'n his back" and that corpses had not affected him, neither did sleeping nor eating near the dead, nor had anything else that profaned them. But this day had forced him to reexamine his values. He hadn't liked what he saw.

"The war ain't honorable no more," he said, "and I'm sick a'the killin' and what it done to me inside. As fer as I'm concerned, we oughta put ar bayonets t'the throats of all them damned politicians on both sides who wanted all this and force THEM t'do the fightin', if it be so all-fired important to 'em. It be their sport, ana'way, not 'arn."

He said he no longer believed in the war, that both side's had "sold their souls to the Devil."

Twenty yards away the body of a Federal soldier looked untouched. Curious, the tall soldier stepped around other bodies until he came to it, and looked down at the angelic face of a very young private lying on his back, still clutching his rifle. The youth's eyes stared skyward, his pupils dilated. Though mottled with dirt and dust, his face remained smooth and unlined. We initially detected no wounds, though each of us had long since learned that the slightest sliver of iron, rock, or wood, lodging in the brain or a vital body organ or nerve, can kill a man. Obviously, canister balls had ripped and mangled those around the youth, but what had killed him?

The tall solder knelt next to the lad, having then spied small amounts of blood that had pooled in his ears. A small droplet had turned maroon in one nostril. Undoubtedly, concussion from an exploding shell had brought him low. And now he slept in touching purity, though his parents would spend the remainder of their lives enduring joyless days, their treasure gone. I judged the youth's age to have been no more than sixteen, and possibly less. How was it that a boy of his tender years had been recruited? Federal recruiters, I supposed, could be as heartless as ours.

"You were too tender to perish in this damned war," the tall soldier lamented, speaking to the boy and reaching out to close the lids of those sightless eyes. He placed a hand on the lad's arm: "Lord, this here boy was too young to be my enemy. Tell me why ya took him. Tell me why ya let his kind wear a uniform. It weren't right. How ken we older men depend on ya when ya permit this kind thing? If I gotta fight, give me evil men to kill, not tender boys! Tell us why ya 'bide this madness, Lord. What's it all for?"

A growing breeze now circled the battlefield, disturbing the boy's long brown hair.

"Why don'tcha answer, Lord?" the tall soldier suddenly raged, looking skyward. "Why don'tcha eva speak?"

I had seen war break other men when they had witnessed and felt too much of it. I now saw the same stress eating away the tall soldier's soul.

"I want ta cry," he said to me, "but the tears won't come. They quit comin' a long time ago. I used t'be young, too. I used to admire soldier's uniforms and were moved by the drums. Thought war was the most excitin' thing when we was taught 'bout it in school. Didn't know nothin' 'bout it, but that be what I thought. I b'lieved in noble causes, but b'lievin' don't justify all this. These Yanks b'lieved in noble causes, too. There's shame in what we done ta this here boy, but least he went to Eternity pure and young. None of US eva will, not ana'more. I surely won't...maybe ta Hell t'kick the Devil's arse, but not ta Heaven."

"It shoulda been HIM layin' there, not the youngin," he complained. Why, he asked, did the young ones "always get took" while the Lord kept his kind "a'hangin' on foreva?" THAT, he objected, was the greatest injustice of it. He said his kind could cozy up to the muzzle of the biggest cannon on Earth – and the "damn thing'd misfire, but boys like this one fall eva time. Why? Lord. Ya owes this boy! In the name a'justice, Ya gotta take care of him and comfort his maw and paw and give 'em peace, ya hear? And next time, 'stead takin' one like HIM, ya take ME!" Then, regaining his composure, he turned back to the young soldier, his voice softening: "Sorry, son. Trula am. No doubt, they're gonna bury ya in a big hole with a passel of othas, but don't let it botha ya none. Yer soul's free. You jest rest now and sleep...jest rest and sleep and wake up in the arms a'beautiful angels. You jest was a face too young."

He stood, shouldered his rifle and, pausing, said, "Hell, guess he actual be a damn-sight better off than the rest of us. He's goin' t'the Lord pure, not like worthless killin' trash like me."

Then, he walked on, obscured by the burning caisson smoke blown across the meadow by a rising wind. I might have wagered that he would walk back through our lines into the wilderness beyond, quit of war, a soldier no more.

Rebel Doodles

In the midst of our march today, a lone fife sounded from somewhere in the company behind us, playing Yankee Doodle Dandy.

Sore feet and lagging dispositions immediately found renewed vigor as rank after rank took up the tune, and began singing with resounding volume, but with slight word-changes...

"Rebel Doodles went to war, didn't own no ponies, showed them Yankees how to fight, skerd Lincoln and his cronies..." etc., etc.

Many of our ancestors had fought in our first Revolution, and it appeared that the spirit of those times found resurgence in OUR ranks. Even I discovered myself being swept-up by their enthusiasm.

I don't believe anyone had reinvented more than a single verse, but we repeated it until the tune died of its own volition.

Then it began raining, and the march continued in absolute solemnity, as vigor gave way, this time to sore, muddy feet and soaking dispositions. The bewildering contrast left me and most of us in a fog of melancholy worse than before all the gaiety. Shoulders stooped, heads hunkered down, hardly anyone spoke for two more drenching hours until our column halted to bivouac in the wet for the remainder of the miserable night.

.

Pie in the Eye

Here we were, brigades divided into regiments and further divided into companies, trekking wearily through the countryside, feet blistered, legs aching, sleep assaulting us from every direction at every opportunity – and then, wafting into our nostrils from points unknown (or, perhaps, from a tiny little homestead just up the road) came the rich, familiar, warm and tantalizing home-reminding aroma of fresh baked pies – too much for some mere mortal soldiers a long away from home and hearth to endure without gastronomic gratification!

Such was the case that morning, as the company in which I labored, part of five-thousand-man column, passed that little house. It appeared from our position, as we shuffled by, that on the sill of its one open window rested the magical endeavors of uncelebrated magicians within. Perhaps the fare were cherry pies, or apple pies, or peach pies flush with delicious warmth and sweet satisfactions, or perhaps they were of mysterious ingredients, but whatever they were made of their aromas were overpowering.

All around me, grimy, disheveled and hungry soldiers looked longingly in the house's direction, salivating, no doubt, as did I. But strict prohibitions against breaking ranks kept them at bay save for two who could not deny themselves the possibilities that stealth might afford them. Handing their rifles to comrades for safekeeping, they set off. And since, being a civilian, I came under no such restrictions, I followed them while at the same time warning them that they chanced stern punishment if caught. They in turn advised me that they did not intend to BE caught. I admired their courage but doubted their wisdom.

Their temporary desertion could not have been more observed, since the entire company and the next one behind us jealously noted their exit, all watching as the would-be thieves sneaked toward the cottage, using trees to mask their approach. As we neared the cottage I held back, since I did not wish to be associated with their felony. It was plain that they would have to crawl the remaining distance to avoid detection by the cottage's occupants. For a time it appeared they would succeed, and sneak back with everything from the sill. I wondered if, in that case, the regiment would cheer them, thus causing the occupants to realize a part of the army was passing by and come out, perhaps noticing the theft and remonstrating to our officers, which would lead to our thieve's arrest. What punishment would then be enforced?

As the two were nearly to the sill it struck me that it was almost impossible for the occupants not to have heard our noisy column sixty yards away – the troop's chatter, the snorting of horses, the clinking of equipment, the grinding roll of wagon, caisson, and artillery wheels all being quite audible. Then, at the very second both men rose from their crawl to grab the pies, two other creations flew from the window, splattering into both men's faces in a rainbow of steaming fixins' and crust. The cottage door flew open and out raced a diminutive, broom-wielding woman whose vocabulary would have wilted lilies! Our two ambushed thieves, screaming in pain as they struggled to wipe away the pies' oven-hot contents, fairly danced a jig as she pelted them with her broom, a second female face appearing at the window urging her on. Our troops roared as the two plotters stumbled toward the road, the woman, with a little mutt's tenacity, striking at their back-sides.

The two stumbled and fell as, yelping, they raced back to ranks, with the little lady swearing at them profusely before retreating – except for the two pies she and the other woman had used as heavy artillery, the remainder and their pride were secured.

There is no describing the jibbing both men received upon reentering ranks, except to say both were thoroughly humbled and mightily embarrassed, their sore faces comedically reflecting their humiliation.

"Taste good?" they were repeatedly baited. "You went for a mouthful, nary a face-full! Ain't nobody eva' showed ya darned fools how t'eat? Goes 'tween yer lips, not like hogs up yer snouts!"

We came away with new respect for the back-country citizens of that back-water parish. Indeed, they were nobody's fools. Our two failed villains, as their reward, got the infamous rear of the column, there to eat dust and sidestep horse droppings until the column bivouacked that night, compliments of their company officers – who, all things considered, figured the dust plus the pair's bruised egos and smarting expressions served military justice well enough.

Unto This Hour

I look into the faces of soldiers around me preparing for battle and weep within. At no other time do I feel greater and more intense empathy for their bearers than now. I study their facial details, feeling such close association with their humanity and such sympathy for it, knowing that only a short time from this moment many will be forever consigned to the earth, that humanity shattered upon bloody soil and dissipated within it. How can that be? Why should it be? For what purpose had these human beings been conceived and nurtured unto this hour, for this?

What motivates these men, each knowing what might happen to them when their ranks advance into the murderous unknown only minutes from now? What steels them? What assurances persuade them that they will survive and that only the "other man" may not?

I watch their hands and fingers nimbly handling and fidgeting with the paraphernalia of their trade, and I realize what marvelous and wondrous creations hands and fingers are, too much so to be stilled and destroyed by hot lead and iron and to rot away in the earth. How precious, I realize, is the human body that only a genius beyond our comprehension could have designed. Even more precious is the energy within it that thinks and feels and wonders and speaks and prays and hopes. And I ask myself, what are we doing? Do we fully understand the titanic principle we are blaspheming?

At present, I am too emotional to continue this entry. Perhaps my cup has at last filled. Perhaps my soul and being have at last rebelled against this colossal civil tragedy Americans are so willfully perpetuating. Perhaps my conscience can no longer tolerate the damnable waste of it all.

I cannot reconcile all of this holy life being so carelessly risked and soon sacrificed upon the fields to our front. My humanity cries out against it, but, as always, God is reticent about responding and remains silent, His mind being inscrutable. But for this volatile free will by Him to us freely granted, like poison into a child's hands or beguiling jewels tossed away by that child into the sea, I desperately ask Him (and believe I and these souls have an imperishable right to know at last), "Lord, in your Holy name, why?"

Equine

It can be said of our civilization that it has advanced on the backs of these patient, gentle beasts whose bodies and souls we criminally and inhumanly abuse in this war, these ill-fed, ill-cared for and callously overworked entities who look into our consciences with their large, doleful eyes.

Personally, I cannot return their gaze without pangs of remorse and shame for MY human species, or without believing that God will surely bring down retribution upon us for what we have done and daily do to these servile creatures, our neglect of their welfare and dignity being unforgivable.

This mount, a wagon-hauler, stands with ribs protruding, back swayed from straining against too much weight, head bowed with miseries. For lack of feed and hay, our Army cannot nourish him and his kind as it should, yet we push him and the others to their limits and beyond until they often drop dead in their leathers. In battle, to destroy our human enemies with bullet shot and shell, we carelessly or purposely shoot out these gentle animals' guts, put holes in their bodies, fill them with shrapnel, blow off their legs, blind them, tear off chunks of their bodies, decapitate them or otherwise leave them thrashing and writhing and screaming in agonies too horrible to imagine – exactly as we do to our brethren in differently colored uniforms. Still, these innocent subservient victims do both armys' heaviest labors.

For men, they are indispensable to war, their innocence exploited to make war possible. Indeed, we treat them as pure chattel and worse, no better than collected firewood, having no regard for the life-force and spirit within them – as if we had any regard for our own species's. How can humans who express a love of horses at the same time expose them to injury and death, especially the men who fight on horseback in search of glory? And yet they do so consistently, often eager for and relishing combat at their horse's brutal expense?

Never, for the remainder of my life, will I look at a horse without feeling obligated to it, without remembering what we've done to the equine race, our crimes against it. Even now, I feel such pity for this animal that tears seep from my eyes, blurring what I write. Perhaps others would call me foolishly sentimental. Let them. If I were able I would make this horse mine. I would care for it and honor it and give the rest of its natural life into God's trust that, in some way, I would pay it the debt my kind owes it.

It gazes at me now with such innocent eyes, even after all we have done to it, and, in private, I would weep sincerely for it and its sublime purity of heart. Would that MY species were as noble and grace-filled.

Until Now

I studied General Matthew Stiles with great sympathy. It appeared that he had never understood the depths and profundity of weariness until now.

He sat slouch-shouldered in Atlanta's small candlelit concert hall, engrossed in the sonata being played that evening by the city's chamber orchestra, his eyes closed, with the war's stresses appearing to drain from his troubled soul.

Having known him for a little more than four weeks, I had come to appreciate the spiritual burdens he and his kind silently and secretly endure, sending men into battle and watching them lost beneath clouds of lead and iron. A less compassionate or sensitive man would not have been so plagued. And, perhaps, men like him should not have been generals commanding combat troops. But his men worshipped him and his kindred nature. His brigade had lost heavily in recent months, having been in the forefront of the Army's efforts to oust our plundering Northern brethren from Southern soil.

It is said that through a man's eyes one can measure his soul. This man's were transparent, his manner gentle, his demeanor proud and dignified, yet tinted with spiritual fatigue. Had I not frequently conversed with him about the war and the rigors of command, I might not have appreciated what I now observed about him. And I wondered how, if he survived the war, it would change him or as with so many others, claim him as well, its residual effects and spiritual wounds breaking him eventually.

Yet upon the sonata's conclusion, it being the orchestra's last presentation, he rose to his full height, his back straight, to participate with the audience in a standing ovation. As I looked around I perceived many faces belonging to personages who so very obviously had suffered loss in this war – loss of loved ones, and also of spiritual strength which the orchestra had attempted to reconstitute. More and more we were becoming a war-weary people who, if our heart of hearts were revealed, sensed defeat. The general more than sensed it. He daily felt its inevitability's crushing weight. Pride had sustained our war effort to date, but now futility's vapors infected the air, causing many, including the infant nations' leaders, to belatedly consider the price. How many more lives, how much more misery, should be devoted to The Cause? How could we continue to hold out against an enemy with virtually unlimited human and material resources? How could we prevent our society's total destruction?

So many of us, in 1861, had feared such an eventuality, but now its reality was no longer theoretical. It savagely approached our nation's core. Hunger and destitution stalked the land. At one time our soldiers' uniforms and garb had been clean and neat and our officers' impeccable. Now, our diminishing fortunes were evident in even our senior officers' worn, stained, and tattered appearance, which gave our people no encouragement.

That was why that evening, the general's proud posture and charming manner reflected much welcomed and still prized gallantry that so stimulated the audience's admiration. Despite our dire military situation here was a courageous, enduring symbol of the South's statement to the North, of its faithfulness to the Revolutionary's Founder's Constitution and the Confederacy's and the righteousness of that stance – to deal with its internal issues and social inequities unimpeded by the dictatorial tyrannies of a federal anti-Constitutional colossus.

These matters aside, when the evening's diplomatic theatrics ended and the General proceeded to his command, his shoulders once again sagged with weariness, as he once more envisioned the war's costs. At one time, he and I had stood humbly viewing a battle's aftermath – bodies, bodies, bodies, young and middle-aged, the enemy's dead mixed with ours – the wounded of both sides calling, crying out, crawling, limping, stumbling, writhing, each image burned indelibly into memory. So vacant had been so many of those young faces, appearing so innocent in their eternal slumber. How many times could a man maintain his sanity viewing his decisions' results, and those of tragic necessity?

The General, for a time, had found escape in the evening's musical fare, having been treated to programmatic images of peace and serenity. I know he wondered what sleep would bring him this night – restful oblivion or tortured restlessness. I prayed that unto him God would be gracious and to all our sleeping valorous.

Infamy

I debated whether I should write about the following, owing to the public's extreme sensitivity about such things, and its abhorrence over the mentioning of such. But, I will detail the essentials of the incident, and nothing more.

Two older soldiers, during a bivouac, forced themselves on a young soldier of fifteen years who had wandered into the woods while innocently chasing butterflies, which he collected. Bleeding and literally savaged, the boy made his way back to the bivouac before falling in near unconsciousness in front of soldiers cooking their evening fare.

Enraged, the soldiers began an immediate search for the perverts, the crying boy having related his molesters' descriptions. Word quickly spread throughout the company until virtually every man in it joined in the hunt. The offenders were trapped in a thicket an hour later, unceremoniously pulled out and severely beaten before being bound like hogs and dragged back to the bivouac by their ankles.

By this time the regiment's commanding officer had heard of the molesting and was on the scene. He asked the boy to identify the culprits, and then ordered that they be tied to a tree on the edge of the woods. Pleading for their lives, the two begged for forgiveness and leniency, citing their long and loyal service to the Cause. But on the officer's orders, a firing squad was quickly assembled. The two were advised of the charges against them and what their punishment would be. Owing to the shame and gravity of their crime, prayers for their souls were denied them, and they were refused blindfolds. Minutes later they were summarily shot. They were then cut down, their bodies dumped into shallow graves without markers, and the graves covered with weeds and leaves to mask their locations. They boy was given to the care of regimental physicians and our Chaplain. I was later told that he was discharged and sent home, having been too young to have been in uniform in the first place, in itself an offense to God and decency.

It had been a short-lived but singular drama. So help me, had they handed me a rifle and assigned me to the firing squad, I would have felt no compunctions about pulling the trigger. In this case, justice swiftly rendered was justice justifiably served.

In the Beauty of the Lilies

**The Wartime Journals
of Confederate Correspondent
Royal K. Chapman
1862-1864**

Journal Fourteen

Contents

A Thought

Some men resolved
that if going home at last
meant going home to God,
they would prefer it
to going home to heartache,
travail and nothing.

Tribute to a Leader

Honor and devotion are powerful matters.

Captain Tyler Smith lay dying on a cot in the dimming light of a failing day. Having taken two minie-balls in the chest during afternoon fighting, his men had brought him to the regiment's outdoor hospital beneath a spreading oak. Around him, hundreds of mutilated men twisted and turned in their agonies, some whimpering for water, some having baked all the sweltering day beneath the indifferent sun and its fiery mercies. But now, the drizzle and cool evening breezes graced the survivors.

I stood the grim watch with Smith's subordinates as this respected company commander coughed and spit blood, his breathing complicated by a fatal gurgling. He had lain on the cot for hours, his chest ripped open by shards from an exploding enemy shell. Regimental surgeons had pronounced him beyond help and had encouraged us to make him as comfortable as possible, since their overwhelming work with other wounded they could not consistently attend him. And thus, his men had covered him with a blanket, having placed a bedroll beneath his head. Yet he had lost much blood and trembled untrollably with terrible chills.

I cannot begin to adequately express the feeling of helplessness I and those around me experienced that evening, awaiting his last breath. To view life so laboriously departing a soul depressed us all, though we had watched it all that very day upon the battlefield. Yet now the full weight of war's tragic consequences once again gnawed at our consciences, giving us to consider the profound and poignant waste of it in honor's name. It was not so much that we held his officer's life above those of the enlisted wounded in that makeshift hospital that day. In his suffering, he represented them all.

The Captain had passed into semi-consciousness, having told his subordinates earlier that he felt little pain. Some men so wounded often grow delirious and babble as if speaking to invisible spirits. He did not. Aside from his gurgling and trembling, he appeared at rest and without severe discomfort, his eyes only occasionally opening slightly, as if, in partially lucid moments, he wished to be assured that he was not alone and still in touch with the physical world. On those occasions his second in command, Lieutenant Jakes, took his hand, speaking to him softly with those very assurances. It was a sad and touching scene that compelled me to walk about to relieve my emotional strain. At least, Smith would not lay in an unmarked grave, as would so many of the enlisted wounded fated to expire without identification upon their persons. Loved ones would never know their resting places nor be able to pace flowers and offer prayers over them for their gentle deliverance.

When the Captain's breath became dangerously labored and his face assumed a bluish tint, we knew the end was close. Surgeons had stripped him to his waist to drain his gaping chest wound of corruption, remove pieces of lead from one mutilated lung and remove pressure on his damaged but still functioning second. That he had survived this long baffled them. Physician Edmund Page came by to inspect the wound. He pulled back the blanket. The Captain's torso had turned deep blue. Both lungs lay exposed beneath his shattered ribs. The lone working organ weakly heaved and shrunk, while its counterpart, torn and pulpy, remained inertly covered with pinkish foam.

A short distance away exhausted company survivors stood by in silence, awaiting the inevitable. Feeling helpless to do more than pray for him many others milled about, remembering how their Captain had led them in a dozen awful charges since recruiting and organizing them in 1861. Each time, so they related, he had braved the enemy's wrath to set the example for them, leading out front, where he chanced enemy rifles sighting him first. They revealed that he had always cared for them, looking to their warfare and writing faithfully to the families of those who could not write, or those killed in battle, or those who had passed of sickness. Regularly, he had found them scarce or extra rations, and just as often had brought them medical assistance for their pains and aches. Whether they suffered bunions or blisters, rashes or chigger bites, indigestion or dysentery, he had found them relief.

Said Private Abner Hill of North Carolina, "He most often calmed ar' fears and sympathized with 'ar loneliness. Why, I person'ly knowd of several times when he gentle-like discouraged men from desertin' cause a'fam'ly concerns that growed too unbearable."

Simmering with frustration, many now wondered how to show their respect and affection for Smith before the end came. How could and would they honor his memory? What act or ritual would convey their loyalty that would remain undiminished by his death? Whatever they decided, they would have to express it in the rain.

Overwhelmed by suddenly arising storm clouds, the setting sun now vanished. The breeze brought rain's telltale scent and for so many of the wounded, the promise of at least a measure of blessed but soaking relief, not to mention cool, fresh water to satiate their parched throats. Thunder rumbled like cannon fire to the west. Subtleties, the veterans had learned well, distinguished thunder from artillery. Besides, true thunder did not threaten them, while, when artillery raged, men perished.

Rain would add both a soporific and introspective quality to the moment, prompting guilt-ridden soldiers, who regretted having occasionally cursed their Captain over petty inconveniences, to deal with their consciences. All solemnly listened to his gasping for breath, their worried glances communicating their concern. Most feared he would pass without seeing their devotion to him. Many waiting while treating minor wounds or staring into nothingness, craved sleep but refused to succumb.

Wiping his brow, Dr. Page stepped away, his expression grave: "Gentlemen, if your men wish to pay the Captain their respects, you'd best arrange it now. Perhaps he might yet sense their intent."

Slowly, the men queued up, waiting for the physician's nod. Then they shuffled by, staring at the bloodied soul on the cot. Tears traced muddy trails down some men's grimy expressions. Others looked on stoically, afraid to see their leader's wounds lest they break down in front of him and their fellows. Some men, respectfully bareheaded, briefly paused, recalling, they later told me, how Smith roughhoused with them and led energetic snowball fights at winter camps. All contemplated their loss, for they had depended upon him for so much. Who would they depend on now?

Thunder grumbled anew as raindrops tapped gently through the oak's verdant boughs. Said a nearby soldier to me: "They say it's a good sign if it rains when a body passes ova. It's 'spose to mean the soul will be welcomed by kin and loved ones already in Heaven, his spirit bein' cleansed."

Others who overheard remained silent as they pondered his words, hoping, I guessed that, if true, rain would fall when their time came.

The breeze played more energetically around the tree as raindrops fell in greater numbers. I wanted to believe they did so in deference to the suffering officer. When the last man filed by the Captain's breathing appeared to cease. Seeing the working lung fail, Dr. Page examined the body, putting his ear to the Captain's chest: "Not yet, gentlemen, not quite yet. He is keeping himself alive by will-power alone just long enough to acknowledge your loyalty. By waiting until the last man he has thanked you all. I've encountered this kind of reciprocal loyalty before with dying soldiers."

I listened to the gently rumbling thunder, wondering where, after his breathing ceased, his spirit would go. A few of his subordinates looked skyward, letting the refreshing rain settle over them, perhaps wondering the same thing. Feeling, they said, like children abandoned and lost, all vowed to remember this mystical moment as the rain now fell in earnest. Humbled, their caps and hats in hand, they stood christened in sadness. Never had I or they felt lonelier. Never had the war felt as cruel.

Our dreaded watch continued until late, when, at last, as the sun set, the Captain's eyes opened wide, drizzle dotting his cheeks. Turning toward us, as calling night birds swooped overhead and the breeze stirred wet leaves in the boughs above him, he feebly extended one hand toward us and affectionately gestured "good-bye." He softly gasped, laid back, his arm slowly descending beside him, his eyes closing, lines of strain upon his dusty, beardless face fading until they melded into a flawless portrait of sublime peace.

Comedy to Tragedy

Today, I watched our bucking artillery pieces pour out fire and eye-burning smoke with concussive force, suffocating the battlefield. The enemy answered with his until entire fields and meadows where butternut and blue clashed were nearly hidden in white. Our men furiously served their guns, each side determined to prove that theirs was best.

You cannot stand near active artillery and not put your hands to your ears, otherwise the thunderous, gut-shaking noise is deafening. A courageous breeze might have carried the smoke away, but it appeared any breeze would have been too intimidated to interfere.

Hot gun powder smoke is acrid. It scorches one's eyes until they water. I could imagine troops of both sides mechanically loading and firing their rifles blindly into the virtual fog, their eyes watering as men fell all around them, sheets of rifle fire bringing men down by the score, some ranks melting away into piles of both still and writhing humanity, the voluminous smoke from their rifles adding to the misery. I cannot see how the commanders of companies and regiments, even brigades on both sides could have seen to maneuver their troops, let alone keep track of them. What a confused Hell it must have been – eyes, throats, nostrils burning – men coughing and gagging as bullets whined around them, men falling unseen by comrades – Americans against Americans in a fierce, gory family debacle.

I saw some of our officers emerge from the smoke, running back and forth encouraging troops I couldn't see, trying to maintain cohesion and momentum as the fighting, I was later told, turned into contests between small groups. This became a rare occasion, I learned, when bayonets and rifle butts became each side's prime weapons – a bashing, stabbing marathon of sheer maddening, physical endurance. How many men on both sides must have run away from it I cannot say, but many of our boys drifted out of the smoke here and there without rifles, as if too stunned to know where they were anymore. They were corralled, when possible, and directed back into the maelstrom, urged to use their fists and feet and elbows and knees to attack their opponents and defend themselves. Some staggered out only to fall on the spot, severely wounded or dead.

How could our artillery or theirs see targets to blast, I wondered? Yet I detected the elevated paths of their explosives and ours that began arcing above the struggling infantry and falling on rearward positions, probing for each other's batteries. Enemy guns began dueling with ours, their shells falling among our pieces, smoke drifting just enough for their gunners, obviously using field glasses, to have spotted our artillery and for us to have spied theirs.

"Get back to safety, Mr. Chapman," a lieutenant called out to me, a fellow named Rittenhouse I had met earlier. "You'll be killed if you persist in staying with us!" He could not have been more than twenty years young. No sooner had he motioned for me to move away than, in a red spray of uniforms shreds and viscera, solid shot tore him in half.

Stunned, I moved away slowly, watching the careening shell bound toward me, tearing a furrow in the turf, then bounce over my head, disappearing somewhere to the rear. I remember thinking at that moment, as if my mind insisted on fantasizing to escape its shock, "What if the lad's destruction was only a mirage? What if he is still alive?"

Rittenhouse had been the officer who, the day before during the brigade's march, had disciplined two soldiers for bloom-picking along the roadside and passing the flowers to their fellows for adornment behind the ears, a popular fashion for plodding infantry. The Lieutenant had the two not only stick flowers IN their ears, but up their nostrils and between their teeth and keep the flora there for the remainder of the march – to the uproarious laughter and continuing amusement of their company. The opposing faces of "comedy and tragedy," I ruminated, a Shakespearean point brutally made this very day. The image of the Lieutenant's boyish face that instant before his death would remain with me for the duration.

Now in the midst of its fiercest crescendos, the fire from both side's artillery began to slacken, diminish and fade away, our guns falling silent. In the field beyond tattered companies, regiments, and gaggles of butternut-clad soldiers began drifting back to their starting lines, as a strong breeze asserted itself, moving the fog of smoke away to expose a body-strewn cauldron of equipment, still and writhing souls, and incredible amounts of debris. Enemy lines moved rearward as well. I am not a tactician and cannot guess the reasons for the interruption, but the battle had reached a mutually condoned hiatus, both sides temporarily withdrawing to the tune of myriad bugles and shouted commands. Errant enemy shells came our way but hit nothing vital, many failing to explode. Behind me fresh ammunition-filled caissons, drawn by straining horse teams, replaced empty caissons being drawn off to rearward areas for replenishment. Artillery crews worked feverishly, cleaning gun barrels, some men stripped to the waist in the summer sun, some drenching themselves with buckets of water and scrubbing off sweat, gun grease, and powder residue. At the Lieutenant's gun, they worked around his body's remains, as if it were two piles of sandbags or discarded canvas. And as fresh caissons came on line far to the rear of the guns soldiers emptied them of shot, shells and canister, bringing them to the guns and stacking them at each gun position. I had noticed during the firing that men constantly ran back and forth to the caissons to bring each gun the powder charges crews would use to fire individual loads, not risking them to vulnerable exposure in stacks along with iron ordinance. Seeing the young officer's remains left me wondering why I did not vomit with revulsion, the war having hardened me to its carnage to the extent that I had begun to fear for my humanity. I understood my spiritual vulnerability as I assumed the young Lieutenant had understood the physical quality of his.

It has often been the case that caissons struck by enemy shells would erupt in terrible volcanoes of exploding powder and shells, flinging intact munitions skyward on smoky tendrils that eventually arced to the ground all around, the unexploded iron bouncing and careening amongst the guns and occasionally bringing down cannoneers – those serving the struck caissons vanishing or their instantly roasted forms coming to rest in smoldering pieces here and there. Such is the artilleryman's peril. And I have seen artillery pieces struck by enemy shot and shell disintegrate in instant explosions, wheels, traces, barrels, truncheons whirling, fated crewmen somewhere in the blinding mix. Such is also an artilleryman's peril. I have witnessed guns explode of their own volition, their weakened barrels splitting, chunks of iron scything their crews. Again, an artilleryman's peril.

In one instance, standing behind a tree near a battery a few months previously, I observed a crew leisurely serving its gun, laugh at something humorous one of them either said or did, only to be obliterated a second later by an enemy shell that struck the gun's barrel, sending it, along with gun parts, whirling through them, the barrel striking my tree with titanic force, cracking it through and knocking me senseless to the ground. I recovered with a two-day headache. Five of the nine-man gun crew perished. Three were mutilated. One escaped unharmed.

In battle, rare laughter can be both treacherous and expensive. Fate enjoys humor perverted, and often sees to it. I view it with great suspicion knowing that, like hawks, the gods of war circle the fighting man, watching and listening for perverse comedy they can prey upon and the humored they can fiendishly devastate. I could not rid my mind of the young Lieutenant's countenance. In essence he had given his life to encourage me to save mine. Ironically, he had warned me not with humor but with heart. Perhaps the twisted gods also had found mirth in that, a joke on HIM. Regardless, I would forever owe him for a conscience-plaguing debt I could never repay.

Neva Yer Back

He was too young for war, yet in a fit of adventure, but unknown to his parents, he'd signed for soldier and now, at fifteen, faced the fiery gorgon.

He understood nothing of the war's issues, nothing of states rights, nothing of union, only that a great war raged across the countryside. He had not understood the meaning of civil war nor the war for Southern independence, save for uniforms and the opportunity to carry a shiny new rifle like the adult men around him. Fear now wound 'round his gut like a slithering constrictor. His fright-parched mouth craved water. His legs turned rubbery, as if he were unable to control them. More than all else, he feared he would soil himself, to his mortifying humiliation.

His brigade awaited the bugle call that would sound the army's advance into torrents of hot lead, shot and canister that would tear huge gaps in advancing ranks. Furtively, he glanced at the veterans to either side, finding neither comfort nor encouragement in their grim, stoic expressions. He pitied himself, unable to believe that life – his dear, fragile, innocent life – could be so cheaply and callously spent upon these fields, even as the sun shown brightly and billowing clouds paraded by, supernaturally indifferent to his youthful existence, and caring not that he was more than a mere weed.

Now came the call. He froze, ice shooting the length of his spine. Though not yet a man he was being summoned to what he was told would be manhood. But war would not make him one. It would merely form his soul's unformed clay into its own savage image.

"I cain't move," he cried, "m'legs won't move!"

"They'll move," the veteran next to him responded above the ongoing battle's din. "Come, boy, ya gots t'go. Ya signed fer it and tuk the uniform. Now, ya gots t'honor it."

"I cain't...!" the boy protested, "I cain't! I wanna t'go home!"

"Ya cain't go home, boy, and yer mamma ain't here fer ya t'hold to. And don't be figurin' on runnin', 'cause the army'll gitcha fer it. There ain't an offense worse than turnin' yer back to the enemy. Neva yer back!"

The boy felt warmth running down his leg, darkening his threadbare trousers. The veteran stared, but not accusingly.

"Don't be shamed, boy," he said, "early on it done happens t'lotsa men. It don't mean nothin' ceptin' yer human."

They'd fallen behind the others: "You there, you two men," an officer shouted at them, "git up with the resta the ranks b'fore I put this sword to yer backsides!"

Tentatively, the veteran took the boy's arm and moved him forward, the boy's embarrassment appalling. Missiles buzzed by him like menacing demons, thudding into flesh and bone here and there, eviscerating men and sending gore splashing into his face. He wiped it away, then retched, then wiped more away. Thick smoke blinded him with acrid intensity. Iron shells and solid shot whooshed by him. Canister hummed and sang through ranks, carrying away other's arms and legs, sending entrails whirling. He looked back for the veteran, but saw only a headless body writhing as its life force drained into the tortured earth.

Now the brigade ran forward bent against that iron wind, its ragged ranks furiously screaming, challenging the hundreds of small orange and pinkish points of light spitting invisibly spinning minié-balls from enemy rifles far ahead. His mind swirled. He felt sorry for his flesh and body. Terror threatened to turn him catatonic but he dared not let it, dared not again display even a hint of cowardice. He had never fought hand to hand with anyone. Adventure was not hand to hand. Nor was it killing nor maiming. This was not what he had anticipated. He hadn't wanted THIS!

Too many men were falling – bludgeoned to the ground, twisting downward, staggering before collapsing, holding and cursing their wounds, screaming and crying out – too many. There would never be enough left to carry the enemy's breastworks.

Then, another bugle blew. The brigade slowed, its survivors halting. The boy halted with them. Now they began to withdraw, some men turning and running, others retreating slowly, deliberately, defying the missiles searching them out, their faces still to the enemy and firing back.

The boy didn't know why, didn't know how, but he had begun to drag a wounded man with him.

"Lemme go, son, lemme go," the man begged, his face twisted with pain, blood pouring from his belly. "I'm dead. Save yerself." Slipping from the boy's grasp, he disappeared in the thick smoke tearing the youngster's eyes.

The boy backed away, his face toward the enemy, remembering the veteran's caution, feeling his continuing presence: "Never yer back, boy...never yer back"...his unfired rifle leveled, its unblooded bayonet glinting in sunlight that futilely attempted to penetrate the battle's gloom. Feeling uplifted, his rite of passage completed, he grew suddenly braver, sunlight pooling around him. The enemy's guns had ceased their havoc. His body violently shook, as if it were shedding its soul's torment.

"Ya done good," the veteran said, putting his hand on the boy's shoulder.

Surprised, the boy looked up: "You ain't dead. Thought y'was kilt!"

"They cain't kill me, boy," he responded. "This here hide's too thick, and the critter inside it be too ornery."

They backed away together, turning around only a hundred yards later when turning their backs to the enemy was no longer dishonorable. The weed had grown.

He looked up, the sun's warmth bathing his face, sensing that if he were not yet a man, he was no longer a boy.

Perceptions

"Battle? It ain't ever'thin' there be t'warrin' – but it be what it all comes to. It be emotion, simple and pure. Those who ain't never know'd it cain't 'magine it. And them's what HAVE cain't nearly s'plain it t'all them what ain't. If'n I was t'say it be madness, I doubt ana'body'd argu' me the point, 'cause it be a horr'ble dance – a curiousness and a puzzlement, too – all them things and a hun'erd more. Now, the little 'ole mind of a virgin soldier who ain't neva' seen the elephant yet, don't wanna' b'lieve it 'til he's a piss'n his britches in the middle of a fight. Then, he starts a'askin' God fer hep'. But he ain't learned yet – God ain't near where men's a'tearin' each otha's throats out. No, God be a way's off – a'weepin. And if'n y'listen t'yer conscience real close, y'ken hear Him plain anuff'.

Engineer Private Autry Small

"T'ween attacks, when yer s'pectin' the enemy t'come agin', time's the most precious thing you ken imagine. Yer soul demands that y'consume ever' tiny drop of it as a man dyin' of thirst consumes even a single drop a'water. But there ain't neva' 'anuff t'slake THAT kinda thirst – not in ALL Creation. Waitin's the hot flame that dries it away and withas' yer soul even as yer silently cryin' t'God for mercy – and more a'that rar'afied water..."

An Infantry Sergeant

"Some soldiers stand steadfastly in ranks, no matta' what's comin', bravely facin' the enemy and their own doom. Sometimes, they openly weep, castin' away embarrassment and shame t'cherish a last genuine and earthly emotion. Like as not, their tears are for loved ones they know they shall neva' see again. No bullet's ever as painful as that agaonizin' emptiness. No wound eva' goes so deep."

A Company Commander

"First time I saw the enemy charge, I froze. The fierceness of their yellin' and the contortions on their faces r'minded me of m'nakedness b'fore God and nature – like I were small prey about t'be torn apart in conformance with natural law! And when m'rifle fired, it was a pure, 'skerd accident. Din't know I even pulled the trigger, s'great was m'fear. Saw m'bullet explode inta an attackin' man's chest. He done went down right away, then groveled a second b'fore disappearin' unda' his comrades' feet. Was bayonets after that – them damned things – and t'this day it's all fuzz. Cain't rememba' no details, but still feel bad 'bout killin' that man. Wonder if'n he'da felt bad 'bout killin' ME. Killed some more that day, I reckon. Felt bad 'bout THAT, too. Din't know it were in me. Got over it, though. Guess it were jest instinct and jest a natural matta' instinct n'all that. Wonder how I'm gonna s'plain it t'ma children afta' the war – if'n I survive it – when I cain't even s'plain it to m'self.

An Infantry Private

"In a battle's aftermath, men's thoughts linga' on their fiery passions. They r'call sounds and images tender upon their souls, and lightly tread around conscience, lest they endure more torments tryin' t'flee the wrath of terrible giants they fear t'awaken – guilt, mostly. War steels the hearts of some men and destroys the souls of otha's. War's unfair."

Chaplain Elmer E. Stone

"Sometimes, I git t'feelin' like I weren't human no more. Dead people don't bother me none, and me and the otha' boys find ourselves laughin' among the dead and wounded when we oughtn't t'be outta' common decency. But, y'see, we don't have no decency n'more. Lost it somewheres. War puts a hide on ya that thickens ya agin' other's sufferin' and the sufferin' YOU'VE done caused. That there's the worst of it! Makes ya 'shamed of yerself and wishin' y'could do fer someone agin', so y'could feel good 'bout yerself like y'used ta – and 'git yer humanness back. Lordy, I doubt I'll eva' be the man agin' I were b'fore this here damn war. Ain't worth much ana'more and too tuckered t'care."

Medical Private Lawrence Carey

"It ain't always all bad, the fightin' n'all. Sometimes, it' could be as near t'sport as ana'thin' you'd eva' want. And sometimes, the enemy's jest a'hankerin' fer ya t'give 'em a bad day. Does foolish things outta pride 'er worse y'jest cain't ignore and gotta satisfy – and y'wanna give it to him jest outta general principles fer bein' s'stupid. Ain't no r'spect there. Lotta men's lost thata' way on both sides. Sometimes, though, when y'lose good men 'cause of the enemy's stupidness – like attackin' us when they ain't got no hope of succeedin' – it hurts a lot, 'cause none of it needs doin'. Nobody wants t'die fer nothin'! But, sometimes, y'ken lose yer best men thata' way, and there ain't no sport to it no more. It jest be cryin' sad."

Infantry Private Edward Reed

"When a soldier sees his best friend fall, and when that friend dies in that soldier's arms, something profound inside that soldier dies as well. If eva' God was to minister to a poor man in his most vulnerable hours, it'd be then. Foreva' afta'ward, that soldier's soul's changed. God's got to nurture him back t'the Faith with patience and infinite love, for the hurt's vera'deep, the scar pronounced, and the soldier's trust in the Lord shaken. The change is a natural thing, though the soldier neitha' wants it nor wishes it. Simply occurs."

Physician Major A. Harwell

"A soldier neva' truly knows who he is inside until battles forces him t'see himself in the pure nakedness of his bared soul. Strips him down – gives him no quarta' – shows him what's there and what ain't – or it leaves him too devastated t'care. Makes men outta' some, confirms the manhood of others, and 'jest plain destroys a good number who ain't neva' good fer much afta'wards. Understandin' comes from all that. Don't know where God comes inta' it, but I know where the demons and devils do – and it 'ken be a SU-preme triumph for a man...or a punishin' tragedy. Y'see, not all the worst wounds a man can suffer come from iron and lead."

Infantry Lieutenant R. Rustin

"Men'd get t'talking 'bout things, 'bout themselves and the war and what they'd seen n'heard. Sometimes, they'd talk 'bout the horror a'fightin' and dyin', as if the subjects be the weather – sorta' casual and unserious. Always strikes me that it shouldn'ta be so, but it is – 'cause it's war – and war is their sleepin' and wakin' business. As a preacher, though, I can't get used to it."

Rev. Henry Kaul

"There is always so much standin' 'tween God and the individual soldier that chaplains can neva' cut through. The men always look at preachers as bein' outside the reality of things – nice men but not part of the actual world – THEIR world. In the end, most chaplains neva' are accepted – and can neva' truly be considered one of 'em – fighting men, that is. The individual soldier seldom lets them into their most private souls and circles. You'll hear this from other chaplains. Sad."

Chaplain F. Cahill

"If I were to tell my readers the things they want to hear, I could never accurately report this war. They don't want to know about things as they actually are – but about things as they imagine and want them to be. Privations, shortages in all ways, massive casualties, misery, death en masse – all these applicable clichés of war – are constants, but not appreciated by the public. If I were to write the plain truth – that commanders cannot supply their troops with even rudimentary amenities because the army hasn't got them anymore because supply has broken down – that our battle lines are bein' mercilessly bullied by the sheer mass of our powerful enemy – because all wagons are bein' used to carry our tremendous casualties – because the war isn't going well – I would be excoriated, never mind never bein' read again. And, if I were to write, that our common soldiers are sufferin' terribly and that our senior officers are as frustrated, humiliated, and embarrassed by conditions as any soldier in ranks – and sometimes more so – I would create a political firestorm that would sweep the land – a much NEEDED firestorm, I maintain. Yet, would it be good for our war effort? It's a quandary, but no. Instead, it would be VERY good news for our enemy – and, thus, I am obliged never to write so!"

Correspondent George Everette

"Men won't always say they talk t'the Lord, 'cause they're embarrassed 'bout it in front of otha' men – generally speakin'. But they see and talk to HIM ever'where. Guess it's like this: a man'd like t'have God standin' right in front of him, or sittin' next t'him, so's he could talk t'Him straight out, like a friend on a peaceful day. But, God don't come down t'talk t'men thata' way, so some men pick out natural things He's c'rated – like trees 'er stars – and talk t'Him THATA' way. Don't 'xactly pray t'Him, but it's the same thing – means the same thing. Most always, though, God's silent. Y'gotta sometimes figure out if He's a'listenin' t'ya and if y'think He'll answer ya. Most times, though, a man's jest glad t'be a'talkin' t'Him. Wants answers but don't actual'need 'em jest then – 'cause the talkin's 'anuff."

Artillery Corporal Jamie Nagel

"I'm sitting here looking from my window at the autumn landscapes beyond, finding it difficult to believe that somewhere beyond all that magnificence, war rages unopposed by Providence. Our loved ones exist where the fires of regional hatreds blaze so fiercely while we, who are left behind to care for their children and property, wait and fret, some of us beside ourselves with worry – and still others desperate to hear from husbands, sons and brothers, while terrified for their safety and lives. Already we are widows, our warring kin silent and dead to us between all too infrequent letters. And even when letters arrive we go stoically if quietly mad at the thought that our kin might have perished since sending them – and we frantically crave the next ones that we might be fleetingly reassured. This is Hell – OUR very special Hell."

Mrs. Autry Small

"I count on you, gentlemen, to 'rememba that we have pushed our men to the utmost. They're good men, the best infantry in the world, but they're also human and not invincible. Daylight flees. You have your orders. If conditions mandate, they WILL be changed accordingly. Now, go prepare your troops with respect and kindness, for we shall leave many behind this day – and pray to a merciful God for their deliverance. Include yourselves in your devotions, for it is God that we offend by warring at all."

General Wm. Hostead
Addressing His Officer Corps

"How'd it feel t'git hit? Like I got thumped hard by a kickin' mule – and I know what THAT feels like, too. Bad pain didn't come 'til later, then it come on the wings a'Hell. 'Fer a spell couldn't figure out who I was 'er where I be. Oh, I know'd I got hit, but right off, didn't know what in, 'ceptin' it was above m'waist fficest'. Jest felt numb all over. Couldn't breathe hardly ffices' a'tall. Ever'thin' were blurred. World were a'goin' 'round and 'round. Works out, I took a minié-ball through m'side – in the front and out the back. Lord, it was a mess – and how the pain did come afta'wads. Din't care who found me 'er even if I ended up a prisoner a'war. Jest wanted a generous soul t'put me outta m'misery, if'n he couldn't fix me quick. Lord, I din't much give a care 'fer nothin', save I wanted t'die and DIE right then."

Infantry Sergeant Otis Gilmore

"If there's anything most soldiers hate more than being wounded or dying it's hospitals and surgeons. You can't imagine how surgeons are despised as butchers and fiends, very often unfairly. Some ARE incompetent but all are overworked, and for even the best among them to professionally fulfill their jobs is impossible. They must cut and hack quickly so great is the volume of wounded after every battle, limbs and lives that might have been saved in calm civilian times must be sacrificed to speed if any lives are to be saved at all. Yet the common soldier, suffering the agonies of hell and facing amputation and operation without anesthetic, remains unimpressed. Some refuse treatment and prefer death to the surgeons' saws. Others drive themselves into catatonic states from which they never recover. Even I must admit that THESE poor souls often are the most fortunate."

Correspondent John Houser

"We commit a great injustice when we forget the civilians who suffer in this war – those made homeless by our marauding armies – who are burned out, their farms destroyed, their possessions looted, their fields savaged and salted, and their livestock slaughtered and left to rot for the evil amusement of it. I have seen such atrocities committed – people shot down for the mere fact that they're Southerners – acts that would infuriate those up North who support this war yet remain criminally ignorant of its details. I say now – there CANNOT be reconciliation after this war – not after such crimes. How COULD there be? Are these people who have suffered them simply to say to us – "All is forgiven – it was war, after all?" – and go on as if nothing occurred? So many of these depredations are vindictively committed, with neither necessity nor reason, but out of sheer mendacity. It leaves me wondering why our best officers are sacrificed in noble battle while the army's commissioned degenerates are purposely relegated to renegade actions requiring no courage and even less honor. Someone must be made to answer for these things, whether or not we are victorious. Yet, I know in my heart they will not be – for victory is, and has always been, its own exoneration."

Captured Union Cavalry Captain Ira Johnson

"Sleep r'mains the general coin of the realm in our bivouacs, though sleep is not universally cherished. For some, it's escape into a brief oblivion – a time when a man suffas blessed nothingness. But, for others, it's a time of hauntin' by cruel temptations or sheer terror – fantasies that remind 'em of inaccessible things – such as family or lovemaking – or reanimates every second of battle's horrors. Some men refuse sleep, for even in wakefulness their terrors can be as painful as cold bayonets. I've seen some haunted men actually terrified by the very prospects of goin' t'sleep. They dare not, for fear of visiting demons they can escape only in wakefulness. Some fight it so terr'bly hard, they spend days without it and ultimately collapse. Yet, I have also seen men transformed by dreams and the visions that come to them in sleep as if they've received inspirin' insights or messages from the Great Beyond. It's all quite arbitrary, actu'lly. But war's teachin' us more 'bout the human mind than peace would eva' taught us – yet at a terrible cost. Perhaps, it's knowledge we could well have afforded to receive far less speedily and abundantly – considerin' that much of it we'll neva' unda'stand. Unda' these circumstances, I'll have t'admit that such expensive ignorance often amounts t'sheer waste."

Dr. Wm. Talmadge

"I have been asked…if one man works for no pay and another works for a penny, is it that penny that makes him free? If, t'survive, a man must be a slave t'his pennies while another is admittedly well cared for chattel, which one's truly freer or the GREATER captive? If true freedom's merely to be defined in a physical sense, isn't it a narrow definition? Consida' the difference 'tween the exploited immigrant and that well-cared for slave? Think, now – which is freer? True, the immigrant can walk away and the slave cannot – that bein' physical freedom and freedom of a kind. But the immigrant, on his own with that freedom will be allowed to starve if that be his lot. ON the otha' hand the slave in his physical bondage, will not. If'n a man's well-cared for might he actually b'freer than an incompetent man who cain't care for himself? By the same token, then, should a competent slave be allowed physical freedom before an incompetent white man who would make a better ward of the state? Take it anotha' step: if a gova'ment provides for all its people's wants and needs, are such people freer than under a gova'ment that does not? Soldiers ask me about these riddles agin' and agin', but it's a quandary. The ansas' used t'be clear, but no longa'."

Chaplain David Hobbs

"Did y'eva' wonda' what it trula' means to a soldier when he r'turns home from this war to a demolished life? For some it's soured wine, for othas' an oppa'tunity t'search for nectar, if'n, a'course, he's whole or his wounds have healed well. But when a MAIMED man's released from the Arma' and r'turns t'civilian life, what then – 'specially a farma' on whom a familia' must fulla' depend for its subsistence? Despite what he's given to his nation, his gova'ment generalla' makes no useful provisions thereafta' for his fam'la's welfare nor his own. Or, if'n ana' effort's extended to him at all it's usa'lla' a pittance. I grieve for such men. They and soldiers gen'ralla are the true chattel of circumstance. I know, 'cause everyday I trek with 'em and share their mis'ries. How naively and innocently they have otha'wise come to the slaughta' we've led 'em to – 'specially the young ones – God's rifle-carryin'lambs. Like all youth, they see t'day but seldom t'marra, and it's t'marra that does 'em in...on the wings of our crim'nal neglect."

Chaplain Custis Spencer

"I 'spose, afta' this war, the Lord's gonna chastise us fierce for the horses we done kilt' in it – both sides – poor dumb critters. I shudder recallin' what I seen of 'em – the mutilatin' and manglin' of 'em – those innocent creatures a'strugglin' and a'kickin' and screamin' after ever' battle – hun'erds of 'em – thousands all across the land fer years – writhin' in their death throes cause a'what we'd done to 'em – shot t'pieces and sufferin' – leg's ripped away, innards a'hangin' out, bleedin' t'death with it comin' out of 'em, a'hangin' out of 'em like pourin' water – and the terror in their big, wide, innocent eyes, a'pleadin' with us t'help 'em and askin' us why – and men havin' t'walk among 'em afta' ever' fight a'shootin' 'em in their heads by the score ever' time t'put 'em outta their miseries! I tell ya, I cain't sleep at night fer thinkin' of it sometimes and a'hearin' them executions. Sometimes, I duly cry fer 'em. They d'served betta'. We got no right to do what we done to 'em – wagon horses, artillery horses, cava'ry horses – no right in God's sight. Feel bad, I do – like m'soul's a'rottin' away fer it. It's a fficest' pain in m'heart, I swear. Beautiful souls theirs be – graceful creatures a'God – and we done fficest agin' 'em right up to our sad necks. Somehow, some way, He's a'gonna make us pay fer it – I know it. Cain't blame Him none. Forgiveness be too good. Whatever my punishment be, I'll take it – 'cause me and thousands a'others like me done earned it – without a doubt – we done earned it."

Cavalry Private Thomas Applegate

"The boys is always talkin' 'bout reunions – reunions with their fam'lies and youngin's, wives, and sweethearts and jest goin' home. Goin' home – y'think 'bout it all the time. It always be there in yer mind, and yer always a'wonderin' 'bout it. Keeps men a'goin', though. If'n they didn't have it t'keep a'hopin' fer, they'd give up and die t'God and ever'thin' else that's good."

Infantry Corporal Mason Jeffers

"Y'ken ask me what I think a'politicians and their ilk and likely as not I'll spit in yer eye. Y'don't see none of 'em HERE, do ya? It's THEIR damn war, but they ain't HERE are they? How come? Cause they're back THERE, getting' writ'up in history books whilst' most of us is jest getting' buried in big, stinkin' pits. We oughta' march back there and GIT' 'em ALL up HERE – and put 'em RIGHT OUT FRONT in ever' assault we make – that's what we OUGHTA' do! You know it – and so do ever' sufferin' man in this here army! In the meantime, they betta' watch out and hide good and hard b'hind their little wive's petticoats at night – keepin' an eye out their damned windas'! 'Cause we jest might be righteously a'comin' fer 'em some day, if'n this here war lasts much longa' – or afta' it ends. Yes, suh, we jest might be a'comin' fer 'em – like the LORD a'comin' afta' the Devil!"

Cavalry Sergeant Alvin Hayes

"I miss the past – the balls and cotillions – the waltzes and polkas and beautiful ladies and the sheer pageantry of the old peacetime army. That was the army I joined but – outta conviction – had t'leave. I once reveled in it, but neva' intended to be involved in a war – 'specially THIS kinda war. How what we most wish to avoid eventua'lly stalks and finds us in the end despite ourselves. I must sit out the waltzes and polkas, THESE days, now. A one-legged dancer makes for an awkward partner."

Former Artillery Captain Leslie Corso

"Know'd a vet'ran who runned once't...Wilcox, be his name...when all the leaves was a'fallin' one year. Fought in many places, he had; seen many horrors...a quiet, rev'ent man...a married man. Done his duty good from '61 'til '64, then, one day, casual as y'please, sittin' by our campfire drinkin' some hard chicory, he jest upped and dropped his cup and done walked away...that look in his eyes...jest walked away. Neva' saw him agin'. They say he went back home, sick of all the killin'. Don't know...could be. I mighta'. 'Cause what he done we'd ALL thought a'doin' – and all WANTED doin'. I r'memba how the leaves sorta swirled afta' him in a gentle breeze that evenin', like outta kind affection, like they was wantin' t'follow him where eva' he was a'goin'. Neva' thought ill of him, though...nobody did. Jest thought he were the bravest man we ever know'd...fer doin' what he done."

Infantry Private Thadeus Tuttle

"Faces...it always be about faces...somes they be clear in yer mem'ry and somes they be misty. Sometimes the details be sharp and sometimes they ain't...somes bein' hidden and mixed up with otha sights and sounds ya remember in all the action ya seen and in the stillness ya remember that come afta'wards. They be frozed-up foreva, like on them glass picture plates I seen. It always be like these things eva afta', and no matta yer age afterwards er watcha doin' in life, it stays with ya strong...and I spose it will 'til MY last measured breath. It were that a'way after the Mexican War and it'll be that a'way afta this one, cause the echoes remain and neva cease. A man might confine 'em to the backwatas of his mind but they neva quit. And when life's strong winds blow or its quiet moments come, they flow by, like you was standin' by a stream's edge and a'lookin' across it to yer whole life – and they swirl there and eddy 'til yer taken-up with emotion...and time jest drifts away. I ain't no poet, but it seems this way to me and always has. Now, in this war, I'm gonna have more t'rememba, and sometimes I wonda if'n I'll be able to deal with it ana'more or, if someday, it'll finally take me, my heart gived-out. Right now, I don't know...I jest don't know.

Artillery Sergeant
Eustice Colby
Mexican War Veteran

Lookin' Back

"I'm thinkin' the saddest thing I ever seen was the rainy day when kinfolk come t'the hospital t'take their dead boys home. Rain was a'pourin' down and y'cud barely see yer hand in front of ya, but they was there – come from Lord knows where t'cart away the coffins. They come on wagons, mostly, some on buggies with long beds. Seemed unkindly and unfittin' the way the sky din't welcome 'em better, leastwise fer the sake of decency. But Nature don't care none fer what man does and it sure held him in no high r'gard for the warfare he was a'makin' 'mongst 'hisself – so I 'spect we shouldn'ta hoped fer better. Mud was eva'where – deep and ponded up – and we was mortified by coffins what was leakin' gaggin' corruption from the inside, but there weren't nothin' we could do 'bout it then. Mosta the dead wasn't embalmed. And there was only us medical orderlies (me among 'em) and a few enlisted men and officers to do the amenities – and, a'course, the honor guard. Was all cold and soaked and shiverin' that autumn day. Women was a'cryin' and their menfolk was grim-faced, and they brung a few children along – Lord knows why – which were a'sufferin' bad in the rain and cold damp, some of 'em cryin', too, and I' soaked. But, whatever the weatha' that day, it were a might better than what most dead soldiers got in the field on days jest like it – nothin' but floatin' holes in the ground. Still was sad, though – them long lines a'wagons and buggies and all them poor people come fer grief, with them coffins numbered for their kin t'match-up and the officers pointin' out which one was which. Sad day, I'm tellin' ya – and the thunder din't make it no betta', with lightnin' crackin' 'round – and that honor guard a'twenty soaked-through men riskin' the fever and worse bein' out in it for houts outta' r'spect. But, the Army had t'do the honorable thing, y'see, even if it couldn't be much. But what more COULD they a'done, after all, even if they'da had a thousand men in that honor guard? Wouldn'ta brought a single dead soul back, would it'a? No, sir...not a single, solitary one. Sad day, that were...sad day."

Private Josie Miller
Medical Corps

"Seen devotion durin' the war – oh, not t'Cause and Country s'much as t'loved ones and sweethearts back home. Even among the dyin', their last thoughts was often fer THEM. I remheba' this one lad – had a tintype of his sweetheart and were a'grippin' it somethin' 'turble – wouldn't let nobody touch it, let alone take it from him. His body was a'tore t'shreds by canister balls and he was all bled white, with his innards hangin' out ever' which way – and how he was still alive was a mystery to all his comrades in arms and me that was a'hoverin' over him afta' the fightin' ended. Were chalk white, he were, as white as y'cud get chalky t'be, but he were a'fightin' death with all his spirit like a tiger, 'cause that's 'bout all the fightin' left in him t'do. Kept sayin', "Tell her I love her, boys...tell her I love her...!" And the boys kept a'replyin', "We will, Tim, we will, don'tcha worra' none," us all bein' from the same parish, y'see. And then he jest seized up and quit, his eyes a'starin' t'the Heavens with his pupils gettin' bigga' and bigga'. But a team a'mules couldn'ta got that tintype outta' his hands...no, suh'! So, they buried him a'grippin' it tight – the way he'da wanted it. Talk 'bout d'votion. Tim Oliver were his name...Tim Oliver... all a'eighteen tenda' years. Wonder how they broke it t'her when they got back home. Wonder if'n they left her knowin' how MUCH he truly cared for her. Hope so. Would be an outright shame if'n they din't.

Corporal Travis L. Quay
Infantry

"Like as not, y'was tired all the time. More a tiredness in yer mind than body, through yer body was gener'lly wore out and painin' bad. But, y'got used to yer body. Never quite got used t'yer mind, if'n y'know what I mean. Y'never know'd what it was a'goin' t'do t'ya – make y'feel good 'bout things one minute and terr'ble des'prate the next. Got t'worryin' 'bout little things like they was all BIG things...and ever'thin'd git y'nervous and snappin' at yer friends. They called it the jitters. Yer temper'd git short and y'couldn't sleep fer beans and y'ud git t'shakin bad sometimes and cryin' fer yerself like y'was a little youngin' again' a'skerda the dark 'er jest plain feelin' so sorry fer yerself y'ud be a'bawlin' in yer sleep, if'n y'COULD sleep. The more fightin' y'saw the worse it got. Couldn't b'lieve y'ud survive the next day, never mind the next week 'er month – like the angel a'death was a'bidin' next t'ya ever' wakin' and sleepin' minute a'the day, jest a'cruelly waitin' t'take y'over. That waitin' fer it was what got t'ya. Jest the snap of a twig'd git'cha jumpin' and make y'wild-eyed with terror – and y'never wanted t'hear rifle shot or cannon report eva' agin' in yer life. Some men'd come through it fairla' well – but not others. I know'd a man once't who went a'screamin' off inta the night like a banshee with a flamin' tail and we never heard a'him agin'. Lookin' back, I git all skerd and sick inside all over agin' jest thinkin' 'bout it. Guess it'll be with me 'til they put me under – and maybe even afta' that. I'll duly need the Lord, then, by God...I surely will."

Sergeant Jeremiah Peck
Infantry

"Singin' soothed a lotta the boys, singin' and story-tellin', mostly tall stories. Mosta' the time in bivouac we'd do one 'er the otha'. Some boys had mighty fair voices, and it made y'wonder how come they joined up 'steada comfortin' othas' with their nice tones...what I mean is...y'wondered whata waste it'd be ifn' they got kilt' and nobody but us'n's eva' knowed about 'em. Lotta boys died that'a way, though, what coulda' give'd the whole world powerful good it coulda' sorely used. Damn, shame, y'know. Wonder if'n y'could figure it all up how much it'd come to. But, mayba' it's better if'n we neva' know."

Corporal Will Cully
Artillery

"I was very often taken with the love men showed for the land. Common infantrymen, whose educationa' levels were low t'nothin', would lay or sit for hours in camp or in bivouack in the shade of summer days or the warmth of autuman sunshine, drawin' great comfort in studyin' fields and hills and woods. And just as often, even in the company of othas', they'd do so quietly without conversin' for long periods, studyin' the land's features in d'tail. I 'spose that for them the land was a kind of music or great lit'rature on levels men a'my inculcation will never quite 'preciate. I'm from the city. The land, therefore, does not hold the same meanin' for me, though, while on a diff'ernt spirit'chul level, it holds great beauty. But I don't b'lieve they and I'll eva abide on the same plain, visa vis the land. I mean no arrogance nor to imply any class super'ority by this admission. I trula' admire and enva' those men. I merely state a fact a'life. We come from two diff'ernt worlds yet are thrown t'getha' inta' the same cauldron a'war. When it all ends, a'course, we'll have more in common, and p'haps a greata' 'preciation for life and each otha'. We'll have seen the elephant t'getha' and smelled its hot breath and, in that sense, will eternalla' share a common brotha'hood. I HAVE met enlisted men whose common sense and native intelligence s'passes those a' half the gin'rals and senior officers I've met in this war. And just as mana' times I have owed my s'rvival to their superior instincts. No, I have learned through hard experience to make no class distinctions otha' than those which celebrate the fraternity of the enlisted man – and humble mine."

Major Collin Gray
Infantry

"Stood on a mountain once't. Seemed like I could look out 'cross the whole world from up there. Where ere' I looked, there weren't no war – jest land all colored up with autumn, and trees as far as y'cud see. Was a right most beautiful time a'the year – like in standin' there I was above the world we know'd – even above of fightin' and killin' n'all – like it never were. Still cain't git' over that we was in another world up there – maybe Heaven 'er close to it – like, if'n y'looked around a little farther, y'mighta found the Golden Gate with the Lord a'standin' right there t'let 'cha in, if'n y'deserved it. Couldn't see man from up there, jest Nature. Oh, it were a lovely world up there, with nary a single smell a'powder smoke and no cryin' out of the maimed and dyin' – jest quiet and silence and peacefulness only the Lord cudda' created. Didn't wanna leave – didn't wanna go back t'that other world – feared it 'til m'knees shook and m'legs got weak. Already had three year of it. If'n I cudda' gone back and closed m'eyes t'it and shut out the sound of it, it wudda been better. But, I know'd I wouldn't be able to, a'course – and that were the horr'blest part of it. No, I din't wanna leave – jest wanted t'walk through that gate and sleep in a quiet place in Heaven for a hun'erd years is all. Weren't much t'ask. Was kinda hopin' the Lord was hearin' m'thoughts. I swear, He were up there. Swear I could feel Him a'standin' right next me."

Corporal George Ivy
Infantry

"Ruma' is the fightin's all ova' – the war and ever'thin' else – ova'. Doubt it, though. They's always ruma's. B'sides, our regiment and brigade sure ain't actin' like it, even knowin' it be endin' sometime. But I b'lieved it's got a blooda' ways t'go. Mayba' we ain't got a whole lot left t'fight with, but we ain't a'givin up yet. I did agree it shoulda' ended long ago...leastwise, shunt' neva' a'got started. Din't realla' matter at that point 'cause it HAD and we'd been a'sufferin' with it fer four long year. Ana'more, winnin' 'ner losin' don't appear t'matta' none, eitha'. Maybe it neva' did. Maybe it were alreada' been written, was how WE feel. Jest so it ends soon and don't neva' happen agin'. We all jest want t'git home. We're tired of it. Feel a thousand year olda' – maybe more, and all m'friends is gone…dead and buried onla' God knows where and in some places no one'll eva' rememba. Nothin' much is left a'me save fer a little pride, m'wife, m'kin and m'youngins' a'waitin' fer me – and m'sick horse. Guess that be anuff'. Hoped so, 'cause it'll be all I git t'take home with me when it do end. I rememba m'horse's face better than m'wife's. Don't even r'memba what m'youngin's look like – jest a hazy impression's all that's left. Been three year! Hope t'be I' home in time fer plantin' – if'n there'd be ana' seed left t'plant. Trust so. Is fixin' t'be a hungry season if'n there ain't – yes, suh – a vera' terr'ble hungry season."

Private Harold Fenters
Cavalry

"You cannot imagine the scourge of enemy horsemen who fired our small town. I am writing to you, dear brother, Collin, that you might know our suffering here and the madness of it. They were vandals in the uniforms of our enemies, yet I cannot believe our enemies would stoop so low or revert to such barbarism. Therefore, I have concluded they were red-legged trash and completely outside our enemy's authority. They stole, burned, looted and attempted rapes until our cavalry drove them off and captured a half dozen of their wounded, whom they immediately hanged from the loft of the only stable in town as yet unscathed. Dirty and disgusting they were – animals in manner and appearance and smelling like hogs. They hang there even now. No one wants to touch them, let alone bury them anywhere near here. Lord!"

Your loving sister,
Gwin

"Mosta us stay n'fight cause we b'lieve in Heaven – that life contin'yas beyond all mortal trib'alation. W'trust t'God's Word and what we be a fightin' and willin' t'suffa fer – but w'dare not question Him ner doubt His Word. Fer us, death be no mystery, but the door – jest like the Word promises the faithful – t'Eternity. And w'trust the Word 'cause it be anuff."

Anonymous

What Realm is This

Sojourning with the Army through a woodland wilderness with a breeze lovingly caressing its langorous, verdant depths and the sun dappling flora with ponds of gold large and small, and a sky so brilliantly blue and cloud-tufted that it appeared conceived and hued by a supernatural artist's hand, every intuition confirmed to me that I was a mystical part of it all and it a part of me.

I realized as if having an Epiphany that all things human and of nature's realms are, by mysterious design, linked to a vast matrix that will forever transcend human comprehension, that it derives from the province, in every minute detail, of a daily, guiding intelligence. Compared to a mountain all of man's accumulated knowledge unto this hour from all of his Earthly strivings amount to a thimble that only a drop has dampened, let alone filled, and that if comprising a sulfurous match could not produce flame enough to light the smallest candle.

And thus I trudged along with the column as if in a dream, as if I had been suddenly liberated from my body's incarceration, free to soar to imaginary heights in a dimension far beyond myself and this Earth. I cannot otherwise explain the experience except perhaps to proffer that the fatigue of our long march might have influenced my perceptions. But whatever the circumstance I would not refuse a repetition. On the other hand, perhaps because of my fatigue I entered into a realm thus far secreted from all of us for reasons we have yet to discover when we pass from the only world we know.

How beautiful were the lilies where I wandered today.

To Neither Does He Respond

Honoring a request by the Colonel commanding the brigade to which I had attached myself, I met on neutral ground with a chaplain from the other side to exchange the effects of one of their officers killed in yesterday's fighting. It is common for both sides to do this, conditions permitting, a last surviving pretension of chivalry in this war.

For a moment, as we met, we stared at each other, he being as grizzled as any combat veteran and I being the same. His eyes betrayed a weariness born not necessarily of physical exhaustion but spiritual pain. Immediately I perceived him to be a man who, for too long, had witnessed inhumanities his faith could not reconcile. What he saw in my eyes I can only guess. But I assume it was something similar, for just as immediately we understood each other. Never before had I experienced such a quick and poignant bonding, let alone with a supposed enemy.

"I believe I am to place these in your safe keeping," I remarked as I handed him the effects.

"Yes, I was selected to receive them," he responded.

"As I was selected to deliver them," I replied. "I only wish it could have been a declaration of peace to be signed by both of us."

"I would sign such a document without hesitation," he confided, "if it would mean a sudden end to all of this. Are you military?"

"No, I am a civilian following the war and documenting what I see. I think you and I have seen more than we would have wished to."

"Much too much," he confessed, "my soul aches with it."

"And mine," I responded.

"Would that the common soldiers of both sides could put down their weapons and simply walk away..."

"And why could they not?" I rhetorically asked. "Perhaps men of God like you and those of the pen like me should insist upon it, and prevail upon both side's leaders to end it. Our persuasions might deliver our peoples at last to peace."

"I have prayed continually for just that," he revealed. "As yet, the Lord has seen fit not to answer. Perhaps, He believes our common folly is our just chastisement."

We studied each other for a moment more, he, I'm sure, wishing to talk more with me, as I wished to talk more with him. Talk is what the rank and file of both sides wished for more than all else, that it might lead to a cessation of all hostilities in lieu of negotiations. But he and I knew well that neither side's leadership would accede to any such movement. If negotiations were to be realized at all, they would have to result literally from mutiny on both sides, from common soldiers by the thousands telling their leaderships, "Enough! No More!" and walking away... throwing down their tools of war and boldly walking away.

"Too bad we must hastily end this conversation," he said. "I would have wished to have treated with you at length."

"And I with you," I replied. "I wish there had been a covenant granted at the war's outset to those of our outlooks to work for peace in the Lord's name. I wonder if the powers that be would have honored such an arrangement."

"I believe it would have troubled them greatly," he conjectured, "knowing the aims of some. But it would have evoked a noble enterprise."

"Indeed it would have," I replied and bade him good-bye, saying I hoped we might meet again in pleasant times. "My name is Chapman."

"And mine is Collingsworth. Somehow, I have a feeling we will," he said with conviction that gave me pause; "if not in these mortal climes than, perhaps where lions lie down with lambs and Earthly tribulation shall be no more for us."

"Perhaps so," I replied. "I look forward to it."

We shook hands, turned and trudged back to our respective lines. How futile, I mused, that both sides pray to the same God, that He might side with them against the other, while widows on both sides are left desolate or perish with grief. We on our side, see our homes and farms and cities burned or turned to rubble and our kin and livelihoods destroyed, while our enemies have but to turn around and return to all they left safely behind. But I know that men like the Union chaplain and many others would condemn such atrocities if they thought their voices would be heard.

We both fight for liberty by different definitions, and condemn the motivations of the other. They condemn slavery, for which the bulk of our men at arms do not lay down their lives, yet Union politicians would subjugate us and our land as if we, not they, were a foreign invader to be smashed. We, in turn, must respond. And yet despite all, in intervals of quiet escape from the slaughter, such as that which the Chaplain and I concluded, our men and theirs often meet on neutral ground to greet and speak as old friends engaging in friendly discussion, eying each other not as enemies, but as Americans in common. By what right have both sides brazenly exceeded their authority in the very sight of God?

Perhaps Collingsworth had been correct. Perhaps God, in His wisdom, permits us, via our abuse of the free will He has given us, to unwittingly chastise ourselves for it with our own mutual violence that we might someday realize the waste and corruption of what we've done, and thereby grow in our spiritual commitment to His Word. For even now, unto this very hour, to neither side's prayerful lip service does He respond. Perhaps sincerity supported by action is what He craves from us, action in exchange for His blessed intervention.

The Plains of Mars

The ragged roads over which we have marched thus far have led here, to this nighttime valley and these hills. From this promontory I look down upon the hundreds of watch fires all around me and consider the thousands of common soldiers who sleep by or near them, or within their now diminishing glow. The hour is late and most of the army is at rest.

I cannot vouch for the depths of their sleep. Some, undoubtedly tormented by the thoughts of battle come daylight and loved ones they may never see again, lay restlessly, their misgivings and regrets tormenting them. They wonder, perhaps, about sentiments they should have expressed to their families or sweethearts but did not, or debts they should have settled but did not, or letters of love and sweet good-byes they should have written home, but either did not or could not because they could not read nor write – or a thousand other matters to which they should have attended. For now, depending upon their fortunes after sunrise, it is too late, unless Providence spares them yet another day. In war there are no tomorrows as we commonly consider tomorrows. There is only fate's eternal night whose dimensions extend empire-like beyond man's ken and far into the dark unknown. But for those rare individuals internally at peace with themselves, sleep is a blessed balm that grants them time away from war and war's haunting specters and anoints them with a blessed, if brief, oblivion.

The air tonight is benevolently calm with only a slight affectionate breeze to embrace their dreams. To the west only the slightest trace of daylight remains, now tenderly in the firmament's care. Tree-lined hills about us remain silhouetted against a blue-black curtain embroidered with a thousand brilliant sequins. One might think, "There cannot be war here. Man cannot be so callous and unfeeling as to produce his mayhem beneath and surrounded by such mysterious splendor." But he is well capable of ignoring the gifts written by God in land and sky for him to correctly interpret. I fear our arrogance is a heresy that shall stand against us when, on that last day, the Lord judges us all.

Now as I stand bereft of sleep studying the sky, I realize there is music to the night, unheard except within, a celestial orchestration of ethereal composition that only the soul can interpret – a gentle, soothing language of its own connoting a beautiful somewhere beyond that bids one "Come to me and I will comfort and enrapture thee," its effect mesmerizing and hypnotic. It is not in mysticism that I now indulge my pen but in spiritual discovery, what I feel at this moment being as real in its own right as the physical world in which I write. It is as if Creation attempts with its transcendent voice to communicate to us the wonder of it that exists beyond our meager senses and our intelligence to interpret. I have discussed this on occasion with soldiers who feel as I do but who have never found words to describe it, though within they understand its effects.

And now as the aroma of smoldering and burning pine wafts through every bivouac, I appreciate more than ever nature's majesty.

Across the landscape, these plains of Mars, myriad campfires dot the growing darkness, too many to count. Sentries walk their posts. Invisible boughs above me rustle in the breeze, and I close my eyes as I breathe in the Earth's saccharine breath. Weariness blankets me. Sleep stealthily seeps into my tired brain. I feel its velvet-like tentacles reaching deep and caressing me. Shall I honor sleep tonight, or will my haunted mind hold it off? You see I, too, fear the morrow, the reaper being ever closer at my side, for when the army goes into battle I go with it, without a rifle, yes, but once more to see the war in every way as those about whom I write see it, my civilian status granting me no privileged protection. But before I sleep, if I sleep, let me tell you what I have learned about the common soldier unto this hour.

For the moment he is quiet as he approaches battle. As his sullen regiment files into position along the battle line, the clinking of his equipment and other's mixes with the dull boom and crack of distant artillery. With musketry's rattle escorting his shuffling footsteps he begins to think, sometimes dully, sometimes feverishly...will he die today or will it be the man or men next to him? Will he see the sun at this time tomorrow, or feel the rain, or hear the songs of wild birds, or feel the wind upon his face, or see his wife again and loved ones and know the comfort his home and hearth – or will he be feeding the worms somewhere beneath the earth with untold others? How does death feel? Will he experience excruciating pain before he succumbs? Will his innards or limbs be shot away? Will he endure the surgeons' saws? Will he be able to love and be loved again?

Suddenly, his tactile senses intensify as never before, every impression and sensation heightening until his body trembles. He sees the dead and the carnage in the fields before him and the maimed and horribly maimed struggling rearward or being carried by wounded others, some passing through his company's ranks, that silently and with death-like stiffness make way. Instantly, he loves and craves life as never before, yet feels profoundly sorry for himself, offended that a living and breathing being with the grace of God within him should be so ruthlessly sacrificed. He wants to scream out, to proclaim its unbelievable injustice and incredible waste! But he remains silent because all those around him remain silent, and he does as he's told because THEY are doing as they are told, and if he trembles, he wants not that they should see him trembling lest they think him cowardly. He melds with and hides within the group, his individuality suppressed, and awaits his fate, perhaps self-consciously mouthing a prayer for salvation, for which he feels no shame as, all around him, others feel no shame for theirs.

He stands next to a grim-faced veteran whose apparently steel determination tenuously strengthens him. Yet, he cannot see the fear and turmoil within that veteran's soul because that veteran will never dare to let it show, pride being his sustaining bulwark.

For those moments before the order to advance, he isolates himself from the gruesome realities before him, as if they belong to a non-existent wasteland. He imagines it is all a mistake yet to be rectified, that at the last moment his regiment will be recalled, that a chance remains that he will avoid whatever catastrophic destiny would otherwise await him out there. Of course he knows it is a futile hope, but hope, at that moment, is all that is left to him. He frantically cocoons himself in conflicting worlds of quiet terror and tender reveries of home. He fears a savage, crippling wounding even more than death, death suddenly becoming too abstract to consider, and he dreads returning home less than a man having to encounter a wife, frightened children or a sweetheart devastated by his appearance who might reject him.

Trembling within as without, fear smothers him and shortens his breath. He lets on to no one, though he would cry like a child in his mother's arms if she were there to hold him at that moment. At the same time he does all he can to take heart in what only appears to be the strength and apparent resolve of those around him. He tells himself their stoicism connotes indestructibility. He passionately recalls all he holds dear and whatever good about the life he has left and WILL leave behind forever, if fate so decrees that day. And once again he silently rages that fate is about to auction his flesh and blood so cheaply to hot lead and iron in violation of all that's holy.

He becomes a child again, momentarily regressed to wondrous innocence, his tactile and psychic senses bayonet sharp and heightening. Yet he feels miniscule and inconsequential against the vast universe of chance incarcerating him as he steps into the unknown, as if he were a valueless plaything vulnerable to its whims. He wonders about the nature of eternal oblivion, about Heaven and Hell. He feels that he is expendable mud in the hands of an all-powerful perversity exceeding God's benevolence. And he grows angry with God for not interceding on his behalf, a God to whom for a lifetime he has loyally devoted his fealty. In the next breath he chastises himself for his blasphemy and apologizes to God. But still he does not run, as some have done. He stays to face the gorgon, every instinct bidding him flee, his soul demanding, "Why do you not?"...his ego countering, "Because I cannot."

"Give us the fifes and drums," a veteran demands, that it may stir the blood and propel weak knees forward.

Whistles blow and "Forward" shouts the regiment's commanding officer. "Forward" passes down the line from company to company. In front of his command the officer raises his sword, jabs it toward the enemy, and the regiment and its parent brigade advance. Now come the fifes' jaunty notes and the drums' stirring cadences, as if each were an inviolate shield. Now the soldier will earn his bread. Hundreds of yards later as the brigade nears the enemy's lines it will be expertly leavened with Lincoln's iron and lead.

If he survives, his ears having been bludgeoned with titanic noise and painful concussion, exhilaration will carry him to heights of spiritual ecstasy, and for a time he will believe he's immortal. But when his mood passes, as it surely will, he will collapse against a wall of mental exhaustion, craving sleep's blessed relief. And when he awakens sober and reflective he will discover that he's become a veteran ever more appreciative of the simplest pleasures and all things of beauty. His mind will temporarily refuse to recognize the horror he's witnessed. Forever more as he wears a uniform he will guard his ever greater appreciation of life, keeping it treasured securely within, while secretly revisiting it during introspective moments. He will commune with it and, like a child, peer into its sunsets and vistas as if it were a crystal of mesmerizing spectral light. Eventually, he will withdraw into himself where his soul is known to God alone.

In the meantime, the roads he marches will be barren of beautiful lilies.

*   *   *

Addendum To

In the Beauty of the Lilies

Chaplain's Confess

**From the Wartime Journals of
Confederate Correspondent
Royal K. Chapman
1862-1864**

By

R.A. Busse

A Thought

Some soldiers saw Christ among them
and remembered that He was weeping.

In The Beauty of the Lilies

Explanation

Royal Chapman's endeavors during the War Between the States were not restricted to commenting upon the perspectives of combat troops but extended to the wartime Clergy as well.

He sought out priests, preachers, ministers, and deacons, somehow encouraging them to reveal their innermost feelings about the war and their responsibilities. Always he kept his promise not to disclose their identities, and to observe strict confidentiality in that regard. Otherwise, for obvious reasons, he could not have gained their cooperation, let alone their trust. Names were never as important to Chapman as sentiments. To him they represented the Army's collective soul. It was that soul he constantly sought to define and explain, no matter where.

While searching the landscapes of human tribulation on myriad battlefields and encampments large and small, Chapman became part of the humanity he immortalized. Though we know few of his subjects by name, he has given us an alternative means of recognizing them by their revelations, confidences and confessions, clergy among them. Our curiosities may have been more conventionally satisfied had he put names to their commentaries where appropriate, but it cannot be denied that the words of chaplains in essence were collectively more important to history – and to that end Chapman has diligently rewarded us.

The Editors

Chaplains Confess

They were honor-bound to serve their Faiths
but could not confess their truest feelings
except to God or their confessors – or to
civilians like Royal Chapman who, like them,
saw the war through a non-combatant's eyes,
but looked sympathetically into their weary
souls that daily endured the whirlwind beneath
war-stained Crosses.

Chaplains Confess

From Regiments in

The Army of Northern Virginia and the Army of the Tennessee

The Army of Northern Virginia

Part One

"It is unfortunate that so many of our men are illiterate. That so many cannot communicate in writing the thoughts they eloquently express to me in their homespun ways will leave much of this war's most poignant essences untold. Whether they sit in their bivouacs observing Nature or simply woolgathering, I am compelled to ponder to what depths they consider life's mysteries and most salient quandaries, for their intellects should not be undersold. I long ago reckoned that their quaint accents and uneducated personae often mask disarming intelligence. Perhaps the truer case is that while educated men study reality, uneducated men perceive it with alternative insights. In many respects, their brand of spirituality surpasses purely intellectual reasoning, owing to lifetime circumstances that produce keener, if more earthly, perceptions. We should hear them, for no less are they the Lord's own."

"Had I arrived on these scenes at the war's commencement, harboring an innate prejudice of social and intellectual superiority, such arrogance would soon have been quickly humbled. Even now I serve alongside men of simple dignity and countenance, who although without high-born status or means, comprise our Army's soul and sinew. New to the chaplaincy, and ignorant of matters, I formerly stood in civilian boots beside barefooted farmers and shopkeepers who faced mutilation and death with bewildering stoicism. But made guilty by their dedication, and that I enjoyed footwear at all, I forsook the boots to don sandals instead, as did our Christ. Sadly and for the most part, whether these soldiers presently alive survive or perish, their nation and the world will probably never know let alone remember their names, yet they are content with that. And when considering these things, and as I look upon the poorest and most bedraggled among them, I must fight back tears, for their spiritual strength overpowers my emotions. As another regimental Chaplain explained to me, "They may possess nothing but honor, yet they believe that if they perish, they will gain everything – the Kingdom of Heaven – and will not be spiritually destitute if and when fate should claim them.""

"The word of God would be made plainer for our troops, and my work made surer if the Scriptures were written with more understandable construction. The Bible's venerable syntax is foreign to the ears of our illiterate, to whom we must preach in lieu of that illiteracy. That syntax, though common to a bygone era, often is a puzzlement to my flocks. I would rather have it in straight English to better communicate the Lord's message. As it is they listen dutifully, comprehending little on most occasions and nothing on others. Duty to their faith compels them to politely listen, trusting as they do that the Holy Spirit will intervene to compensate them for their good intentions. I pray that he will convey to them the essence of the Master's Words, thereby enlightening them even as antiquated English cannot. I have learned in my work that God often teaches by indirection."

"It is in the half-light of mornings such as these as the army still sleeps that melancholy overtakes me and I weep. There is a soulful innocence about a slumbering army condemned to the fate violence has created. God knows many ARE yet children, and I weep because many will breathe no more by this hour tomorrow, and though I am a holy man who believes in the afterlife their deaths will sting me no less severely, for their resting places will not be only unconsecrated but sordidly anonymous, as if each man had never existed. Hundreds will die perish known only to God. And I will wonder why and for what purpose their mothers endured the agonies of their births if it was only to these pitiful ends that their progeny were destined. Why then, does not the Lord – if only for the sakes of those poor women – put His restraining Hand upon both armies and convert their hearts instantly to peace? No, I have seen too much to ever again relinquish my conscience to the spiritually satisfying enticements of simply herding flocks in war. I came on a mission – to relieve, with God's help, the souls of soldiers suffering this war's tribulations, yet I find my task one of loneliness. Now it appears my epitaph may read: "He perished of wounds his collar could not heal.""

"Many times I have sat with my face in my hands, having been unable to reconcile Faith and reality for a poor soldier who has witnessed a good and decent friend torn to pieces by the day's violence. In such cases my intellect is impoverished and my soul emptied, for such cases are too typical and occur too often. I am frequently shamed when ordered not to accompany our troops into battle; I must content myself to wave after them as they move forward or bless them as they pass me by, while battle rages beyond. It is my calling to go with them, as I would to the doomed aboard a foundering ship. And when they brush by me, their faces grim and their eyes haunted, and humbly reply, "Thank-you, Father," I am reduced to desolation. The Lord could not have chosen a more effective manner for humbling His servants."

"Many men look upon chaplains as privileged persons who are neither soldiers nor civilians, nor obliged in any way to share their dangers. Thus our credibility, despite our calling, is suspect, for why should they not think that God protects us – before them – from all harm? And thus we are marked men, avoided by some and resented by others. Consequently, I have long since abandoned my collar and ministerial garb to wear instead the trappings of the most common infantrymen – my only religious badges being the Bible I carry and a Cross on a chain 'round my neck that hangs to my chest. Thusly dressed I am not only a curiosity but better accepted. And thus I am better able to disseminate God's Word and bring hope to the star-crossed that they shall find themselves in the court of the Almighty's select should their fate be so adjudged. My superiors have called me too unconventional and much too "theatrical," but in my heart and in my soul I am neither. No, in this war one serves God best who does so by the most practical means."

"Soldiers gossip about what they see and hear, sometimes laughingly recollecting the horrors of battle and the grim details of other's deaths as if casually speaking of the weather. It always strikes me that ideally it should not be so, but there is little about war that is ideal, and my naïveté about its nature was rife when I first came to it. War is a soldier's living and waking business, paradoxically as much so as any peacetime pursuit. He cannot be expected to treat it otherwise. I often feel that I am an interloper when I attempt to cautiously insert myself into his inner circles so that I might nurture souls. Sometimes I am rejected, but I expect rejection. Still it troubles me when in my presence they speak so humorously and in such graphic ways about their friends' terrible death throes, as if flaunting their disrespect for and protesting my collar. As a pastor I've never gotten used to it."

"If I were to confess that I occasionally drink it would not be to relieve by conscience but to honestly admit that drink is my earthly haven in this warring Hell our combined peoples have ignited. But I have never preached in a state other than sobriety, though perhaps a touch of the creature at those times might have better provided inspiration. I give it to you to decide how YOU would manage, looking daily into fear-tortured eyes and young and old faces wrung out by ferocious fighting, all permanently scarred by too much killing. Their distress crushes me, for I feel it as surely as if an impossible weight were upon my chest. Sometimes, contrary to my faith's ethic, I feel the war is not a place for chaplains, or even for religion."

"People have asked me my views concerning the politics and morality of this war. I have demurred only because it seems futile at this stage of the conflict to do other than contend with matters as they are – the foremost being the spiritual health of our soldiers. Yet some have rebutted that concern, protesting that God is obviously absent from the affairs of men – and this affair in particular. What does it matter, they ask, since so many have been lost despite millions of prayers uttered daily – and will be lost despite my work, the grave being the grave? I concede that to these souls who have abandoned their faith nor have never possessed it, my work appears pointless – and that because I spiritually prepare men for death, I appear to enable the war's prosecution. Perhaps it is because they are right that their criticisms disturb me greatly. My conscience, not my pious superiors, tells me that perhaps we chaplains of both sides should have long-ago put ourselves between the guns, not behind them."

*   *   *

Part Two

"I cannot conceive of a more complicated matter than faith. Neither intuition nor empiricism substantiate it. So, despite my growing doubts, I am left to convince my charges that what their eyes cannot behold or their fingers touch is nonetheless a solid truth beyond doubt. Despite all, and if these soldiers only knew, I am a fraud, for I must daily struggle to sustain my faith even for a second, fearing my spiritual destruction lest I become too shamed in my conscience to utter a single prayer even for Divine guidance."

"I must often beg and cajole men into attending services whether on Sundays or other days. When not drilling they tend toward lethargy and rest. Still, they cannot be blamed. Their nutrition is poor, their physical exertions greater than the body's tolerance, and their long marches exhausting. And then there is battle itself that doubly empties them of emotion. To ask them to further spend themselves by attending services – or to encourage them to comprehend anything other than their own dissipation – taxes them beyond words. Yet I do reach some, for many who do attend services return to their bivouacs reenergized for short periods, especially when they hear me assure them that the Almighty understands their plight and hears their souls cry for solace. I tell them that what they endure is not His work but man's and the product of man's free will spent for war – and that God's Kingdom awaits all of faith who trust in His Word. I am sometimes asked if I truly believe what I preach – the question stemming from their harsh experiences, not from contentiousness. Yes, I reassure them, or else I would not have donned a white collar and followed them to war. They accept my goodwill and in turn show me respect. I have preached to hundreds of spent souls after battle who are low with the loss of friends or who, once away from services, collapse in sleep before reaching their bivouacs. At those times I feel guilty for having obligated them despite their weariness, but am sustained by the hope that they sleep more soundly as a result, their burdens lightened."

"For some of our boys the Sacraments are more important than their wounded, bleeding bodies. They crave the Word, and many have died searching me out for Confession even before medical attention, my masses having been beyond their physical reach. They yearn to unburden themselves. All around me war contradicts all evidence of God's love and compassion for man and His Church, but even then these dedicated souls will not let the guns persuade them that He is false. They thirst for that final taste of assurance, and I am honored to help them see Heaven as the truth of His Word paints it."

"Today a Private – a mere boy – died in my arms, his legs mangled by round-shot. He quickly bled to death, surgery having been impossible. I found him lying next to a fence he was attempting to scale when struck. All that he was able to convey to me was a single agony-free confession: 'I see it. I am going there now. It's all so beautiful.' Although so little time existed to affirm his faith, he affirmed mine."

"Occasionally as a courtesy to the Cloth I am invited to attend staff conferences. They occur in tents, the out of doors or, in rarer instances, within the largest rooms of private homes those staffs temporarily occupy. I cannot always follow the military details discussed, but I AM intrigued by the faces and demeanors of those officers around me, most of which usually show signs of stresses related to crushing responsibilities – and to grinding exhaustion. The depth and intensity of their weariness appears to correspond to their rank – the most senior appearing the least harried, junior officers the most, especially those closest to the fighting who lead their men into battle. These officers, their uniforms covered with dust and grime, are a most debilitated class, their health sometimes marginal and their fatigue sometimes incapacitating. When staff conferences are called every day during heavy campaigning or after equally heavy fighting their endurance is sorely tested. On these occasions I feel helpless and ineffectual, for my instinct is to minister to those most in need of spiritual support and uplifting. Yet protocol prohibits it. I stand only as an observer, a functionless appendage until afterwords when, ironically, those officers have no time or patience for religious matters, but must speed to their commands. Many of our chaplains believe our attentions fall too commonly among the enlisted ranks but too uncommonly upon their officers – whom some erroneously assume are supernaturally immune to the same fears and terrors. Of course, they are not. Yet the very fact that they must daily display unshakable resolve and courageous leadership out front in the face of carnage and death makes their spiritual maintenance equally imperative, if not more so. Though a shambles within and spent in every way, many persist in their shams of invincibility for the sake of their troops, holding together only by the most dangerously frayed threads. It is no wonder they've grown estranged from God and exist within a detached, mechanical state. I could not say what MY daily state of mind would be if I lost numbers of men upon every battlefield for whom I felt conscience-stricken and personally responsible. Even Christ's Cross could not have felt heavier. These men, too, have been spiritually scourged by the whims of this greatest of all human tragedies. I pray that He grants them His Grace, for I am helpless to reconstitute them."

"Chaplains are not always able to penetrate all that stands between God and individual soldiers. The men look upon preachers as being outside of their reality–special civilians hardly a part of their world. In the end, most of us never are fully accepted, nor are we truly considered kindred spirits, let alone fighting men. Only rarely are we freely permitted into their private lives and souls."

"I have confessed many times to God that I do not always understand Him nor his methods; that although I am honor bound to represent and preach His Word, I cannot always reconcile his lack of love and mercy in what I daily witness, man's free will not always being a convincing explanation. My confusion often drops me to my knees, for how can I convincingly preach His Word when reality betrays it? How can I then persuade my sheep to disregard what their eyes and experience tell them that counters their faith and trust in Him? When prayers go unanswered, when faith is not rewarded and devotion goes for naught, how am I to rationalize and repair such damage? My quandary is that of countless chaplains, many of whom have surrendered their vows to the ethers and have walked away, not only from the war, but from all religion. I have clung to my collar only because I have clung even harder to my intuition – that despite Holy Writ, Heaven is a natural part of Creation, has always been so and WILL always be so – and not the exclusive province of religion, or religious faith, nor a reward for fidelity to any corresponding theology. Does a tree owe its existence to the wonder of faith, or does faith derive from a wondrous tree? What then should be my conviction? And how do I therefore present myself to spiritually hungry soldiers? What ends justify what dogmatic means? Forgive me, please. My misgivings and ramblings are merely those of another weary laborer in the vineyards of Salvation."

"I have heard soldiers in their post-battle depressions doubt the Lord, disparage religion and disavow all Faith. At the same time, ironically, I witness many of them search for all three not in the Word but in Nature, as they contemplate, say, the most magnificent works of sky, land and sea. I attempt no competition with these venues for they are much better persuaders. Instead I am content to accept such Divine assistance and to watch the wonders of His Nature speak to their souls when they are most off-guard. Men so naturally attuned to the land turn to it reassured, and also to that which they more easily understand. It is then that they spiritually commune with that other dimension apart from man's, from which God speaks to them with therapeutic certainty."

"It is not always possible on the march to plan a coherent sermon, though one has convenient time to consider it. It is enough to try to follow our troop columns in a covered buggy, my advanced age requiring it, with my dozing assistant at the reins, as we bump over every state of road – and often no roads. My years no longer permit me to walk without extreme difficulty. However, it is cause for celebration when a pause allows me time to speak to resting soldiers willing to listen. Many, being exhausted, are not, and one must exercise discretion by treading lightly among all. As it is, my impromptu conversations with willing listeners cannot be sermon-like, for I am constrained – and always obliged – to use the time to reassuringly answer religious questions, or write notes home for the illiterate, or counsel the most war-weary concerned about their families and domestic matters. On such occasions I am more a comforter than a minister, yet I trust I serve an equal mission. But I am content that the Lord will always provide other opportunities to impart His sentiments more formally."

*   *   *

The Army of the Tennessee

Part One

"Of late my preaching responsibilities have given way to more practical matters. I and other chaplains devote ourselves to the wounded, working as medical orderlies in field hospitals under the sky and roof. We can do no less, for help is vitally needed. Never are there enough medical personnel to assist physicians and surgeons, much less the staff in the daily drudgeries of hospital care and management. But chances also arise to minister. On Sundays we preach to convalescing soldiers and encourage hymn-singing. While general hospital work is tedious and demanding and often discouraging when we daily deal with so much death, Sundays can be uplifting and constructive for the wounded, raising them from both their depression and discouragement. Perhaps in suffering us to endure the stench of human waste and gangrenous flesh that our evergreen-soaked masks do not entirely overcome, the Lord establishes a humbling, practical ministry for us that fulfills His Will. Do not think that dealing with wounds and toilet is not as spiritually, as physically, taxing. They are, yet He gives us endurance when we seek it. Care is our calling, for which we are grateful, our hearts being compensated when our efforts help to preserve life. I cannot conceive of not being available to administer last rites to those we cannot save. It has even been the case that the fated refuse to let go of life until we are summoned to their sides. Thus we are encouraged, knowing that in serving them we are serving Him."

"I am continually overwhelmed by the insights of the common soldier – so much so that I'm positive the Lord's angels speak to them on occasion more clearly than to us of the clergy. This morning, on the eve of battle, a soldier asked me: 'Padre, if I die today, what'll happen to me? I mean, who am I?'

'You are a soul who will live again,' I responded.

'Where?'

'I'm sure it will be in a gentler and more beautiful place we call Heaven, which is now invisible to us but which is all around us.'

'How can that be?'

'It is a mystery too great for our poor minds to fully understand. Only when we arrive there will all be made clear to us?'

'You mean, it be a s'prise?'

'Yes...if you will...a surprise.'

'Well, Reverend I got the bad feelin', like someone done whispered it in my ear, that I'm gonna be s'prised in just a while 'cause I don't reckon I'll be a'comin' back from this here contest t'day.'

Despite my attempt to dissuade him from thinking so, he didn't."

"In battle's aftermath, soldier's thoughts linger upon their fiery passions. They recall sounds and images tender upon their souls while, when it comes to the killing they've done, they tread lightly around their consciences lest they endure giant torments in trying to flee the wrath of terrible guilts they might awaken. War proves the character of some men while destroying the decency of others. God is not unfair – war's waste being a lesson we must eventually learn only through our collective pain."

"I stood one night upon a treeless knoll. Save for sparse undergrowth it was bared to the sky. Until I arrived a breeze had blown gently across the valley the knoll overlooked, where the Army slumbered amidst a thousand dwindling campfires. I went to the knoll to pray beneath an ebony firmament alive with celestial brilliance. As I prayed for the strength to stay the war's course and remain true to my duty to God, a quiet becalmed the night, leaving me cocooned within a deep yet almost audible silence. Immediately I was taken by a chill throughout my body that disrupted my prayers, leaving me divorced from the world, as if I were immersed in a realm apart from it. It was an Epiphany. God was assuring me that all of mankind's tribulations are trivial, if not to the battle-maimed and suffering. But when I looked into the heavens I was convinced that sentient and intelligent stars heard my thoughts and confided to me, saying that suffering would mean the salvation for the fated slumbering in the valley below. My Faith was further encouraged when I was shown landscapes of indescribable peace and beauty, transcending all mortal experience. Even now I wonder why I, a lowly country ambassador of the Lord, was so honored with such stunning precognition. If it was to convince and reassure me of the dead's continuing existence, I have done so every day since – abundantly and with conviction."

"Inevitably, because I am a cleric I am asked my opinion of slavery and if I believe it is this war's most compelling issue. What, I am queried, is God's instruction? At the risk of stepping beyond my collar's bounds I avoid discussing politics with our troops, assuring them that I know no more than do they, which is the truth. I DO know with surety little more than they do about the whys of this war. Personally I believe slavery is NOT the most compelling issue but that, for political expediencies, Lincoln has made it so. The true issue as I see it, if a clergyman is allowed contentious commentary, is that of unconstitutional and overbearing federal authority threatening to destroy the principle of dual sovereignty and the division of authority championed in the Constitution; in other words, that federal authority should never be permitted to, in all cases, override the will of individual states, nor of all states collectively. I cannot offer a religious perspective concerning slavery, though Scripture is oft cited as a rationalization against it. But when does not "interpretation" put biased meanings into God's mouth and upon His compassion? I am here like all chaplains, to encourage neither side in its violence, but to collect

456

these arguments' spiritual wreckage and attempt with good heart to mend and reassemble the pieces. It is only through God's Grace that we chaplains persevere even when we are soaked in the dying's blood, listening to their cries."

"Cruelty, tenderness, vindictiveness, generosity – this war produces all in confusing proportions. I have found that if a soldier is close to God, he accepts his conditions with baffling calm and composure, if not fatalism, and struggles to retain his Faith amid war's terrors and inhumanities, often showing the enemy great charity. If he is not, then after seeing and experiencing too much war he gives quarter to few and charity to none, as if hounded by the basest animal instincts. Some men, bad to begin with, are chastened by war and made mellow. I search for those the Lord has strengthened, for they replenish me and give me heart enough to minister to those it has weakened. But, even upon the strongest war etches indelible scars."

"They who fight experience much that transforms their hearts and transfigures their souls. And what of the chaplains who follow them? If the truth were admitted they, too, are transformed and transfigured. Some being only human beneath their collars are spiritually demolished. Yet there is a general assumption among rank and file troops that Chaplains fall under a special Grace –that they are impervious in every physical and spiritual sense to the infirmities war heaps upon mind and body.

That some of us comport ourselves with dignity enough to impart this impression pays tribute to men of the Cloth much stronger than I. In fact, only we realize how spiritually fragile we truly are and how close we often come to the edge of futility – and sometimes of madness."

"At this moment, the Lord must be weeping into His hands for the manner in which this land He has blessed has profaned His hopes. Sometimes I wonder if my participation in this war has contributed to His disappointment, for I have gone along to save souls when I might have protested the war beforehand, and thereby attempted to save every soul now in it – and those countless we've lost."

* * *

Part Two

"We chaplains and warriors alike, in an awful, single aggregate, cannot be more than disappointments to God. To see and hear a battlefield after a fight, and smell it and walk through it, is enough to sicken one's soul for a lifetime. But do we protest it loudly and with vigor? No, even though we cannot help but acknowledge that what men are doing to one another in the name of principle and idealism is not only unforgivable, but obscene. My patience with myself and my kind, as with generals and politicians, grows ever-thinner, and I fear that I daily fall short of reclaiming the souls of those who kill and those who die seeking grace, weighted as my calling is by so much self-righteousness. Of late I've grown confused, not knowing if, in my sermons, I should chasten the makers of this fratricide on both sides, and encourage my brethren in uniform to lay down their arms and return home, or simply adhere to comforting their souls when they gather to hear me. And thus I fear to become what I criticize - an opportunist venting his politics instead of remaining true to his calling. I am torn between God's Word and patriotism, and I despair of finding neutral ground, between compromising my calling and being more practical. I ask myself, "Does being true to God mean that I must defy my government?"

"We non-combatants who have waded through the bloody viscera of countless fields, small and large, can only hope that, ironically, the massive killing now occurring brings this war to a swifter conclusion. Either the public's revulsion with it will intimidate its makers into ending it or there will no longer be enough manpower remaining, especially on our side, to persist in it. Admittedly many men of the Cloth, spiritually desperate to be of positive consequence, are so darkly encouraged. Yet God help us, we cannot go on forever laboring in these gardens of infamy. Someone must stop this war."

"Anymore the point is not who wins or loses, for no rationalizations can justify the slaughter we've engaged in for four, insufferable years - not in God's eyes - and He is all that matters. We must end this misery before it consumes us all. How many more graves must we preside over and look upon before the Devil's bloody appetite is satisfied?"

"For the men I serve peace is a temple in the mist, a mystical place in an ethereal valley of autumnal splendor deep in their imaginations - illuminated there when in quiet moments they look for and ponder the improbably - war's end. Secretly they worship within that valley, trusting that their prayers for that final tranquility will be heard and honored. Still being human, they fear that, in the interim, they might cross too soon upon that distant field beyond all mortal understanding, whose portal is yet unknown to them. They fear because they remain so fiercely attached to Earth, but walk each day in the shadows of the frightening Eternal. And they also wonder - if they survive this carnage, what then? Who will they be?

What will remain of the decent souls they once were? We chaplains must endeavor to reconstitute them, lest when the violence ends they leave their weapons behind, but not their war within.

"The most eloquent testimony concerning this war, and the one I will illuminate to my congregations when peace comes, will never be printed nor spoken, but will survive in this mortal vessel of mine containing four convulsive years-worth of my most private tears."

"When I stand in the privacy of my own solace and look skyward I imagine I hear a celestial trumpet softly calling me to prayer. Yet after years of appealing to God for peace I am weary of prayer's futility. Why, I now ask the Lord, do You continue to respond only with Your stubborn silence?"

"I went among those fighting in the front ranks, blessing all I encountered as they repeatedly fired their weapons, reloaded and fired them again, enemy bullets whining through the air around them, the din ear-shattering, until a terrified soldier, his eyes wide with fear, turned to me, shoved his rifle into my hands and yelled, "Here, God won't be a'killin' you...you fight..." and tore away to the rear and disappeared into the smoke."

"I cannot reach many of these veterans. I mean I cannot heal their ravaged souls with the Word of God for they have been so hardened by this war. And I fear this hardness more than all else, for the scars it will leave upon their souls long after the fighting ceases. It will make their adjustments to civilian life difficult, if not tragic, and leave us Chaplains defeated in our work."

"When I appeal to their humanity, to these men who have seen and felt and experienced what they have for so long, or when I preach to them from the Bible or read them Bible verses some glare at me with cold and even condemning indifference, as if I were an object of an alien realm or simply a dribbling fool. Many smile resentfully and turn away."

"So many have become completely indifferent to the killing and carnage. Friends fall around them in battle yet they come away with no emotion, as if they suffer a terrible stunning of sorts that leaves them numbed to all sympathy and loss. Some, I'm afraid, have absorbed this perverse conditioning deeply and into every fiber of their beings - until it is now who and what they are."

"Some say the war and the killing is God's retribution for slavery and its evils, and for not having sought His guidance to abolish it. Many God-fearing men in ranks, even anti-slavers and those who have never owned a slave believe this, that the Lord is using the war to punish and chastise us. I cannot say that they are wrong, for what mortal truly knows the mind of God? But in believing this they are fatalistically committed to their destruction, believing that the war will end only when He is satisfied that His punishment is complete. Yet I cannot truly believe that His lack of intervention is due to anything more that His already understood commitment to allow men free will to accept or reject His general stewardship and thus to experience the consequences, good or bad. Still I admit this war does appear to be an extreme lesson contradicting His teachings concerning mercy, and therefore making His tolerance for it also appear hypocritical. I am at a loss to defend Him."

"Two days ago I intervened to prevent one of our commanders from harshly prosecuting captured white officers. The troops were for it, so heightened was their outrage that their white enemies would command black men to do their fighting for them instead of facing up to their white Southern foes like honorable warriors. I apparently flabbergasted them by revealing that our government in Richmond was at that very moment considering using black troops by the thousands against the Federals, and that punishing these prisoners would be another egregious affront to God while solving nothing in our struggle for independence, when we would be obliged before the international community to rid ourselves of our peculiar institution. I explained that some of those black men who would soldier for the South would be freed men, farmers and property-owners, and would fight to prevent the Federals from destroying their homes and farms. Black freed men have suffered some of the worst of Sherman's destructive predations upon Southern citizenry. My testimony appeared to help cool tempers and restore order. I therefore conducted a prayer session to which I invited all, including our prisoners, to participate in asking the Lord to swiftly end the war and restore all to their peaceful Christian commitments."

"I have found very often that I do not have to utter a single word or prayer to encourage men to come to God in their way. Sometimes I merely have to pass among them, and they meekly follow me as if seeking solace from the Almighty Himself, whom I represent. At other time, I merely sit among them and they gather silently about me, and we gaze together into beautiful vistas in the countrysides around us, words being unequal to the inspiring peace and equanimity we all feel on such occasions. In that sense we all momentarily escape the war, and nothing I could say could be more spiritually nourishing."

"Preaching does not always involve the Word of God. It just as often involves lifting spirits through laughter, through encouraging men to speak of home and their families, to reminisce about their lives before the war and to express their hopes for their lives after the war. Men leave such sessions spiritually revitalized, trusting that, perhaps, it is good, after all, to believe that they will survive to see their homes again."

"Often I bless sleeping men who lie exhausted after battle, oblivious to my presence. On such occasions I trust that God will pass along after me, anointing their brows lightly with His affirming touch. At those times I feel the reassuring presence of His angels at my side...and I am encouraged."

*　*　*

In the Beauty of the Lilies

**The Wartime Journals
of Confederate Correspondent
Royal K. Chapman
1862-1864**

Miscellaneous Journal

Entries discovered
in Nov. 1864
on the Franklin Battlefield
and retained
by Infantry Sergeant
Coltin Morse

In 1885, upon learning
of Chapman's greater works
& their imminent publication,
Morse forwarded his find
to Publisher
Jay Albright Fuller

*   *   *

Contents

Testimonies From:

Private Charles Britt, Infantry
Herman Stoddard, Merchant
Captain Edmund Wells, Navy CSA
Private Lester Scherer, Artillery
Mrs. Hattie Marquette, War Widow
Sergeant Theo Spencer, Cavalry
Corporal Jesse Wade, Prisoner USA

Also

The Advance: A Captured Yankee's Remembrance

Patchin'

Child of Light

Serpent

*   *   *

A Thought

Their spirits are upon the land,
never to leave nor war again.

Private Charles Britt, Infantry

"The scene will be foreva with me. It cannot be that I could eva forget the deaths of so many, even be they my enemies. I am bothered about it to this day, for I, in the company of hundreds of othas, was responsible.

"Each of us contributed to the carnage that accursed mornin'. Our company and regiment, guess it be 'bout a hunerd and twelve-hunerd respectively, was entrenched b'hind a wall of dirt we'd thrown up to protect us. We had reinforced the protection with heavy branches to make it Hell for enemy infantry to get over and through even if they ovawhelmed us. The logs and dirt made it impervious to minié-balls and all but the most powerful artillery shot and shell.

"Knowin' we was unda enemy observation, we waited confidently for him to decide that, havin' studied our postion, he'd consida an attack futile. So none of us trula expected it to come. But by God, it did.

"He come outta the woods a half-mile away in impressive numbas, all aligned in pretty ranks with his flags and bannas flappin' in the breeze, and fife and drums snappin' out livela tunes, his bayonets glintin' brightly in the sunlight. Then he come on, with no artillery fire against our positions havin' preceded him. We couldn't b'lieve his lack a'care. He was gonna try to carry our works with infantry alone! Shurla he couldn'ta thought we weren't ready for him and that we lacked artillery of our own, which we shurla had loaded and had waitin' for him. In fact, we enjoyed the support of at least sixteen Napolean cannon in four batteries all masked and filled with explosive shells for long range targetin'. But when and if'n they got close, then the boys would fill the guns with double-charges of canister. Canister takes down men in ranks like a scythe takes down wheat.

"On he came, through knee deep mists clingin' to the damp earth, his pace measured and his alignment precise, maybe three thousand more, I couldn't be sure - right across fields of stubblin' corn and pastures where frightened cows were a'grazin'. The closer he come, the clearer his fifes and rattlin' snare drums become, beatin' out a defiant cadence that was inspirin' even to us. But then an odd thing happened. The breeze quit sudden-like, leavin' his flags and bannas hangin' limp, like the fight had suddenly gone outta 'em. At the same time, his ranks faltered a bit, like the breeze quittin',' and his flags a'droopin' was a fearful omen to his ranks.

"His officas began shoutin' up and down his lines, getting' up their men's courage and urgin' 'em on. Fairly quick, they all was shoutin' huzzahs and cheerin', their pace quickenin'. The fellow to my right looked at me and said, 'This ain't a'gonna be a merciful thing, I'll tell ya. Them people's gonna rue this day.' I knew his meanin'. A lot a good men out there was gonna perish foolishly or s'vive with terrible mutilations. Seemed a pity to have to pull a trigger on 'em - would much ratha a'traded 'em tobacco for coffee.

"On they come more rapidly, now, the distance closin', their cheerin' upon our ears. We admired their pluck as the distance continued to close. Then our artillery opened fire. Shells whined and streaked inta and above their ranks, some failin' to explode, but takin' out men like rag dolls. The shells that did explode, especially over their heads, bludgeoned men to the ground with shrapnel, crushin' skulls like eggs. But the survivas kept a'comin', like they was blind to the destruction around 'em. The noise was ova'whelmin', it bein' more fearful than them iron tearin' 'em apart. Why, we asked ourselves, had those brave men been so foolishly committed? We actually grew angry for 'em at their leadership for the waste of it, they bein' infantry like us. Elan not withstandin', it was criminal foolishness and they were sufferin' dearly and tragically for it. But they would suffa more.

"When they were within range, our artillery paused, as gunners quickly loaded double charges of canister. We cringed at what was comin'. Canister is the most terrible of all artillery rounds, bein' absolutely devastatin'. It tears bodies to pieces, throws innards and arms and legs and heads in every direction, includin' straight up, like confetti. What was more hauntin' was their facial details becomin' eva plana, makin' the carnage to come even more painful and personal for all of us. How could I have compassion for the enemy, I been asked. Well, they bein' of flesh and blood like mine, and able to feel the pains and agonies of Hell, they become kin in arms regardless. It is a terrible thing to see the faces of men you're about to obliterate. Someday the men who make war are goin' to realize that we should no longa fight wars this way, that the costs are just too appalin' to soul AND body, and the means too inhuman to tolerate ana'more. They might even conclude that there's more merit to talkin' things out than fightin' 'em out. Those faces out there would become images fixed on my rememberin' mind.

"And then, upon a single coordinated command, the artillery along with our infantry fired, our rifles addin' a chatterin' staccato to the cannon's thunder in a great, single roar that accompanied spittin' lead and iron in a pulverizin' cloud of rollin', acrid, eye-stingin' smoke. Onla reluctantly did I pull my rifle's trigga, feelin' the piece buck sharply against my shoulda. Boilin' smoke obscured our vision, but we knew what was happenin' out there. We kept on a'firin', hardla seein' to target ana'thin, but we knew our minié-balls were a'cuttin' down most of whatever was still standin'. The cheerin' out there had ceased - so had the drums. And their flags and regimental banners had disappeared like ships havin' gone down to a deep six.

"We were ordered to cease firin', and when the smoke cleared a deep, heavy, ominous silence reigned eva'where. I was sweatin' heavily. Hadn't noticed I was 'til that point, my nervousness havin' gripped me mightily. Out there beyond, piles of humanity, some still as rocks, some undulatin' in mortal agony, revealed themselves. Down were their flags and banners, sure anuff, with bearers here and there still clingin' to busted staff or shredded fabric. Yet to our amazement and horror more ranks advanced far behind those just smashed. God, no, we thought, not more insanity! I was possessed by the urge to abandon my position before participatin' in any furtha slaughterin'! But then, just when our revulsion and emotional panic mounted, and as our artillery and infantry hastily reloaded, bugles sounded in those ranks. The ranks halted and reversed themselves, slowly and methodically meldin' back into the treelines from which all had fatefully emerged - their army's assault havin' been a bungled waste of blood and bone.

"And then came the cries and shrieks from those piles of humanity we had brought down, pitiful, gut-wrenchin' pleas for wata and help and mothas and the Lord and somethin' to ease and end their agonies - from bodies torn and shredded and unable to move - survivas now helpin' wounded rearward - wounded helpin' wounded, limpin' and usin' rifles for canes and crutches and tryin' to comfort those thrashin' and writhin' where they'd fallen.

"'Maybe we oughta finish 'em off' an unsavory and unlikable fellow in ranks remarked, a sneer crossin' his lips as he began to take aim on a limpin' survivor.

'You jest try that,' another fellow to my left said, cocking his rifle and puttin' its muzzle against the man's temple, 'and I'll spread yer calculatin' matta all across this here countra'side.'

"To this day I cannot know where my bullets went or who they mighta struck. Yet I still hope, as I did when the smoke lifted that day, that I missed completely since I aimed high. You see, after three years of war, I was tired of killin' and tired of imaginin' the families and sweethearts of those I killed sufferin' such terrible grief for it. Some of our boys hardened like iron by the war, had no feelin' or emotion's left for such fantasies. I felt sorry for 'em but I understood. Maybe if'n I had killed one more time my soul woulda died, too.

"Strange what we hope for when our actions savage our consciences. Got wounded two days lata - shattered arm. It didn't come off, but it ain't worth much ana'more. Got discharged after two months in hospital for that and the dystentery and infections I contracted. Almost died from 'em. Guess the Lord give me more time to ponder what I'd done for three year, 'cause there were a moment back there behind that wall when I knew I shouldn'ta pulled that trigga at all, but did ana'way in violation of the voice inside me that said 'Don't'. God had spoken to me through my conscience - but I'd ignored Him."

* * *

Herman Stoddard, Merchant

"This day, as we often did, we silently watched our soldiers file wearily through the countryside. Late in the war, with our country so depressed and set upon, these were reverential occasions when the costs of the war came stunningly home to us in their ragged appearances and quiet demeanors.

"The hurting flesh and smashed bone in the columns' ambulances reflected these costs and were always what war came to. It had been that way in Mexico seventeen years earlier when I had served. I still carry them with me as I stand on my one leg with my crutches. It saddens me that I had fought under a different flag then, that so much had come to pass in the interim to make old friends enemies by virtue of unfeeling borders and prideful politics.

"That day, as our soldiers filed through our settlement, they passed in front of my general store, which I willingly emptied for them of all necessities and dry goods they had long since given up. I did not care that I would spend the next few years making up my so-called losses, for I did not consider them as such. They constituted my belated contributions to the relief of their sufferings.

"We had been aware of their approach the day before, since the column had bivouacked no more than three miles from the settlement the night before. Our residents had gathered what foodstuffs they could spare to pass to them, knowing the men's dilapidated conditions. And the column appeared so. Company by company, regiment by regiment, brigade by brigade, they came trudging along, a certain élan still apparent in each man's gait despite their physical conditions, many with a mischievous smile or glint in their eyes. And so they proceeded until the column's van extended far beyond the settlement while its rear still remained a long way off.

"Then they were halted by a series of commands originating in the van and tumbling rearward, unit by unit. We were duly impressed by the precision and discipline displayed in this exercise. In minutes General Henry, the column's commanding officer, proudly mounted on his sorrel, galloped into the settlement with his mounted staff, directing that our offerings be collected and put into his supply wagons for later distribution - as equally as possible - to the whole of the column, by regiments.

"Though disheveled, dirty, and skinny from obvious malnourishment and deprived of material needs, the troops behaved kindly toward us and with the greatest deference, making us self-conscious that although they had done the lion's share of suffering in this war they were treating us as if WE had. To a man, they behaved particularly chivalrously toward our womenfolk of all ages, which earned them profound respect from our menfolk. We would never forget them. They rested for perhaps two hours.

"When I recall that day, admiration swells within my aging breast. For every child who looked on that day, those proud men embodied the finest possible examples of Southern manhood and courage."

*   *   *

Captain Edmund Wells, Navy CSA

"I remember how our man-o-war slipped by the enemy's coast, leaving behind large fires in the fort our fleet had just bombarded, not to mention a Union gunboat blazing and sinking.

"Along the shore, in the half-light of dusk, enemy civilians watched our progress. Through a spyglass, I studied their sullen forms, feeling their hatred for us pass along the waters to permeate our vessels' very timbers and all aboard. They might as well have been in a land thousands of miles from mine, but they were not. They were only miles away from it and attached to it by both geography AND history.

"To my mind, and although technically enemies, we still were one people, divided in common - both imperfect - our lands both guilty of our divorce and this genocidal tragedy which both should have morally avoided, if for no other reason than loyalty to and love for the Almighty and His blessed Son.

"Yet I well appreciate that the side that wins will feel no compunctions for it, while the side that loses will be unable to feel anything."

* * *

Private Lester Scherer, Artillary

"When y'march behind a man for a couple of year, y'get to know the back of his head and neck pretty well. Y'ken tell a lot from the back of a man's head and neck. First off, y'ken tell if'n he's got lice 'er somethin' that's crawlin' around up there that oughtn't to be. And y'ken tell if'n he bathes regular, which none of us ever do, and I swear some men ain't never done.

"There ain't much time 'er opportunity to do much bathin' in the army durin' wartime. And some boys cain't figure what the Lord made water fer anyway. Y'ken also tell if'n the war's a'turnin' him gray, which it does to many a man quicker than yud think - and y'ken tell by the tilt of the head if'n he's a'sleepin' on his feet, which we all do at some time 'er other. Most s'prisin' of all, y'ken git to tellin' what a man's a'thinkin'.

"Now, most folks would scarcely believe that, but that's 'cause they ain't never walked b'hind somebody fer two year, like all his thoughts was a'tumblin' outta his ears and bumpin' inta ya on their way to the rear. Why I got to knowin' what ole Cully Watson was a'thinkin so well that he'd git the powerful jitters jest knowin' I was b'hind him.

"'You pickin' on my brain agin, Lester,' he'd ask over his shoulder.

"'Well now Cully,' I'd say, 'them thoughts a'yours keep a'slappin' me in the face! Why don'tcha put some cotton in them big flappers a'yours?'

"'Lester,' he'd say, 'if'n you'd really knowd what I was really a'thinkin', yer face'd be a'blushin' bright red.'

"And another thing - y'sure git to know when a man's havin' stomach and gut troubles, and fer that yer always sorely regretful, if'n yer a'knowin' what I mean."

* * *

Mrs. Hattie Marquette, War Widow

"I can divulge now that we women of Atlanta, and no doubt, of Charleston and Richmond, as well, are not ashamed to give their essence to the war effort and to the wagons that daily come by to collect it.

"That by doin' so we are assistin' in the manufacture of gun powder for the army's armaments, and it makes us soldiers, too, as much as women have eva been allowed to BE soldiers.

"Of the thousands of chamber pots emptied inta those wagons eva' mornin' and evenin' by women of eva social description on eva street and neighbahood, none have been dispatched with ana'thin' but pride. It has neva been a d'gradin' experience as much as a patriotic one.

"Afta this war, I'm sure it will contribute to the sheddin' of certain hypocritical social airs and financial distinctions, if'n I may so describe them. I spose what I DO mean is...for a genaration on we once uppity daughtas of privilege wont' be able to look each otha in the face, no matta who were are, without seein' a vera humblin' bare bottom!"

* * *

Sergeant Theodore Spencer, Cavalry

"Got leave and went home on foot. M'troop couldn't spare me m'horse.

"M'city were a jungle a'despert people made homeless by the war. They come from parishes all around. The city folk was hardla betta off - no smilin' faces, no friendla words - engaged in the humnblin' business a's'vival. Lord, Lord, it weren't the world I'd knowd. Liked t'neva got ova it.

"S'vival for them folks meant tryin' t'feed their youngins and theirselves with eva'thin' bein' scarce, includin' all otha necessities of well-bein' and comfort. Even folks what knowd me dint have no time for neighborness, all bein' kinda skerd and jittery. Couldn't blame 'em none, like they was nervous that if'n they paused long anuff an enemy shell'd come over and blow 'em t'pieces, which weren't no unreasonable fear, since the enemy had jest ceased a bombardment of the city two day long - there bein' smoke and fire in most places, with folks a'fightin the flames as best they could.

"Naw, I were jest pushed aside most often, jest one a hunerds a'soldiers in the streets and generaly ignored otha'wise. I see'd ragamuffin youngins beggin' eva'where, and thievin' goin' on with nobda tryin' t'stop it, and loose ladies plyin' their trade in the open without shame - and general despair and confusion all ova. Couldn't afford t'buy what soma the boys gived me money fer - like comforts the sutlers couldn't get t'us back at the war, the greed bein' terr'ble.

"When I reached m'house, it be abandoned by m'famla and looted and otha'wise wrecked inside, and what couldn't be took be smashed. Refugees from the countr'side was all over the place and beddin' down in eva room. Some was in a panic cause a'the bombardment and a'fearin' it were gonna start up agin ana minute. Weren't no riotin' in the city but there were violence a'breakin' out here and there - people a'fightin' ova what they was a'stealin'. Couldn't git a meal nowhere, 'cause all the eatin' places been stole-out.

"Seemed t'me the whole cita was on the edge of panic, though. And I neva see'd such a flood a'wounded men ana'wheres - men comin' from the fightin' upcountra - hobblin' bein' carried, some half-dead and hunerds more a'lyin' in the streets and allyeways - most untreated and sufferin' and mana alreada in the Lord's arms beyond human help.

"M'heart sunk to m'feet that day. No one knowd where m'folks and m'sista'd got to. Neighbas I know'd couldn't help me none eitha, sayin' that all my kind left fer the countraside with all they could find after the house got looted. So, I wandad around for a while lookin' for 'em 'til I plumb gived up in the confusion. Spent the rest m'leave huntin' fer 'em in the countraside, t'no avail.

Dint wanna leave without 'em, but there weren't nothin I cud do. Hadn't et nothin' in two day and m'stomach was a'gnawin' on m'backbone and painin' me somethin' fierce. So, I jest walked all the way back to m'troop that be bivouacked with m'brigade 'bout eight mile north. Did a passel a'thinkin' along the way 'bout the famla, the war and things I seen in the cita. Neva HAVE found m'kin, though, not even t'this day."

*   *   *

Union Corporal Jesse Wade, Prisoner

"I joined the Union Army directly from my university studies. I was not for war, but I followed my dearest friends into it who believed profoundly in its legitimacy.

"Being in ranks did not interrupt my search for the war's meaning, as I considered the human fallibilities that had lead to it. I saw myself as merely passing through it as might a student his schooling.

"Then one strange day upon a battlefield, I experienced what some might have termed a coincidence. Yet I intuitively felt it to be God's intervention, His sign to me that He exists and that He sees us all in our spiritual nakedness and rebukes us for our violations of his intent, even if more reluctantly than we deserve.

"A priest in his cassock emerged from the smoke in front of me, a specter, staring into my eyes with disarming compassion, and then like a vapor he was gone. His look had shamed me into putting down my rifle, my conscience too wounded to carry it any longer. From that moment on I could not shoot anyone. The mere thought of doing so sickened me. I've wondered since if he appeared only to me or to others as well. I'm convinced that had he appeared to both armies, the war would have ended there and then."

*   *   *

The Advance: A Captured Yankee's Remembrance

"In the midst of battle, with our ears assaulted by a thousand furies, we paused.

"Preoccupied with the day's killing, we had not noticed a new army advancing beneath the direction of its Supreme Commander. Yet the rumble of its celestial guns now caused the Earth to tremble. Beneath our feet we felt its power about to humble the worst our pitiful arms could boast. And then came its missiles, millions upon millions, large and stinging, hail in rifle-sized calibers - painful, punishing, savage.

"The Earth had darkened. Now, the sky turned black.

"Our enemy also paused. The slaughter slackened as their troops, like ours, could do no more than cower. Horses shied, protesting and panicking. Our guns stilled. Suddenly like primeval creatures put to fight, we vainly sought every shelter - opposing uniforms be damned - but found none, our rage and blood lust blunted, our adrenaline pumping.

"The sky raged. Clawing lightning sought us out. Cyclonic winds stole air from our lungs.

"By the thousands, we fell to the ground, friends and enemies curled in fetal desperation, absorbing our hapless lots' pitiful agonies, yet those much less malevolent than hot lead and iron.

"The previously wounded screamed for succor, the dead ignored the day. With hands and arms over our heads, we endured our scourging. Opponents of only moments ago suffered side by side, weapons forsaken, lashed by frozen bullets that stung our senses even as they bruised our bodies.

"Fear balled in our throats. The wounded laid face-up, hidden beneath their hands. Hail pounded the immobilized, pulverizing their vision.

"Cracking lightning, crashing thunder - the sky cast down its anger relentlessly, our souls rent by the ear-splitting volume. We had offended God, insulted Him with our butchery, hurt Him with our arrogance. And now the bouncing missiles of His retribution buried us, blanketing the bloody earth, sending our chastened generals flying.

"How foolish must we have looked to Him, we whose mutual malice had motivated our hearts' contempts. How criminal and futile the war's insanity appeared to us. How stupid we appeared to ourselves, the icy bombardment driving home the point that by having subscribed to the violence we had acceded to and perpetuated the war. The ice and rain and tornadic winds ripped away our pridefulness and made us see a lesson that couldn't have been better taught.

"This was the way of the Old Testament, of its forceful God, who suffered men not who transgressed His Word. He was aloft in the heavens commanding this supernatural force. We knew it, felt it, and understood it. He was Father - chastising his errant children.

"And then, when the tempest became unendurable, it abated. The ice sheets vanished, the rain turned to a trickle and the following winds caressingly warmed us, as if reassuring us of His transcendent parenthood. But the shrieks and wailing from those damaged by His anger overpowered even those laid low by our weaponry, whose tormenting burdens his wrath had amplified.

"I opened my eyes. Another's peered into mine. The color of his uniform remained dissimilar, but his eyes told me such differences no longer mattered.

"The sky's blackness retreated, pursued by golden sunlight magnified a million times by suspended moisture not yet evaporated. Billions of tiny droplets reflected our disgrace. Physically drained, we sat or laid or stumbled with bewilderment and spiritual lethargy, our senses still held prisoner.

"Hurting, my body having been savagely assaulted, I eventually stood. So did my "enemy", and so did countless others across the whitened landscape that day, man by man, too humbled to reassert their antagonisms. He and I stared at each other, not knowing what to do next, except to accept our mutual punishments and walk away, our antagonisms momentarily nullified. And that is what those multitudes did - turned away and returned to their respective lines, carrying back their wounded while leaving their dead to God - retrieving along the way their weapons and battle flags, pride abandoned. Too bad the storm had not come sooner, before the killing had begun, before so many bodies lay wasted upon that earth.

"I walked away from war that night, understanding that my presence in ranks no longer represented idealism, let alone nobility, but the perpetuation of that which the Lord had protested that day. He had awakened my conscience, having given me the strength to defend it to the world. His message had been clear. I had made myself a brick in a false wall, but false walls cannot stand without bricks to support them. Why had I run from home in search of glory?

"The next day, I gave my life to Him.

"Weeks later, I roamed the countryside, seeking my place away from the warring world. Our warrior leaders, as I told my eventual Rebel captors, remained abroad pursuing violence against a Southern people I no longer cared to destroy."

* * *

Patchin'

We've become the most threadbare and patched-up Army on Earth. And that is why, given the chance, our men will spend much bivouac time sowing and stitching and trying either to put their abused uniforms (or what passes for uniforms) together again or reconstructing wearable items, using recovered civilian garb or military issue taken from the enemy. The boys call it "patchin."

Colors vary - gray to butternut (after bleaching and dying) to civilian patterns of all descriptions, with patches on knees, elbows or wherever needed. Coupled with patched blankets (for those who have blankets) roped over their shoulders, plus any number of hat and cap styles, jackets, and britches too short or long, we are a memorable sight.

"Patchin's" a constant activity. Early in the war, we were more uniformly butternut or gray or both, with a modicum of civilian wear, plus occasional modifications. Now we wear whatever we can using whatever we can find and repair. Only our kaleidoscopic diversity is uniform.

Besides sleeping at most opportunities, our men patch. They work at it diligently, demonstrating domestic skills otherwise attributed to their wives and lady folk.

Enemy uniforms are a boon no matter how obtained - from the dead or the reluctant. Naturally the other side's boys do not appreciate the humiliation of being stripped and held captive in underclothes, but necessity is necessity. Of course, not all of our boys enjoy the luxury of wearing underclothes, most of theirs having rotted away without available replacements. Enemy uniforms are easily bleached, the surviving color tending toward butternut or tan when bleached or mixed with natural nut dyes. Not always having a choice, we wear whatever colors result when dyes run out. Dying resources must be used sparingly.

Being as patched as the rest, my sewing skills have greatly improved. Shirt and jacket elbows are quick to wear away, and britches eventually lose their knees and seats. Although it can be a chore to find material enough to cover minor holes, it usually is a hardship to find material enough to entirely patch what goes over the fence last - or thread enough to repair torn seams, let alone tent-flap sized tears. Thread and needles are as valuable to us as gold to a banker, and every man jealousy guards his cache. I only wish the souls of the most exhausted and depressed among us could be patched as handily.

*   *   *

Child of Light

For every bird that sang in the trees of this forsaken Wilderness as many thoughts of home whispered in the tired Corporal's memory.

He laid against a tree, abandoned by his army and left for dead, his rifle across his lap, his shirt and jackets blood-soaked, his wounds aching. Yet all of his life had not yet pulsed from his body, and even now he felt renewed energy coursing through his limbs and vitals. Was Nature fooling him? Was he truly recovering, or were these his body's last desperate stirrings before it succumbed? He didn't know.

Around him the refuse of vicious fighting lay amidst the perished of both sides. Fires burned everywhere, consuming dry tinder, the screaming wounded and the mercifully dead. Those among them not yet claimed by the fire struggled for life - coughing, smoke-gagged, spitting, vomiting, crawling, agonizing, whimpering - most as much in need of water as salvation, water not at hand, but in the canteens of the dead, the wounded having long since exhausted theirs.

"My name is Alfred," the soldier mumbled, trying to convince himself that he, his name, and his life still existed, still possessed meaning; that he would not die an unknown soul among so many anonymous souls, never to be buried, his charred bones to fall apart amongst all the others that would lie hidden forever beneath the leaves of a hundred seasons.

"I am alive," he said and repeated many times, convincing himself, as he choked on smoke, that he had not yet passed into the realms of the horribly anointed.

Incredibly, screeching birds flitted from as yet untouched trees to other untouched trees, as if terrified that their sacred domains were being consumed. Their flight lifted the soldier's spirits, as if something of his soul were reaching out and away from his body, preceding his thoughts of places filled with cool waters and sublime safety. He felt as if he were moving unhindered through this dreamlike state surrounded by beautiful, boundless lands. Yet he still possessed awareness enough to know that delirium follows quickly upon loss of blood.

"Come, Alfred," voices whispered, "come to us where the immortal dwell."

He walked in this new dimension of brilliant flora, pausing here and there to touch a leaf, admire a wild blossom, commune with forces and energies unseen. Never had he so appreciated a flower's graceful intricacies or the teasing messages live overhead within swaying boughs of exotic descriptions. Never had he sensed such mysterious immensities.

He came upon a brook and listened to its playful waters that harbored a crystalline glaze, sensing a sentient aura about it, alive with innocence. He strolled between sunbeams, wondering what made them golden and why they pooled with molten majesty at his feet. He studied an ant scurrying across a slender tendril that reached skyward from the loam beneath, and wondered where it was destined. Reaching out to it with a diaphanous hand, he saw it merge with the light and realized that he, too, was light, a child of light.

He no longer hurt. No longer did he suffer wounds. No longer was he afraid that his mortal life was passing. And it mattered not to him that he might return to his mortal world of pain and fire before his transition was complete. For now he had glimpsed something greater and was satisfied that Earth amounted only to a moment of temporary value. Existence, he now understood, reached its zenith beyond his five Earthly senses and the hobbled knowledge they imparted. And then magically he was home again - his boyhood home. Once again, he WAS that boy.

Free once more of care and responsibility, he retraced his youthful footprints still embedded upon the past. Once more he wandered there, wondering as he used to about the origins of land and sky, stars and sun. Even his parents were there, but no longer aged but oblivious to him. He saw himself playing on the floor near their cabin's hearth, ever warm in the glow of its perpetual fires. The wondrous feelings and impressions of those exciting days of youthful exploration flooded back as he observed himself, his mother at their stove and his father at their table cleaning a hunting rifle. The soldier was happy again, as happy as he had ever been. But then the scene faded.

Now he drifted over majestic panoramas, still free of Earth and Earthly mortality, his dreamlike state continuing at one with everything above and below, his heart as light as cotton. But God balances all things. Moments later, the soldier settled upon a less happy scene, his adult home in the present, where his wife and children toiled in a corn patch - hoeing, raking, and weeding, their hands caked with reddish soil, the sun blazing down, his children's hands too small for such arduous but vital labor, all three souls too frail for straining in such heat. He studied his wife's face now sun-weathered and aged, her femininity dissolved in sweat, though she had been young and vibrant when he had left for soldier. He could see, in hurtful detail, how severely farm work had reduced her in his two-year absence - how it had bent her back, wrinkled her face's once graceful contours and shrunken her frame. This was HIS doing, he belatedly admitted to himself. Overcome with guilt, he faced the truth - that he should never have gone for soldier, that he had abandoned her and his progeny and secretly had gone to war for the adventure of it and to seek escape from his mundane existence, all the while feigning patriotism and noble intent. THAT had been the truth of it. Patriotism be damned, he had selfishly sought diversion!

He might have paid someone legally and beyond societal reproach to have served in his stead. Somehow, he could have found the money, perhaps borrowing it on the season's crops. Other farming couples had found ways around this issue when duty to country versus duty to family had raised its contentious head. But not with him, though she had begged him to consider their children's welfare first. And what had been his bogus rebuttal? That his conscience would not have permitted him to let others do his fighting for him? No, he had sought glory, in war the most foolish of pursuits. And as this scene faded, his heart throbbed with guilt for his family, Earth's realities now returning to condemn him.

He opened his eyes.

He had come back with agonizing suddenness, the tree trunk's bark digging into his back. His wounds savagely ached. Once again, he beheld in front of him and all around mortality's hideous human postures - men dead, others tortured with pain, fear, and threatened by fire. Smoke once again choked him. He coughed violently, doubling his torments. Before him, a strange wreck of an enemy soldier crawled up to him, reaching for his canteen!

"Water if'n y will," the man's parched throat croaked, "jest a little water...I promise."

The man's reddened eyes begged; his tortured face pleaded. Blood-caked dirt clung to his clot-dripping nose. Saliva oozed from the corners of his mouth, both conditions forming a topography of ongoing suffering. His face, ears, and both hands were badly burned, his uniform singed to rags.

"Please," he gasped, "jest a little..."

The Corporal, his pain lessening somewhat, stared back, his facial muscles taut, seeing mirrored in his enemy's face his own wretched fortunes. What difference did it now make that this poor fellow had been an enemy by Richmond's and Washington's edict? He was hardly anyone's enemy anymore, just another Devil-begotten mortal in this endless war whose insides dragged along in the dirt and tinder beneath him, collecting corruption and beset by flies, his humanity devastated.

"Cain't help ya none, soldier," the Corporal mumbled. "It be empty, I b'lieve."

Even if it hadn't been empty, he couldn't have helped the man. He couldn't have moved to access the canteen on his belt and pinned behind him against the tree. The wounded man would have to try to loosen it, though his weakened body might defeat him. And what of the intolerable pain the effort might cause both? Yet the Corporal felt compassion for this so-called "enemy" who, like him, was now made of damaged flesh and diminishing blood.

"Bless ya anyway, Corporal," the man stammered; "I guess it wouldn't do me no good nohow. Gonna die in a minute. I ken feel it. Woulda gimme jest a little comfort, that's all. My thirst is so great. How come, if I'm dyin', I'm still so thirsty? Don't make no sense, do it?"

"I'm dyin', too," the Corporal confessed, "but I got no thirst left, jest an addled brain and many regrets."

"We all got THEM," the soldier agreed. "You seen Glory yet?"

"Ya, I seen it. You?"

"No."

"Don't be a'worryin' none. It be a lovely place…peaceful and kindly. We'll both be there presently."

The man dragged himself closer to the Corporal, as if seeking the comfort and temporary security of being close to a fellow human in these final moments of his life. Yet, in his near-delirium, he reached again for the canteen, forgetting that it was supposedly empty. With his remaining strength, he yanked it away, pulled out its plug and, with trembling hands, put it to his lips. Tilting his head back, he gulped as if it were filled, as if it were overflowing down the sides of his mouth and chin, as if it were cool, refreshing and life-sustaining."

"Let him be," the Corporal thought, having felt no pain upon the canteen's release, "let him think he's a'gettin' want he needs."

Then, the Corporal looked down, amazed. There HAD been water in the canteen after all! Embarrassed, he realized that the bullet that had pierced its neck had not emptied it, as he had assumed. Powerless, he watched water actually spill down the man's chin, fearing the man might now believe he had been deceived and take revenge.

"Din't know," the Corporal mumbled…"believed that bullet had drained it. Don't consider me badly, friend."

"I don't," the man mumbled in return, his words bubbling out. "I don't hold nothin' agin ana man n'more."

"Where ya be from?"

"Kentucky."

"Me, too," the Corporal revealed. "How come we're a'fightin' each otha?"

"Don't matta n'more," the man responded, his lips barely parting. "Fools we been…jest fools. Got water now. That be all I care fer."

But drinking water was not what the man should have done, thirst or not. Momentarily, as he was about to thank his benefactor, his eyes widened in shock. Fiery pains laced through what remained of his savaged innards. Grimacing, his lips stretching wide in agony revealing his tobacco-stained teeth, he clutched his belly and rolled over in mortal agony. Straining to save himself the shame of howling like a mangled cur, he yielded nonetheless to this most primitive of Nature's imperatives. With a final agonized convulsion, he screamed-out his life and then laid still, the water he had drunk seeping from his shredded stomach.

The Corporal looked on, feeling cold, his vision dimming. Regretting the man's passing, he realized his time must also be near.

"Where eva you've gone ova there in that beautiful place," he told the lifeless man, "I'll be a'followin'. Thought I might make it through...but don't look like it. Skeer'd a little. Shouldn't be, cause I seen the Glory I be comin' to, but I'm still a might. Can't feel nothin' from the neck down, not even my hurt. Shuttin' down, I reckon. Be stiff in an hour, if'n the fires don't be get me first."

Flames crept closer, their heat intense.

"Guess I won't be seein' my family agin...not in this life. None of 'em'll eva know where my bones be...prob'ly be right here all cov'd in weeds and the like foreva. But I seen Glory...you, too, b'now, m'friend. Won't be enemies there. We ken chaw t'getha on good tobaccy and jaw 'bout whateva's our notion...jest friends in peace and rest...sheda fear and safe agin."

He listened to the birds, noting that long after he would hear them, and long after the fires died, they would twitter as now, as if they understood that his passing had not meant oblivion for him, but merely a change of form.

Tuckered, his breathing shallow, he closed his eyes once more, craving the sweet dreams he had dreamed only minutes earlier. And then he was staring at himself from outside of himself, noting how poignant he appeared lying blood-soaked against the tree while bathed in pools of golden light.

"Come to us, Alfred," a new, youthful but recognizable voice gently urged him; "come to our side for a moment more."

He turned his head. His brother, Connor, killed a year earlier in another battle near this very wilderness, stood in another pool of golden light: It's all right, Alfred...everything will be all right."

But, Connor was not twenty-eight anymore as on the day of his passing. Now, he was only eight.

"We will be children again, Alfred," his brother assured him. "It'll be a miracle."

To reassure himself that he, too, was no longer alive, the Corporal studied his own hands. They were small again, those of a seven year-old, as they had been in his and his brother's "wonder" days, when the world and their lives had been made of the the richest and most exciting adventures.

"Come with me, Alfred, come with," his brother persuaded him. "'Tis no longer a dream. We have a new friend...once a soldier, too. You gave him water, Now, he, too is seven."

"But my family, Connor...what will become of THEM?"

"They will be well, Alfred. They will survive and their lives will be good. Elsa will always love you and Billie and Liz will prosper and think of you proudly."

"How will they know I have died, Connor?"

"Bye and bye, Alfred. Come, now. Let's run."

"But, I deceived 'em, Connor. I was wrong t'leave 'em."

"You are forgiven, Alfred. Everyone here has been forgiven."

Reassured by his brother's sincerity, the Corporal studied his mortal body once more, reluctant to leave it behind, much like a personal possession he had known well for so long.

"It will not know the flames," Connor promised. "Your new body is for here."

No longer did Earthly attachments matter. In all respects, Alfred was a child again.

He and Connor raced together through the wilderness of a new world where amazing discoveries and ceaseless wonders thrilled each, while another seven year-old boy named Henry, formerly a Union soldier, tagged behind them. Mysteries abounded, exciting their boyish curiosities. They were "forever' children in a dimension replicating the mortal haunts of their youth, but this time boundlessly, their innocent souls rejoicing. They played in golden light permeating an infinite sky and stood before limitless vistas, where there had never been, and would never be, wars.

"You will see Billie and Liz grow, Alfred," Conner revealed, "and you will be with them and Elma always. Come on...let's have more fun! Time doesn't exist here. It will be day when we want it to be day and night when we want it to be night. Let's go see Ma and Paw and Gramps and Meemaw. They're waiting here to see YOU."

Save for Elma and his children, Alfred let go of everything mortal in mind and memory preventing him from giving himself completely to his new experience. Ironically, despite his new youthful countenance, his love for his family thrived anew, and he sensed that this playful realm of warm, benevolent light, a Providential gift, would forever fill him with good cheer and spiritual strength - with the youthful Connor and Henry there to accompany him.

———

How do I, Royal Chapman, know this story is true in all of its details? Because Sergeant Alfred Williamson told it to me and others around a campfire the night before he left on furlough. Yes, rescued from the fires by men from his regiment, he returned to Earth and to that body against the tree by special dispensation from countermanding powers governing such things. In fact, his mortal wounds healed within two weeks, astounding hospital physicians who declared his recovery "miraculous". I spoke to one later who, still incredulous, confirmed it.

Anxious to see his family's welfare, he sauntered away from our encampment waving good-bye, his eyes tear-filled, his knapsack bulging with rare provisions his respectful friends in arms had donated for his children. His positive presence had left all uplifted and joyful, though overwhelmed by his story's implications. I must admit that never had I met a more inspiring soul.

His beaming face and eyes had conveyed every assurance of the immortality he had described. To those seated around the campfire that night and facing combat soon, his tale could not have been more comforting, even reassuring, though many there pondered its probability.

We watched him leave, our eyes misty with wonder. One veteran, a religious soul, turned to me saying, "He be bound fer somethin' the Lord be wantin' awful bad. Don't know what, but you ken feel it."

I knew what it would be because Williamson had confided it to me - the "Powers" having confided it to him. His destiny would be a church and a simple white collar.

* * *

Serpent

Today I stand in the midst of a field hospital in a meadow beneath the open sky. As I gaze upon the poignant scene before me my thoughts drift to such scenes in the past and I weigh the awful costs of this war, my senses offended by the suffering all around me; the stench of gangrene and mangled viscera, the moaning, the cries, the occasional screaming of those tormented's intolerable pain. What price hubris, I ask for these two nations of common blood? What incurable maliciousness have each unleashed upon the other that has withered our pity for each other's agonies? What mutilations have we wreaked upon each other's souls that will mar and prejudice us against each other for generations? Perhaps the opposites who suffer here are the ones in this war who have found common ground at last and belatedly would reject all that has brought them here. Would that both capitals' leaders were moved by them.

Unattended, little protected from the broiling sun, their numbers overwhelm medical personnel, our Southern and their Federal lying mixed by the hundreds, enemies no longer. Moaning and squirming in excruciation, countless beg choruslike for water, for their mamas, for God to take them. Others lay pleading for Heaven's mercy. Still others writhe in pitiful contortions. The delirious crawl over one another like snakes in a nest in search of succor, heedless of all but their miseries. Many vomit and evacuate their bowels and bladders involuntarily. Unable to tend to bodily functions or savaged by dysentery, they soil themselves with devastating embarrassment while many bleed out, confused and inconsolable. We are compelled to tolerate the putrid stench of it all, and therein lies our curse - we have accustomed ourselves to it and thereby have accommodated it. The entire human panorama undulates like a vast carpet of restless serpents. Medical orderlies pray for gentle winds to waft the smells away, the air being still, the humid heat oppressive. But now as if answering them, the atmosphere begins to move to the west beneath a darkening horizon threatening rain. Building thunderheads march eastward in a boiling alliance sure to result in a deluge that will bring cooling relief to many in the meadow.

Cannon fire from the battlefield three miles way has died away, as nature's artillery booms and grumbles, vibrating the bloody waters beneath this sea of human discord. Many now fear that lightning, the bane of infantrymen and the helpless wounded, will threaten those suffering clusters who shelter in the shade of strike-inviting trees and wooded copses dotting the landscape. Others remain too pained to care.

I overhead an agonized soldier nearby, barely able to form words, confess to a man next to him, "Hope lightnin' takes me. Cain't abide m'pain no more. Don't care if'n it bakes me black." His legs, a pathetic tangle of flesh and bone, have taken the full impact of solid shot. Festering tissue has blackened with gangrene. Shattered leg bones protrude, all attesting to his impending mortality.

"This is hopeless," an exhausted surgeon complains to me. "We cannot possibly attend to them all. Our medical capabilities have never been up to this war."

No, they have not. We haven't the manpower nor the necessary medicines or anesthetics to repair but a modicum of all this mutilation. Sometimes I think these surgeons cannot go on without mentally and spritiually disintegrating. For hours they probe and dig for bullets and shrapnel. They suture and amputate until all becomes a blur.

"I fall asleep on my feet," he relates, "then awaken, yet I cannot remember what I'm doing even as the anguish of the wretched souls beneath my knives and saws torments my ears. I've had enough of this insanity, but I cannot cease my work. My oath compels me to stay the course."

I look on, depressed by the waste of what we witness. The surgeon confessed that initially he had not been for war, yet the gods of power had made his reservations moot, his protests akin to a child weeping in the wind.

Yonder a newspaper artist busies himself sketching an overview of what he sees so that his readers might better appreciate what hubris in high places has wrought here. Yet not with charcoal, ink or pencil could he convey the sounds and the smell of it. Knowing his readership, he must understand that no matter what draws, much of the self-consumed public will consider it only passively. Yet should he attempt to accurately portray the reality of it by starkly detailing the gore and suffering, he would offend that same conservative public. I consider such public hypocrisy obnoxious. It is their war, after all. Their kin are here. This is their investment, their currency buying their fledgling Confederacy its threatened existence.

An artilleryman, middle-aged Corporal Ezra Pike, one of our boys, is a simple scratch farmer who has lost a leg to shrapnel. He told me a story yesterday. It concerns another artilleryman, a private who lost his arms in the same incident that felled Pike – the exploding of a cannon's breach upon firing.

Said Pike, the Private awakened from his delirium in this very meadow, but miraculously without the pain he had endured for two days. Nor did the Private awaken with the odor of gangrene in his nostrils that signified to him that he would spend the rest of his days without arms. Originally disoriented by the concussion of the exploding cannon's breach that had torn his arms away, the Private had not initially appreciated the severity of his injuries. The blast had burned and broken eight men the instant a gunner had pulled the weapon's lanyard. Having perceived his stubs while writhing in fleeting moments of lucidity, the Private had cursed his fate, passing in and out of consciousness, praying for death. But this time upon reawakening his pain had vanished. He found his arms were whole again. He could move them as freely as before, when only hours earlier he could not have moved a finger without Hell reerupting across his roasted body. Feeling rejuvenated yet not understanding why, his legs conveyed strength. That very morning he had not the strength to lift a fork.

All around him, he witnessed the nearly colorless images of men of both uniforms slowly trudge in the same direction. Odd, he thought, that they should be doing so. Why did they appear as they did? Was it drifting smoke from the battlefield that clouded the Air? They carried no weapons. Were they now orderlies assigned to assist medical personnel and on their way to receive more wounded to carry to still vacant areas in this once flower-graced meadow? Then with sudden clarity he realized the truth. Although he had heard of amazing recoveries among wounded elsewhere in this war, how virtually dead men revived to return to ranks or, eventually, home, this was different. These men, unless receiving special dispensation, would not be returning to Earthly homes. It had to do with "the book", that supernatural archive of names soldiers believed was kept by Heavenly monitors who listed in separate columns all destined to perish or survive the war. No man could escape the book's edict. If it indicated that on a certain date at a certain time a man would pass, even in his sleep, so it would be. It was the Lord's way of permitting His celestial servants to affect a soldiers' destiny in accordance with His wishes, such times and dates having been preordained by Him at the time of every man's birth. Superstition, you say? No, the Corporal insisted, instinct.

The Private cautiously rose to his feet, balancing himself with his now unaffected arms. He could not have seen how he resembled the men he beheld, while far and wide the prostrated human condition he also observed remained substantial in appearance. Why had they not all been killed outright, he wondered, those torrents of hot lead and iron pouring across the battlefield that day had been unimaginable! He had seen so many felled en masse, whole companies devastated before even nearing their objectives. That anyone has survived unscathed defied reason. It did no good for him to lament his peculiar fate. That artillery exploded upon firing was not uncommon, that state of metallurgy being what it was.

"Where is ever'one goin'?" he asked a passing soldier, a boy in federal garb. "Over there", the boy responded, pointing.

The Private looked: "Where? I don't see nothin'!"

"You don't?" the boy remarked. "Why, it's as plain as you are to me."

The Private looked again, intensely studying the area being pointed to: "Still cain't see nothin'," he admitted, "'ceptin' all these here fellas headin' in that direction."

"I believe that means you are not quite ready yet," the Union boy advised. "You will be in just a bit after your sight has adjusted to our new world; then you will see it, like I did."

"New world? Do the war be quit?" the Private asked. "That be why? They be a'musterin out and a'headin' home?"

"Truth be known," the boy answered "That IS where they are headin' ... home."

"Lordy," the Private responded excitedly, "that mean you and me ain't enemies no more. Neva' shoulda been anyhow. That be the work a'men who oughta be shot fer it." Then, he looked down, noticing a curiosity; a boot he recognized, then another. Looking more closely, he realized they were his, belonging to his body that lay there with its two fire-blackened arm stubs bent upwards like charred claws, the remains of burnt muscles locked in rigor. Remarkably, he was neither alarmed nor shaken by the horror of it and no longer concerned, beset instead by a restful calm. He looked pleadingly into the young soldier's sympathetic eyes, realization bleaching his bewilderment.

"It took me a while, too," the boy said, "when I awoke and my pain was gone and my body was whole again, like yours is now. I believed I was dreaming. Then it come to me; I wasn't. Look yonder to where I'm pointing; see it now?"

The Private stared. A ball of shimmering white light, brilliant yet soothing to the eyes, hovered just above the ground, golden hues outlining a portal in its midst. Side by side, soldiers of once opposing allegiances filed through it, but to what, the Private wondered? Beyond the portal beckoned the most beautiful azure sky he had ever beheld, a shade that transcended the Earth's most memorable.

I see it now," the Private said, "but what do it be?"

"Home," soldier replied, "yours, mine and theirs. Out true Home."

In that moment the Private instinctively understood: "I know now," he said. "I unda'stand. But m'family? What'll b'come a'm'wife and youngins? Youngins be jest four and three."

"They will live out their destinies just as your is now being fulfilled," the soldier answered. "That is what I was told about my kin by an old soldier walking toward the light. Come, let us go Home together."

The Private followed the young soldier through the portal, unseen by those still in the physical. A shining figure, his luminosity distinct from the portal's, stood in its arch, welcoming all. His nearing presence warmed the pair, ingratiating both with an overpowering sense of peace and well-being. As they approached, the figure held out his arms to them in a paternal greeting. In the breathtaking background, well beyond the portal's entrance, where indescribable colors of inridescent intensity graced an ethereal landscape, soldiers by the score singing old hymns gathered by a glimmering and equally beautiful river. He remembered the words. The war had not diminished their meaning.

And there the single-legged Corporal's story concluded.

"But how do you know any of this?" I asked him. "How could you know, even if it were true?" "Oh, it be true enuff," he guaranteed me, "'cause I were there. I be one of those the man at the doorway turned back, said my sit'ation were rethought and they was a'givin' me back m'life. Wouldn't tell me what fer, but fer some purpose I 'spose I might discover lata on or neva know.

But I told him I done all ready know'd I bled out back there. So's I asked him how they intended t'put life back in a man like me with no more blood in him? He said t'me, as the Lord had produced wine from nothin'ness, y'all shall have blood agin. And here I be, one legged maybe, but alive t'Earth agin' and goin' to m'home down here. I ain't complainin'. I got lovin' folk anxious fer me and waitin'. Gonna eat a hot meal agin and sleep in a actul bed, maybe fer a hunnerd year."

He related one thing more: before entering the portal, the Private and the boy soldier paused, each observing the Earthly sky for the final time. Sodden clouds embraced the sun while thunder rumbled distantly. A breeze of Heavenly origin caressed them gently, its fragrance spellbinding. The rain fell – not in a deluge, but softly, wetting them not.

And so his story ended.

*   *   *

In the Beauty of the Lilies

Testimonies

From the Journals
of Confederate Correspondent

Royal K. Chapman

1862-1864

With collected Post-War Commentaries

added by

Jerrod Cushing

Department of History
The Citadel

Testimonies

Chaplain Willard Hayes

Major Tory Smith

Front Rank

Viewpoints – Confederate Veterans & Southern Civilians Speak

The Rank & File Speak – Conscientious Objections to War

From a Chapman Letter to Jefferson Davis

Chapman's Last Entry

Afterthought

The War Between the States - No Matter the Cause

*   *   *

In the Beauty of the Lilies

"They served, fought and saw much that, in the
end, gave them pause and caused
them to wonder much about God."

Chaplain Willard Hayes

A Time of Leaves

It is said the past is prelude.

"I, for one, say this...we
all are mere pawns in the chess
games of mad gods."

Major Tory Smith

Infantry-CSA
1863

Front Rank

"Things come back to ya in passing...things ya thought about or seen...and they come back jest as clear as they was then...and ya cain't b'lieve ya neva forget 'em,...that yer mind a'kept 'em all locked away...like it wanted 'em saved no matta how hurtful they was...like they was worth savin'. Some was, but most not. Neva liked bein' in the front rank--always got 'deefened or m'hair signed by the boys firin' over m'shoulder b'hind me. Near lost m' head oncet! Weren't b'cause I lost m'mind, though. Some fool r'cruit b'hind me's rifle went off b'fore he were ready. Spoil't a good slouch hat, it did - and t'think I traded a feller a tote a'good t'bacca for it, too! Poor r'cruit were kil't in the head an hour later. Was when we got within range of that enemy works, the storms of lead that come out of it tore men around me to pieces. The Yanks turned us around, they did, and I drug back to our lines covered with otha' men's bone chips and guts and brains and blood and feces. The gods laughed at us that day. Yes, I b'lieve they be as mad a some say they be."

Corporal Thomas Lynch
Infantry

Viewpoints
Confederate Veterans & Southern
Civilians Speak

A Senior Officer: "The war was never about slavery, sir, but about economics, tariffs and the fears of Northern business men that the South might eventually have provided them with dynamic economic competition domestically and via foreign trade. I never owned, slaves, sir, therefore I cannot speak too openly about it for fear of reprisals by fanatical Northern authorities occupying us."

A Colonel: "We, the Southern states, fight to maintain the right to chart our own destiny concerning our peculiar institution, free of federal coercion either by law or force that does not understand it. Slavery will erode of its own inertia despite all appearances to the contrary and in far shorter time than anticipated by Northern Abolitionists. As it is, it is proving an expensive, failing instrument of economic means. The South wishes to mechanize and will, if left alone. But I doubt that Northern industrialists who fear the competition from such economic expansion wish to patiently abide us, but push Lincoln and his party instead for ever-more war, lest they sacrifice their gigantic war profits and their monopolies be cleaved."

A Captain: If I were a Northern industrialist, how could I lie in the face of obvious truth, plain to any observer, by saying that I am not a salve master, when, in fact, I own factories filled with exploited white immigrant captives of my avarice and neglect who live and work virtually incarcerated in their work places. And consider the great Northern drafting of thousands of innocent, non-English speaking cannon fodder fresh off the boats and conveniently ignorant of our national politics? How moral their exploiters and the god-like Lincoln.

A Major: "Yes, I am a slave-owner, as prejudicial in all cases as that term is. But had not I acquired them, someone of lesser conscience might not have treated them with the same dutiful considerations. Your Northern industrialists treat their ignorant immigrant labor with far less concern. I am not the vicious sort portrayed by Northern propagandists who incite and inflame the Northern population against us, and neither are those owners with whom I associate. Many of my plantation people are virtual family members, are considered as such and have always been. There are abusers, I admit, and they should be punished by law, but what morality would it serve to release every black man in the South into the winds without provisions made for their equitable absorption into society? Contending that summarily doing away with the institution would produce a panacea for them is absurd. Any such abolition must be instituted gradually to accommodate the economic transformations that must result. The omniscient Lincoln does not appear to understand that nor care. To do so would be politically inconvenient. It is unbelievable that so contemptuous of reason is he that he would send armies against his own people to expunge it."

A Lieutenant: "My family, too, owns what Northerners would term slaves, but none are coerced into staying on. Yet where else could they go and what else could they do? All are well cared for in all respects and some paid modest stipends yearly as befits their needs. Does this make us devils or any less moral than Northern employers who even now bind their workers to them (and to their company stores) with inadequate pay and no amenities? My family taught black children and certain of their parents to read; they also taught rudimentary accounting principles that they might oversee certain elements of cotton production. True, not all plantation-owners do what we do for our people, but neither do Northern factory owners do for theirs and those immigrants who cannot speak or read English - all of whom are virtually indentured servants in every respect, save for the meager pay that so many are forced by economic necessity to put back into company stores for vital commodities at inflated cost."

A Sergeant: "Well, them there Abolitionists got their way, and now millions of Black folk with nothin' save their skins is bein' loosed on Northern soil among white folk who don't want 'em and will neva accept 'em into their ways as equals, and the Yankees damn well know it. Lincoln jest cruelly used 'em as political tools. But to accuse me a'fightin' for big plantation owners is the same as sayin' that all the Yankees that was felled by our guns died t'keep them big Northern factory owners rich and fat. But, I wager that if the facts be known, that'd actually be the truth of it. I fit the Yankees 'cause they come down here to put their boot on our necks. If they'da stayed t'home and in their beds, a half a million boys, theirs and ours, would still be alive with their loved ones this minute."

A Corporal (college educated): "Even now, the assimilation of Negroes into Northern society can be accomplished only after generations of arduous tutelage, that even then may never be fully accomplished. We are dealing with a people who, generally, because of their circumstances, will be seen as alien to white society and culture and who Northerners will resent having to accept. The souls of black folk will eternally scream to be released to their ancient ethos but they, in turn, in order to adapt, will experience turmoil in rejecting it. Imagine yourself struggling so within in forced circumstances comprising your present existence. Imagine your dilemma and confusion. Physical freedom guarantees them not much else, except perhaps a limited freedom of choice and may prove a cruel burden for generations."

A Private: "I ain't no slaver. None of us vet'rans I know is. Wouldn'ta wanna t'be one and neva had no d'sire fer it. I fight 'cause them Yanks come down here t'burn us out, which they're proceedin' t'do with a vengeance, simple as that. No, back home, I were m'own slave master. You try t'work the land I got and you'd be a'slavin' fer it, too, night and day. Why, some of them plantation Blacks I know'd lived betta than I done then 'er do now, and had it easier. My land whipped me unmerciful ev'ra season. Them Northern people don't unda'stand us down here ana betta than we'uns unda'stand them. Since that were fact, I reckon them and us was a'fightin' a war of plain ign'erance."

A Physician: "Yes, my generation of slave-holders lives with an institution that exists not of their construction but by their business culture's perpetuation, nonetheless making them and their forebearers equally responsible for it. It must eventually go the way of Rome. Yet wounded Northern soldiers frequently tell me that despite their government's propaganda, they fight not to eradicate slavery but for three general reasons: simply because they were marched down here, because they enlisted for the adventure of it and the pay, and due to social pressures. Like most of their kind, save for a scattering of idealists, the educated and non-educated confessed to being indifferent about our institution. Some will admit, as we believe, that the issue has been exploited by Lincoln's government for purely political purposes, and to disguise the Northern business's economic designs. I find that intriguing but am too involved with attempting to mend mutilated bodies to concern myself with politics."

A Sutler: "Being a practical man and not and idealist, I would ask our Northern invaders this: Why should any of you have risked your lives and, thereby, the possible destitution of your families for the debatable sake of any particular race? Why should anyone have done so when both our societies should have trusted to God to have found better ways to resolve the issues between us? And why was invading our lands so necessity . . . to stifle rebellion and prevent, for altruistic reasons, the South's independence? We believe Fort Sumter was Lincoln's excuse and the North's purpose to destroy us in order to prevent us for generations from becoming a strong economic competitor. Big businessmen have no conscience. The dollar is their flag. They will always submerge the weaker merchant. Slavery is a decrepit institution that would have perished on its own, simply because the trends of our Southern society and economy were pointing in other directions, but its black labor force is a prize I'm sure Northern industry covets. Still the common man, not the big businessman, suffers for it. Why should you and we have killed each other by the countless thousands, and continue to do so, year in and year out, before demanding solutions short of war? That the cream of both our youth have perished or been maimed at each other's hands for the sakes of a people who can in no way compensate either of our societies for the loss of that generations' promise and talents makes sense only to Abolitionist zealots - most of whom, I would say, have done little of the dying. In principle, it is akin to emptying the wells of two entire cities for one man's thirst - Lincoln's."

A Chaplain: "Religion gives legitimacy and impetus to the war only in the wildest of imaginations. I've heard Lincoln speak candidly concerning slavery, as much as we can depend upon any politician to speak candidly about anything. Based upon his views as I heard him express them and despite his oft-used reference to Providence in relationship to the supposed purity of the Federal cause, I would vouch that he planned, after winning the war, to return as many as possible of the South's black population to Africa or to Caribbean colonies. In either respect, he would remove them from white civilization, believing the Black man could never successfully amalgamate. Despite his wartime talk, I am convinced he does not believe the Negro can blend with white culture. I overheard him say as much in prewar utterances, some of his asides being confidential. He must have comprehended that if white plantation owners could have affordably replaced their people with mechanization they would have considered federal compensations in exchange, thus ending the institution, the people becoming wards of the federal government for repatriation and resettlement, an astronomically cheaper solution for the North than the costs of war. But I'm told Lincoln would have rejected such a plan had it been proposed by Southern emissaries, sending troops south instead having always been his intent. Despite Sumter, for him to have discouraged secession by force of arms was hardly an imaginative option for such a supposedly intelligent and compassionate icon. I see his military response as having exposed two sinister truths: this war continues to be the North's ruthless political theater with Lincoln its leading thespian."

Another Chaplain: "Unfortunately, the war was human nature falling into its own trap of resorting to human devices before appealing through long meditation to the counsel of God. Yes, Northern intransigence on any number of matters aggravated Southern patience, but trusting to Him gave way to guns, though history records that incidents of shooting by both sides occurred long before Sumter. I believe Lincoln's minions stampeded him into war by constructing the inevitable scenario for it. This would require hours of explanation from my point of view. But I am convinced that, had the matter been given to God, a solution would have come. I've heard Lincoln was a railroad attorney before the war and therefore associated with many Northern tycoons. Is this true?"

A Wounded Veteran: "They say up North that I'm fighting down here to preserve slavery, as if I would give up my life for it or, as it has happened, my leg for plantation owners' profits. I would ask, what truly is every Yankee who burns our crops and farms and pillages our villages and towns for his side's criminal element up north? Makes about as much damned sense. Let Northerners come down here now and see what their armies have wrought. Let them see the destroyed bridges and farms and granaries and homes and mills and shops and cities and so much more, all this supposedly conducted to speed the war's conclusion by destroying our society's capacity to

497

support the war. I think it was simply, as was the war they began by their invasion, an excuse to destroy us and keep us down for a century. Let them nobly seek victory in our destitution."

A Seaman: "That's right! Let them Northern folk see what their generals - Sherman and Sheridan and the like - done down here for God and country before they condemn us fer what we's fightin' fer, like they trula know'd 'er cares, and maybe they'd start t'fall off'n their high horses. If'n they'd turn theirselves around and skeedadle back home, the war'd quit faster than you can jumped a stump. Anotha thing that bothas me sorely 'bout all their righteous flag-wavin' - just so's they do a little thinkin' 'stead all that self-righteous caterwaulin' - I be a genuine, bonafidee American as ana creature a'God in Union blue and always were and jest as fiercla' proud of it! By they way, I were a powder monkey aboard the CSA Merrimac."

A Farmer: "Never gived a damn 'bout slavery. Neva know'd much about it. Had some black friends who was poor scratch farmas like me, freed men they was and good farmas, too. We traded and socialized back then. Called ar'selves the Dirt Grays, 'cause if'n y'mixed us t'getha, that's what yould git. In the war, I had two good friends, a shop keepa and a school teacha, both shot standin' right next t' me and dead now. I s'vived when there was lots a'times a shouldn'ta, but don't know how come. Guess the good Lord was a'wantin' me t'keep farmin' and t'take care of m'liitle girl and stay loyal t'my wife, which I always done. They been damn-near starvin' these last months. My wife took bad sick for ova'workin' our land and the hard labor she done with me gone fer two year. If'n I die sick in the war 'er be kilt on some field somewheres, and they send my carcass home - which they'da never be doin' fer a private like me - she'd have t'keep plowin' and plantin' right ova' where she buried me,'cause she'd have t'use eva inch a plantin' soil jest t'keep 'ar youngin' whole."

Cavalry Officer: "Take mana prisoners now and then "Mazes me, those Yanks do, when say they neva seen a black man before. They's usualla big fellers from up in the high North, not them littler fellows from the East. Hell, I ain't neva seen them big farm fields up North, eitha', that' 'sposed t'be so rich and black I hear so much about. The Yanks is decent fellows mostly. Neva have a hard word fer us. They ask why we was a'fightin' them and we asked them why they's a'fightin' us. Mostly, when ya git right down to it, thems and us don't really know, ceptin' that they be down here n'all. We hear what 'ar politicians is tellin' us and they hear what theirs is tellin' them, but maybe b'tween us, I suspect we neva had no real differences, not man t'man. Christian farmas be a'talkin' t'Christian farmas 'bout plantin' and crops and soils and seeds, and we d'cided that we's both a'dyin' fer mattas b'tween highfalutin' men and concerns that they oughta be doin' their own damn fightin' and dyin' fer. No, we jest be little toy soldiers they kept a'movin' around on their big chess boards for their own greed 'er pride 'e both - and we poor folk both got weaseled inta killin' each other for it. So, we smoked 'ar tobaccy t'gtha and talked about 'ar homes and familas. And when they'd have t'go back to their lines afta prisoner exchange, we's all thinkin' the same thing . . . if'n we eva git each otha in our rifle sights, are we gonna pull 'ar triggers?"

A Confederate Congressman: "I am convinced that early on, but for the feuding and infighting among our generals, governors and politicians, we possessed the military power to have won the war. Personal grudges, including Davis's, snatched victory from our teeth on several occasions,

Davis, having toted the heaviest cares, being principally responsible for our misfortunes. He should have tolerated none of the dissension. These deficiencies, plus the machinations of incompetent appointees, have resulted in lost opportunities and outright blunders, personal considerations having on occasion taken precedence over the war effort and policies that should have assured victory. But even should we win, the South will face great political difficulties, what with some states desiring to rejoin the Union, our case on the battlefield having been successfully made. Others, especially our deep South states, might stubbornly elect to remain separated and independent. And, even then within those states, opinions might radically vary, economics being a principle factor possibly resulting in chaos. It is not fanciful to suppose that, at some future time, fiery sentiments one way or the other might cause a split within the Confederacy itself, possibly leading to a Southern civil conflict. Some of our more mischievous governors never, or refuses to concede the fundamental principle that to assure a successful national war effort, all our states must unselfishly pool their resources, not horde them. Within limits, our vaunted ideal of independent state governance, perhaps appropriate in peacetime, should be subordinated to a single common goal. By acting as sovereign entities unto themselves, and selfishly withholding vital war supplies from our armies in the field, they materially collaborate with defeat."

A Discharged Army Surgeon: "I saw the costs of war from the grimmest aspects, having spent three years sawing away mangled arms, legs, feet, hands, fingers and toes, probing tissue and viscera for bullets and shrapnel while my patients writhed and kicked in the agonies of absolute Hell. Their cries still haunt me while awake and sleeping. We never possessed enough anesthetics or anything else of absolute medical necessity. Our methods and means were hopelessly crude. I lost countless men under my scalpel and saws, stuffing guts back into shredded abdomens and eyeballs into sockets and repositioning shattered stomachs, bladders, livers and kidneys and brains slipping from shattered skulls - all the while praying these organs would magically heal and revive themselves. I excised gangrenous flesh, picked bone splinters from smashed muscles and attempted to reconnect sinew. But infection was always our bane. I worked in appalling stink and countless hours, covered with my patients' gore, smeared with their feces and soaked through with THEIR urine and blood. Never could or did I save as many lives as I would have wished. Had we had more time with each soul, we might have better and more professionally attended their wounds, but always after battles, there were too many needing quick surgeries and life-sustaining amputations. We simply couldn't give time to skillful and prolonged repair procedures. Do I believe our fledgling nation's struggle was worth all that? I am not a politician. I understand nothing of violence save its aftermath. Ask me instead if I believe prayer would have been worth more - and do so before I escape again today into my whiskey."

A General: "If we had Grant's manpower, resources and coffers to rely upon, we could drive those people from the Confederacy and could have done so early on. Though we have not yet gained our independence free and clear, our South has made its point, though at a supernatural cost we did not foresee. We've stood against Lincoln's invasion and his usurpation of federal power, not to mention His violation of his own Constitution's spirit and intent. We created and fight for a Confederate Constitution of superior quality, yet I and my fellow former generals are frequently accused by some of being profligate with lives, of throwing too many men into the grinder of battle because generals are heartless by nature. Let me declare to those critics that I will feel the blood of every man and boy I've lost on my hands until I, too, die. We were forced into this war by Lincoln. Someone had to make battlefield decisions. I admit that some of those decisions were unfortunate, but we are only human. Such results are every general's Cross to bear. But let me tell you what is truly heartless; heartless are powerful, profiteering men who have no country though they pretend the opposite, who only pose as politicians so they can manipulate government for their own purposes and also only pose as patriots for personal political or financial gain. No, these men are leeches and blood-suckers. They know loyalty to only one flag and its three colors . . . power, greed and gold. Such men have always existed. They do so now and always will. It is men like me and those I command that fate places in harms' way, the safe and secure always expecting us to transcend ourselves, as if our authority has made us supernatural. In the name of profit, not patriotism, such men encourage and begin wars, set in motion the causes for them, support violent reactions to them then reap the personal benefits. Sumter gave them the excuse to begin their infamy in earnest. Always, because of them, and in the South's case, firebrands who took their bait, men like me and hundreds of thousands of others came forward to preserve the Confederacy and save its lands from the depredations and miseries we knew our enemy would eventually attempt to wreak upon our peoples. And I and my kind are heartless? If I am so, what monsters are they? Lincoln's legacy should be about these infamies he cannot escape. They should be attached to him like the stench of putrefaction to a corpse, for it will be the only scent Southerners will remember of him. Perhaps, history will reveal or hide his collusion with those who profited, the South's remaining manpower, white and black, soon to be cheaply available for exploitation, its dreams of economic transition and prosperity dashed and looted. But then what do I actually know? I was a heartless general."

A Married Woman: "My husband's come safely home. Was all I and ar' youngin's ever asked of God."

The Rank & File Speak
Conscientious Objections to War

I can tell you very personally that war wears dearly on a soldier's soul. No matter what the cause nor his dogged dedication to comrades and country, deep down his soul eventually rejects the conditions of mind and body under which he daily labors. Months and years of combat produce a cynicism that bores into every fiber of his being. All seems to him an interminable dirge, a waste and a sacrilege. Realty has become a stalking threat. He tires and sickens of the killing. He has seen and absorbed too much. He has killed and witnessed the bloody obliteration of those close to him, their humanness made coldly irrelevant. His conscience quietly but incessantly screams, "Enough," but his incarceration persists, the only escape for him being impossible except by desertion, an option honor abhors. For harried civilians, wartime experiences can be no less grim, not even desertion being possible. The following observations should be considered in these contexts, for beneath their veneer of apparent desolation, soldiers and civilians alike nurture their patriotism and loyalty to the South and its striving for Independence. And until Lee stands him down, Johnny Reb will stubbornly resist the Federal invasion and destruction of his land, as his ancestors withstood the armies of George The third.

Corporal Quinton Dobson
Infantry

"I pulled the trigger, then felt m'conscience pang. There was somethin' wrong in this work . . . somethin' very wrong . . . and then, m'conscience scourged me 'til I wept in shame. The man I jest shot groveled in the agonies a'Hell and I was the Evil."

Anonymous

Sometimes, y'don't wanna' think 'bout war no more. Sometimes, y'jest wanna' let it lay. Y'ain't the same man no more, ana'way, and y'don't wanna recall the killer y'was. Y'wouldn't do it agin' no how, no way, but it eats on ya that y'cain't figure why y'did it a'tall when y'did. Y'd'cide y'was jest too young t'uv know'd better then and y'get frustrated and powerful angry 'cause y'wanna' choke the gen'rals that used yer youth and yer ideals and yer tender years, and yer awful, dreadful ign'ernce t'start and finish somethin' terr'ble neitha side shoulda' got inta t'b'gin with.

Corporal Otis Gentry
Artillery—CSA

"Yes, my conscience also torments me greatly for doin' what I know'd in m'heart I shouldn'ta done - gotten inta' this mess a'tall. The onla' thing this war's gonna do is quiet all its pertinent issua's by force of arms, nary b'reason 'ner necessary compromise - as it oughta' be. Time was on ever'one's side even afta' Sumta', but Sumta' was not the cause - not even the spark. The fuse'd been set so long ago in Jeffa'sons' time and was burnin' eva' since. Sumta' was the excuse. No, the fires'd been lit in Congress years b'fore, where selfish and cowardly men was a'feared t'take off their prideful coats and roll up their sleeves in good faith for peace - and crim'nally, cast the America's fate to the mendacious winds."

Lieutenant E.G. Edmunds Infantry

"Some say it were all inevitable, that no matta' how much talkin' we might yet have done, it still woulda' happened. They say it was somethin' we were fated to r'move from our craw - the diseased pride of sectionalism, that is. But the states' rights issua will return one day to haunt our successors, I guarantee it - when the power of federal gova'ment suffocates people. And then, as Jefferson advised, they'll feel compelled, even against their hearts and betta' 'natchas, to cleanse, if necessary, their house and kill its corruption with the lime of belated r'form. Yet the damage done in the interim - the lost national potential and missed oppa'tunitas' t'do great things - will take its toll. There'll always be that kinda' price t'pay for a Democracy's maintenance. Yes, our 'futcha history might yet r'sult in anotha' civil war - class agin' class, race agin' race - b'cause even then, the lessons of OUR war t'day will a'been lost t'memora' - and no one in those times'll unda'stand what it meant to us and cost OUR misled generations."

Captain Hubble Baline
Cavalry

"I might be only a private, but I chose t'be one, t'know the war from the common man's view. It has taught me about conscience and sacrilege in ways none of the philosophers at university could. The sacrilege of having killed men in this war will have forever changed me - the cost so many of us have grudgingly paid for not daring to bring shame and disgrace upon the good names of our families and loved ones, lest our conscientious objections make them and us outcasts in decent society. You and I know how strong the compulsion can be to avoid that eternal stigma. But a man should never go against his conscience, never. He does so only at mortal risk to his eternal soul. For conscience, I've learned, is God's Divine spark within man. Quench it, and one proceeds forever in darkness."

Private Quentin Eastman
Infantry

"Violate conscience? To do so is worse than whatever disgrace one might encounter for doing so - for standing up for one's beliefs. At least, when one stands for something even against war - one has something solid to hold to. A man can take heart when he knows the right despite enduring the worst and most profane criticism. But, going against oneself eventually leaves a man with nothing but emptiness inside and terrible loneliness. And it is such loneliness and emptiness that goes down hardest of all."

Major Andrew Smith
Surgeon

"When I take stock a'the killin' I done in this war and the widas' and orphans I made, I feel I b'trayed God."

Corporal Owen Stanley
Sharpshooter

"The Lord, at this moment, must be weeping into His hands for the way this blessed land, North and South, has profaned His hopes by resorting to war instead of His Word. And even I, in my participation, am a contributor to His disappointment - for I have gone along to save souls, when I should have protested the war beforehand to have saved every soul now in it. We are all disappointments to Him in a single, awful aggregate. To see and hear a battlefield after a fight, to smell it and walk through it, is enough to sicken one's soul for a lifetime. What we do to one another in the name of principle and idealism is not only unforgivable but obscene, and insanely so. Those of us who cause the bloody viscera or wade through it can only hope that the monstrous killing now being done ironically brings this war to a swifter conclusion.

Yet what a blasphemous rationalization even THAT is. But, anymore, the point of who wins is moot - for we ALL have lost and ARE lost anymore. No rationalization on Earth can justify what we do and have done to each other for four long years - not in God's eyes - and He is all that matters."

Cornelius Everett
Chaplain

"Today, I spoke to prisoners taken in the latest fighting. They are like us - fellow countrymen, with so much in common with us that I cannot be anything but ashamed of our contentiousness. One was a school teacher, as was I; the other, a farmer - simple men and both glad to be out of it. We were glad FOR them and wished we were them. We took no pride that we had won our skirmish with their fellows, nor did we take pride any longer in winning at all. We are long past that, for winning no longer is the point. Survival is - purely and simply. The original issues of this war have been clouded with too much blood and made profane by too much suffering. And the nobility of causes has long since been lost to the battlefield's impartial brutality and further dissipated by the agonies both sides have mutually shared."

Captain Benton Talmadge

From a letter to his wife, Andrea,
from Sergeant Jeffry Stark

"The otha' day somma' our boys simpla' went home, Andy. They jest put down their rifles and walked away. They was finished with it all - with the sickness and constant hunga' and the senseless' of the killin', ana'more. We watched 'em go, includin' our officas', all of us envyin' their courage and conviction - 'cause I know'd ever' one of'em and none of 'em done it outta' cowardice. They all been three-year vet'rans who done more for their land that ana'one coulda' asked of 'em. Captain Moore, our commandin' offica', said that in a 'poignant way, they spoke'd fer all of us—in a pra'fond way too, he said. Our offica's coulda raised their pistols and shot'em all down right in their backs and been just'fied unda' military law - and woulda' been exonerated by the arma' for ana' wrong-doin'. But they done watched 'em go, like they was wishin' they coulda' gone with 'em. They jest stood there, their shoulders stooped like they was mightly tucka'd, and I thought right then that they was carryin' some 'unbarable weight—like for the mana' dead already per'ashed under their command. And, Andy, I swear - I firmla' b'lieve the Lord neva' woulda' let 'em shoot - even if they'da been hankerin' to. No, mam, neva."

Your lovin' Jeffry

"Would that the peoples of both sides could be forcibly marched through these fields after a single day of slaughter. This war might there and then be ended, when the politicians responsible for it sniffed the putrifyin' bodies and the people's anger and sensed the desperate malice in their recriminations. We are so manipulated by propaganda from political institutions. Why do we let ourselves be led so, even in violation of our own good and common sense? It is very much a mystery."

Daniel Passford
Correspondent

"By perverse and aboriginal standards of honor and Comradeship - which, on one hand, shame and embarrass me, yet, on the other, form a compelling imperative I can neither ignore nor turn from - I am condemned to the present course of things where ever they lead and for however long - to my comrades and their faith in me and to my fidelity to them - and to my loyalty to our bonds of eternal friendship, which have made us alter egos through these terrible war years, one with the other. For, by all standards, we are brothers as never before and made companions in common suffering. And, thus, are we so with our "enemies" across the way - our American brothers for whom we silently consider in quiet moments, as we do for ourselves, when both sides' tears of conscience wash away the petty hatreds each have been obliged by shameful circumstance to embrace. By these mystical threads linking me to those of my uniform, I can do no less, even while expecting nothing more from my conscience save constant reproach for the costs of it all - and despite my misgivings concerning the war and my rantings against it that you knew so well. I am, in a sense, an eagle in a cage - an officer sworn to his mystically confining oath. Forgive my hypocrisy, if you can, Anna - and may God forgive me more."

Captain Warren Sikes
From a letter to his
Sister, Anna

"I apologize for these maudlin introspections, my dearest Alta, but you above all others have always been my rock. If my brother Joshua still were alive, I would not burden him with these thoughts, but would trust to you to know my soul in these matters, since the war has affected us both and our thinking is such similar ways. I have had the privilege, if it can rightly be called such, to confirm our convic convictions about this war in the mud of it, as it were. Perhaps for that reason alone, if for no others, some constructive value has come from it. It is, and has been, all we feared and detested. There is no nobility to it and even less chivalry. No, it has degraded into a killing contest that tries men's souls to the utmost and reduces most I've seen to only shades above animals. But they have been driven to that state by those conducting the war on both sides - who refuse to come to the table to compromise for peace. Generals have no concern for lives, which, to them, are no more than leaves to be consumed by fire in the pursuit and conduct of operations - else there could not possibly be a contest of this horrendous butchery and scope. For contest is what it is - one of egos at the highest command and political levels. You, in volunteering your time in our military hospitals, see the war from its most poignant aspects. I see it in the context of bridge and fortification-building. But I also see it in the aftermath of battles, which - with all my resources - I would prevent YOU from seeing, lest your very sanity be jeopardized. It is enough to witness the wounded streaming back from the fighting bearing every state and kind of wound - from light to hideous. But I assume you see enough of these from your perspective, as well as all other insidious shades and shadows of battle's aftermath. Keep well, Alta, and bide. We shall endure to protest this war afterwords lest we shirk our moral obligations to the maimed and the dead. Hug our little Billie, who, by now, must be six. May he and his progeny never know the tragedies you and I have witnessed."

Your devoted husband,
Patrick

"Today, in the dusk followin' the fightin', jest afta' we made our bivouacs, the regimental band come through. Guess they were tryin' to boost-up our morale - some ign'ernt offica's notion, we reckoned. But we was in no mood for entatainments, bein' sick and hungry and alotta men hurt and cleanin' and patchin' their torments. Our offica's shoulda' know'd our mood'd be like that afta' ever' fight - and that the men onla' wanna' be left t'themselves and quiet. We done LOST a whole THIRDA' our compana' - dead and wounded! Some of our boys shoulda gone t'hospital but r'fused, bein' resentful a'surgeons and otha'wise suspicious. Those of us who did listen t'the music did so more outta' curiousity than inter'st - glum with little r'action. Was thinking' of friends now gone and silent. And I spose that b'cause of it, the band figured they wasn't bein' 'preciated like they oughta' been and was bein' put upon instead. A smatterin' of clappin's all they got fer their r'ward, as mosta' our men thought they was jest a purely damned nuisance. And since they wasn't getting' no attention 'er compliments, they done quit in the middle of a tune and walked off - and good riddance, somma' our boys called after 'em. Guess we done sunk 'perda low in the last few months. Guess the whole arma' has. Tired, we are - and wore out - jest plain wore out and sick a'this life-suckin' war."

Private Hubie Nance
Infantry

"We was fishin' outta' this here creek. Was a nice day in the countra'side, 'cause the arma' weren't getting' us nothin'. Our whole hungra' regiment was bivouacked 'bout a mile back. Was three of us there by the creek, and we'd already hooked some nice ones that'd fry-up real good. Then, comes this sound a'talkin' from the other bank 'about fifty yard downstream. Figured it were somma' our boys that'd been scoutin' 'round out there - but it weren't. Was somma' the fellers we'd been a'fightin' fer nigh on to three year! They come a saunterin' to the creek with their own poles and a'fixin' t'do what we was a'doin'. They din't see us right off, 'cause they was lookin' anxious t'git' to it. Well, we wasn't 'bout to up and run, 'cause the fishin' was good—and since they was downstream, they wasn't gonna' bother our catches. So, we jest sat there. They din't have no guns along and we din't neither. And I 'spose none of us was gonna' fight each otha' with fishin' poles—well, actualla', they was small tree branches we was usin' fer poles - and them, too. Then, they seen us - sorta' jest stood there froze fer a spell, not knowin' what t'do. Well, we done waved to 'em and they done waved back. Then, with us eyein' them and them eyin' us, they got t'puttin' their lines in the wata'. We kept a'watchin' each otha' fer a spell, then, Bill Jenks, one of OUR boys, done hollered for 'em to come with us but they hollered back that they didn't think they oughta', seein' as how they'd have to cross over t'our side of creek and didn't wanna' git' captured. Well, what ended up was, we both moved closer', 'til we was directly across from each otha'. Nice fellers they were, and we talked and fished 'fer an hour more. Got t'speakin' 'bout a lotta' things and found out we shared a whole lot in common - so much so that it were a damn shame that we'd be a'tryin' t'kill each otha' the next day. They thought so, too. Got t'thinkin' 'bout it alot afta'wards and feelin' bad 'bout it - I mean, 'ceptin' for them talkin' a little funny with them Yankee accents n'all, they was decent folk. Next fight the arma' got inta' was a hard one for me - got a bead a sev'ral of our enemies but jest couldn't pull the trigger - kept a'seein' those fishin' fellers we'd met and come t'like. Wasn't much for soldierin' afta' that - got t'viewin' all the killin' and slaughter a diff'ernt way. Got t'botherin' me bad that we shouldn't a been fightin' each otha' a'tall. We was ALL Amer'cans, wasn't we? Was all the same blood in the Lord's eyes! Yes, sir . . . it got t'botherin' me real bad."

Sergeant Robert Burrows
Infantry

"Had a bead on one of our enemy yesterday - had 'em plain in my sights at sixty yard. 'Course, he had a bead on ME - same distance. We was lookin' at each otha', eyeball t'eyeball. I din't wanna' kill him and he di'n't wanna' kill me - could feel it, and I know'd he coulda, too. Jest pointed our rifles down and stared at each otha' a minute, then hunka'd down in our trenches agin'. M'hands was a'shakin'. They din't wanna' do what duty told 'em they oughta."

Corporal Raford Sutton
Sharpshooter

"Carried ona' their wounded inta' our lines last night. Poor feller' be gut-shot. Dead he were jest a spell lata, but I felt good 'bout what I done—betta' than I have this whole damn war. Hell, he was a poor private, jest like me."

Private Henry Kendall
Infantry

"Was spoonin' last night 'cause a'the cold. Frost was ever'where and the boys were a'huddlin' close by fires, what wasn't sleepin'. Them's that were was a'spoonin' up agin' each'otha' t'keep warm, but the last man on each end was the most miser'ble, bein' warm on one side and cold on the otha', if'n y'ken 'magine it. Somma' 'em was a'grumblin' that there be hardla' no blankets t'go' round n'more—somma' 'em not havin' ana'. Well, with no food t'et fer 'bout three day, 'ceptin' what they'd hoarded 'er picked off'n the land, their moods was bad. Most was sicka' the war and reada' t'go home. Don't know what makes 'em stay, 'ceptin' pride and plain 'ole feisty stubbornness. That's what makes ME stay - 'cause I ain't givin' up 'til I ain't got but rock t'throw at them other people - and then I'll be a'throwin' plenta'! This here war could end right now if'n they'd jest pick up and go home - then we could jaw at each otha', 'steada killin' eachotha' ova' what we cain"t settle right off. I got my share a'killin' and I'm sicka' it - and so's the otha' boys. But if'n more fightin's what those otha' people want, we still got plenta' left—and 'anuff amm'anition t'make 'ar point. Ain't no thoughta' winnin' n'more, if'n y'git right down t'it with mosta' our boys, the fightin's the issa'. As long as we be a'fightin', we ain't a'losin', not t'OUR thinkin'. Lot'sa folks might not be understandin' that, and some's lost heart, but that's ''cause they ain't here. Still n'all, I'd much ratha' be quit of it and t'home. But, it be plain that it all be up t'them otha' people - w'got n'choice n'more."

Sergeant Leslie Kurts
Infantry

"What do I thinka' this war? Rub two sticks agin' yer arse . . . that be what I thinka' it. We been a'killin' each otha' fer three long year, and whata' we got . . . a torn-up country with nothin' t'show fer it 'ceptin' rottin' bodies in a hun'erd-thousand graves - and a lot not even buried. Y'asked what I thinka' it . . . well, THAT be what I thinka' it. I think we oughta 'git Davis and Lincoln out here, give 'em fifty-yard start and go 'fer 'em BOTH with double-canister . . . and end this whole damn thing!"

Private Ben Duggan
Artillery

"I ain't been home in two year . . . no, two and a half. M'wife's dead five months and m'kin's got m'youngins' . . .and ona' THEM be deathla' sick b'the last letter I got. Cain't read none, but our offica's ken. Worra's been eatin' m'soul t'the nub, but I gotta' stay r'cher. Cain't be sparin' a man - that's how bad things be. That's what this here war's come 'ta. Cain't be sparin' a man . . . . Lordy, it ain't right . . . ain't right a'tall."

Corporal Burt Watley

"Last leave I got's onla' 'cause they done shot m'ship out from unda' me. Swum' ashore, I did. Ain't got any otha' ships's FER' us . . . not even an old ram. I'd take ana'thin' right now t'git back on . . . even a barge . . .'cause I don't like what I see ashore. People's des'pert here - a'stealin' and a'cheatin' from each otha' - done lost their fear a'God. Bad ashore, it is. Quakes a man's spirit."

Seaman Chill Davis
Navy

"The cold nights in winter and the damps . . . that's what keeps stickin' with me . . . on my horse on picket duty in the darkness or twilight or dawn . . . my horse a'shiverin' so bad I thought he'd fall . . . and me n'better . . . no warm clothin' . . . nothin' warm t'eat 'ner drink . . . my hand 'bout frozen to m'scatta' gun . . . m'feet numb . . .'skerd t'move out from b'hind cova' . . . m'horse too froze and weara' to move ana'way . . . stuck t'm'saddle . . .m'face a'frosted 'bove the bandana coverin' ever'thin' b'low m'eyes . . . lookin' for the enemy, if'n he be out there . . . Lord, Lord, that be what I rememba' most . . . misera' plain and simple . . . ever'boda' miser'ble, the whole reg'ament . . . bivouacked in ice and hunka'd' round fires a'tryin' t'stave off the cold . . . but it be a'creepin' inta' 'yer bones as sure as sin . . . that be what Bein' on vidette in the winter's ter'ble duta' . . . bones still ache from it . . . but we gotta' . . . got n'choice . . . got t'suffa' it 'cause I be a soldier . . . and sufferins' be what a soldier does best. Wonda, now, if it's all been worth it."

Corporal Willie Shepherd
Cavalry

"Troops trudgin' along, their heads bowed agin' the wind and rain and cold and snow . . . it be what I see when I close my eyes and r'memba' back ana'more . . . all that d'votion t'Cause and countra' . . . all them lives and s'mana' fellers buried where nobody ken r'call. Seems s'long ago, now, but ain't it weren't . . . and one day it'll all be gone like it neva were but eva' afta be a'hauntin' us. I got out wounded. Was luckier than most."

Sergeant T.R. Judd
Infantry

"I look at m'gone legs and wonda' if'n I shoulda' run the otha' way that day them r'cruiters come t'get me. But the bastards - they come with all the men they already hooked . . . shamed me, they did, inta' comin' with 'em. Slick, them fellers was . . . damn slick . . . and m'honor cost me m'legs."

Private Victor Sigo
Infantry

"Jest stand, now, at m'wife and youngins graves feelin' shamed . . . that I left 'em t'go fight, when I shoulda' stayed t'home. Disease got 'em while I was away. There be nobody t'help 'em . . . the docta' gone for soldier, too . . . so they died alone in their agonies with me n'where when they needed me . . . fer somethin' bein' lost ana'ways. Now, I jest stand at their graves; nothin' left in me t'weep out, like I be mada a'wood and cold inside. Seen s'much dyin' . . . s'damn much dyin' . . . got nothin' left inside. Shoulda' stayed t'home, like she wanted me to . . . like she begged me t'do . . . if only . . ."

Lieutenant Justin Maples
Artillery

Buried our Chaplain today. Looked at his dead body and begun thinking, which, I'm told, a man in war should never ever do. Poor critter, he was - 'kilt by a ball plum through his skull; went in below his left eye and come out the back of his head with most everything in it - a common occurrence when the head takes a ball. The Lord sure pays his servants in hard currency."

Sergeant Porter Thomas
Engineers

"Sad how there'll be a man in yer outfit y'kinda ignore' or never take serious. Lost a man like that t'day, and we're all kinda sad about it. Never paid him much heed while he were ALIVE, but now he's getting' to us in death - and we're a'feelin' ashamed of ourselves - us vet'rans - and low 'cause a'what we done to him and the way we done it - jest 'cause he weren't no vet'ran like us and we din't think he d'served no r'spect for it - like we was gods 'er somethin', a'judgin him the way we done. Hell, I ain't never cried fer no man, not even 'fer a kilt friend let alone the likes a HIM, not since this foul war begun, but I guess I ain't as hard as I thought this war's made me, 'cause I been sheddin' tears all day fer that feller - like the whole damn war was a'fin'lla comin' outta' me - and fer that I thank the Lord, 'cause I were sure my conscience done turned t'rock even three year back. He were a'smilin' feller, never had no bad word fer no one - was patient and kindly - and we shunned him, ana'way. Lord, I feel terr'ble 'bout it and jest plain sick inside. And I ain't the onla' one. The Lord done brings y'low fer yer vanity and pride - I mean He truly brings y'low for the sin of it - like a lesson to ya y'ull never 'fergit - and y'know y'truly d'serve ever'bit of. We need this damn war t'quit - b'fore it turns us all t'rock inside."

Corporal Alias Thatcher
Infantry

"Got a letter from m'wife t'day. M'brother, Karl, was killed last month. Hope it weren't my bullet that put him under. He was on the otha' side of this here argument we been fightin over, but he was a good man. Got caught up in conscription. Didn't want war no more than me. Shame. Damn, shame. Were a man of fine words. Spoke alot 'bout religion. Never made as much sense t"me who weren't as faithful as it done t'him, though - and the war's done killed off what little b'lief I had left. Seen t'much in all the fightin' and sufferin' that contradicts the Good Word, seems t'me - 'specially 'bout love and mercy and such. Couldn't figure no more - and still cain't - what kinda' love let's so much death and misery abound. I know we got free will - or so says our Chaplain. He lays the whole war to it. And I spose Karl woulda' 'greed. But, no, it jest be too confusin' and deep fer me, ana'more. I got a simpler brain. But he were a brave man and died a b'liever, I reckon. Feel pity fer him, though. He were such an innocent feller in his faith - like a poor dumb lamb a'tryin' t'outrun a stampedin' cattle herd. But I'll miss him . . . surely will."

Private Able Dalton
Infantry

"Corp'al Billie fell t'day. Never thought nothin' could kill that man. Been with the troop two year and never once wounded. I 'spose even HE got t'blievin' in his own immortality, 'cause we sure did. Was the kind of man who could walk down the barrel of a Howitzer jest b'fore it went off and come walkin' back out without a scratch. Weren't the fightin' that killed him, though. Lightin' hit a tree near where we was mounted durin' a storm t'day - a branch come down and took him clean off his horse. Skull and neck crushed. Heck, that weren't no way fer Billie t'go - not HIM! Ain't nothin' fair in war, damn it . . . nothin'."

Corporal Joe Chance
Cavalry

"Ever'time we see a man pray b'fore a fight, sure as not he ends up bein' buried the next day. Makes us superstitious, sure does. Get t'fearin' t'pray 'cause of it - like ifn y'do, the Lord'll take a likin' t'ya and take ya home! Makes y'think—the war's gone on fer so long that maybe bein' dead's the onla' way yer gonna' get out of it.

Private Wilbur Leach
Infantry

"I thought sure I'd lose m'faith b'fore the war ends, but I haven't yet. The longer it goes on, the more a mystery God becomes, 'cause the more I see, the less I understand Him until I give'd up tryin'. Now, I feel calmer 'bout things. Put everything in HIS hands. I figure whatever will be, will be. A great peace came over me when I did. Weren't afraid of livn' no more and weren't as afraid of dyin'. It were like I seen a beautiful place somewhere - a special peace and loveliness - and I r'membered it - or thought I did. Was my home, but not my Earthly home. Had m'doubts b'fore I felt and seen that, but not afterwords . . . never afterwords. The boys said I were a changed man after that. Guess they was right. Am still changin'.

Private Junior Evers
Medical Corps

"Passed a lot a dead feller's t'day. Was off the side of the road as we was trudgin' by. Whole brigade was on the march after the fightin' of yesterday. Poor fellers. There'd been fightin' 'cross this here road we was on, and these boys was still where they fell, there's and 'arn, the battle's leftovers all around 'em in caps and canteens and papers and jackets and trash and the like. Somebody'd already picked up their rifles. Was jest a'layin' there in all sorts a positions, they was, some contorted up - some jest layin' peaceful—some on their backs with their arms up and kinda stiff, like they was reachin' fer somethin' - others face down so's you could hardly see their 'espessions—some with their eyes wide open and their bodies startin' t'bloat, tongues a'swellin' outta their mouths - some with their legs crossed at their ankles and their clothes all tusseled up, like a bunch a'human vultures'd done gone through their pockets and seams a'searchin' fer valu'bles and stealin' what they could get. Was always des'acratin' the dead like that, they was. But leafs was already a'coverin' them boys up, jest a'blowin' up next to 'em by the genteel wind - sorta' protectin' their privacy, y'see, outta' decency, y'might say. Figured they'd all be covered b'fore nightfall, and if'n nobody buried 'em - which they prob'ly won't - their bones'd be there next year at this time, somewhere in the grass n'weeds fer somebody t'stumble over. Flies was a'buzzin' 'round 'em ever'where - them damn things - a'crawlin' in and outta' their ears and noses and mouths and gatherin' where they was mutilated - a'layin' eggs. Wondered if I'd be a'lookin' like that some day. Prob'ly would, odds makin' it likely. But these boys - mostly . . . well, sir . . . they be so young, y'see—so very, very young. Lord, God, it don't seem fair . . . not fair a'tall. Oh' their mothers'd be a'weepin' when they never come home. And somma' them poor women'd never know what happened t'their sons. They'd jest gone fer soldier and done vanished.

Don't never wanna' hear all that wailin' back home . . . don't never wanna' hear it ever. I b'lieve it'd break me. I'm a hard ole vet'ran, no doubt . . . but, yes, sir . . . I b'lieve it would."

Sergeant Mervin Douty
Infantry

"I can't explain how the rain brings me into melancholy when I think of our boys beneath it somewhere beyond our ken. The soporific patter of it upon the roof and the gentle rumblings of distant thunder are mesmerizing, and I wish only to sit and close my eyes, trying somehow to part time and distance in these autumn times before winter, that Johnathan, my husband, might hear me and return my most private meanderings of mind and care. To be married to a soldier this late in the war heightens my fears and apprehensions for him. Please, Lord, not now, at this late date - not disaster for him now when this tragedy must be ending soon, after three years away. I could not bear it. I could not survive it."

Mrs. Anna Madison
From her Diary

"We know the end is coming but cannot bring ourselves to face it. The men speak of it not, remaining glum and grim and withdrawn, lest the costs of the past four years seem futile and the dying for nothing - as if all those sacred lives are being thrown away, our dead surely to be forgotten in time by succeeding generations. We cannot believe it has come to this . . . surely not to this. My hand trembles as I write, my stained journal already having absorbed its sad four-year share of silent tears. Four terrible years – yet in truth, who wins this war or loses it no longer matters as much as the end of the blood-letting. Too long it has gone on - far too long and far beyond both sides' most grievous expectations. Triumph or defeat - we who survive it will be going home . . . home . . . the sound of it is as the siren call of a haunting angelic chorus."

Captain Hubert Holt
Infantry

"Be it all worth it? Doubt it. The most weary among us is lookin' for the end a'things. Ever'body's tuckered, worn down. Ain't n'sense to it n'more. Was once, but n'more. Lot's boys are willin' t'go on, but I ain't. Both sides shoulda' spent four years doin' more talkin' and less shootin'. But arrogance, pride, and stubbornness - all contributed, y'see. Somma' the boys say we made our point - that we wouldn'ta been worth nothin' as men if'n we hadn't. Well, we surela' done that, and I ain't a bit sorry fer it. But there be an end fer ever'thin' unda' Heaven. I'm jest a'wonderin', though . . . who's gonna' care for all the graves we done left along the way . . . and who's gonna' r'member' the one's w'never had time t'marker 'ner bury?"

Sergeant Alvin White
Infantry

"No more sufferin, that's what the war's end'll mean. No more sleeping in damp and cold 'er walkin' freezin' picket lines in the winds a'winta' . . . no more hunga' and starvin' er' vomtin' out rotten rations when they DID finalla' git food t'us . . . no more dysentery and bein' sick all the time and otha'wise feelin' poorly . . . no more people tellin' y'what t'do and when t'do it . . . . no more havin' t'kill and bein' kilt' . . . no more watchin' canister and minié-balls rip and tear yer friends t'pulp 'er watchin' 'em dyin' in yer arms 'er seein' boys die who b'too young t'serve and shoulda' neva' been let to . . . no more losin' 'cause y'ain't got anuff' amm'anition t'fight with . . . no more listenin' to the shriekin' and cryin' of the wounded at night . . . no more dreadin' if'n y'was eva' gonna' see yer wife and youngin's agin' or if'n y'd be alive by sunset the next day 'er if'n y'd git' a decent burial 'er get dumped in a hole like most done . . . 'er

511

if'n yer kin'd eva' know'd where they dumped ya t'plant a flower in r'mem'bernce of ya . . . 'er wonderin' if'n yer famla' were well 'er sick 'er needin' y'sorely . . .er if'n yer mail's got through 'er the torture a'why y'weren't hearin' from 'em fer months . . . 'er dreadin' the damn surgeons and all the maimed a'layin' in them open hospitals in the agonies a'Hell and damnation afta' a big fight with most of 'em knowin' they'd never be got to b'fore they died a'screamin' out their pain . . . 'er the quiet sufferin' t'themselves and silently slippin' away 'cause they be ova'looked . . . and no more drillin' all day and marchin' 'til yer feet bleed and pain terrible and y'sleep on 'em as y'trudge along miles afta' miles, neva' knowin' where yer goin' and maybe t'Hell . . . and no more r'treatin' ' . . . no—jest t'home and quiet, and real beds agin' and peacefulness . . . and sleep."

Anonymous

"If'n peace comes, mosta' our boys won't know what t'do with it . . . 'cause they be SOLDIERS . . . some of 'em fer' four long years. Peace'll come as a scary mys'try, 'cause they'll b'havin' t'try t'be human agin', like they used t'be b'fore the war . . . but half 'em won't r'memba' what that be like n'more . . . hell, most cain't r'memba' even now!"

Sergeant Bill Courtney
Mule Skinner

"When they done furl our flags, it'll come outta me in a gush . . . won't be able t'stop it . . . couldn't fer nothin'! I won't be the onla' one, though, and none of us'll be ashamed fer it. It all come t'the same thing - we din't wanna' t'quit . . . t'give up . . . but quitin's all we'll have left—it and painful memor'as a'duty faithfulla' p'formed and honor valiantly served - as our livin' could swear to and our dead could testify. 'Ar army's fortunes is goin' so bad . . . the terr'blest kinda' low there eva' could be."

Sergeant Walter Sine
Artillery

"Dear Mandy - we was a'headin' back home, crossin' some fields we done fought ova' a year back 'er more - found a tintype in the grass. Some bones was still around where it laid with a dried-up belt and cartridge box, a canteen and a half-rotted kepis with a hole right through it and bloodied 'round the edges with rusty leavings. There be a soldier's shirt under the hole and a weathered image of a pretty young miss next to it. I see there was hope frozen in her eyes and faded likeness that would never come true anymore. Takes no need saying anything 'bout the way his ended up, I'm thinking . . . like a hundred other souls I remember who perished alongside me."

From A Fragmentary Letter - Author Unknown

"When I return home to you, Dora, I will try for both our sakes to put the war behind me, but I will need your help and, more vitally, your generous forbearance. There are many images and sounds of war that may haunt my sleep and days and come between us. Just give me time, Dora. Just give me time."

Colonel Archie Travis
Army Surgeon

"I must somehow explain this war to my students. God help me sort the truth of it, lest to them I cannot explain it nor to myself reconcile its immensity. I doubt if we shall ever be able to reconcile any of it even a century from now."

Captain Calvin Hobbs
Infantry

"Fer us when we git back, there prob'ly won't be no parades, jest folks tryin' t'survive and bein' down and desperate. We'll jest drift back quiet like but not as a unit 'cause there ain't anuff of us left of 'ar regiment to be a unit. No, we'll jest drift back lookin' no betta than scarecrows and some of us not lookin' THAT good. We'll come back by ones 'er twos threes n'fours with nobody taken much notice, I'm, figurin', like what we gived fer our country neva meant much to 'em, but it ain't gonna be their faults. They'll still be a'fightin' their kinda war and there's won't be ova when ours be. They'll be a'fightin' to keep body and soul alive and their youngin's, too. But, fer us, it'll be a sorry feelin', the worst sorriest and loneliest feelin' we eva knowd."

Anonymous

From a Chapman Letter
to Jefferson Davis

Sir,

When this tragedy ends there will be mourning and cries in the night from the anguished who will see their sons and kin no more. And there will be waiting for word from those at arms who may never come home, their fates unknown. Lord, I cannot imagine a crueler ordeal for those who wait for them.

For years there will be wives who hang on every approaching footstep and upon the opening of every door. Their existences will be haunted by worry and, later, by uncertainty and eventually by desperation. For they will know not whether to conduct their lives as wives or widows, and their children will grow without the fathers they once knew or had yet to meet. Nor will their mothers know whether to remarry or risk their former husbands' eventual reappearance. Some men, their souls twisted by war, will abandon their families forever.

Win or lose, reconstruction will require years and, perhaps, generations. If conducted in victory, the challenge will be welcomed. If undertaken in defeat, then we must rely as never before upon God's charity.

Men will come home to ashes and fallow fields. They will stand over the graves of children they have never held nor seen and find wives destroyed by by years of the arduous, physical labors their men unfairly left to them. And they will curse themselves for abandoning all to answer adventure's "glorious" call and duty's stern imperative. To various degrees, the war will have changed, for good or ill, every veteran. None who have challenged the elephant will return free of wounds within, let alone those countless thousands who will return maimed for life.

Victory will enable most to overcome and put into perspectives the tribulations they endured. Defeat's bitterness will linger in the bones of others, making each day another trek across spiritual wastelands,

If victory be ours, then we who put pen to paper must do all to inspire our people to create a more just society. If defeat be our lot, then we must do all to resurrect them. Victory will make all good things possible. Defeat will exacerbate every ill and defer change within hardened hearts for decades. We will require leaders of charisma and talent. But, for all who participated, and for all those who endured at home, their lives will henceforth be measured in two halves - before the war and after the war - while the war itself will remain a time unto its own.

Those who lead us, no matter our fate, must transcend all who went before.

Your Obedient Servant
Royal K. Chapman

Chapman's Last Entry

Near Franklin, Tenn.
29 November 1864

Tonight this regiment sleeps. I gaze upon their hundreds of slumbering forms silhouetted against the darkness of dying campfire light and, unseen by sentries, I weep.

Many will perish tomorrow in the fighting surely to come, yet they rest in such innocence, as if nothing must concern or trouble them. I will join in the fighting, too, but now I cannot sleep. Why can they?

As a soldier of sorts, I have steeled myself to hardship and sacrifice, for I have understood since the beginning that I must eventually pay a soldier's price for my participation. Yet tonight, at my shoulder for the first convincing time, I sense the Reaper's presence. Why I am not panicked or trembling with foreboding? Because a strange equanimity enfolds me. It is wonder, not so much fear, that chases away sleep. I wonder in what Kingdom I shall dwell tomorrow at this hour. What revelations about Creation and mankind's Earthly purpose and destiny shall I comprehend by then? Or shall I reside in my present ignorance? Can a soul truly comprehend Eternity? But what also of oblivion?

The stars tonight offer no answers. Yet, at this moment, the almost supernatural contentment I feel - which I do not understand - convinces me that I am being spoken to by unseen messengers to assure me that death, apart form its attendant pain, is not to be feared. Still, my emotions concerning it remain paradoxically jumbled.

In this candlelight by which I write, I study my hands and fingers and realize what amazing creations they are. Likewise, the candle's flame and the stars themselves, and I sense that I am detaching myself from them and this Earth in bits and stages, preparatory to my final leave-taking. I am becalmed and the tensions of my life are stilled. I welcome the respite but ask is this how it is for all destined to perish in battle? Surely, then, I am not alone in my feelings tonight. Why, then, are all around me able to sleep while I contemplate eventualities?

How will the end come . . . by bullet, bayonet, shot, shell or canister? For it must come by one or the others. And what will burial teams grant me . . . a separate resting place or an unmarked hole with scores of others surrounding me? Will I die recognizable or unknown, as many thousands of others have died known but to the Lord? Or does it matter to Eternity? Yes, though I remain homesick for this Earth I have known since birth, my hands are steady.

I look forward to a last sunrise, hoping it will be magnificent, for I shall study it intensely and as never before appreciate all life around me. And with new humility in the time left to me, I shall breathe the precious air of this present dimension and listen with more thankful hearing to the songs of morning birds vibrantly alive in the nature around me. And I shall savor the mysteries of the coming morning mists and their touch upon my face, and the aromas of sweet grasses - and, with equal acuity, feel the rasp of tree bark upon my fingertips. For my last impressions of physical life must be both spiritual AND tactile, though my last thought will remain heavily upon my new nations' fate.

In the meantime, the nation's soul shalll remain where it has always been since Sumter - with its men at arms. For those who return, it shall be left to them to rebuild and reconstitute our land and provide for all. In victory, they shall cherish the task. In defeat, they shall be severely tested. Yet either way, into their hands shalll be placed our people's ultimate fate. I am confident they shall put away their tattered banners and threadbare uniforms but never their honor. Their strength must derive from that.

So now, I will dedicate these stained and worn journals to the men of this army who survive tomorrow and the war, and to the still living spirits of those who gave all. Each journal has honestly and candidly chronicled their parts in it. Therefore let each one be to them and theirs my humble tribute - as inadequate as each remains. If I am struck down tomorrow I am positive some part of my consciousness will survive to embrace the unknown. And I will follow the living invisibly from battlefield to battlefield and beyond, ever welcoming those who are passed to my side.

All this the angels tell me - so it must be true - where the lilies flourish eternally with unstained beauty.

*   *   *

Afterthought

Dearest May,

"I write you, my sister to rejoice in the war's end. It is over and our long darkness has become light, though some might yet say, dimly. But our husbands are home and with us, and that is all that matters now. We have them back, at last. Some women still are waiting and worse. Some will never know their men's fate while others know they will never see them again. How bitterly tragic. I cannot think of a greater torture . . . children now fatherless by the thousands or who must wait, never knowing if that someone - ever more dimly familiar - might yet appear on their door-steps. Yet you and I have our children and you, your Timothy and I, my James. They have been through so much, and so have we. I am aged beyond my years and no longer attractive, having cared with arduous labor for our land in his absence. But he cannot see my awful deterioration and blessedly remembers me as I was. Still, even now, you and I must do and be more. You must be your Timothy's legs and I must be my James's eyes. In that sense the war continues for us, but we will endure as we have endured before - have no doubts . God Bless us all and protect you and your dear children. Write when you can."

Cora

May's Reply

Dearest Cora,

"We must now love our families as never before and trust such love to see us through. God will provide in gratitude. I know not what I will do when I see and meet those in the uniforms we have feared and fought for so long, but I will put my faith in His Hands to temper my heart and fill it with charity. They and we are yet countrymen, estranged though we've been by war. But to survive, we who struggled against them must compromise or perish, and we who have not directly born the battle must unite to feed our children and succor those who have. Great hardships portend, but, yes, we will proudly endure undefeated within, for endurance is within our peoples' hearts and blood. And, indeed, we have our husband's back and all now is possible again. Those who have perished for the South will forever have engraved the scrolls of our heritage with poignancy and honor. We shall miss but cherish them. May God's guidance and renewed blessings, dearest sister, have graciously begun."

Lovingly, May

The War Between the States

1861-1865

We were not there . . . we did not see it . . . we could not hear it nor feel it nor could we know . . . and yet, it haunts us still and we remain prisoners of its times.

R. A. Busse